IN THE CROOK OF THE ROCK— JEWISH REFUGE IN A WORLD GONE MAD

THE CHAYA LEAH WALKIN STORY

Jewish Identities in Post-Modern Society

Series Editor
ROBERTA ROSENBERG FARBER (Yeshiva University, New York)

Editorial Board
SARA ABOSCH
(University of Memphis, Memphis, Tennessee)
GEOFFREY ALDERMAN
(University of Buckingham, Buckingham)
YORAM BILU
(Hebrew University, Jerusalem)
STEVEN M. COHEN
(Hebrew Union College, New York)
DEBORAH DASH MOORE
(University of Michigan, Ann Arbor)
BRYAN DAVES
(Yeshiva University, New York)
SERGIO DELLA PERGOLA
(Hebrew University, Jerusalem)
SIMCHA FISHBANE
(Touro College, New York)
UZI REBHUN
(Hebrew University, Jerusalem)
REEVA SIMON
(Yeshiva University, New York)

IN THE CROOK OF THE ROCK— JEWISH REFUGE IN A WORLD GONE MAD

THE CHAYA LEAH WALKIN STORY

Vera Schwarcz

Boston
2018

Library of Congress Cataloging-in-Publication Data

Names: Schwarcz, Vera, 1947- author.

Title: In the crook of the rock : Jewish refuge in a world gone mad : the Chaya Walkin story / Vera Schwarcz.

Description: Boston : Academic Studies Press, 2018. | Series: Jewish identities in post-modern society | Includes bibliographical references and index.

Identifiers: LCCN 2018006730 (print) | LCCN 2018007337 (ebook) | ISBN 9781618117878 (e-book) | ISBN 9781618117854 (hardcover) | ISBN 9781618117861 (pbk.)

Subjects: LCSH: Small, Chaya, 1934- | Jews—China—Shanghai—History—20th century—Biography. | Jewish refugees—China—Shanghai—Biography. | World War, 1939-1945—Jews—Rescue. | Shanghai (China)—Biography. | Shanghai (China)—Ethnic relations.

Classification: LCC DS135.C5 (ebook) | LCC DS135.C5 S39 2018 (print) | DDC 940.53/18092 [B]—dc23
LC record available at https://lccn.loc.gov/2018006730

©**Academic Studies Press, 2018**
ISBN 978-1-61811-787-8 (e-book)
ISBN 978-1-61811-785-4 (hardback)
ISBN 978-1-61811-786-1 (paperback)

Book design by Kryon Publishing Services (P) Ltd.
www.kryonpublishing.com

Cover design by Ivan Grave

Published by Academic Studies Press
28 Montfern Avenue
Brighton, MA 02135, USA
press@academicstudiespress.com
www.academicstudiespress.com

In memory of Rabbi Shmuel David and Rebbetzin Tzivia Walkin—
their wise visages accompanied me through many worlds.

Table of Contents

Preface

A VOICE KNOCKS:

   Chaya Leah Walkin's Story Finds Me   viii

Acknowledgments   xiii

Introduction   xv

THE VIRTUE OF ONE VINEYARD:

   Jewish Refuge Reconsidered

CHAPTER 1   1

IF SHE BE A WALL:

   Pohost and Lukatch Before Disaster Strikes

CHAPTER 2   24

WATCHMEN PATROLLING THE CITY:

   Escape from Vilna to Japan

CHAPTER 3   53

AN APPLE TREE NESTLED IN THE WOODS:

   Respite in Kobe

CHAPTER 4   79

TENDER KIDS BESIDE THE SHEPHERDS' TENTS:

   Starting Anew in Shanghai

CHAPTER 5   113

IN THE CROOK OF THE ROCK:

  Expanding The Meaning of Survival

CHAPTER 6   146

THE VINE HAS BUDDED:

  Schooling, Bombings, and Beyond

CHAPTER 7   174

UNDER THE APPLE TREE:

  End of the War, End of Refuge in Shanghai

CHAPTER 8   208

BEFORE THE SHADOWS OF NIGHT ARE GONE:

  Starting a New Life in America

CHAPTER 9   242

UNTIL IT RIPENS:

  Marriage, Community, and the Arc of Return

CONCLUSION   279

  Seeking Your Voice for the Sake of the Unborn

BIBLIOGRAPHY   294

INDEX   302

Preface

A VOICE KNOCKS:

Chaya Leah Walkin's Story Finds Me

> *I sleep, but my heart wakes,*
> *The voice of the beloved knocks...*
> *I have removed my cloak,*
> *How shall I put it on?*
>
> Shir Ha'Shirim 5:3

The world was mad enough in 2015, the year in which this book project found me. This was the year in which Reuters reported that 65.3 million people were uprooted worldwide, many of them fleeing religious wars and terrorism. This was also the year in which the Islamic State of Iraq and Syria (ISIS) attacks were carried out on three continents. At the same time, China was building artificial islands in the South China Sea to ratchet up its bellicose claims against Japan. Though aware of these events, I was not planning to write a new book that would juxtapose global madness and the inner resources of refugees in catastrophic times.

In spring of 2015, I thought that my academic and writing career had come to a natural end. It was a period of personal reckoning about how to face the unknown path ahead. I was ready to wrap up four decades of China studies.

The afternoon that I finished the retirement address was drenched by cold rain. I allowed myself to ask for the first time without dread: "What next?" Not five minutes later, my cell phone rang. The caller was David Sokal, the son of a refugee from Vienna who kept in close touch with the community of "Shanghailanders." David started to speak enthusiastically about a special *rebbetzin* (wife of a distinguished rabbi) named Chaya Leah Small who had moved him deeply with her story, her warmth, and her unique open-mindedness. He said that this special lady wanted to write a book about her experiences during the Holocaust and that she had asked David for help. Not being a writer himself, he thought of me.

Looking at the pounding waves beyond the beach house, I agreed to help. It was too odd to have gotten this call out of the blue just when I had reached the end of what I thought was my public purpose. Here, it seemed, was someone who could use my skills. Since I had mentored beginning writers before, perhaps I could advise the *rebbetzin* how to jot down something enduring for her children and grandchildren.

David surprised me by the depth of his admiration for this woman whose roots stretched deep into world of Talmudic scholarship before the war. He told me that Chaya Leah's mother had grown up in the home of the Chofetz Chayim (1839–1933), the venerated sage of Radin. Her grandfather had been the chief Rabbi of Pinsk. I listened, aware that David was praising the kind of Torah wisdom that had shaped my own life.

On April 28, 2015, Chaya Leah Small came to visit my home. I had emailed her about my willingness to help with the memoir. I knew from David Sokal that Chaya Leah had broken her leg and that this was going to be a daunting journey for her. The day of the visit, I ran around cleaning the house, preparing some soup, arranging flowers. I felt as if the great Chofetz Chayim himself had deigned to come to my house.

As the hours stretched and Chaya Leah was stuck in traffic, I had second thoughts: Why was this life-seasoned woman making this great effort to come to me? If we were to speak about her remembrances and how I might help in the writing process, we could have used Skype and saved all this trouble.

When Chaya arrived, I was surprised to see a petite, marvelously stylish woman step out of the car driven by her son, Shaul Small. She was carrying a gift, a hand-painted vase, which she handed to me saying:

> *This is for your tears.*
> *I came to visit you because you are widow, like me.*
> *I know how painful this time is for you and I came to offer you some* nachama *(comfort).*

This is not what I had expected at all. Chaya Leah's use of the Hebrew expression for relieving grief after death touched me to the core. I realized that this visit was not about her memoir, not even about Shanghai. This was something more personal—an encounter more generous than I could have imagined from a stranger. Tears welled up even before I could serve the tea, and later some soup.

In the end, we talked for a few hours and I suggested strategies for Chaya Leah Small to start a rough draft of the memoir. She was determined to try. In an email, which I received after Shabbat on September 17, 2015, Chaya Leah found the words, again, to speak of our losses, about the ongoing grief that binds us more deeply than her childhood refuge in China, which was also the locale of my academic studies:

> *I felt every ache, pain, emotion, farlorenkiet (a feeling of being lost) as you.*
> *I felt like a wrung out rag.*
> *I felt I was drifting.*
> *So alone, so lost, and yet surrounded by so many...*
> *Like a child who learns how to walk even though the child can do it alone, the security of holding a finger is all that is needed to go.*
> *Now we have to walk alone without even a finger.*

In this email, a mother of five children who had endured a traumatic childhood as a refugee speaks in the voice of a forlorn widow. The line breaks, the punctuation are Chaya's. They are poetic without any conscious intent. And they hit their mark—they helped to mobilize my own resources in the service of a new narrative.

Yiddishisms like *"farlorenkiet"* had been one ingredient peppering the various mother tongues that surrounded my childhood in a city in Romania, densely populated by Hungarians and Germans. This city was also home to survivors of the *Shoah*. Two of the neighbors who shared our communal kitchen and bathroom had Auschwitz numbers on theirs arms. Thus, I came to understand Yiddish almost without trying.

Chaya Leah's story was a different, yet familiar, continuation of fragments I first encountered in my mother tongues. I responded to them out of familiarity with both Chinese and Jewish history. As in King Solomon's masterful poem, *Shir Ha'Shirim* (*Song of Songs*), I found myself addressed in a state somewhere between sleep and wakefulness.

In the spring of 2015, I was just trying to wrap my China studies, not start a new book. Yet, being that child of survivors from Romania, I could not turn away from recording, shaping, and vivifying one more voice from the Holocaust that is slipping away from us with the passage of time.

Over time, Chaya Leah became for me far more than yet another witness's voice. As I began to craft her story, it became a unique window into the world of a Jewish child who withstood the madness of the world in a way that remains compelling even today. Along the way, I also discovered that my social science training about "objectivity" had to make room for something else, something that I came to accept more readily through Chinese terms such as *zhuguan* 主觀 ("host perspective") and *keguan* 客觀 ("guest perspective").

This discovery came several months after our meeting in April 2015, as I gave Rebbetzin Small some concrete suggestions to jumpstart a book of memoirs. I shared with her a technique that I have used with my students over many decades. It is called "junking." In this process, I urge the writer to spew forth a first draft that is rough, unorganized, and wrestles with bits of concrete information. Later, we could sort through the rubble to excavate some major themes. I told Chaya Leah to send me her jottings and that I would help her in the revision process further down the road.

The energy, skill, and vision with which she plunged into the junking process amazed me. Within weeks of our meeting, Chaya Leah started to send me pages that rivaled the best of my graduate students' early efforts. These pages were filled with details about her childhood, her adult years, and the trauma of becoming a refugee in times of war. In one of first pages of this draft, I found an entry that revealed Chaya Leah's determination to give voice to her unique, and obviously subjective story:

> *The phone is ringing off the wall.*
> *No, I am not answering.*
> *My neighbors are worried.*
> *They are knocking at the door.*
> *You guessed it.*
> *I have started writing this book.*

By July 2015, Chaya Leah had written about 70 pages of so-called "junk." As I started to edit them, I saw immediately that they contained gems of historical importance combined with powerful spiritual and personal insights. I also began to glimpse an altogether different book that I could write, which would add historical context and thematic breadth to Chaya Leah's jottings.

I was not sure that I really wanted to commit to such a project or that Chaya Leah would agree to the change in the direction of our collaboration. This was something that we had to discuss in person. So, five months after our first meeting, I flew out to Chicago for three days of conversation and research. During the first hours after our warm reunion, I asked Chaya Leah the question that I was asking myself: Do we want a book by an orthodox *rebbetzin* that is likely to reach only a limited audience interested in the religious outlook of Jewish survivors who took refuge in China during the war?

Or do we want a book that will reach a broader audience by addressing more objectively various themes beyond the framework of the yeshiva world? Chaya Leah's response was unequivocal and also surprising. Yes, she was willing to let this become my book, one in which my voice and my concerns would shape the meaning of Jewish refuge in times of war.

She trusted my research and analytical skills and had been overly generous in praising the literary value of my previous works, which she had read before our meeting in Chicago. More importantly, she stressed, she did not want the book to be *"fa'chnyoket,"* which is a Yiddish term for someone who is unctuously religious.

This was an old-world expression that I did not know. Chaya Leah explained to me that it connotes an overly scrupulous attachment to the details of Jewish law without consideration for the larger context. This was the kind of book that Chaya Leah did not want. This was the kind of book I could never write.

Thus, a different project began between us. I would research and write the story of a Holocaust survivor focused upon the voice of a little girl of distinguished Torah lineage who witnessed a world gone mad. Chaya Leah would be my interlocutor while her jottings provided the morsel of living memory that I needed to flesh out the theme of Jewish resilience during the journey from Poland through Vilna and Kobe to wartime Shanghai, and beyond.

In the process of trying to make sense of Chaya Leah's story, I found myself going back again and again to the Chinese lexicon for "objectivity" and "subjectivity," which have been translated poorly in modern social science parlance. 客觀 and 主觀 are four characters which were borrowed in twentieth-century China from the dense language of classical poetry to suggest a marvelous interaction between the "guest's view" and the "host's view."

The guest, the outsider, the traveler passing through, is privileged with knowing an object from without. The host is within, limited by the partiality of her knowledge derived from an intimate world that the guest can never fully share.

In this book, I was the guest warmly invited in, like you, my reader. Beyond our gaze and grasp lies the subjective world of *zhuguan*—which I am tempted to call here the *"Jew guan."* This is Chaya Leah's universe of Torah roots and Jewish faith that sustained not only her family but may also provide a key to our own survival in a world that shows no signs of lessening madness.

Acknowledgments

The first and greatest debt of gratitude for this work is due to the Rebbetzin Chaya Leah Small. She has been a constant, devoted, caring companion along the journey of this writing. Her friendship is more precious to me now than I could have ever imagined possible when our paths first crossed in the spring of 2015. My hope is that this work will bring her *nachat ruach*—comfort and joy of the spirit—and that she will be blessed with long years and good health in the midst of her loving family.

Rabbi Chaim and Rebbetzin Henny Walkin, Chaya's brother and sister-in-law, respectively, have also been treasured advisors as I delved more deeply into the subject of the Walkin family legacy in Pinsk, Vilna and Shanghai. It has been a great privilege for me to be invited into Rabbi Walkin's gracious home in Jerusalem, where I witnessed personally the enduring generosity and open-minded commitment to Torah values that stretches from the pre-war world in Europe to all parts of the Jewish world today.

Chaya Leah's extended family has been supportive of this project all along. Her children, especially Sarah (Dubby) Pollack, responded with alacrity and kindness to my requests for information as well as driving Chaya Leah to meet me whenever and wherever time permitted. This kind of dedication speaks volumes about the values that Chaya Leah embodies and has conveyed meaningfully to future generations.

In Jerusalem, I have received research help from Ms. Rita Margolin of the Yad Vashem archives. A native of Pinsk, Ms. Margolin went beyond the call of duty to help me find original documents about the death of Chaya Leah's grandfather, Rav Aharon Walkin, known as the Pinsker Rav.

Closer to home, I am greatly indebted to David Sokal for introducing me to Chaya Leah in the first place. Having interviewed David's father—Dr. Robert Sokal (a refugee from Vienna)—twenty years earlier when I was writing about Shanghai's Jewish life for the first time, I knew of David's interest in the stories of kin who had crowded the alleys of China during the Shoah. Although I met with David's parents and sister often, it is his own ongoing commitment to the legacy of the Shanghai refuge that moved me to start this project. His learned comments inspired me and kept me going all through the writing of this book.

Unexpected generosity and research help also came my way from Professor Yoshiko Samuel of Wesleyan University. She was supportive and helpful in this project, especially as I began to probe Chaya Leah's sojourn in Japan and the rope-jumping song that she carried from Kobe to her own children in America. Yoshiko was so moved by the memory of a Jewish child refugee that she contacted Professor Masahiro Iwai, a well-known ethnomusicologist from the University of Kobe. These two scholars puzzled over Chaya Leah's childhood snippet with marvelous empathy and insight—thereby encouraging me in the larger effort of understanding the fractured meanings of Jewish refugee life in China and Japan. From Chicago, Dr. Khane-Faygl Turtletaub provided linguistic support with the transliterations of key Yiddish phrases in Chaya Leah's narrative.

I am also thankful to Hebrew University, especially to the Mandel Center for Advanced Humanistic Studies, for a Visiting Professorship that enabled me to revise this work in a truly beautiful and inspiring landscape. My research assistants—Yochana Storch, Hadas Sharon, and Gleb Diorditsa—were resourceful in accessing sources and in the creation of a Powerpoint presentation that enabled me to share preliminary findings from this work in the spring of 2017.

Last, but not least, I want to express my gratitude to the staff of Academic Studies Press for their skilled and visionary approach to this book. Professor Roberta Farber, acquisitions editor, was the first to respond warmly to the manuscript. Eileen Wolfberg did an extraordinary job as copy editor while Alessandra Anzani helped with images and moved the book along toward publication expertly.

Without all this kindness and help, Chaya Leah Walkin's story might have remained a fragment of memory sheltered by the Walkin family alone. Now, it has a chance to reach the wider audience that it deserves. Needless to say, any errors in the book remain my own responsibility, for which I beg the reader's forgiveness at the start.

Introduction

THE VIRTUE OF ONE VINEYARD:
Jewish Refuge Reconsidered

> *Solomon had a vineyard,*
> *He let others guard it...*
> *My vineyard stands before me.*
> *You Solomon, keep your thousands.*
>
> Shir Ha'Shirim 8:11-12

Each story of refuge with dignity is worth telling. Each has a different melody, a different message. Once Chaya Leah Walkin's story found me, I knew that I was obliged to convey its undertones in a way that sets it apart from many other narratives of survival during the *Shoah*. Through the writing of this book, I became the guardian of a unique vineyard, unlike the "thousands" that the *Song of Songs—Shir Ha'Shirim*—attributes to King Solomon. He owned many fields and could afford to allow others to watch over them. For me, the act of listening to one particular voice in the fullness of its emotional and historical details transformed yet another Holocaust remembrance into a life-nourishing garden from which, I hope, others may draw nourishment as well.

Judith Miller had already pioneered this narrative strategy as early as 1990 in a book entitled: *One by One: Facing the Holocaust.* In this work, Miller sought to counter the dullness of the past that accosts us when we survey the huge field of atrocities in the twentieth century. The best antidote against the urge to either summarize or deny the lessons of the *Shoah* is to rescue singular fragments one story at a time:

> Abstraction is memory's most ardent enemy. It kills because it encourages distance, often indifference. We must remind ourselves that the Holocaust

Rebbetzin Chaya Leah Small in her home in Chicago with collage of Jewish refugee.

was not six million. It was one plus one, plus one… (Only thus) is the incomprehensible given meaning.[1]

Judith Miller's project honored the singularity of the dead and challenged other scholars to similarly vivify the lives of those who survived atrocity.

Deborah Dwork and Robert Jan Van Pelt embraced this challenge as well in their study, *Flight from the Reich: Refugee Jews 1933-1946*.[2] Published in 2012, this work combined documentary evidence with personal accounts to paint a more vivid portrait of various pathways of refuge out of Europe during the *Shoah*. Fleeing, as Chaya Leah Walkin's journey shows, did not evict one from the Holocaust experience. Rather, it shifted the locale, embedding Jews into geographies and temporalities that were unfamiliar and often terrifying.

---

1 Judith Miller, *One by One by One: Facing the Holocaust* (New York: Simon and Shuster, 1990), 123.
2 Deborah Dwork and Robert Jan van Pelt, *Flight from the Reich: Refugee Jews 1933-1946* (New York: W. W. Norton, 2012).

It was flight itself that tested the innermost resources of Jewish life in a world gone mad. What did refugees carry with them to survive with dignity? In Chaya Leah's Chicago home, I found a piece of artwork that sharpened this question in my mind. It is a collage hanging in a hallway quite apart for the many lovely Chinese vases and cloisonné-decorated cabinets that recall Chaya Leah's childhood in Shanghai.

This work centers upon an aged man in a black coat and hat, walking stick in hand, grasping a roped-up suitcase. Old-fashioned bags and trunks are strewn all about him. A dismantled room looms in the background. The white bearded figure does not look back at all that loss and destruction. He has grasped only what he can carry with fierce determination. He will move on.

At first, I only noticed the haunted gaze. This does not seem to be the first time that the man—clearly a Jew—has been chased out of his home. Nor has he become inured to the pain of leaving precious bits of the familiar past behind. Yet, the more I looked at the collage the more I came to appreciate the moral strength it takes to select what to carry.

Even in a hurry, grab what is most precious, make a choice about which valuables go into that one suitcase, which values will keep you strongly Jewish in alien worlds. This is also the leitmotif of the Walkin family's refugee experience. It is a history-seasoned strategy for meaningful survival that stretches all the way to the Spanish Inquisition and, before that, to the Babylonian exile.

One could say that Jews became expert refugees by force of historical circumstance. But that is not quite the truth. There were innumerable small and large acts of choice that shaped survival, that lent it meaning beyond physical endurance. In Chinese, the term for raw tenacity—*ren* 忍—is comprised of an ideograph showing a knife over the human heart. Here, endurance requires one to submit to violence, to outwit its brutality by simply going on. Chaya Leah and her family did more than endure.

Reflecting upon the meanings of their Jewish survival, I found myself coming back to the philosophical meanings of "agency." This overused theoretical term does, nonetheless, capture something essential about Chaya Leah's journey. It highlights the autonomous resources within a person or community that facilitated survival with dignity in harsh times. Even as a small child, Chaya Leah Walkin understood that Jews were more than victims of a vicious fate. In the effort to understand this sense of an inner fulcrum for action, I turned to the work of my Wesleyan colleague, historian Gary Shaw, who argues:

> It is time for historians to show how attempts to understand the self are essential to historical work... For it is the agent in concert with others who is the one sure place where meaning gets made and unmade, and where history is waged and witnessed.[3]

Shaw, from his position as editor of *History and Theory*, dared to take issue with the various theoretical frameworks, including Marxism and Postmodernism, which took the agent out of history. He pointed out that the responsibility for making meaning out of the debris of the past remains compelling for each of us who writes history. We cannot shoulder this task without taking into account how individuals and groups fashion survival into something more than naked endurance.

Philosopher Emil Fackenheim, in contrast to Gary Shaw, tackled the question of endurance in light of his own experience as a survivor of the Sachsenhausen concentration camp. Decades before *History and Theory* debated the problem of agency, Fackenheim forced himself to look into the ashes of the *Shoah* and declared:

> A Jew endures because he is commanded to endure instead of going mad... Whence has come our strength to endure, to affirm our Jewishness against the forces of hell itself? The question produces abiding wonder. It is a commanding Voice without which we would have perished in our affliction.[4]

This "voice" can be heard in Chaya Leah's jottings about China and Japan as well. These places allowed Jews to outwit the madness that engulfed Europe during the Holocaust. The voice described by Fackenheim was also audible in Kobe as well as in Shanghai. It echoed forward in time and continued to strengthen Jewish identity after the war.

BUT DO WE LEARN FROM HISTORY?

For Fackenheim, the voice commanding endurance emanated from Auschwitz and had to be heeded as an additional commandment beyond the 613 that

---

3 Gary Shaw, "Agency and Language in the Postmodern Age," *History and Theory* (December, 2001): 1-9.
4 Emil Fackenheim, *God's Presence in History: Jewish Affirmations and Philosophical Reflections* (New York: Jason Aronson Inc., 1970), 182.

form the core of traditional Judaism. For Chaya Leah, survival with Jewish dignity was an essential outgrowth of the Torah itself and of the distinguished legacy of Talmudic scholarship that had shaped the life of her parents before they became stateless refugees.

Born in 1916 in Halle (Germany), Emil Ludwig Fackenheim was a Western-educated intellectual in his 20s when he was arrested during Kristallnacht. Chaya Leah, by contrast, was merely a child of five when she had to hide in a wagon to escape the murderous hatred of Jews raging in Europe. Her expression for the Holocaust—*Churb'n*—draws upon an older, more traditional lexicon than Fackenheim's philosophical reflections about Auschwitz.

This Yiddish term builds upon the Hebrew term for "destruction" associated with the ravage of the First and Second Temples in Jerusalem. *Churban*, which connotes a fiery ruination, also calls to mind the biblical concept *korban* used to describe the sacrificial burnt-offerings that sanctify both God and the Jewish people. By the late 1940s, the expression *Churban Eyrope* was on the lips of most Yiddish-speaking survivors who sought to fathom the destruction of the world that they had left behind. Looking back at her own family's survival, Chaya Leah marveled at the legacy of scholarship that had carried Jewish life forward from the ashes of the Holocaust:

> *The churban destroyed all the yeshivas, yet the Mir is the only Yeshiva that was saved whole, as after the second churban, Yavne remained whole.*
> *And we see what followed as history repeats itself.*
> *The Mir in Shanghai was saved as a whole and look at what they accomplished, and the blooms of their work.*
> *History repeats itself.*
> *But do we learn from history?*

Here, Chaya Leah is paying tribute to the extraordinary renewal of Torah learning that followed the survival of the Mirrer Yeshiva in Shanghai during the war. Her own family's links to the yeshiva are discussed at length in this book. For now, it is important to see how Chaya Leah placed her own experience as a refugee in the larger context of Jewish history going back to the destruction of the Second Temple in 70 CE.

Her reference to Yavne is no accident. It shows a conscious continuation of the legacy of Rabbi Yochanan Ben Zakkai (30–90 BCE), who (according to the Babylonian Talmud) asked Vespasian, the emperor of Rome: "Give me Yavne and its sages." Ben Zakkai was not immune to the horror and pain that beset Jerusalem after the destruction of the Temple. Yet, he also understood that continuing Torah scholarship in the hamlet of Yavne would ensure Jewish survival despite this catastrophic loss. Chaya Leah looks back and sees both Yavne and the Mirrer Yeshiva as beacons of hope, as sources of spiritual flourishing for the Jewish people as a whole.

At the same time, her scorching question stands: *"But do we learn from history?"* This question rang loudly in my mind as I was working on this book. Looking around the world today, I saw very few signs that we have learned enduring lessons from *Churban Eyrope*. I think back to Max Kaufmann's heartrending work entitled *Churban Lettland* (The Destruction of the Jews of Latvia)[5] published in 1947 and realize that the twenty-first century continues to besmirch the memory of Jews murdered during the Holocaust. As recently as May 2016, a major memorial to the Lithuanian *Shoah* was vandalized in honor of Adolf Hitler's birthday. News flashes of Jewish names defaced with swastikas deepen for me the searing doubt in Chaya Leah's question: *"But do we learn from history?"*

I have no answer, but I do know that there is a terrifying moral and historical myopia afoot in the world today. Wanton cruelty reigns undiminished after the Holocaust. Hatred and murder of Jews, alas, has not become a matter of past history. So Chaya Leah's question and Emil Fackenheim's injunction about endurance have lost none of their bitter force. One way that this book addresses ongoing madness in the global context is by detailing the inner resources that enabled refugees to survive with dignity. Restoring "agency" to victims of hatred helps us, quite literally, to see them and ourselves in a fresh light.

The urgency of this task became apparent to me as I looked at a loudly publicized art exhibition entitled "Love Without Boundaries—Jewish Refugees in Shanghai." First opened in China in 2011, the exhibition also arrived with diplomatic fanfare to the International Convention Center of Jerusalem on May 10, 2015. The show revolved around forty oil paintings depicting various aspects of Jewish life during the war in China. Here was a glossy, sentimentalized version of Jewish survival that veered toward historical distortion again and again.

Official commemorations in Jerusalem, as in Shanghai, often depict child survivors in Shanghai as helpless beneficiaries of Chinese benevolence. One of the paintings in the exhibition that evoked this falsified pathos was

---

5   Max Kaufmann *Churbn Lettland: The Destruction of the Jews of Latvia*, ed. Gertrude Schneider and Erhad Roy Wiehn (Kostanz, Germany: Hartung-Gorre, 2010).

entitled "True Emotion Breaks the Blockade." This work showed Jews behind barbed wires—something that never happened in Shanghai. The text that accompanied the painting embroidered an agency-denying narrative in the following terms:

> The Japanese authorities did not want to slaughter Jewish refugees directly. Instead they isolated the Jews, restricted their freedom and persecuted them. Once the Japanese authorities kept more than 2000 Jews in an area and cut down all power and water supplies in order to starve them to death. In the hard times, caged in the Ghetto, true emotion (sic) break the blockade. The kind Shanghai residents and some charity organization could not see them suffering from starvation. So they discreetly sent food and water to these Jews. In this way, the Jews behind the layers of metal fences could barely survive.

Chaya Leah was never one of the hungry girls receiving a handout behind barbed wire, even though some features of her childish face are recognizable in the painting. In fact, there were no such Jewish children in Shanghai during the war.

By trying to augment retrospectively China's role in the rescue of Jewish refugees, the painting portrayed a lie. The role of Japanese authorities in actually saving Jewish lives is an inconvenient truth that continues to be ignored on the Chinese mainland and denied in the painting.

Another aspect of the Jewish refuge in Shanghai during the *Shoah* that is literally being painted over here is the social and cultural distance between Chinese and Jews. In Chaya Leah's recollections, as well as in the writings of many other survivors, we learn that contacts between Jewish refugees and ordinary Chinese were rare and made awkward by language and religious barriers. "Love Without Borders," by contrast, emphasized the ties between charity-minded Chinese and helpless Jews. In the process, it robbed the refugees of their own agency by portraying them as victims of a cruel fate ameliorated by China's kindness.

In fact, the various Jewish communities in China had numerous cultural, spiritual, and financial resources to ensure survival with dignity. The Jerusalem exhibit, much like the one in the Shanghai Jewish Refugees Museum, which opened in 2007, diminishes this aspect of history. Survivors of that period, most notably Dr. Lotte Lustig Marcus, have been publicly critical of these distorted, politically self-serving depictions of Jewish survival.[6]

---

6 Marcus, Lustig Lotte. "Contradicting Revisionist History." *Points East* 29, no. 1 (March, 2014): 1–3.

How to give voice to the agency that was accessed by Jewish survivors in China became one of the core challenges of this book. Digging beneath the "painted history" being currently produced was the first step in meeting that challenge. A more difficult narrative task awaited me as I sought to convey Chaya Leah's distinctive cadence and vision, especially in a field dense with autobiographies and memoirs about Jewish refuge during the war.

The very multiplicity of personal and scholarly accounts enabled me, in the end, to listen more keenly to Chaya Leah's own voice. As Alphonso Lingis noted in his study called *First Person Singular,* "voice is a matter of slow paced, often traumatic embodiment."[7] In Chaya Leah Walkin's embodied voice I heard the scars, hesitations, and hopes of a child who came of age in wartime China. References to Torah observance and to the distinguished Talmudic scholarship of the Walkin family peppered her recollection, and therefore also color my evocation of the unique timbre of Chaya Leah's voice.

This book, however, is not an act of ventriloquism. Chaya Leah Walkin does not speak through my voice. Instead, I have sought to create a different kind of middle ground between our disparate visions and versions of history. It was my decision, for example, to frame Chaya Leah's story with comparative reflections about history and trauma. After decades of recording the voices of Chinese intellectuals who survived the Cultural Revolution, I turned with a seasoned ear to the voice of the child who lived through the war in Shanghai. It was my choice to deepen the echoes between the child's voice and other survivors of historical trauma in order to augment the reader's understanding of why this narrative continues to matter in the twentieth-first century, many decades after the war ended in Shanghai in 1945.

NOT A BOY NAMED 6881

To enter Chaya Leah's world required me to carve a distinctive path through the thick forest of existing works about Jewish refuge in Shanghai. Chaya Leah herself was mindful of this large body of commemorative work, and wondered how one more account would add to or change the story of the *Shoah.* I told her that, in time, I would find the themes and the narrative strategy needed to make this book stand its own ground.

In the course of our collaboration, Chaya Leah sent me a volume of memoirs that had moved her deeply. It was written by Israel Starck and was entitled

---

7 Alphonso Lingis, *First Person Singular* (Evanston, IL: Northwestern University Press, 2007), 264.

A Boy Named 68818.⁸ Here, a Torah-observant Jew born in 1929 retells his survival in the death camps to his daughter Miriam. The work is consciously crafted as an educational tool for students in Jewish day schools. Its goal is to guide young minds in fathoming both the horrors and the spiritual heroism possible during the Holocaust. With specially commissioned drawings, the book speaks about the commitment to observing mitzvoth in the toughest circumstances imaginable, including Auschwitz. After reading through this artfully crafted project, I told Chaya Leah: I am not going to write a work like *A Boy Named 68818*.

Yes, my subject was also a child, but she was not a survivor of the death camps. Chaya Leah's story led me to think more deeply about refuge across cultural landscapes that were far from the Torah world of Eastern Europe. Fathoming these journeys required an act of imagination that went beyond the trials of Auschwitz. The focus of this work is a very young woman and her experiences demanded attention to events beyond the war.

Early on in my conversations with Chaya Leah in Chicago, I thought of Margaret Mead's work, *Coming of Age in Samoa*. This anthropological study stands in sharp contrast to the book by Israel Starck. Published for the first time in 1928, it also appears at first glance to be far afield from the life of a girl raised in a prestigious rabbinical family. Yet, looking at photographs of Chaya Leah as a young teenager with budding breasts at the end of the war in Shanghai, I began to think differently.

Margaret Mead helped me look more carefully at the details that mark female lives without falling prey to the condescension palpable in subtitles such as: "A Psychological Study of Primitive Youth for Western Civilization." The happy and chatty natives who populate Mead's version of Samoa have no counterpart in Chaya Leah's world. Yet, those girls took on adult responsibilities much like Chaya had to in caring for, and later protecting, younger siblings. As Mead writes:

> The chief nursemaid is usually a child of six or seven, who is not strong enough to lift a baby of 6 months old but can carry the child straddling the left hip.⁹

As a six-year-old, Chaya Leah had already become a refugee who crawled through winter snows into Lithuania with her terrified mother and two younger

---

8 Israel Starck, *A Boy Named 68818* (New York: Feldheim Publishers, 2015).
9 Margaret Mead, *Coming of Age in Samoa: A Psychological Study of Primitive Youth for Western Civilization* (New York: William Morrow and Company, 1928), 128.

siblings. By age seven, she had survived the scary journey from Vilna to Kobe in Japan. By the time she turned eight, Chaya Leah had also learned to bargain for food in the cacophonous alleys of Shanghai. All along, responsibility for younger siblings was clearly on her mind.

Turning from Kobe to Shanghai, I found no shortage of childhood memoirs written by women and men alike. Each tells a snippet of the refugee experience as seen through the eyes of displaced families, mostly from Germany and Austria. Too numerous to list here, I want to mention only those that shaped my own understanding of what was unique in Chaya Leah's experience as a girl embedded in the small Torah-observant community that had traveled together from Lithuania to China.

Among the many female voices that can be found in Shanghai memoirs, Vivian Kaplan's *Ten Green Bottles* captures most vividly a young woman's pre-war exploits in Vienna before being thrown into the maelstrom of war-torn Shanghai. Margaret Blair's *Gudao: The Lone Islet* is more firmly anchored on the Chinese terrain, with startling details about the Japanese occupation of the International Settlement as well as the internment camps where British citizens suffered deprivations and fear.[10] These terrors also loomed over Chaya Leah's world on Liaoyang Road.

Both Vivian Kaplan and Margaret Blair were older and more secular than Chaya Leah Walkin. This holds true also for the male voices recorded in refugee memoirs, such as that of Sigmund Tobias, entitled *Strange Haven: A Jewish Childhood in Wartime Shanghai*[11] and Samuel Iwry's *To Wear the Dust of War*.[12] Both Tobias and Iwry shared some of Chaya Leah Walkin's background. Both men had been on the margins of the yeshiva world in China.

Sigmund Tobias, born to Polish Jews in 1932, had spent his early childhood in Berlin. He came to China with the wave of German Jewish refugees and ended up briefly at the Mirrer Yeshiva in Shanghai. As he wrote in his memoir, this school offered more food and money, but the rigors of learning proved too daunting.

Samuel Iwry was born in 1910 into a religious family in Ukraine and had received the best Talmudic education available to young men of his generation. Long before his arrival in Kobe in March 1941, Iwry had embraced a secular

---

10 Margaret Blair, *Gudao: The Lone Islet: The War Years in Shanghai—A Childhood Memoir* (Bloomington, IN: Trafford Publishing, 2009).
11 Sigmund Tobias, *Strange Haven: A Jewish Childhood in Wartime Shanghai* (Champaign, IL: University of Illinois Press, 1999).
12 Samuel Iwry, *To Wear the Dust of War: From Bialystock to Shanghai, to the Promised Land—an Oral History* (New York: Palgrave, 2004).

intellectual climate strongly colored by Zionist beliefs. In Japan and in China, Iwry focused on Jewish emigration to Palestine. Yet, when the end of the war came, it was Chaya Leah's father, Rabbi Shmuel David Walkin, who helped Iwry to come to the United States. With a starting job teaching basic principles of Judaism to Jewish students Iwry went on to become America's foremost academic researcher on the Dead Sea Scrolls.

Kaplan, Blair, Tobias, and Iwry (along with dozens of other Jews who survived the war in Shanghai) penned memoirs focused on their brief China years in order to honor those who had perished in the *Shoah*. This work about Chaya Leah Walkin, by contrast, is neither a memoir nor a narrative focused solely upon the China years. Although I am a sinologist by training and have written previously about the Jewish communities in Shanghai during the war, I wanted to create here a broader canvas.

As a result, this narrative follows the broad outlines of Chaya Leah's life, from her birth in 1934 near Pinsk to the building up of a Torah community in Chicago. Through this broader time frame, I aim to capture the voice of the child who became a seasoned survivor as well as a highly respected community leader after the war.

With this more complex portrait consciously in mind, I reconstructed various fragments of Jewish as well as world history. By combining Chaya Leah's story with that of a world riddled by atrocity and moral myopia, I was able to discover the inner art of a distinctively Jewish refuge that went beyond survival in China. This effort to contextualize the experience of one particular refugee was greatly informed by existing academic scholarship on the Jewish experience in Shanghai. In recreating Chaya Leah's worlds, I drew much information from David Kranzler's path-breaking work entitled *Nazis and Jews: The Jewish Refugee Community of Shanghai 1938-1945*.[13] This early book has now been augmented by critical studies authored by Marcia Ristaino,[14] Steve Hochstadt,[15] Maisie Meyer,[16] and Gao Bei,[17] just to mention those that

---

13 David Kranzler, *Japanese, Nazis & Jews: The Jewish Refugee Community of Shanghai, 1938-1945* (New York: Yeshiva University Press, 1976).
14 Marcia Ristaino, *Port of Last Resort: The Diaspora Communities of Shanghai* (Stanford, CA: Stanford University Press, 2003).
15 Steve Hochstadt, *Exodus to Shanghai: Stories of Escape from the Third Reich* (New York: Palgrave, 2012).
16 Maisie J. Meyer, *Shanghai's Baghdadi Jews: A Collection of Biographical Reflections* (London: Blacksmith Books, 2015).
17 Gao Bei. *Shanghai Sanctuary: Chinese and Japanese Policies toward European Jewish Refugees during World War II* (Oxford: Oxford University Press, 2013).

I consulted most frequently. My own approach to Jewish survivors in China also draws extensively upon the research of Irene Eber, especially her collection of original sources entitled *Voices from Shanghai: Jewish Exiles in Wartime China*.[18]

In discussing the rescue of rabbinical leadership during the war, I drew upon Ephraim Zuroff's well-documented study: *The Response of Orthodox Jewry in the United States to the Holocaust*.[19] This book focuses upon the Vaad ha-Hatzala Rescue Committee, which was instrumental in aiding Chaya Leah and her family. In fact, there is evidence that Rabbi Shmuel David Walkin was one of the people who helped to distribute funds among the refugees in Shanghai, along with chief Rabbi Meir Ashkenazi.

The funds for this organization had been raised with great urgency and self-sacrifice in the United States during the *Shoah*. Responses to Zuroff's work have been both appreciative and highly contentious. No one challenges his scrupulous inquiry into the original documentation of the Vaad ha-Hatzala archives, which provides for the first time a clear chronology of the fundraising initiated by American rabbis at a time when the US government was doing very little to help victims of the Holocaust.

Questions raised by David Kranzler and Jonathan Rosenblum[20] (among others) center upon Zuroff's critique of the "particularism" of this rescue operation. Was rescuing Torah scholars the only goal of the Vaad ha-Hatzala's exceptionally committed efforts? Did the funds that managed to reach Shanghai provide dignified survival solely for orthodox Jews, such as Chaya Leah's father and the students of the Mirrer Yeshiva?

Without entering into the details of this controversy, I am hoping that this narrative of Chaya Leah's life will cast new light upon these questions and thereby illuminate the inner landscape of Jewish survivors. The time is ripe now, I believe, to look more deeply into how Shanghai as a locale that shaped the meaning of life for Chaya Leah's generation. On the simplest level, the Chinese word *shang* (上) connotes an upward direction that also suggests something elevated or worthy of respect. When coupled with the Hebrew and

---

18 Irene Eber, *Voices from Shanghai: Jewish Exiles in Wartime China* (Chicago: University of Chicago Press, 2008).
19 Efraim Zuroff, *The Response of Orthodox Jewry in the United States to the Holocaust: The Activities of the Vaad Ha-Hatzala Rescue Committee 1939-1945* (New York: KTAV Publishing House, 2000).
20 Jonathan Rosenblum, "Anatomy of a Slander," *The Jewish Observer*, August, 2005.

Yiddish term *chai* (חי), the name of this city can be seen as the site of an enlivened existence, one that depended both upon endurance and ethical agency.

Combined, שנחי—*Shang-chai*—is more than a place in time. It becomes a pathway for understanding how Jews managed to shape history rather than being its victims. For the Walkin family, this sense of agency was deeply rooted in an abiding faith in Jewish destiny. The music of Talmudic learning never ceased in Chaya Leah's world, whether the place was Lukatch, Vilna, Kobe, or Shanghai.

Among the many sources that comprised this regimen of study were biblical texts admonishing Jews to set up cities of refuge. Long before the crisis of displaced persons overwhelmed Europe during the *Shoah*—and again in our own times of war and terrorism—we read about the commandment to establish cities of refuge in chapter 34 of *Bamidbar* (the *Book of Numbers*). In these verses, Moses is instructed to designate certain cities in the Land of Israel to which anyone may flee who kills a person accidentally.

Called *irei miklat* these cities are meant to protect the killer from the vengeance of blood relatives of the deceased. These places were meant to harbor only those who truly did not foresee the consequences of their actions.

With due respect to historical and cultural differences, these *irei miklat* may yet provide a new paradigm for thinking about refugees. In a recent essay entitled "Refugee Awareness," Rabbi Jacob E. Fine argues for the heightened relevance of ancient Jewish teachings in the wake of the wars in Iraq, Afghanistan, and Sudan. Using the Talmud's elaboration of the biblical injunction to build cities of refuge, Fine points out:

> A Jewish court is obligated to straighten the roads to the cities of refuge, to repair them and broaden them. They must remove all impediments and obstacles… bridges should be built (over all natural barriers) so as not to delay one who is fleeing. "Refuge, Refuge" was written at all crossroads so that the perpetrator of manslaughter should recognize the way and turn there." These teachings reflect something remarkable about the rabbinic attitude toward cities of refuge. The emphasis on the great width and sound condition of the roads leading to cities of refuge, coupled with the injunction to widely publicize the existence of such paths, illustrates the seriousness with which the rabbis approached this biblically mandated communal responsibility.[21]

---

21 Jacob E. Fine, "Refugee Awareness," My Jewish Learning, http://www.myjewishlearning.com/article/refugee-awareness/. Accessed August 13, 2017.

When Chaya Leah's family was forced to flee their home in 1939, there were no clear signposts directing refugees to safety. Their pathways were torturous, filled with fear and uncertainty.

Every bit of kindness along the way was deemed a miracle of divine providence revealed through the hands of specific human beings. From an exit visa signed by Japanese consul Chiune Sugihara to the caring ministrations of a Chinese *amah* (a young country girl brought in to help with housekeeping chores), the Walkin family benefitted from the generosity of strangers. Yet, the meaning of life that they affirmed throughout their years of refuge was all their own. It is this act of conscious affirmation that became the central theme of my own book about Chaya Leah Walkin.

IN THE CROOK OF THE ROCK

There is a world of difference between being simply a refugee and crafting one's own destiny in an inhospitable world. Refugees are constantly at the mercy of others. They are uprooted, cast out, defined by labels pasted upon their documents, their faces, their souls. Chaya Leah's childhood was also marked and marred by such degradation. But neither she nor her family became what they were labeled—stateless persons simply drifting according to the whims of a world increasingly consumed by a crazed hatred of Jews. They remained deeply, fully Jewish. They also remained humane toward others, with powers of giving and nurturing that one would not have expected among the dispossessed.

Simcha Elberg, who was one of the younger Torah scholars in Shanghai, recalled this combination of despair and kindness in an essay that pays tribute to Chaya Leah's father, Rabbi Shmuel David Walkin. Entitled "An *Ish Chesed* Whose Hospitality Knew No Bounds," this work starts with the author's poignant recollection of terror and loneliness before the Walkin family responded to the pain of an orphaned Jewish youth:

> When World War II broke out, we were forced to flee from our homes and cities and we became refugees. We roamed from one country to another and could not settle down anywhere. We arrived as temporary uninvited guests. As a refugee, I was dreadfully lonely and learned about the misery of a person living by himself as a person whom the Torah decreed had to live in a City of Refuge far from his father and mother, and far from friends to whom he could reveal the sorrow in his heart… One man substantially

relieved my loneliness. Who was that noble character who strengthened me and infused me with hope, who always found the right word succor for my limbs with drops of solace and vitality? It was Rabbi and *gaon* Harav Shmuel Walkin, zt'l... The amazing hospitality he showed me gave me the feeling that I have found not only a devoted and faithful friend but a father figure."[22]

Here, a noted Torah scholar (who became the founder and editor of the journal *Pardes* after the war) looks back at himself as an orphan in Shanghai. Elberg recalls the loneliness of a homeless refugee as well as the exceptional humanness that shone forth from the Walkin family, especially Chaya Leah's father. The quest to understand the wellspring of such solace in times of darkness led time and again to the words of *Shir Ha'Shirim*, Solomon's poetic *Song of Songs*.

In this ancient love poem, I found a fount of metaphors that helped to illuminate my work as the interlocutor of Chaya Leah's story. Initially, I had not expected a narrative of Jewish survival to have such a fruitful dialogue with a series of songs focused upon the passionate relationship between a man and a woman—a relationship that, according to rabbinical commentaries, also mirrors the devotion between the Jewish people and the divine. Over time, however, I have found that the verses of this poem were uniquely well suited for every step in my writing about the Walkin family.

A passage in chapter 2 of *Shir Ha'Shirim* has been especially useful as I sought the main themes of this work. I have used it both as the title of the book and as the key to a pivotal chapter about Chaya Leah's life in Shanghai. Here are the verses in the masterful translation of Ariel and Chana Bloch:[23]

> My dove in the crook of the rock,
> In the hiding place of the steep,
> Show me your visage,
> Let me hear your voice.

"The crook of the rock" and "hiding place of the steep" convey the difficulties of surviving in the midst of hardship, the loneliness of being embedded in a foreign world. The Hebrew words in the last two lines were especially apt as I was redefining my own calling as a historian:

---

22 Simcha Elberg, "Hagaon Harav Shmuel Walkin zt"l," *Hamodia* (August 14, 2014), 1.
23 Chana Bloch and Ariel Bloch, *The Song of Songs: A New Translation, Introduction and Commentary* (New York, NY: Random House, 1995).

> *harini et mareaich*
> *hashemini et kolech.*
> *show me your visage*
> *I would like to hear your voice.*

Here, the vulnerable dove is asked to show her face, to sound her call in times and places inimical to song.

I, too, had sought the face of history in Chaya Leah's narrative and found that it was the question of voice that accosted me. This question carried the sound of both anguish and hope and it demanded that I find words to convey its complexity.

On Chaya Leah's childhood-resident certificate in Shanghai there is a face, but no sound. A small girl gazes out seriously, frozen in time. Two English words "*Polish Refugee*" stick out amid rows of Chinese characters. The child's name on this fraying piece of paper is typed simply as C. Walkin, a diminished hint of the complex self, much like the thumbprint beneath the photograph, personal and utterly generic at the same time.

In other documents, the girl is called "Chaja" or at times more fully "Chaia Leah." Each different spelling reflects an awkward, official attempt to place this eldest sibling among the Walkin children in a box where she might stay for a while. The boxes changed, the names changed, none conveying the inner struggles that define meaningful survival. None of the documents labeling this refugee give a hint about the passionate engagement with the sources of Jewish learning that remained a lifeline in the Walkin family's darkest hours.

So, I kept turning to *Shir Ha'Shirim* in order to hear better the music of affection between Jews and their life-sustaining traditions. Rabbinical tradition teaches that the words of erotic intimacy between the "*Dod*" (the Lover) and the "*Raya*" (the Beloved) reflect the love affair between the Jewish people and their redeemer. Without limiting it to a single event in history, commentators suggest that *Shir Ha'Shirim* encompasses key moments in the exodus from Egypt, in the building of the First Temple, and in the Babylonian exile as well during the long dispersion that followed the destruction of the Second Temple.

The human lovers in the poem seek one another, like the Jewish people ceaselessly in quest of protection throughout their trials and tribulations. This description of an intensely intimate relationship was incorporated into the traditional cannon through the advocacy of Rabbi Akiva, a foremost teacher and martyr who lived in the early second century CE. The Mishna (in *Yadaim* 3:5) records a debate about the status of this erotic poem. None of the other rabbis of that period doubted the value of *Shir Ha'Shirim*. But few were ready to grant it sacred status.

Rabbi Akiva, who had lived through persecution and endured a horrifyingly cruel death, was able to summarize the fullness of light and hope in *Shir Ha'Shirim* as follows: "The entire Bible is holy. But the Song of Songs is the Holy of Holies." It was in this most exalted chamber of Jewish learning that I found fresh words to reimagine Jewish survival during the *Shoah*.

Far from being a passive victim of fate, the *Raya* in *Shir Ha'Shirim* is a strong-willed young woman who is confident in her quest for the Lover's ardor and protection. She called to mind Chaya Leah and her descriptions of a community that managed to affirm its humanness even during the darkest hours of the war. In settings that were more daunting than the cliff alluded to in *Shir Ha'Shirim*, I glimpsed the face of kindness, the sound of delicate hope.

Following that glimmer of light, I came to understand more deeply why rabbinical commentators chose to link the trembling dove to the hour when Jewish people stood terrified at the Sea of Reeds. With the Egyptian army coming at them from behind and the watery depths looming in front, they, too, had given voice to both fear and awe.

While sheltered inside a steep cliff, the dove is invited out to show her visage. This invitation, I felt, was addressed to me as well as I entered more deeply into Chaya Leah's narrative. My own voice had to be heard in our conversations. It was not enough to seek the face of the past. I had to make room for its shadows in the present with unvarnished words.

In an email sent to me early in our work together, Chaya Leah described as follows the feelings of piecing together fear and hope. Speaking about the challenge of putting together a collection of photographs for this book, she wrote:

> *Yes, the pictures are beautiful …*
> *and the masks are going to be removed,*
> *the makeup will be washed away*
> *and the nakedness will be exposed.*

My goal was never simply to remove masks, since there was little that was presented to me that was made glossier than the reality had been. Nonetheless, it was a delicate challenge to enter a survivor's world where vulnerability still reigns supreme.

Anchored by the words of *Shir Ha'Shirim*, I tried to tread delicately into Chaya Leah Walkin's world. All along, I had to remind myself that this is a history more complex than I can possibly fathom today. How can I come close and stay respectfully distant at the same time?

One answer to this query came from Rabbi Joseph Soloveitchik's masterful work entitled: *And From There You Shall Seek*. In this book, the *Song of Songs* is linked to a larger human quest for revelation. According to Rabbi Soloveitchik, this journey leads man to confront "realities unsought and often unwelcome."[24] One of those realities is the repeatedly failed or deferred communication that marks every chapter of *Shir Ha'Shirim*. Linking this process to the darkest historical events of the twentieth century, the author concludes that we have no choice but to live with what we cannot fully understand.

In an age captivated by theories and abstractions, I believe that our challenge remains the recovery of the complexities of lived experience. Rabbi Joseph Soloveitchik identified a key aspect of this challenge as follows:

> Living experience of God, who transcends our human conceptions, confronts us as a philosophy-denying Other even as he addresses and makes himself available to us.[25]

In Chaya Leah's story, I also encountered such philosophy-denying otherness. I was privileged to be addressed by a woman who had faced the darkness of being a refugee and also stood her ground as a builder of Jewish community after the war. Recovering the fragments of Chaya Leah's story and placing them in a fuller context was, I now see, a truly sacred task for both of us.

---

24 Joseph B. Soloveitchik, *And from There You Shall Seek* (New York: KTAV Publishing House, 2009), 32.
25 Ibid., 42.

CHAPTER 1

IF SHE BE AS A WALL:

Pohost and Lukatch before Disaster Strikes

> *If she will be like a wall,*
> *We will build upon her*
> *A fortress of silver,*
> *And if she will be like a door*
> *We will enclose her with cedar.*
>
> Shir Ha'Shirim 8:9

In the spring of 1934, when Chaya Leah Walkin was born, the world was already headed for disaster. Not all the signs were evident as a chilly spring swept over the hamlet of Pohost in Poland, a day's cart ride drive from Pinsk. The town had about five hundred and fifty Jews who made their living through crafts, fish from the Pohost Lake, and the sawmill. There was a modest shul; Chaya Leah's father, Rav Shmuel David Walkin, was its spiritual leader. As the first child of Rav Shmuel David and his wife Tzivia, Chaya Leah would learn to shoulder the joys and responsibilities of the oldest sibling during her years as a refugee in China and Japan. For now, the infant rocked in a pram sent as a gift from Chaya Leah's great-grandfather without an inkling of the darkness to come. On May 20, 1934, Chaya Leah's birthdate was officially recorded in the city of Pinsk.

To the west of Pohost and Pinsk, the winds of war were gathering despite talk of peace. On January 26, 1934, Germany and Poland signed a non-aggression pact that was to change the face of Europe and alter the fate of the Walkin family. Until that time, it was France that had orchestrated diplomacy in central Europe. Poland now shifted away from the French

Chaya Leah as an infant with her parents Rabbi Shmuel David and Tzivia Walkin ca. 1934.

influence and became the first country to reach an understanding with the National Socialist regime, already heavily affected by Hitler's ambitions. By June 20, 1934, on a Saturday that would be celebrated as Shabbat in Pohost, Hitler's SS launched a killing operation called, euphemistically,

"Kolibri" (hummingbird). It led to the assassination of more than seventy top officials of the German government.

From that day onward, it was clear that the Nazi's "Night of Long Knives" would be harsher and longer than anyone had imagined. In time, this brutality would reach even the small town of Pohost and lead to the murder of the vast majority of Jews, including those who lived in nearby Pinsk.

In Asia, where a fragment of the Walkin family would find refuge, violence also reigned supreme. Jiang Kai-shek's government, which had been hounding and hunting the small communist remnant that survived the White Terror of 1927, appeared to have achieved its objectives. Five encirclement campaigns later, the Nationalists succeeded in dismantling the Communists' Jiangxi Soviet. A tiny band managed to escape and started what would become the epic 6,000-mile Long March that eventually brought Mao Zedong to power in 1949.

In early 1934, however, this was an inconceivable outcome. German advisors had helped to plan Jiang Kai-shek's campaigns against the communist enclave and they had every reason to celebrate the collapse of resistance in Jiangxi. Yet victory over the communists was embittered by the Japanese aggression in Manchuria. On March 1, 1934, during the spring when Chaya Leah was born, the last scion of the Qing dynasty, Puyi, ascended to the throne as "Emperor of Manchukuo"—a Japanese-controlled puppet state.

In Japan itself, the 1932 assassination of the moderate Prime Minister Inukai Tsuyoshi had consolidated the influence of bellicose army officers. Reigning emperor Hirohito lacked both the power and the will to stem the tide of events that would lead to the invasion of China, starting with the Mukden Incident of 1931. China's shame and her losses would lead to chaos in Shanghai. This defeat, in turn, saved the life of the Walkin family and that of more than 20,000 other Jewish refugees.

AZOI WILL DER ZEIDE

Chaya Leah Walkin came into a world in which the ancient words of the *Shir Ha'Shirim* had become building blocks of personal and communal identity. The little girl, like her nearest kin, basked in the security of knowing that the God of Israel was a constant protector, who would enclose his people like a fortress of silver. The vulnerability of walls and doors, so explicit in the poem, was a familiar predicament in daily Jewish history, but it was assumed that assiduous Torah scholarship would keep most grave dangers at bay. Unlike less learned Jews, who kept the commandments out of fear while going on with daily chores, Chaya Leah's rabbinical family had built up a framework for understanding divine will through prolonged engagement with sacred texts.

This framework proved to be both resilient and life nourishing in the dark times that lay ahead. Even during the years in which the world turned its back on Jews, when children of Chaya Leah's age could not be protected by their parents during the *Shoah*, the *Song of Songs* lost none of its evocative tower. Even as *emunah* (the art of faith) and *yirat shamayim* (trembling awe) were battered by war and the hardships of displacement, the ancient words remained an anchor of hope, a point of return—if not to a physical home, then to the scholarly traditions that had nourished the Walkin family in Pohost and beyond.

Chaya Leah's parents and grandparents were heirs to a Judaism fortified by centuries of Torah learning. Tzivia Walkin's father was Rabbi Avrohom Socharow, the spiritual leader of the hamlet of Trabe, in Poland. A letter penned in his careful Yiddish script bears testimony to his tireless efforts to strengthen the physical and spiritual well-being of his fellow Jews. Dated February 4, 1932, two years before the birth of Chaya Leah, this letter was addressed to the Central Committee for Religious Education in Vilna (which was part of Poland at that time) urging cooperation with the Society for the Safeguarding the Health of the Jewish Population in order to establish a religious school for Trabe youths.[1]

Rabbi Socharow had used coded language about bales of dry goods to hint at the funds needed for this urgent task. Even as he celebrated his daughter's wedding in 1932, this Torah leader did not turn a blind eye to the needs of his impoverished and persecuted community. Eight years later, in 1940, Trabe's Jews were accused of a blood libel—an old excuse to launch wholesale attacks against the entire population. When Reverend Waclaw Rodsko, a pastor in Trabe, was found dead, it did not take long to accuse three Jews of murder as well as crimes against the Dominican monks in the Czortkow monastery. By July 1941, the arrival of German troops in Trabe sealed the fate of the Jews as victims of the *Shoah*. By that time, Chaya Leah and her parents had begun the frantic search for a way out of their hatred-riddled home terrain.

In 1934, however, this heavy dread had not yet fallen upon the young couple who became Chaya Leah's parents. Theirs had been a marriage arranged

---

1 Abraham Sacharaw, "Letter from Rabbi Abraham Sacharaw of Traby, Poland addressed to Chjrew," *YIVO Digital Archive on Jewish Life in Poland*. February 4, 1932.

with great care and concern by the eminent Torah luminaries of that time. As Chaya Leah recalled in one of her earliest jottings for our project:

> *Rabbi Elchonon Wassermann spoke to Reb Moishe Landinski (my mother's grandfather) about the Bais Aharon's son. Reb Aharon Walkin, my grandfather, went by the name Bais Aharon after one of his sforim. So my grandfather Avrohom Socharow took his daughter Cila to meet the Pinsker Rav.*
>
> *The father and daughter met the Pinsker Rav, halfway from Trabe to Pinsk at an inn. My mother was 16 and very beautiful. My father was at least eighteen years her senior. The four of them spent some time talking and then the Trabber Rav and the Bais Aharon left the room.*
>
> *My mother and father spent time talking. They spoke about a new sefer that had just come out by the Gerrer Rebbe. After some time, the Trabber Rav came in and asked how it went, and my mother said it was very pleasant.*
>
> *"But," she said, "I am so young and he is so old. Why would you want me to marry him?"*
>
> *The Trabber Rav answered, "Azoi will der Zeide" ["This is wish of the Grandfather" (Rav Moishe Landinski)].*
>
> *My mother consented and her father said, "Tochterel du bist ah kallah" ("My dear daughter, you are now a bride").*

The last line of this conversation would be uttered again with as much love and respect in New York when Chaya Leah became engaged to Michael Small, seven years her senior. By that time, however, the fires of history had opened up the eyes of the little girl who had been a refugee in Shanghai. Like her mother, Chaya Leah was privileged to have a long marriage marked by deep affection and mutual attraction. Her husband, like her father, knew (as Chaya Leah put it) "how to put a woman on a pedestal and worship the ground she walks on."

Although this is an American-sounding colloquialism, Chaya Leah's sentiment grew out of a long tradition in which Jewish men recited King Solomon's praises of womanhood in a Friday night song called *"Eshet Hayil"* (A Woman of Valor). In this poem, the valiant wife is deemed more precious than pearls, stronger than all the ships that crossed the oceans in search of rare goods.

Far from being disposed of as unimportant merchandise, Jewish daughters in rabbinical families such as that of Tzivia Socharow were cherished, cared for, worried over. The encounter at the inn between Trabe and Pinsk was dignified, well planned, and allowed the young people the autonomy of decision making. To be sure, the wishes of "der Zeide" mattered. Rabbi Moishe Landinski was a renowned Torah scholar and Rosh Yeshiva in Radin. He had been entrusted to guide an entire generation of scholars by one of the most respected figures the Jewish world, the Chofetz Chaim. The Bais Aharon was also a much respected scholar and a communal leader whose son was a student at the Radin Yeshiva.

Yet, as it became clear in later recollections, Rav Shmuel David Walkin was not suggested as the groom simply because of his illustrious lineage. Rather, as a student in Rabbi Moishe Landinski's yeshiva, he had distinguished himself through his exceptional *midot*—personally cultivated character traits that centered on giving to and caring for others. In a recent children's story entitled "Feeling a Friend's Pain," Rav Shmuel David is recalled as a young *bocher* (yeshiva student) who literally gave the coat off his back to another student who was poor and had nothing to wear under his own *chuppa* (marriage canopy). Another time, Rabbi Landinski's own son noticed the young rav Walkin banging upon a tree in the forest, begging aloud for the healing of a sick friend.[2]

This spiritual fervor as well as selflessness drew the attention of the Rosh Yeshiva (head of the Radin Talmudical academy) and led to the receptive response that met the marriage proposal put forth by Rabbi Elchonon Wasserman. These *midot* were also noticed and cherished by the community of refugees in Kobe and Shanghai who considered Rav Shmuel David Walkin to be the *Rosh Ha Golah* (*leader of exiles*)—the unquestioned father figure who cared for the well-being of each and every Jew who ached with homelessness during the war.

Rabbi Wasserman (1874–1941), who had ignited the conversation that led to the marriage of Chaya Leah's parents, was himself a towering figure in both scholarship and moral courage. A follower of the Brisk style of Talmudic learning pioneered by Rabbi Chaim Soloveitchik, he had also studied in the early years of the twentieth century at the Radin Yeshiva before taking on the leadership of Novardok Yeshiva in 1921. After a fundraising trip to the United States for his students displaced by World War I and the Bolshevik Revolution, Rabbi Wasserman returned to Vilna. In the summer of 1941, on a visit to Kaunas (Kovno, where thousands of refugee were struggling to obtain visas out of the Nazi-occupied Poland and Lithuania), Elchonon Wasserman was arrested by the SS. He was condemned to death along with twelve other rabbis. Before being gunned down inside the Kaunas Fortress, Rabbi Wassermann was heard saying:

> In Heaven it appears that they deem us to be righteous because our bodies were chosen to atone for the Jewish people… With fire was she

---

2   Chani, "Feeling a Friend's Pain," *Binah Bunch*, July 4, 2016, 3.

(Jerusalem) destroyed, and with fire she will be rebuilt. The very fire which consumes our bodies will one day rebuild the Jewish people.[3]

Little did Rabbi Wasserman know in that dark hour how true his words would become, literally. The ardor for Torah learning that he had glimpsed in the young Rav Shmuel David Walkin would indeed become part of the conflagration of spirit that sustained Jewish life in Shanghai and also helped to renew it on America's shores after the war.

When he first proposed the marriage between Tzivia Socharow and Shmuel David Walkin in 1932, Rabbi Wasserman had no way of anticipating the murderous events that consumed his life. Yet, he already understood the importance of this young couple's commitment to strengthening the Jewish people through Torah learning. Tzivia, who called herself Cila, was a highly educated woman who matched her groom's accomplishments. In an era in which schooling for girls was not deemed to be a very high priority, she was well versed both in Jewish and secular knowledge. Tzivia Socharow had gone to a distinguished *gymnasium* and was fluent in Russian, Polish, Yiddish, and Hebrew. In her friends' circles, she was known for strong convictions as well as for her gentle, nonjudgmental way of expressing them. Cila's gift for calming people in distress was noted early and came in handy as she became her husband's partner in caring for the spiritual and physical needs of refugees in China and Japan.

Rabbi Shmuel David and Tzivia Walkin ca. 1932

---

3 Yitchok Grodinsky, "The last moments of Rav Elchonon Wasserman Before His Murder," *The Yeshiva World* (April 10, 2010).

The invitation for the Friday afternoon wedding of Tzivia and Shmuel David Walkin was traditional and modest. Three names appear in large print amid the Hebrew abbreviations for "bride," "groom," and "rabbi" and "Aharon Walkin"—the eminent father of the groom. Interestingly, on the lower left, there are three non-Hebrew words: "Rabin Walkin" and Traby (the Polish spelling of the hamlet where the wedding took place and which Jews referred to as Trabe).

Clearly, this was an event that reached beyond the insular world of the yeshiva community that had nurtured both groom and bride. What representatives from that broader Jewish world attended the celebration is not clear. The surviving photos focus only on two tables: that of the groom and his friends and that of the bride with her siblings and friends.

In the photograph of the groom's table, Shmuel David Walkin sits beneath an iconic portrait of his mentor—the Chofetz Chaim—surrounded by a group of young men wearing stylish hats. Most are clean shaven, as was also the style of the Mirrer Yeshiva in Shanghai. The custom in the Walkin family was for the groom to grow a beard, *hadrat panim* (facial glory), only after he became betrothed to his bride. Rav Shmuel David looks serious and dignified and sports the same trim beard and new suit that had adorned his formal engagement photograph with the young Tzivia. In that portrait, the bride faces the camera sideways, eyes looking forward with hope. She is dressed modestly and elegantly in a dark dress trimmed with a gleaming white collar.

At her wedding feast, Tzivia stands robed in a white dress with a lace veil draped around her uncovered face. Surrounding her are a group women friends and little children—a far more crowded image than the groom's table. Chaya Leah mused in one of her jottings about this photograph with the following words:

> *The young bride surrounded by friends and family, the chain of links, each more precious than the other, each link a circle of infinity, never knowing the beginning or the end.*
>
> *My mother and her friends.*
> *And on the floor her siblings.*
> *The twins.*
> *I always remember my mother mumbling:*
> *"The tzviling (twins) were only eight years old."*
> *The weddings in Poland were usually on Friday so that on Shabbos they would have sheva brochos. Usually it was not for seven days, but just Shabbos.*
> *Poverty was a major factor in not having a week of sheva brochos.*
> *It was right after the sheva brochos that my mother and father went to their first stele (job/position).*

I think it must have been Pohost.
My mother was beautiful, cultured, and highly educated for that period.

Here, in Chaya Leah's words, we sense how the future darkness came to shadow a bridal portrait. Many of the young women surrounding the new Rebbetzin Walkin did not survive the *Shoah*. The four little children on the floor below the well-appointed table also did not survive, including the *tzvilings* so dear to Tzivia.

These links in what Chaya Leah terms the "chain of infinity" were severed but not forgotten. The wedding moment thus endures beyond all the trials and suffering of the Walkin family precisely because it was so firmly rooted in Torah traditions. Furthermore, this moment would carry forward in time and lead to the creation of more Jewish families that would continue to celebrate weddings with the dignity glimpsed here in 1932. Even after there was enough wealth to have a full week of nuptial celebrations (*sheva brachot*), the ideal couple remained a paradigm of learning and dignity as in the photograph of Tzivia and Shmuel David on their wedding day in Trabe.

Both the groom's and the bride's tables are decorated simply and graciously. A few cakes and candles are set out upon handmade linen and lace. Poverty was clearly a factor here despite the rabbinical position of Tzivia's father and the eminence of the Bais Aharon from Pinsk. Later, after the war, the Walkin families were able to host many *sheva brachot* celebrated with wine and seven blessings. Chaya Leah's own wedding to Rabbi Michael Small became Tzivia Walkin's grandest affair, with nearly 800 guests. Nonetheless, the focus on *kedusha*—the inner holiness of a Jewish marriage—extended directly from the modest gathering in Trabe to the large ballroom in New York where Rav Shmuel David's oldest daughter became Rebbetzin Small.

In 1932, the young Walkin couple left immediately after the wedding to their first rabbinical post, their first *stele*. The 18-year-old Tzivia accompanied a more seasoned husband to his first job. Her natural grace and her education helped to smooth their transition into a small community where they were expected to fill many roles. For a few short years, it was possible to maintain close contact with parents and grandparents who provided ongoing mentoring and support.

Before the winds of war blew across Poland and Belarus, Tzivia and Shmuel David had six years to build their own family, to welcome three children into the world: Chaya Leah, born in Pohost in 1934; Esther, born in Rav Shmuel David's next job in the town of Troki in 1935; and Moshe Yoel, born in 1938 during his last rabbinical *stele* in Europe in the city of Lukatch.

Three years after the birth of this son, a much grayer Rav Walkin was photographed in Shanghai. One of the images found in the United States Holocaust Memorial Museum's archives carries the following label: "A group of Jewish refugee yeshiva students gather around Rabbi Samuel Walkin former rebbe of Lukatz Kreuz (near Poznan)." It was the hardships of displacement that led the young man who had married Tzivia in 1932 to become a beloved "rebbe" for refugees in China. One of these yeshiva students who donated the photograph to the Washington Museum identified the name of the Walkins' last hamlet that, like all the others, had been consumed by the fires of the *Shoah*.

EINE ENIKLE FUN BAIS AHARON

Before China, before Japan, before harrowing weeks in Vilna and on the trans-Siberian railroad, the young Walkin family had time to bask in the security of family roots. The condensed geography of Jewish life in Poland and Belarus made it possible to maintain links between Trabe, Pohost, Troki, Lukatch, Radin and Pinsk. A young bride could go to rest at her parents' home after the birth of a child. A newly minted rabbi called upon to serve others could return to his own yeshiva and receive valuable counsel from a former rebbe, from his learned father, and from friends.

Tzivia and Shmuel David thrived in such a network of support. In one of the first photographs of Chaya Leah's life, a well-bundled infant with a beribboned bonnet sits in the lap of her stylishly dressed mother. A fur collar and finely tailored suit frames the face of the young Rebbetzin Walkin. The proud new father stands to the side in a long winter coat and sporting the beard of a newly married man. It is winter; the mood is somber, yet far from the dread that would fall upon this family a few years later. Another photograph, also taken in winter, shows the child inside an elegant, old-fashioned baby carriage:

> My mother had loved that picture of me in the pram and always reminded me: "See my child, this if the gift from the Alter Zeide." I was zhoche (privileged) to know my great grandfather and cherished the connections to the Yeshiva in Radin. Although the pram did not make it to Shanghai, the cherishing of our family legacy did. It nourished our darkest hours during the flight from home and in Shanghai…
>
> Winter has always been serenity for me. It was not just being home and watching the world rest, seeing the trees covered in a white blanket, and the earth a virgin white. Winter is so very calming for me.

How much could an eight- or nine-month-old infant remember from the winter of 1934–35? It was the photographs themselves and Tzivia Walkin's often-repeated memories of Rabbi Moishe Landinski that built up this "nourishment" that sustained Chaya Leah's family in Shanghai.

The little girl had indeed met her great-grandfather. As a grown woman, she understood how important the gift of the elegant pram had been, coming from an elder who had cared enough to suggest the marriage to Rav Shmuel David in the first place. The pram, the fur collar, the well-cut winter clothing, the beribboned infant—all this speaks of a world at peace. Looking back, Chaya Leah dwells upon the serenity that blanketed winters in Poland and later her own home in Chicago.

Rabbi Aharon Walkin, known as the Pinsker Rav and as the Bais Aharon (after his well known work by this title) 1865-1942.

The same wintery peace emanates from the formal portrait of Rabbi Aharon Walkin that graces the home of each of his grandchildren. Here is a stately sage with a tall fur hat, white beard unfurling over a generously cut fur coat, an elegant cane firmly in hand. Round, modern-looking glasses enhance the vivid eyes that had not yet seen the worst of what would befall the Jewish world during the Holocaust. In this photograph, we glimpse the Torah scholar who was already known as the "Bais Aharon" for his highly valued commentary on the Talmud. The prestige of his scholarship continued to extend after the war and to add honor to his descendants long after his tragic death in the Pinsk ghetto in the winter of 1942.

Chaya Leah's brother, Rav Chaim Walkin, recalls visiting the famous Rebbe of Gur as a young yeshiva student in the 1960s. To his surprise, the elder man got up in front of the boy who was only twenty, saying: *ein einkle fun de Bais Aron*—"a grandson of the Bais Aharon." Chaya Leah, a granddaughter who carries the name of the mother of the Bais Aharon, is also mindful of both the honor and the responsibility that comes with being the scion of such an eminent Torah sage.

Born in 1865, Aharon Walkin had already shown great Torah promise in his early childhood. His parents appreciated his gift for learning but had few means with which to support the necessary schooling. In the introduction to his commentary on the Talmud tractate of Baba Kama, Rav Aharon looked back and described his early years as being marked by hunger and material deprivation. Material scarcity, however, was no impediment to his devotion to study and this commitment continued to inspire his son's family in their time of scarcity as refugees in Shanghai.

At thirteen, Aharon Walkin became a student at the famed Volozhin Yeshiva and grew especially close to its leader—the Netziv, Rabbi Yehuda Berlin (1816–93). After the death of his teacher, Rabbi Walkin used his feelings of loss to dedicate himself even more strenuously to Torah scholarship. Married at the age of eighteen to the daughter of the highly respected Sorotzkin family, Aharon Walkin saw himself as a unique channel for strengthening Jewish tradition worldwide. In 1912, he became one of the key founders of Agudas Yisrael, an international organization of observant Jews dedicated to shoring up Torah values and to fighting against the new ideology of Zionism. In the words of Rabbi Berel Wein, a historian of Jewish life in the modern period, Rabbi Walkin was a "particularly effective and influential figure in the Agudas movement precisely because he was not a Party man."[4] He was far less judgmental than other rabbis, and was known for a more open-minded concern for values that would ensure the growth of the Orthodox community in Europe as well as in the United States.

In 1914, while on a fact-finding mission to the United States on the eve of World War I, Rabbi Aharon Walkin again showed great independence of mind by speaking positively about the future potential of American Jewry. While other European rabbinical figures bemoaned the freedoms and the economic opportunities that were leading immigrants away from Shabbat and *kashrut* (laws of keeping a kosher diet), Rabbi Aharon Walkin was visionary enough to emphasize that this seemingly materialistic community would set high standards for Torah learning in the years to come. He even made the "revolutionary" suggestion that Lithuanian and Polish yeshivas should teach English to prepare rabbis to communicate directly with their parishioners in the United States. This "out-of-the-box" outlook continues to characterize his disciples who remain fully engaged in the Torah world while being effective participants in the world beyond the Orthodox community.

In his time, however, Rabbi Aharon Walkin's contemporaries did not embrace these suggestions and the American Orthodox community continued to shrink before the war, as newly arrived immigrants did not want their children to be immersed in the old Yiddish-speaking world.

The high caliber of the Bais Aharon's scholarship and his well-reasoned responsa to halachic questions from around the world continued to gain fame and respect. One example surfaced recently about a *kashrut* dispute that was brought to the attention of Rav Walkin: a *shochet* (ritual slaughterer) was rumored to have visited occasionally a woman suspected of prostitution. Local community leaders wanted to disqualify the man on moral grounds and close his business. Rav Walkin wrote a strongly worded responsum that pointed out that it is strictly forbidden to remove a person from his post on mere hearsay. In his own life, as in his writings, the Bais Aharon urged a careful and generous-spirited approach to Jewish life. This attitude colored every aspect of Chaya Leah's life as well.

The work of scholarship that was to be his most enduring contribution was written while imprisoned by the Soviet regime for his activities promoting

---

4   Berel Wein, "Rabbi Aharon Walkin," in *Guide Through The Dark Years—10 Lectures*. Audio compilation (Jerusalem: RabbiWein.com, 2012).

Jewish life and education. It was also reprinted with great effort by his son in Shanghai, where it continued to inspire and nurture the minds and lives of the young refugees who would become Torah teachers after the war.

Scholarship alone did not account for the high repute of this "uniquely colorful man," to quote Rabbi Berel Wein.[5] His personal warmth and moral courage cast a protective mantle around embattled Jewry between the two world wars. After his release from the Soviet prison in the early years of the Bolshevik Revolution, the Bais Aharon managed to escape to Poland, where he was appointed chief rabbi the town of Pinsk and Rosh Yeshiva of the Pinsk/Karlin Yeshiva—which was one of the important centers of Jewish learning in Poland and later Belarus. A letter dating from 1930 addressed to natives of Pinsk residing in New York (a city he had visited and was impressed by earlier) reveals Rav Walkin's passionate concern for the future of the Polish community under his care. With almost prophetic vision, he wrote: "The situation in Pinsk is horrific. Please save us!"[6]

Addressing himself to "brethren from our city residing in New York," Aharon Walkin described the dire needs of two young men studying in his yeshiva:

> Although their spiritual substance is abundant, the Yeshiva students are direly lacking material needs and are nearly starving to death… . It is painful to observe the dear students studying Torah day and night, suffering from the pangs of poverty.[7]

This same cry would be reiterated repeatedly, as yeshiva students were in danger of perishing in Eastern Europe and later as refugees in China. Such requests were not simply about material needs. To be sure, the well-known adage that "without flour, there is no Torah" was familiar to all, including the young Aharon Walkin, who had himself known the pangs of hunger.

In the tearful tone of a 1930 letter, as well in the manifest courage of the Pinsker Rav under the Nazi occupation, we glimpse a call to conscience: if the young men who embody the Torah tradition perish, the Bais Aharon argued, all Jewry will suffer death throes as well. Far from being an expression of arrogance about the importance of rabbis, this was an appeal to strengthen

---

5 Rabbi Wein, "Rabbi Aharon Walkin."
6 "We Remember Jewish Pinsk!" trans. Ellen Stepak, from the Pinsk Yizkor Book of Pinsk (1966), accessed November 3, 2017, www.zchor.org/pinsk/pinsk.htm.
7 Ibid.

the Jewish nation's soul that was needed to vivify the aching body of world Jewry.

IKH HOB ZIKH GEHODEVET IN SHTUB FUNEM CHOFETS CHAIM

The Bais Aharon was not the only formative influence upon the Walkin family members who managed to escape the *Shoah* through Kobe and Shanghai. An equally powerful inspiration came from Rabbi Shmuel David's proximity to the greatest sage of the Torah world before the war—Rabbi Yisrael Meir Kagan Ha Kohen, a diminutive, impoverished scholar who cast a great light in the Torah world. This sage was known by the name of his first major book, *Chofetz Chaim, Seeker of Life*. Rabbi Shmuel David not only studied at Rabbi Kagan's yeshiva in the hamlet of Radin, he also carried its spirit with him in exile and used it to rebuild communal life after the war in the United States. During his early years in America, Rav Shmuel David edited a book of recollections about the teachings of his mentor entitled: *Sparks of Light: Jewels of Wisdom from the Chofetz Chaim*.[8]

Tzivia Walkin, Rabbi Shmuel David's young bride, had also been deeply inspired by this Jewish leader of her generation. Because her grandfather's apartment adjoined the simple rooms inhabited by Rabbi Kagan for many years, she had ample opportunity to visit Radin, to befriend Feiga, Rabbi Yisrael Meir's daughter. The two little girls had been playmates, learned a great deal from each other, and absorbed the *Kedusha*, the holiness that permeated the home of Feiga's parents. Many years later, Chaya Leah recalls that her mother would often repeat: "*Icho hob zach geodevet in stubbe fhun dem Chofetz Chaim*—"I was raised in the home of the Chofetz Chaim." This was no retrospective pride. There was no gloating here about personal connections to this luminary of prewar Jewry. It was simply a statement of physical and spiritual fact. Tzivia Walkin, who in her own right became a pillar of strength and comfort for refugees in China, had learned the importance of inspiring others through her close proximity to an unassuming sage.

Born in 1838, Israel Meir Kagan was vastly different both in physical appearance and in intellectual approach from the stately Bais Aharon. Throughout his life, the Chofetz Chaim carried an aura of poverty and piety. While all his efforts were dedicated to scholarship and to raising funds for the

---

8 Shmuel David Walkin, *Sparks of Light: Jewels from the Chofetz Chaim* (New York: Kol Publishers, 2012).

yeshiva in Radin, he never took charge of its studies as Rosh Yeshiva. After getting married, he supported his family by opening a grocery story. Working for a living, Rabbi Kagan still managed to make time to write and sell his own books. In 1869, he arrived in Radin, a backwater hamlet that later disciples recalled as follows:

> Only You, Master of the world, could permit Yourself such a great pleasure, to present Your Torah to Your people in all its richness in such a nullity of a town—through one of the greatest personages that have ever arisen among Your people.[9]

Half a century later, after Rabbi Kagan's arrival in the muddy streets of Radin, Shmuel David Walkin would become one of the most promising young men to study with the Chofetz Chaim.

Three iconic images of Rabbi Israel Meir Kagan remain in circulation even today. The most widely reproduced visage comes from a photograph in which we see the eyes of the author of *Chofetz Chaim* gazing outward, begging softly for us to take seriously the often neglected mitzvah of "*shmirat lashon*"—guarding the tongue from slandering others. The beard is white, *peyot* (sidelocks) curl gently upward to frame a hatted figure who appears as a timeless version of the Jewish wise man. Another very different image surfaced recently from 1923, when Rabbi Yisrael Meir travelled to Vienna to open the Kenessia Gedolah (the first large gathering of scholars and communal leaders) organized by the Agudas Yisrael.

In Vienna, the elderly Chofetz Chaim cuts a very different figure from the tall, well-dressed men who surround and guide him into the meeting. They are all dressed in European clothes; some appear clean shaven. The scholar from Radin, by contrast, is wearing an overly large, poorly cut coat, his habitual workman's cap, unlike the chapeaux gracing the heads of men who are obviously paying him great honor. Here is a man on a mission. The task ahead—saving worldwide Jewry from assimilation—is momentous. The grocery owner, who was motivated to raise a huge amount of money to build a new yeshiva building in Radin in 1904, had come to help with a job that continued to animate his students and followers even as they confronted the horrors of the *Shoah*.

---

9   Yoshor Moses Meir, *Chofetz Chaim: The Life and Works of Rabbi Yisrael Meir Kagan of Radin*, rev. ed., trans. Charles Wengrov (New York: Mesorah Publications 1986), 87.

The third image comes from a photograph taken shortly before the death of the Chofetz Chaim in 1933. It is taken in front of his modest house in Radin. The sage himself sits on a low stool, looking even smaller than he was in life. Cane in hand, he is absorbed in conversation with a visitor who seems to have a tattered coat. In this image preserved at the Yad Vashem in Jerusalem, some of the men on the street in front of the house look out of focus. Clearly, they are tall, well-dressed young men, perhaps students from the yeshiva. A very clearly visible Shmuel David Walkin stands to the left, a little apart, with a thin beard and cigarette in hand.

Here is the groom who had married Tzivia one year earlier and would become Chaya Leah's father one year later. He has a determined look on his face despite the hasty motion of the camera. He seems different, more grounded in himself with qualities of mind and heart that will enable him to take the risk of fleeing Europe and rebuilding Jewry in far distant worlds. Rav Shmuel David's children have commissioned a painting based on this old photograph, in which the young Rabbi Walkin is even more clearly a loyal *talmid* (student) of the Chofetz Chaim. At the same time, this painting also emphasizes the apartness of the man who was gathering within himself the strength that would carry him across Soviet Russia to Kobe and Shanghai.

In later years, when he looked back with longing and admiration to the sage of Radin, Rav Shmuel David quoted a particularly illuminating snippet in his book, *Sparks of Light*. Entitled "*Der Veldt iz oich a velt*" (This World is also a world), the essay is built upon an expression used in a conversation between Rabbi Yisrael Meir and his son-in-law:

> The truth is that *only* this world is a world. In the World to Come, we cannot even say one chapter of *Tehilim* (Psalms). He was implying that mitzvah observance and the opportunity to amass merits is possible only in this world. In the World of Truth, no one is capable of adding or correcting what he prepared for himself in this world.[10]

As Shmuel David Walkin's subsequent life showed, he had absorbed this teaching fully. Whether as a yeshiva student in Radin or as young married man in Pohost, this youngest son of the Bais Aharon never forgot the opportunities that must be grasped in *this world*. As he often recalled, the courage and determination to find

---

10 Walkin, *Sparks of Light*, 20.

refuge from the fires that consumed Europe stemmed from the small, bedraggled man sitting on the stool in front of a modest house in 1933.

Painting based on a photograph of Chofetz Chaim in Radin ca. 1933. Rav Shmuel David Walkin is visible on the right.

The photograph of the Chofetz Chaim and Rabbi Walkin also shows two women: a broadly smiling servant girl clearly eager to be photographed and the statelier middle-aged woman, who was Rabbi Kagan's second wife. One day, she showed her husband a dress from abroad, designed in the latest two-tone fashion. The Chofetz Chaim's response, recalled by Rebbetzin Tzivia Walkin was: "Oy, are we so poor that we cannot afford a dress cut from a single piece of fabric?"

Legendary and humorous, the story confirms the simple yet lofty vision of the sage from Radin. This material world was to be used to build up and protect Torah institutions. As a result, he could not imagine a fashion in which different pieces of cloth would be deemed fancier than the functional garb he had found sufficient for basic modesty. On September 16, 1933, the *New York Times* carried the story of his death and called him:

> A figure of almost legendary importance for a half century. Despite his fame as the uncrowned spiritual king of Israel, the Chofetz Chaim was a

modest and humble man. Despite his great distinction, he lived in poverty all his life."[11]

His teacher's dedication to the yeshiva and to community were legendary and left a great impression on Shmuel David Walkin as he, too, struggled to maintain the community of refugees during the war years in Shanghai. In 1903, for example, after a great fire devastated almost all the houses in Radin, the town's people gathered in the courtyard of the Chofetz Chaim. As soon as he saw the people in need, he stopped his Torah learning and dedicated himself to raising funds for immediate aid. When large amounts of money and clothes poured him, his simple house became an aid distribution center. Rabbi Kagan even applied to the Czarist treasury for support for the victims of fire and proceeded to distribute the large amount that was granted a year later to gentile and Jew alike.

In 1912, after Radin Yeshiva had become too cramped to house the hundreds of students who were gathering due to the reputation of the Chofetz Chaim, he took it upon himself to raise the 15,000 rubles necessary for a new building. The Chofetz Chaim's partner in all these difficult undertakings was Rabbi Moishe Landinski, the Rosh Yeshiva in Radin from 1900 through his death in 1938. At the outbreak of World War I in 1914, the Chofetz Chaim feared the German invasion and so moved his students across the border into Russia, leaving a small group behind under Rabbi Landinski's tutelage.

Chaya Leah's great-grandfather was at the train station in 1921 when the Chofetz Chaim returned to hear the terrible news that the beautiful new building erected in 1912–13 had been confiscated and used as a stable for horses by the Germans. After the war, Radin began to lose its luster as a great center for learning, although young scholars continued to congregate there to absorb the quiet, inspiring proximity of the Chofetz Chaim. Shmuel David Walkin was among this later generation who witnessed first hand the hardships of his wife's grandfather and of his own mentor as they tried to promote Torah study in an increasingly hostile world.

LUKATCH—"RUN RABBIN RUN"

In 1938, four-year-old Chaya Leah became an older sister for the second time. This was also the year that the child glimpsed winds of war that she had no way

---

[11] "The Chofetz Chaim's Obituary in the NY Times (1933)." Beyond Teshuva website, accessed November 4, 2017, http://www.beyondbt.com/2006/11/03/the-chofetz-chaims-obituary/

of understanding. She picked up the fear of her parents and other elders around her. Everyone seemed worried, even as they celebrated the birth and the bris of a new baby boy, just one year after the birth of Esther, yet another younger sibling.

In January 1938, the Japanese army in China had already started to seize large chunks of land, starting with the Shandong peninsula. The Japanese prime minister had issued a formal statement about the establishment of a "new order in East Asia." The increasingly brutal Japanese occupation of China cost many lives, while also providing the political framework that would save a smattering of Jews, including the family of the rebbe from Lukatch.

In Europe, the nightmare of the *Shoah* started to unfold with increasing rapidity: on March 12, 1938, German troops invaded Austria. The German Reich started to enforce anti-Semitic laws in all its territories. The influence of these policies extended ahead of the Nazi war machine. In Poland, a young man named Shmuel Iwry, a graduate of Warsaw University, expressed how his school tried to get rid of Jewish students. He recalled the start of discrimination as follows:

> It was in 1938 that the universities decided to get rid of Jewish students and as a first step, they made them sit at the back of the classroom on "ghetto benches." They began pressuring Jewish gymnasia and pre-gymnasia to close. They wanted the middle-class families to send their children—but mostly their money—to the Polish-run schools. I was the director of a Tarbut school and we knew our time was running out.[12]

Three years later, Iwry would be telling this story with even darker hues to fellow refugees in Shanghai. By the time Chaya Leah's father heard his community's warning to run, Iwry was serving as a director of a secular Zionist school in Warsaw. In China, their paths converged. After the war, Rabbi Shmuel David Walkin was so moved by Iwry's predicament as an orphan and a refugee that he helped the budding Hebraist get one of the precious visas to the United States after the war. This, in turn, helped to launch Samuel Iwry's career at Johns Hopkins University, where he became a prominent scholar of the Dead Sea Scrolls.

Chaya Leah, looking back—unlike Iwry—recalls a child's version of Lukatch in the last moments before disaster dislocated her family. She knows the Iwry story. She, too, had learned about Chinese suffering during

---

12 Iwry, *To Wear the Dust of War*, 84.

the occupation. Yet, what surfaced in her recollections was nostalgia for a childhood she never really had:

> Picture my pass out of Poland: I remember wearing a gray and yellow sweater, running around a small mound of flowers, pointing to them all, excited—faces, faces, faces. They were pansies, the early spring flowers.
>
> Nostalgia sets in whenever I see a yellow and gray combination and of course, "faces" are my favorite flower. This is the last I remember of my life in Lukatch. My father was known as Rabbin Walkin, the Lukatcher Rav. The pansies in the garden were in the front of our home in Lukatch.
>
> And the soldier who told my father to run. "Run, Rabbin, run!" took place in Lukatch. My brother Moishe Yoel was born in Lukatch.

A child of four saw pansies in the same breath as the warning "Run, Rabbin run!" So many bewildering faces to take in: some like colorful flowers and some stony and less human, marked by hatred against the Jews. Fleeing Lukatch, crossing borders required papers, photographs. Tzivia Walkin prepared her eldest child for the journey in a memorable gray and yellow sweater.

In the meantime, the Evian conference was convened in France in June 1938 upon the initiative of the American President, Franklin Delano Roosevelt. For eight days, representatives from 32 countries and 39 private organizations debated how to respond to the plight of the many Jewish refugees fleeing Nazi persecution. These refugees had placed their hopes in the United States, which was seen as a champion of freedom and had enough clout to help Jews escape the Nazi trap.

Hitler's response to the Evian conference was cold and revealing. If other nations join it to take the Jews, he would help them leave:

> I can only hope and expect that the other world, which has such deep sympathy for these criminals (Jews) will at least be generous enough to convert this sympathy into practical aid. We, on our part, are ready to put all these criminals at the disposal of these countries, for all I care, even on luxury ships.[13]

In the end, the United States and Britain refused to accept substantially more refugees than the trickle that was already fiercely monitored and limited. By May 1939, the United States was turning away boats bringing Jewish refugees

---

13 Ervin Birnbaum, "Evian: The Most Fateful Conference in Jewish History, Part II" *Nativ: Ariel Center for Policy Research*. February, 2009, accessed August 13, 2017, http://www.acpr.org.il/nativ/0902-birnbaum-E2.pdf.

to American shores. The *St. Louis* was the most notorious of these life-seeking and death-condemned voyages. Rather than luxury ships, the Nazis were preparing mass graves and ovens for the Jews no one wanted. Rav Shmuel David Walkin's family managed to make it out of this nightmare through Stalin's Russia by sheer miracle alone.

The year in which Rav Shmuel David's first son was born also brought terrifying news about the destruction of Jewish life in Germany. November 9, 1938 became known as the "night of the broken glass." The infant's paternal grandfather, the Pinsker Rav, had been fully informed about the murder of 91 Jews as well as the vicious violence that shattered the storefronts of about 7,500 Jewish stores and businesses and damaged by burning over 200 synagogues. No wonder that local folks, according to Chaya Leah's recollections, told her father: "Run Rabbin, run!" The Bais Aharon himself did not run. He stayed and witnessed some of the harshest hours in the life of his community.

WHEN GASHMIUS BECOMES LESSENED

From July 4, 1941 until July 14, 1944, Pinsk was under the Nazi occupation. The last year of the Pinsker Rav's life coincided with the German invasion and was deeply marked by its terrors. At first, this most famous Jew in town took to hiding in attics and basements knowing that the Nazis would target him first. After six months, Rav Aharon Walkin could no longer bear the isolation and the knowledge that the religious and spiritual life that he had nurtured had come to a frightful halt. Dressing up as a peasant, Rabbi Walkin left his hiding place and went around town asking young men to sign up for prayers and learning.

This was a huge risk and many parents objected. Nonetheless, the moral example of the Pinsker Rav led a small cohort of yeshiva students to gather around him for *shiurim* (lessons on Torah topics), prayer, and holiday services. In one of his last letters to his son Shmuel David Walkin (reprinted as part of a *Metzach Aharon* in Shanghai), he wrote:

> After the destruction of the Bais HaMikkdosh (the Holy Temple in Jerusalem), when meals from the Father Hakadosh Boruch Hu (the Holy and Blessed One), which sustained us, are no more, it is sure that the children of Klal Israel (the entirety of the Jewish people) go hungry, empty in the stomach. But in our times that we are presently in, I fear the opposite.
>
> Since the children are hungry with no sustenance, our Father in Heaven, Ha Kaddosh Boruch Hu, is also going hungry, *kevayahol* (in the

language of human analogies), not receiving his quota of *tefilah* (prayer and praise) from Klal Israel…

My body has become weak and my strength has dwindled. Nevertheless, for Torah and *tefillah* I feel great strength.

And you my children don't be saddened or worried about me, for from my own flesh I see that when the *gashmius*, the physical is lessened, the *ruchnius*, the spiritual becomes stronger.[14]

In 1930, when he had to plead for the material needs of the students, the Pinsker Rav had been impassioned about the importance of physical sustenance. Under the Nazi occupation, however, he had returned to the verities of his childhood. Hunger and fear of oppression could not squelch the fires of Torah and of *tefilah*.

This would be his enduring message to his son and his family. This is the mantle of Jewish commitment that would also enwrap Chaya Leah, the little girl who bore the name of the Bais Aharon's mother. Even before she became a refugee in Vilna, Kobe, and Shanghai, the child had already absorbed the lesson that spiritual nourishment is a sustaining force in times of material privation.

During the last season for pansies in Lukatch, however, Chaya Leah could not have imagined how acute these deprivations became for her grandfather before his death in January 1942. For the four-year-old, 1938 marked the end of the kind of security envisioned in *Shir Ha'Shirim*. Neither the walls nor the doors of the rabbi's house in Lukatch were sturdy enough to protect the family within. No cedar beams remained in place to reinforce Jewish life in this time of madness.

Yet, while outward physical structures crumbled, inner resources grew stronger, more resilient. From the inspiring elders of their generation, Tzivia and Shmuel David Walkin drew enough strength and faith to start the journey out of Poland to the East. They carried with them a "fortress of silver" more precious than all the possessions left behind: a commitment to Torah learning and to helping others in dire need. In time, Chaya Leah would become a partner in her parents' efforts to rebuild Jewish life with new walls and new doors on foreign shores.

---

14 Ahron Walkin, "Cheirus," *Matzav*, April 9, 2009.

CHAPTER 2

WATCHMEN PATROLLING THE CITY:

Escape Through Vilna to Japan

> *The watchmen patrolling the city have found me. They beat and wounded me, took off my jewelry.*
>
> Shir Ha'Shirim 4:7

Hitler was not joking when he suggested in 1938 that he'd be glad to pack Europe's Jews onto luxury liners, just to get rid of them. One week before Chaya Leah turned five years old, the *St. Louis* set sail from Germany to the American shores. On the voyage that started on May 13, 1939, there were 937 passengers, almost all Jews fleeing the Third Reich. The oldest daughter of the rabbi from Lukatch would not have been told of the great hopes that hastened the boat onward. She could not have fathomed a world so heartless as to prevent Jews from disembarking in Cuba.

The image of desperate men, women, and children floating by the lights of Miami in June 1939 without a single American official willing to let them come into the country would haunt Jewish memory for a long time. Even those who knew nothing of the Torah's mandate for *irei miklat* understood that this was a world without cities of refuge. Yet, on the other side of the Pacific Ocean in Tsuruga, Kobe, and Shanghai—almost unknown and unpronounceable city names—a few Jews found a semblance of safety. The Walkin family was privileged to be among them.

The road of escape to Japan and China was yet unimaginable when the *St. Louis* was turned back in 1939. Most of its passengers ended up in the gas chambers of Poland. For the Walkin family, all hopes of delaying flight from Lukatch ended with the outbreak of war on September 1, 1939. Two days after the blowing of the shofar on Rosh Hashanah, Soviet Russia invaded Poland from the East. In accordance with the Molotov-Ribbentrop agreement (August 1939), more than half of Poland's Jews now came under communist rule. This was a regime known to be fiercely opposed to the Torah values cherished by the yeshiva communities. Fearing that the Jewish learning centers established with so much care and effort were in jeopardy, the Walkin family, too, began looking for escape routes.

The news that the Soviets planned to leave Vilna as an independent city in Lithuania led thousands of Jews to try to reach this city. That window of hope turned out to be very narrow. Between October 10, 1939 and June 15, 1940, when the Soviet army ended Lithuanian independence, more than 15,000 refugees managed to reach Vilna, once venerated as the *Yerushalaim of Lita* (Jerusalem of Lithuania). Among those who made their way to this short-lived city of refuge was Rav Shmuel David Walkin. At first, he crossed into Lithuania alone. A few months later, he managed to bring out his wife and three young children. By the summer of 1940, the Walkin family had one of the precious few Sugihara visas leading them out of Soviet Russia.

In these times of desperation, the words of *Shir Ha'Shirim* gained new depth. Love of life and love of Torah had been awakened afresh by disastrous events. At a time when Jews felt trapped, wounded, hunted, and despoiled, something kind had also been stirred up beneath the sullen face of a heartless world. One Japanese man in Lithuania, Chiune Sugihara, would rouse himself to help Jews. The yeshiva students and teachers who were Rav Shmuel David's intimate companions were among those who received his aid. Their own devotion to a life of learning sustained them as they queued outside Sugihara's gate. They were lovers of Torah who had realized fully the dangers facing their families and homes. The consul of the imperial government of Japan, in turn, demonstrated the power of awakened compassion. Against all odds, he provided a path of escape for refugees who had nowhere else to turn. The beaten and the wounded suddenly found unexpected help.

For five-year-old Chaya, both the depths of cruelty among the "watchmen" and the compassion being awakened in the Japanese consul became comprehensible only much later. Looking back, she saw herself as a child about to lose the pleasures of early youth. The pain of that loss lingers still. It cuts through Chaya Leah's later years like a knife, accompanied by terrors that have little to do with the events of an aged woman's life. Fragments from the past come up, like angry ghosts. A doll collection or a uniformed official can readily bring back echoes of the darkness that had enveloped Chaya Leah's world before the escape from Vilna to Japan:

> *1938-39 was the year that my childhood was lost.*
> *The trauma changed our mood drastically.*
> *I look back and realize I never had a childhood.*
> *I never had the experience of running around with friends, laughing, playing ball, hide and seek, dolls. Never had a doll. Never.*

Here we see what was irrevocably lost among the pansies of Lukatch. The chance to play, to grow up like other kids. Laughter would not come back for many years, not in Lithuania, not in Japan, and not in Shanghai.

In later years, Chaya Leah confesses to compensatory efforts. The girl who never knew the leisurely maturation described by Margaret Mead among the young women of Samoa tried to collect dolls, but did not play with them:

> *I have come to love dolls.*
> *I collect dolls and tea sets and all the little toys that little girls play with.*
> *I never played at being a grown-up wearing my mother's shoes, dresses.*
> *I guess it is called never really opening up.*
> *I did not have books to bury myself, only my imagination.*
> *No fairy tale worlds or a make-believe world.*

Instead of fairy tales, Chaya Leah learned to live with the shadow of fear that no amount of material security could assuage. Like so many refugee children, she continued to tremble long after heartless officials stopped dictating the fate of her vulnerable family:

> *I knew a world of harshness.*
> *A world in which when we saw a person wearing a uniform, panic set in.*
> *This panic is still deeply engraved in my mind. The fear of the military and the police is something I cannot shake.*
> *Whenever I see a foreign uniform, memories and fear come flooding in.*
> *Travelling to a foreign country even though I am travelling with an American husband, I freeze.*
> *Much later in my life, I had a parking violation once and had to go to court with my husband and with an attorney.*
> *The hearing officer asked me my name.*

I could not answer.
My address?
I did not know.
I am still terrified.
Yes, even today.
I am terrified by a uniform.

Forgetting one's name and one's address reveals the terror of the dispossessed. Being forced out of Europe in 1939-1940 was a nightmare that shadowed Chaya Leah's daytime hours. To be sure, the Walkin family was far more fortunate that those Jews who were led to the death camps. Yet, as refugees they carried and continue to shoulder the kind of grief that many of us have yet to fully fathom in our own times.

DER EYBESHTER ZOL HELFN: BLAYB A YID!

The winter of 1939-1940 was one of the coldest that Europe had experienced in the twentieth century. It was in this harsh weather that Rav Shmuel David and hundreds of other rabbis faced their toughest moral and religious dilemma: is a captain allowed to leave his ship in times of danger? As community leaders, these rabbis were looked upon as an anchor, a source of wisdom and advice. In the Chassidic community, this was an even more agonizing question colored by the well-known adage: "A *rebbe* who is not willing to descend into hell in order to rescue his followers from destruction is not a *rebbe*."[1]

Many non-chassidic rabbis were willing to descend into hell. They also knew that such descent would not necessarily help to rescue their communities. An actual halachic question—a request for the clarification of Torah law—had been posed to the Chatam Sofer (Rabbi Moshe Sofer, 1762-1839) in Germany in the nineteenth century about the right of a rabbi to flee from his post in times of danger. The answer that rang with terrifying implications in the late 1930s was that leadership decisions were to be left up to the individual. Each rabbi had to wrestle with his own conscience, his family, and his mentors before deciding to flee from Poland on the eve of the *Shoah*.

---

1 Eva Loenen, "A Fresh Perspective on the History of Hasidic Judaism," *New Horizons*. no. 20 (September 2012).

Many Torah leaders, as we know, did not leave. Rabbi Elchonon Wasserman and the Pinsker Rav were among those who stayed. In Vilna, a central rabbinical figure was the venerable Chaim Ozer Grodinski (1863-1940)—the rabbi whose first names suggested both "life" and "help." Rabbi Grodinski had collaborated with the Chofetz Chaim and the Bais Aharon in the founding of the Agudas Israel and was active in the rescue of yeshivot at the end of World War I and again in the winter of 1939. Although terminally ill with cancer, he conducted endless meetings with the hundreds of rabbis and thousands of yeshiva students who crowded into Vilna during punishing times.

Since Rabbi Grodinski had left his own community to go to Vilna during World War I (and was wounded by accusations of abandoning the ship when he returned), he was cautious in his advice to Torah scholars seeking both moral advice and material help. He suggested that there was "no need to panic, that every place is dangerous and that Lithuania might remain calm, neither black nor red, but pink."[2] Other influential rabbis in Vilna were more explicit in urging the refugee rabbis and yeshiva students to *sh'ev ve'al ta'ase*—"sit and don't act."

Yet, how could one sit still when one had left a wife and children behind in Poland, as was the case with Rav Shmuel David Walkin? How could one do nothing knowing that the Soviets might invade the so-called "pink" Lithuania at any moment? Panic and confusion ran high, especially in the weeks and days leading up to June 1940, when the entrance of Russian armies ended any pretense of independence in Vilna.

Young men started to sign up for passports and began to search frantically for exit visas out of the Soviet Union. Their elders cautioned patience, but sometimes they also gave their young students blessings for the journey ahead. One such blessing is recorded in an interview with Benny Fishoff, a yeshiva student who took it upon himself to run out of Poland and who became a close friend of the Walkin family during their days in Shanghai.

Recalling his journey toward a new life in the 1939, Benny (whose full name was Yechiel Benzion) focused upon a fateful encounter with the Gerrer Rebbe. Benny had gone with thousands of others to celebrate the Bar Mitzvah of the rebbe's son. Having made up his mind to flee, Benny knew that he had to take leave of his mentor. The Rebbe did not tell the young man either to stay or to go. Instead, as Benny recalls, he gave the boy (who would become an orphan

---

2   Haim Hillel Ben-Sasson, "Grodzinski, Ḥayyim Ozer," in *Encyclopaedia Judaica*. 2nd ed. Vol. 8 (Detroit, MI: Macmillan Reference USA, 2007), 91-92.

during the *Shoah*) a penetrating look and spoke these cryptic words: *"Ivdi as Hashem b'simcha.* Der Eybeshter zol helfn: Blayb a yid!" (Serve the Master of the Universe with joy and He should help you remain a Jew").³

Looking back, this seemed a strange blessing for a traditionally observant young man. But as Fishoff remarked:

> You have no idea how easy it is to become swallowed up once the war began. Suddenly *chassidshe bochrim* whose lives had been guided by the Torah were expected to run, hide, run again. All of Poland was a battleground. We had no contact with our families, no food, nowhere to sleep. We struggled to stay a step ahead of the Nazi beast.⁴

Staying one step ahead of the Nazi war machine was a daunting and bewildering task. Perhaps it is not surprising that those who risked the harsh deprivations described by Fishoff were mostly young men.

Rav Shmuel David Walkin, with a wife and three children, was an unusual refugee in this crowd of boys who had left their parents behind. No wonder that Chaya's father became a mentor to so many. In the harsh winter of 1939-1940, however, no one could have guessed the devastating loss of kin and community that took place during the *Shoah*.

What was the most immediate concern in this first season of becoming refugees was the shortage of food and housing in Vilna. An American representative of the Emergency Committee for the Rescue of Displaced Yeshivot, Dr. Samuel Schmidt of Cincinnati, had arrived in Vilna in March 1940 to report concretely on the situation of students and their teachers. Writing to his wife, Dr. Schmidt expressed admiration for the moral courage of the yeshiva students who were continuing a grueling schedule of Torah learning despite the desperate material circumstances. Even as the cruel "watchmen" hunted their compatriots, these young men were developing inner resources that would sustain them during the war years:

> The heroism of the Yeshiva Bochrim in fleeing to Vilno to pursue their ideal cannot be overestimated... That some 2,400 yeshivoth men are studying with devotion and fervor in various synagogues and towns of

---

3 David Mandelbaum and Yechiel Benzion Fishoff, *From Lublin to Shanghai: The Miraculous Exile of Yeshivas Chachmei Lublin* (New York: Mesorah Publications, Ltd, 2012), 12.
4 Ibid., 13.

Lithuania having recently escaped from hell is a strong manifestation that we are a people of destiny.[5]

Here we see the spiritual commitment underpinning the Gerrer Rebbe's blessing to the young Benny Fishoff: Der Eybeshter zol helfn: Blayb a yid! Remaining fully a Jew during the Shoah was not simply a matter of relying upon divine aid. It required one to continually face material scarcity and political adversity armed with the wisdom of tradition as well as the courage to keep on moving in an endless quest for a safe haven.

Rav Shmuel David Walkin became unusually adept at this kind of survival. Having arrived in Vilna alone after leaving Lukatch, he faced an urgent dilemma: how to bring his wife and children from Poland to Lithuania. Studying all day was no longer possible. Sitting still and waiting for divine rescue was also not an option. Although he knew and respected the great Torah luminaries congregating in Vilna in 1939-1940, the young father had to ensure his own family's safety first and foremost.

Fortunately, Rav Walkin did not have to face this terrible challenge alone. In Vilna, he met up with his older brother Chaim Walkin, who had served as Dean of the Volozhin Yeshiva before its destruction during the war. In one of the few photographs that survived the *Shoah*, Rav Chaim stands in the company of three other Torah scholars and four women who were their wives and mothers. In this formal portrait, the serious and accomplished older son of the Bais Aharon stands behind his wife, who is wearing a simple scarf. Next to him, stands his brother in law, Rav Meir Bar-Ilan, a pioneer of religious Zionism. The only one among the men without a hat, Rav Meir gazes into the camera with the look of a man determined to change the future of the Jewish people.

Rabbi Bar-Ilan had been a student at the Volozhin Yeshiva. He was one of the first to take note of the anti-Semitism moving across Europe early and moved to Jerusalem by 1923. There, he worked arduously for the rescue of Jews throughout the 1930s and 1940s. In February 1943, he undertook a one-man lobbying mission to Capitol Hall to try to persuade American officials to rescue Jewish refugees—including his own brother-in-law, who had a visa for Palestine, but, alas, no papers to leave Lithuania. The failure of this mission foreshadowed the murder of Rav Chaim Walkin and his family during a desperate effort to get out of Vilna.

---

5 Zuroff, *Response of Orthodox Jewry*, 96.

Shmuel David Walkin, younger than both Rav Meir and Rav Chaim, had no visa for Palestine. He knew only one thing: he had to find a way to get his wife and little children across the Polish border. Being in Vilna with his older brother was a source of comfort. Getting the support of the Trabe Rav back in Poland was even more crucial.

THEY BROUGHT US HERE TO KILL US

Later, in September 1945, when word of Rav Chaim's murder reached Shanghai, Shmuel David Walkin would name his second son in memory of his brother. In the winter of 1939-1940, however, Chaya Leah's father had a single goal—to use the inclement weather as a shield for a nighttime rescue of his wife and three young children. As Chaya Leah recalled, she, her mother, and siblings had been sent for safety to Trabe. They were sheltered by Rabbi Sochorow, while her father slipped across the border. Chaya Leah's mother was reluctant to follow. Like the beloved in *Shir Ha'Shirim*, she was worried about the "watchmen" and their known cruelty.

Tzivia Walkin felt safe in her father's home and terrified of the dangers lurking in this illegal operation. Rabbi Sochorow urged his daughter to join her husband. Perhaps he sensed more keenly than Tzivia the deadly fate awaiting the Jews of Poland. As it turned out, however, Rav Walkin's young wife had good reasons for being scared for herself and for her children:

> "But how will I get to Vilna?" She had no papers to cross the border.
> My grandfather, beloved by all the town's people, looked for ways to get my mother and the children out.
> I remember in the middle of the night: My mother came and dressed us in warm coats.
> She, my sister, my brother, and I crawled on hands and knees through vacant land to come to a farmer's house. No one in the house was supposed to know that we had left and we were told not to make a single sound.

Chaya Leah's recollection reveals the affection of the Trabe Jews for their Rav and his daughter's family. Despite the risks, they were ready to help their community leader to send out his daughter and grandchildren from Poland.

It may have been in preparation for this crossing that Chaya Leah's birth certificate was manufactured with the date of May 20, 1934 and the place of birth recorded as Pinsk. Although her mother recalled Chaya Leah's birth at

Purim time in Pohost, any piece of paper was useful as the mother and children got ready to flee in the winter night:

> The first time we tried to cross the border, Russians stopped us. When they saw my mother and saw that she was very beautiful, they said to her that they will take her with them, and put the children in an orphanage and she would have a good life with them.
> I do not know what exactly happened, but somehow she managed to get back home with the farmer.

This was exactly what a husbandless woman had feared in the dead of night—crawling on hand and knees toward more danger. Nonetheless, with the Trabe Rav's encouragement, Tzivia Walkin decided to try to cross the border again. This time, Tzivia's father entrusted his own young son Leibel to her as well, in the hope that at least two of his children might make it out of death-infected Poland.

> The second time we tried to cross the border, there were more people in an open wagon. Again we left in the middle of the night.
> It was already winter and very cold. My mother's 10-year-old brother Leibel was with us. He ended up in Siberia, and survived the war. After the war, he came to America from Germany, where he had married a young girl from a religious family.
> I remember a full open wagon with people, and I remember stopping at different houses along the way.
> In one of the stops, my brother, being little, was wrapped in a blanket. He did not make a sound. When we got off the wagon and opened the blanket, my mother thought she had smothered the infant. One of the men lay my baby brother down on the ground and rubbed him with snow till he came to.
> My mother thought that he had frostbite.
> Here was a tiny person being rubbed with the snow till he revived.

Tzivia Walkin's worst nightmares were coming true during this dangerous escape into Lithuania. Like other refugees in terrible circumstances, she dreaded murdering the very child she sought to save. After the one-year-old baby was revived, other horrors lay ahead:

> On this same trip, when we got closer to the border, still dark and the soldiers shooting at us, my uncle and several other people jumped off the wagon.

> On this attempt, we again had to go back to my grandfather without his son.
> A little later, we made our third attempt. This one was successful.
> I remember the trip, I feel the trip, I smell the air, see the horses with the moist air coming out of their nostrils.
> The scene is alive for me. The scene of our escape is so powerful. Winter, with its invigorating snow, remains my beloved season since it was the start of our survival.

Tzivia Walkin had not imagined this kind of trial. Trying again and again to cross the border, she had "lost" her brother. Still, she was persuaded to try for a third time.

For Chaya Leah, a five-year-old girl, the dangers were less vivid than the winter landscape that held the promise of freedom and reunion with her father. Aware of her mother's terrors (as she would be in later years after the war as well), the oldest child of Rav Walkin was one of the voices encouraging Rebbetzin Tzivia to make one more attempt at border crossing.

> Again we started out in the middle of the night, bundling up with almost no personal belongings. We crawled to the farmer house, and into the open wagon. I remember two horses.
> On the way, we had to stop at another farm; the balagoleh (cart driver) took us into the barn and he left.
> My mother and the three children were huddled in the corner, wrapped in a blanket for warmth.
> A little bit later, we heard a whirring sound. A huge man was sitting on a little bench, sharpening a knife. Maybe some tools. We could not be sure in the dark. My mother's shock was overwhelming. She just tightened the blanket, and held us all together without a sound or mumbling.

Here, a grown woman looks back at her mother's terror with compassion, and fear as well. Chaya Leah was acutely tuned into her mother's feelings without being able to fully understand them. The child must have been even more scared as the mother voiced her greatest dread:

> "They brought us here to kill us," she kept whimpering, shaking quietly.
> I can just imagine the fear.
> A woman all alone, in the middle of the night with three small children.
> A little later, we were back on the wagon going through forests.

> Suddenly, at about daybreak, we heard shooting. The farmer whipped the horses, yelling in Polish.
> Faster, faster, faster, whipping, and whipping, and faster, and faster.
> The white virgin ground, trees blanketed with snow, the horses' moist breath, the whipping, the yelling, the shooting, the speed. I remember all this.

Again, the joys of winter override the child's fears of strange noises in the night. Tzivia Walkin dreaded death while five-year-old Chaya Leah was getting her first whiff of freedom. As it turns out, the little girl was right:

> Then suddenly, very suddenly, he pulled the reins. It took several seconds for the horses to slow down their speed.
> What happened?
> What went wrong?
> Did we get caught?
> Will we be sent back again?
> None of that.
> We had safely crossed the border and were now in Lithuania.

A woman in her early 80s recalled with exhilaration how they survived the terrifying escape from Poland to Vilna. What lingers in the mind is the invigorating taste of being out of Poland. It is one of Chaya Leah's great gifts to focus on the good that came out of terror, even as she vividly recalls the near death experience of her little brother, Moshe.

Like Avraham's wife Sarah in the Jewish bible, Tzivia Walkin was a beautiful woman at risk among brutal strangers. In the Torah, when famine forces the family to go to Egypt, Avraham asks his wife to pretend that she is his sister so that he will not be killed on her account. Rabbi Shmuel David Walkin, in a different context, had faced a similar dilemma. He was determined to get his family out of Poland, yet could not be near his wife in her dread-filled escape through the woods controlled by ruthless peasants.

His father-in-law must have sent off his daughter, son, and grandchildren with a trembling heart. The Trabe Rav knew the dangers of the road as well as the need for the family to be united. A cart driver had ferried this secret cargo across the border for money—not because he loved Jews.

Once in Vilna, Chaya Leah's family met up with Rabbi Chaim Walkin, his wife, and two little daughters. No one knew that the reunion was going to be short lived. None of the children guessed that only one set of cousins would survive by journeying to Kobe and Shanghai. Looking back, Chaya Leah recalls small details that colored their shared months in Lithuania.

> We were in Uncle Chaim's house, with tante and the two little girls, the white tablecloth—I cannot forget. Walking down the street with them for avenbroth (lunch). I saw a bakery in the basement. They were selling Neapolitans (a cake layered with sweet cream). My mouth watered and I really really wanted them, but we had just eaten and had no money for luxuries.
> In Vilna, I also saw a "droshky" like we had ridden during our escape. It was winter—the driver had covered us with a blanket. Riding a dorshka in Vilna was completely different. It was a horse-drawn carriage with coach lights. I felt like a princess.

Just weeks after the terrifying border crossing, a child longs for the taste for sweet cream. Winter, carts, and blankets connoted very different things to Tzivia Walkin and her daughter. During the escape, a blanket had nearly smothered Moshe Yoel. Here, the same object connotes kindness. It did not take much to make the little girl feel like a princess. She understood that money was in short supply. Yet, the joys of family reunion and a carriage ride were enough to lift a child's heart.

Harsher deprivations would become familiar to Chaya Leah and her parents during the war years in China. In the spring and early summer of 1940, however, for just a short while, Uncle Chaim's house, the white tablecloth, and the kind *tante* provided shelter, familiarity, and hope. What augmented hope in Vilna was also the news that American Jews were mobilizing to help refugee Torah scholars. By November 1940, the Vaad ha-Hatzala headed by Rabbi Eliezer Silver was busy awakening the Jewish community's consciousness concerning the dire needs of families such as that of Shmuel David and Chaim Walkin. The renowned Rabbi Avraham Kalmanowitz (1881–1964) had arrived in America from Sweden in April 1940. By August, when Rav Shmuel David lined up with hundreds of other refugees for a transit visa through Japan, the Vaad ha-Hatzala had already launched its urgent *pikuach nefesh* campaign. Following the Torah injunction that one must save life at all costs, Orthodox rabbis in America were willing to break all rules, even Shabbat, to raise the funds needed to rescue Torah scholars from the *Shoah*.

Chaya Leah as a child could not have grasped the magnitude of the dangers facing Jews in Lithuania and Poland or the heroism needed to find a way out. Yet, looking back, she comes to dwell again and again upon the "miracles" of the summer of 1940 when enough love and compassion were aroused to save thousands of Jews, including her parents and siblings.

MY FATHER WAS A REAL SAMURAI

Unknowingly, two children's lives converged in the summer of 1940. Chaya Leah had turned six in Vilna sometime between the holidays of Purim and Shavuot. The Nazi invasion of Poland had uprooted her family from the garden of pansies in Lukatch. Nonetheless, she held on to memories of snowy serenity. During the same winter, five-year-old Hiroki Sugihara celebrated *Kodomo no Hi* (the Japanese Children's Day) in his parents' villa in Kovno, Lithuania. A few days earlier, the little boy had savored Hanukah food at the home of a Jewish family befriended by his parents. While Chaya Leah Walkin was escaping from Poland with her mother and siblings, Hiroki's life remained gracious and calm. Yet, by the summer of 1940, both of these children would become enveloped by the language of a world gone mad.

Being five years old, Hiroki did not understand a great deal about his father's job as a diplomat, much less the dilemmas that he was facing as Japan's consul general in Lithuania. Looking back, Hiroki recalled a scene he witnessed while standing alongside his father at the window of the Japanese consulate in Kovno:

> In late July 1940 something happened that changed everything. It began to happen when large crowds of people began to surround the front entrance of the Consulate. When I tried to peek out of the window to see what was happening, my father told my brother and me not to look out the window. I sensed that my father and mother were confused and a little worried... Later, they told us that all those people were Jews who were trying to escape form Poland. They told us that if they did not escape, they would be killed or put in prison.[6]

The child who looked out the window had no way of grasping the hardships endured by the Jew who had managed to come out of Poland. He could not have imagined the terror-filled cart rides endured by Tzivia Walkin.

---

6 Hiroki Sugihara, *Puppe's Story: A Five-Year-Old Child Remembrance of His Father's Remarkable Rescue of 6,000 Jewish Refugees during the Holocaust* (Sacramento, CA: Edu-Comm. Plus, 1996), 27.

He could not have known how short lived the window of freedom would be for the Jews lining up outside his family's home. Yet, Hiroki's father and mother had conveyed enough information to the boy to grasp that a momentous choice was coming their way. Looking back many years later, Sugihara's son gives himself some of the credit for awakening his father's compassion:

> My mother explained that they believed that my father could help them escape if he signed some special papers for them. I later found out these special papers were called *visas*. When I found that my father could help them, I ran up to him and said: You must do something to help the children.[7]

Without knowing the words of *Shir Ha'Shirim*, a small Japanese boy had spoken in the language of borderless affection.

By August 1940, Chaya Leah's father, the Rabbi of Lukatch, was among those standing outside the Sugihara home, which also served as the consulate of the imperial Japanese government. Rebbetzin Tzivia, Chaya Leah, and her two younger siblings were all included in visa number 1410 issued to "Walkin Szmul" on the 7th of August, 1940.

Hiroki Sugihara did not know Chaya Leah or her family. He could not have imagined a September day in 2016 when Chaya Leah and her family would enter a conference room in the Kitano Hotel in Manhattan to publicly thank the mayor of Sugihara's hometown and the governor of Gifu province for the kindness done in the summer of 1940.

What the eldest son of the Sugihara family did understand, even as a five-year-old in Kovno, was that his father was about to undertake a difficult and dangerous job. In Lithuania's capital, he was learning something new and important about the Japanese ethical code for samurai:

> My father explained that he was going to do something
> that would be against the government of his country, Japan.
> He explained that he would be punished for going against orders. He told us that he must sign the visas because it would be the only way he could save all the people outside our gate… My mother told us that we should be proud because my father was doing a brave thing. I was proud because I knew that that my father was a real *samurai*.[8]

---

7 Ibid.
8 Ibid., 7.

The Japanese child's frame of reference would have been strange to Chaya Leah's ears. Yet, she would have no trouble understanding that genuine morality required uncommon kindness during times of inhumanity.

Looking back upon her own father's bravery in the frantic search for a way out of the cauldron of death engulfing Poland, Chaya Leah could not but marvel at Hiroki's father, who was willing to disobey his government in order to help thousands of bedraggled Jews. With the passage of time, Chaya Leah's questions deepened:

> Why?
> Why would a diplomat on the ladder of success commit suicide by going against the orders of his superiors?
> Why?
> Why would a diplomat spend three weeks working day and night with his entire family to handwrite and document two thousand visas?
> Why?

The intensity of Chaya Leah's question did not diminish with the passage of time. Again and again, Rav Walkin's eldest daughter would ask herself—and others—to explain the reasons behind the actions of the Japanese diplomat in Kovno. Sugihara's post-war disgrace only accentuated her compassion for the "savior" of her own family:

> Why would he become an outcast, ostracized, shamed diplomat who supposedly betrayed his country? A broken man hiding his shame for a deed performed twenty years earlier.
> "Did I save even one person?" he asked himself.
> Did he know he saved a world?
> He asked for nothing and accepted nothing.
> Why?
> These are whys that cannot logically be answered in my generation.
> Sugihara never capitalized on what he did.
> He simply said: "It was the right thing to do."
> My mother taught me to do the right thing.
> True Chesed (Kindness) is doing this without thinking what is in it for me.

The little girl who became a formidable Jewish leader in her own right after the war looks back and asks hard questions. No historian has yet answered Chaya Leah's query.

The boy Hiroki recalls his father with almost the same wonder as Chaya Leah. Somewhere along the way, Chiune Sugihara has also taught his children about the right thing to do. Chaya Leah Small attributes this lesson to her parents. In her recollection, without diminishing the sheer wonder of Sugihara's actions, doing what is right becomes linked to a key Jewish value: *Chesed.*

Kindness for the sake of kindness alone was not part of the samurai ethic. It was, however, the foundation of the Walkin family life even as they became refugees and wandered on to the shores of China and Japan.

THE POWER OF ONE

"Kindness" is a poor translation for this key *mida* (spiritual and emotional attribute) that was imbued in the Walkin family so deeply. In a world so frenzied by the needs of sheer survival, Chaya Leah was taught that it is important to act in ways that are beyond the self, to give to others without expectations of personal benefit. And yes, to go beyond the fold, beyond one's own family and group.

A couple of years after their encounter with the "miracle" of Sugihara, Chaya Leah's family would act with the same *chesed* toward the motley group of refugees who were their neighbors and friends in Shanghai. Rabbi Shmuel David's acts of kindness went beyond the family and the group of the Mirrer Yeshiva scholars. All were welcome in his one-room home, all were treated with respect, kindness. All were helped in whatever measure was possible, including a visa for Samuel Iwry, the future professor of Judaic studies at Johns Hopkins. Iwry did not fit the paradigm of the yeshiva student, yet he was helped nonetheless.

How much did Chiune Sugihara risk in giving Jews visas in the summer of 1940? Hillel Levine concludes his study *In Search of Sugihara* by pointing out that survivors themselves often need to robe their rescuer with more self-sacrifice than might have been the case. Chaya Leah's jottings, like that of many other recipients of transit visas in Kovno, confirm the retrospective narrative of Sugihara's widow and her children. These close relatives of the Japanese consul argue that his hardships after the war were punishments for Sugihara's courageous actions in Lithuania. Levine, by contrast, argues against simplistic notions of the so-called "altruistic personality":

> Altruism is usually contrasted with egoism on one hand and individualism on the other. In so far as rescuers are deemed altruistic, sacrifice and

risk-taking becoming items on their "job description." That heroic rescuers often make sacrifices moves from the descriptive to the normative—rescuers *should* make sacrifices. But making this connection between sacrifice and rescue maybe have more to do with the needs that we, observers, seem to have than with the needs of the rescuer. [author's emphasis][9]

Levine's quest for Sugihara's motivation ends on a very different note than Chaya Leah's. He concludes that the Japanese consul was motivated primarily by a "love of life," which is not quite what is meant by *chesed*. Levine's book gives voice to the questions of a western scholar.

Chaya Leah, as a survivor who feels acutely embedded in the story, digs deeper, going beyond Sugihara's supposed self-sacrifice in the summer of 1940. Instead of the more universally appealing "love of life" (which is also a key Jewish value painted in starker colors when one factors in the urgency of *pikuach nefesh*—"rescuing life at all costs"), she endows Chiune Sugihara with a moral trait that is distinctly Jewish and that colored the rest of her own family's life long after the Japanese consul left Kovno at the end of August 1940.

Before arriving in Kovno/Kaunas in the later part of the summer of 1939, Chiune Sugihara had already been posted to several key positions by the increasingly militant Japanese imperial government. Trained in the Russian language and in Soviet spying methods (with a Russian first wife), he was seen as an especially useful diplomat, first in the newly occupied Manchuria and later in Helsinki. The signing of the Nazi-Soviet nonaggression treaty in August 1939 led the Japanese military and foreign office to decide that they needed "new eyes in Lithuania." Chiune Sugihara, with his language skills and previous experience of spying on the Soviet Union, was a logical choice.

This kind of logic, however, does not explain why he granted 2,132 visas to refugees in the summer of 1940. When asked to account for these actions in 1942, Sugihara was already stationed in Prague. How he compiled this list, which was sent to Japan, is not clear. What we do know is that he cabled the Foreign Ministry saying that only 1,500 of these had been granted to Jews. After leaving Kovno, the Sugihara family was posted to Berlin. No opprobrium seemed to follow him there. In Prague, he was commended for hosting a large-scale exhibition for Japanese crafts attended by over 7,000 guests—this in Nazi-occupied Czechoslovakia. After Prague, the Sugiharas

---

9   Hillel Levine, *In Search of Sugihara: The Elusive Japanese Diplomat Who Risked his Life to Rescue 10,000 Jews From the Holocaust* (Lexington, MA: Plunkett Lake Press, 2012), 283.

continued their grand diplomatic life with a posting in Romania. With the end of the war, they were detained with other Japanese officials by the Soviet government. Chiune Sugihara was repatriated to Japan in the spring of 1947.

At that time, he was ordered to submit his resignation along with many other former diplomats. It was a time of retrenchment for the impoverished Japanese government under the American occupation. Sugihara was given a termination grant of 7,605 yen and a starting pension of 1,613 yen. Not a huge sum. Yet, the Foreign Ministry continued to argue until early in the twenty-first century that Chiune Sugihara was not fired for his actions in Kovno in 1940. Seishiro Sugihara (no personal relation of the former Japanese consul) argues forcefully that the Foreign Ministry "falsified history by concealing its own war responsibility; because of this the Japanese people were trapped in a warped linguistic space."[10] Denying its own culpability, this key agency of the post-war Japanese government made Chiune Sugihara into a "cocklebur"—a constant and unforgettable irritant who managed to act in a humanitarian fashion at a time when few others did the same.

To be sure, Sugihara was not the only Japanese consul to give Jewish refugees visas during the last possible moments before the *Shoah* engulfed Europe in its deathly grip. We now have documentation about several other Japanese and Chinese diplomats helping Jews escape from Europe. A total of 1,477 Japanese visas were issued in Vienna and Berlin alone between January 1940 and April 1941. No other Japanese diplomat, however, gave as many visas as readily as Chiune Sugihara did in a very short period of time. In the words of Pamela Sakomoto, "many Japanese diplomats issued visas that saved Jews… only a few like Sugihara saved Jews by issuing visas."[11]

There is a subtle and important distinction here that made a huge difference in the life of Chaya Leah Walkin and her family. One man in one place at one moment in time mobilized all the resources of his office with the conscious intention of saving Jews in distress. As Chaya Leah noted in her jottings, *chesed* might be the most meaningful explanation of why and how Chiune Sugihara awoke to the urgency of his own compassion in a world gone mad with hatred and confusion. The fact remains that he did awake to the predicament of those lining up outside his gate in Kovno. He acted with an alacrity that surpassed that of most other diplomats in war-torn Europe.

---

10   Seishiro Sugihara, *Chiune Sugihara and Japan's Foreign Ministry*, trans. Norman Hu (Lanham, MD: United Press of America, 2001), 136.
11   Pamela Rotner Sakamoto, *Japanese Diplomats and Jewish Refugees: A World War II Dilemma* (Westport, CT: Praeger Publishers, 1998), 4.

The Soviet invasion of Lithuania on June 15, 1940 had ended all hope for remaining in Europe for Jews like Rabbi Walkin. Torah scholars had flocked to Vilna in order to find a safe place between the Nazi extermination machine and the Soviet violent suppression of Jewish observance. Rabbi Grodinski had told the yeshiva community that Lithuania would remain "pink"—marred neither by the black swastika nor the red sickle and hammer. Alas, his prediction had failed. By the time of his death on August 9, 1940, many yeshiva students chose to stand in line outside Sugihara's villa in Kovno rather than attend his burial cortège.[12] They had held Rav Gordinski in great esteem and they owed him a great deal for his help when they first escaped to Vilna. But on this day, they chose life over death. Or at least the possibility of life—which was synonymous with an exit visa from the Soviet Union.

Rav Shmuel David had just received his visa from the Japanese consul one day before the passing of the great Torah sage whom he admired and had known personally. He had already caught, what Hillel Levine termed *bahalat nesi'a*—veritable travel frenzy which had affected so many other young Torah scholars and students.[13] They were bent upon seeking an escape for all costs. In his own memoirs many years later, Chiune Sugihara pointed to August 10 as his watershed moment. On this day, which was the Jewish Shabbat, he wrote later:

> I decided that it was completely useless to continue discussions with Tokyo, I was merely losing time... I started to issue Japanese transit visas on my own responsibility.[14]

Archival documents show that communication with the Foreign Ministry was breaking down at this point. But as recent research shows, Sugihara had official permission to issue visas to Polish refugees. He simply began to increase their numbers even before August 10. On July 30 alone, he issued 257 visas. On August 11, a Sunday, the consulate was closed. On August 12, the pace of visa signing picked up dramatically with visa no. 1,608 being issued to Olgierd Pawlowitz and his family. By August 20, Sugihara's last day in Kovno, he processed 454 more such life-saving papers.

What happened that Shabbat became so memorable in the rescuer's mind? It was, as Levine pieces together the story, a turning point in his moral

---

12 Zuroff, *Response of Orthodox Jewry*, 72.
13 Levine, *In Search of Sugihara*, 163.
14 Levine, *In Search of Sugihara*, 201.

awakening. Although Sugihara had sent four more cables to Japan seeking instructions and permission to sign more visas, what mattered more was the scene that he witnesses before his eyes. This is what also made such an enduring impression upon little Hiroki and his mother, Yukio. Hundreds of bedraggled Jews, some holding children by the hand, had been lining up the day before.

The photograph that Sugihara took sometime in August 1940 shows a group of men lining up outside 30 Vaizgantas Street. They are part of a larger throng and look well dressed. None of them is smiling. There is despair and also hope in their eyes. Here was a last chance. Like Rav Shmuel David Walkin, they were determined to take it. Chaya Leah rightfully termed this the "power of one"—one man acted. Once awakened, a compassionate person made all the difference in the world.

Sugihara did not wait for permission to increase the number of visas originally agreed upon with his superiors. He saw an urgent need and responded. At the same time, he knew he was part of a larger puzzle. The so-called "Curacao" visas had to be into place beforehand in order for Chiune Sugihara to move so swiftly into action. Who was responsible precisely for that bit of "miracle" is still being debated. Alyza Lewin, author of a recent essay, credits the chutzpah of the Curacao strategy to her grandmother, who had Dutch relatives. In this narrative, it is Jewish persistence that accounts for the decision taken by L. P. J. de Decker, Holland's ambassador in Riga.

It was refugees like Lewin's grandmother who discovered that no entrance permission was needed for Curacao. When de Decker appointed Jan Zwartndijk (Zwartendyk), to be the Dutch consul in Kovno, doors to escaping the Nazi threat became more open. Zwartndijk knew Chiune Sugihara personally. The Dutch consul, like the Japanese one, also mobilized what Chaya Leah termed "the power of one. " He, too, began issuing permits. By the end of August 1940, Zwartndijk had signed 2,345 passports indicating that no special permission was needed to enter the Dutch colony of Curacao.[15]

During the last days of July 1940, two Dutch yeshiva students, Nathan Gurwith and Leo Sternheim, also applied to the Dutch consul in Kovno for permission to travel to the Dutch Antilles since they could not return to Holland, which had been occupied by the Nazis since May. The surprising news of this possibility spread like wildfire in the congested alleys of Vilna. Any individual with a valid passport was thus able to obtain a visa for Curacao.

---

15 Alyza D. Lewin, "How my grandmother's chutzpah helped Sugihara rescue thousands of Jews," *Jewish Telegraphic Agency* (JTA). April 25, 2016.

According to Zwartndijk's son, his father issued 1,200 to 1,400 visas in less than a month before the official annexation of Lithuania by the Soviets. Soon thereafter, the butchery of Jews began. The Dutch consul recalled with horror his last days in Kovno in the fall of 1940 when "someone was seen hanging from every tree."[16]

Following the Dutch consul's initiative, Sugihara was able to act, and he acted promptly. Others, too, became part of the "miracle" that helped a small cohort of Jews to get out of Soviet-controlled Lithuania. The rabbis who encouraged their students to get passports when the general advice was to sit still and wait also stand out in this narrative of salvation. The Mirrer Yeshiva was one of the few yeshivas to urge their students to flee and one of the first to encourage all of its students to procure travel documents. Rav Shmuel David Walkin, too, had been one of those who made preparations. He produced birth certificates for his children and himself, some with the correct information, some not. What mattered was to have documents that Sugihara or his staff could stamp.

When news of the Curacao travel permits and Japanese transit visas arrived in Vilna, a small group of Torah scholars was prepared to act. On the same day that Rabbi Grodinski was being buried in Vilna, a young yeshiva student named Moshe Zupnik was in Kovno activating yet another aspect of the "power of one." While little Chaya Leah was eyeing sweets in a bakery in Vilna, her father and Zupnick had journeyed to the gates of the villa on Vaizgantas Street. Recalling this encounter with Chiune Sugihara years later, Zupnik remembered how the Japanese consul had questioned him about the actual means of travel and what funds they had for travel across Soviet Russia.

Assured that means would be found, Sugihara agreed to give over three hundred transit visas, enough for the entire Mirrer Yeshiva. Then came another practical problem. One man could not process all this paperwork, especially when time was so short, as both the Jews and Sugihara understood by August 1940. Speaking to Hillel Levine, Zupnik recalled his own audacity in solving the Japanese consul's dilemma as follows:

> I said: You know what? I will help you. The Consul looks at me and says: "He's all right, let him help." Sugihara was very friendly; he was a small man. From that day on, for the next two weeks, I used to come in the morning and sit in the room, not with Sugihara but with Gudze. I was

---

16 Zuroff, *Response of Orthodox Jewry*, 123.

stamping and he was stamping. I don't have the list in my memory, I don't remember it. But there were applications that people filled out.[17]

Moshe Zupnik understood the need to take the initiative. The man with whom he worked in Sugihara's office, Wolfgang Gudze, is part of the "miracle" as well. He was a Gestapo operative hired by Sugihara for his excellent language skills.

Prepared to fight for the German Fatherland, Gudze disagreed with Hitler on one small point only: he did not hold Jews in utter contempt. Zupnick recalls a delicate conversation between the yeshiva student and the Nazi official working in Sugihara's office:

> Wolfgang, how can I thank you? He said to me: "Remember the world is like a *rad*." He used the German word for wheel. "Whoever is on top today tomorrow might be down. Don't forget what I did for you." Those were his last words to me, exactly. He was thinking of Hitler and his successes and what might happen to him. I had one thing on my mind: how to get out. I still cannot understand how Sugihara could let me in, a boy. He didn't have any records on me, he simply handed over the consular stamp and allowed me to make visas. He wanted to do good. He told me: "I do it just because I have pity on the people. They want to get out so I let them have visas." ... He listened to us and he knew we were in danger and he did it.[18]

A Gestapo operative and a young yeshiva student are here working side by side. There is more to this narrative than the "power of one." Perhaps Hillel Levine's apt term, "a conspiracy of goodness" makes most sense in piecing together the entire puzzle that came together in the summer of 1940. In an utterly mad world, Chiune Sugihara became a force for mobilizing others in responding to a minuscule moment of opportunity to rescue Jews who were literally running for their lives.

SIBEER MIT TZEN SHLITZER—SIBERIA WITH 10 LOCKS

Getting hold of one of the Sugihara visas was hard enough. Imagining the end point of flight on some island in the Dutch West Indies was even more fantastic. But as options for life narrowed in Soviet-controlled Lithuania, there was no

---

17 Levine, *In Search of Sugihara*, 246.
18 Levine, *In Search of Sugihara*, 248.

choice but to start the next daunting step: getting an exit visa from the USSR. Permission to leave the communist "haven" was beyond the means of ordinary Soviet citizens; Polish refugees had no choice but to try.

After lining up for days at the terrifying offices of the Soviet Secret Service for exit documents, Jews like Rav Shmuel David Walkin faced the next challenge: how to deal with Intourist, the Soviet agency that controlled access to tickets on the Trans-Siberian Railway. Intourist officials demanded to be paid in American dollars. Where was an impoverished Jewish refugee to obtain forbidden foreign currency?

After all that, how was a family with small children to make the four-thousand-mile journey from Vilna to Vladivostok? How to escape the all too common fate of Jews (and other unfortunate "malcontents" within the Soviet regime) of landing forever in a Siberian labor camp? After the war, facts bore out the worst of the refugee's fears: roughly 150,000 Polish citizens had died in Soviet labor camps between 1938 and 1941, many of them Jews.

No wonder that Chaya Leah recalled a special Yiddish saying from that era to convey both the difficulties of the journey out of Soviet Russia and the frightening memories that linger on from that time. The name "Siberia," itself, calls to mind expanses of frozen tundra, with no way out of harrowing darkness. Now add to that 10 locks—*Sibeer mit tzen shlitzer*—and you have a realm in which one is sequestered forever. Jails might have one or two locks. But when something frigid and distant is further buttressed by "*tzen shlitzer*," escape is not even conceivable:

> *Siberia with ten locks.*
> *I started removing lock after lock, digging to remember, Zachor ve'al Tishkach. Remember and do not forget.*
> *So the seed of wanting to tell my story for my family started to germinate in my mind.*
> *As hard as it was to get out of Siberia, because it was as if every gate was locked with ten locks, my memory had a need to tell the story of the miracle of Shanghai and the cast of players involved in the miracle.*

Looking back, Chaya Leah links this vivid Yiddish expression with her own slow process of coming to terms with memories of trauma. Leaving Poland was difficult but exhilarating. Leaving Lithuania was more dangerous and also more memorable. Recollection is a religious duty for survivors of the *Shoah*. It is also a most difficult obligation.

Siberia with ten locks.
Meeting with refugees of the Holocaust who until recently would not talk about their experiences. Suddenly, they are over 70.
Now they are unlocking those locks—slowly, little glimmers of light are coming out to stoke long buried memories.

Chaya Leah's jottings describe the journey across Siberia's daunting terrain with the terror of a child. Nonetheless, the Torah injunction to never forget to recall what Amalek did to the Jewish people on the way out of Egypt becomes a guiding light for an aged woman who dares to look back upon a terrifying past.

This directive to "remember" covers more than mere survival. The difficult weeks that a child of six had spent on the Trans-Siberian Railroad to Vladivostok required more than endurance. It demanded an alertness to danger and humiliation that a child barely fathomed and yet obeyed with scrupulous care.

Chaya Leah uses the intimate Yiddish expression about Siberia's ten locks in order to remind herself that trauma, even retrospectively, must be approached slowly. Only memories unlocked with patience and care might bring forth glimmers of light, and not just an avalanche of unbearable grief. As a small child, Chaya Leah was not aware of all the hardships that had preceded the family's journey on through Soviet Russia. Samuel Iwry, by contrast, was a young man in his 20s who had no choice but to fend for himself. He recalled in detail what it was like to deal with the Secret Police in Vilna, even after obtaining one of the precious Sugihara visas.

Most of Iwry's Jewish neighbors in the crowded alleys had found their name on a list penned to the door of the offices saying "*Nyet*—No more applications for exit visas accepted. The difference between the frenzied kindness that had dominated the Japanese consulate in Kovno and the harsh extortion practiced by Soviet authorities made a deep impact on Iwry:

> But I got my permission before it was too late. It took some time, but the answer was positive. The only thing that Intourist wanted was to be paid for the whole journey—including passport, hotels and even places you will have to stay if the 11-day journey was interrupted—all this had to be paid in cash. Not only cash, but American dollars. The joke is that dealing in foreign currency was a punishable crime in the Soviet Union. Some of my friends experienced this—before and after leaving the Intourist people were searched and arrested for possessing foreign currency... Getting our

money changed was not difficult. We went to the back market for dollars and paid a very high price, almost 30 *lit* to the dollar. The official exchange rate was only five *lit* to the dollar, but this was another fiction.[19]

Coming up with a sizeable fee in US dollars was no easy task. Escaping the machinations of the Secret Police and the tricks of Intourist similarly required nerves of steel. As an intrepid young man, Iwry managed to cope with all this.

Older, but no less resourceful, Rav Shmuel David Walkin also managed to get his family on the Trans-Siberian Railway. Rav Walkin's resourcefulness became the subject of conversation many years later, when Chaya Leah met up with Hilda, who had been a refugee in Shanghai. Being of German origin, she had been called the *Daishike* by the Walkin children even after she married one of the Polish yeshiva boys. It was Hilda's groom who recalled the story that made such an impression on Chaya Leah six decades after the war:

> *The Daishike came to visit today. She was the one who gave my mother the tin can to make a stove in Shanghai, the one whose wedding picture we have. She was here all day. She came to put up a matzeive (memorial stone) for her son, who died in his sleep. She told me that on the Trans- Siberian Train, my father had one hundred dollars in one American bill and he gave it to Yosele, her future husband. My father with a family was afraid to carry the money in case he got caught and would jeopardize his family.*
> *Yosele went to the bathroom and carved out a hole in a bar of soap and inserted the bill. When he came to Vladivostok, he had American dollars.*
> *I think they split the money. I remember the story, but was afraid that it was a fragment of my imagination. Now, I know that it is true.*

Now that I am writing about Chaya Leah's efforts to piece together bits about her father's past, I recall my own father's arrest on the Romanian border just as we were about to emigrate in 1961.

My father was much less savvy than Rav Walkin had been under duress. We, too, were leaving a communist "homeland" in 1961, not as refugees but as emigrants after ten years of waiting for a legal passport. Like the Walkin family, Jews leaving Romania knew they would need foreign currency all along the way. Clever cousins of my parents hid jewelry and dollars in hollowed-out loaves of bread and therefore were able to establish lucrative businesses upon arrival in

---

19 Iwry, *To Wear the Dust of War*, 64.

Israel. Our family had no jewelry, no American dollars. Instead, my father tried to hide the 1,000 Romanian *lei* (maybe worth $50) in his coat lining.

Taking Romanian currency out of the country was as illegal in 1961 as dollars had been in Soviet-controlled Vilna in late 1940. Caught right before we boarded the train to Vienna, my father was placed in jail for six months, while my mother, my sister, and I were forced to travel ahead. The tears and anxieties I witnessed as a 14-year-old remain searing. These memories helped me to imagine what Chaya Leah experienced on the train to Vladivostok, not even knowing that one bar of soap carried all her family's resources for survival.

Rabbi Chaim Shmuelevitz (1902–79), the venerable mentor of the Mirrer Yeshiva, also recalled the dangers and fears that marked the journey out of Soviet Russia. In his testimony for Yad Vashem, Rav Chaim described the efforts of Moshe Zupnik and other yeshiva students in processing the Japanese visas. He also emphasized the support of a young Zionist leader, Zerach Warhaftig, who was instrumental in convincing Sugihara to help the entire Mirrer Yeshiva, even though he was not part of their group. After obtaining Japanese transit documents, there were other daunting difficulties:

> Every person leaving had to present himself to the NKVD (the Soviet Secret Service) in Vilna or Kovno for a formal investigation before receiving his exit visa. Dozens were rejected and held back in Lithuania. It is unknown whether any survived. The yeshiva students and teachers left in groups of 50. From January 1941, five or six groups of yeshiva students left from Vilna to Vladivostok and from there to the Japanese port city of Kobe, where hundreds of refugees were gathered. Payment for the visa to the USSR was 180 dollars per person, was provided by the Joint. The "Curacao travelers" were unable to continue, as it became clear that the visas they had received were not valid.[20]

Rabbi Shmuelevitz's testimony gives credit to the American-Jewish relief agency called the "Joint" for helping with the foreign cash required to travel out of the USSR. How many Polish refugees actually received that aid is not clear. In the frenzied autumn and winter of 1940–41, the Vaad ha-Hatzala was cooperating with other Jewish agencies in trying the reach as many Jews as possible who had exit papers out of the Soviet Union. As Rabbi Shmuelevitz recalls, his

---

20 Tzvi Yaakovson, "Rav Chaim Shmulewitz on his Holocaust Rescue," *Yated Ne'eman*, December 24, 2014.

own Torah community was a beneficiary of this rescue effort, but far from the only one.

All of the refugees who managed to board the Trans-Siberian Railway knew that they could be dragged off at any point and sent to one of the many gulags that they passed along the way. Samuel Iwry was especially mindful of all the dangers along the road of escape from this Stalinist "paradise." By March 1941, when he boarded the train in Moscow, he knew that the fate of European Jews was sealed for death. He also knew that Soviet authorities could take him off the rickety old train at any point. He recalls one officer looking at his documents and noting that Iwry was a teacher, wanted to send him off to Birobidzhan, the so-called "Jewish republic" established by the Soviet regime on the Amur River at the border with Manchuria:

> I almost was taken off the train, and I know that if I had stepped off, I would have never returned. One night, as I remember, we reached the town of Irkutsk, which is high on the Asian plateau, over a hundred miles north on the border of Mongolia... (A Soviet officer) "invited" me to step off the train and from there he said maybe we could find some connections to Birobidzhan... When we headed for the platform, I thought I was going to be taken prisoner. And then I heard, when we stepped out of the train, that the temperature was 72 degrees below zero... that if you stay outside as long as two minutes, you will never have your ears back... So I stepped right back on the train. I went back to my seat and never saw him again.[21]

Freezing cold and the threat of arrest accompanied the fleeing Jews every step of the way toward Vladivostok.

Chaya Leah Walkin, as a five-year-old, knew nothing of Birobidzhan or about the gulags. But she did sense the dread of her parents and fellow travelers whenever the train stopped. It was clear to her, as it was to Iwry, that getting out of the claustrophobic wagons was to risk death. Unlike the more seasoned young man who resisted the "invitation" to get off the train, Chaya Leah's recollections dwell upon the most basic need to relieve herself:

> *I do remember a lot of the train ride.*
> *I remember it being very cramped.*

---

21 Iwry, *To Wear the Dust of War*, 73.

Watchmen Patrolling the City: Escape Through Vilna to Japan • CHAPTER 2 | 51

> *I remember the train stopping in bitter cold*
> *and we were allowed to get off the train to relieve ourselves.*
> *I remember a guard with a gun watching me relieve myself, a little girl.*
> *Where will I run to?*
> *I was so embarrassed.*
> *I was afraid to go the bathroom, which was the cold icy earth.*
> *I remember my father warning us: Do not say anything!*
> *If the Bolsheviks will ask you anything say:*
> *"Die mehe adin stakan tchai"*
> *(Give me a glass of tea).*
> *I remember the cold.*

The cold. The fear. The shame. To be sure, looking back upon this dreadful train ride was much easier than to fathom the cattle trains that took my own grandparents to Auschwitz. On the train to Vladivostok, a child was free at least to ask for a glass of tea, even if it was not given.

Yet, even this cup of tea is part of the terror of the *Shoah*. The dark memories of this child must be recorded in the same universe of meaning and meaninglessness as that of my own kin. Dan Pagis, the Israeli poet who went through the death camps, found the words to frame the dread that binds survivors. Using the language of the Jewish bible, he wrote:

> here in this carload
> i am eve
> with abel my son
> if you see my other son
> cain son of man
> tell him that i[22]

The unfinished, unpunctuated line speaks volumes about how the appeal of the Jews fell upon deaf ears. Pagis's poem is entitled "Written in Pencil in a Sealed Railway Car." Chaya Leah Walkin and her family did not travel across Siberia in a sealed cattle car. Their train was sealed by fears of the unknown. The *tzen shlitzer* of Siberia remained tight upon the heart and mind long after Chaya Leah's terrifying journey ended with a few blessed months in Japan.

---

22 Dan Pagis, *The Selected Poems of Dan Pagis*, trans. Stephen Mitchell (Berkeley, CA: University of California Press, 1996), 24.

By early 1941, the Walkin family had found its way to Kobe. There, they were met with kindness and civility, which had been inconceivable in Nazi-occupied Poland or in Soviet-controlled Lithuania. Looking back on their survival, one cannot but acknowledge that timing made all the difference during every step of their flight from Lukatch to Kobe. Cart rides endured, papers manufactured, visas procured, dollars obtained—all this was part of the ordeal of survival.

During the gruesome journey, there had been plenty of "watchmen"—in the words of *Shir Ha'Shirim*—who had been ready to beat, wound, and despoil the Jewish refugees. Yet, despite the staggering odds against them, a modicum of compassion had prevailed all along the way.

CHAPTER 3

AN APPLE TREE NESTLED IN THE WOODS:

Respite in Japan

As an apple tree nestled in the woods,
So is my beloved among young men.
Under its shadow I sit delighted,
The fruit sweet to my taste.

Shir Ha'Shirim 2:3

The momentous year 1941—which brought the Walkin family to Japan and then to China—shook up the wider world as well. In Europe, the murder of Jews was moving into high gear with the appointment of Adolf Eichmann as head of Jewish Affairs in March 1941. In Poland alone, more than 10,000 Jews died of starvation in the Warsaw Ghetto. In Pinsk, the home of Chaya Leah's father, Heinrich Himmler ordered the execution of all Jewish men, women, and children in July 1941. In only nine months, 11,000 Jews were murdered before the formal establishment of the Pinsk Ghetto on May 1, 1942.

For Japan, the year 1941 brought a bit of respite from the pursuit of conquest in China through the signing of a nonaggression pact with the Soviet Union on April 13. Four months later, on August 14, Franklin Roosevelt and Winston Churchill released the "Atlantic Charter" affirming American support for Britain in the war and for the "self-determination" of all nations—without any promise of help to persecuted Jews. This agreement helped to keep the United States out of direct involvement in the conflict raging across Europe.

By December 7, 1941, all hopes for American neutrality ended with the attack on Pearl Harbor. By that time, the Walkin family's refuge in Japan had ended as well. A couple of months before eight US Navy battleships were bombed and four sunk, Chaya Leah—along with her siblings and parents—had been cast amid thousands of other Jewish refugees from Europe into the dirty alleys of Shanghai.

Chaya Leah's recollections of her nine months in Japan are glazed by a child's delight in a land that seemed both exotic and generous. After the meeting with Japanese officials seeking to memorialize Chiune Sugihara in New York on September 8, 2016, she wrote:

> *The manners and the ways of the Japanese came back to me: the bowing of the farewell was an almost automatic response from me.*
> *Japan has nothing but pleasant memories for me.*
> *The beauty, the cleanliness, the flowers, gardens, the marketplace, the house we lived in, the school I went to, the Japanese friends and neighbors.*
> *I was a young child protected by a loving family.*
> *I did not know what was going on in my parent's hearts and minds.*
> *Ignorance is definitely bliss.*

In the moving aftermath of the encounter in Manhattan, and after she had expressed her gratitude to the Japanese hosts with *Arigato* (thank you) and *Nippon Hai* (long live Japan), Chaya Leah acknowledges that the pleasant memories of 1941 may have been as much ignorance as bliss.

The flowers and gardens of Kobe, Japanese friends and neighbors all come alive when Chaya Leah speaks or writes about the delightful interval between Vilna and Shanghai. Her memories also call to mind the vision of refuge described in *Shir Ha'Shirim*: an apple tree nestled among the woods, its gentle shadows protecting the lover about to taste a sweet, sweet fruit. The longed-for refuge, according to rabbinical commentators give us hints of the sublime delights experienced at Mount Sinai. There, marvels were glimpsed briefly and then became hidden until the end of days. In Japan, Chaya Leah as a child had savored a bit of the kind of peace described under the apple tree in the woods. She could not fathom what lay beyond her shadowed nook.

She knew nothing of the web of politics that led one country in Asia to consciously craft a policy for the rescue of Jewish refugees. However short lived, the "Fugu Plan" had set a tone of welcome that even a six-year-old child could sense, even if she had no clue about the machinations that lay behind it. Named after a poisonous puffer fish, the "Fugu Plan" was conceived by anti-Semitic Japanese officials eager to benefit from Europe's hatred of the Jews. On December 5, 1938, when the Walkin family was still in Lukatch basking in the birth of a baby boy, five top ministers of the Japanese government convened a conference to discuss what should be their country's response to the "Jewish problem." Based on their positive reading of the "Protocols of the Elders of Zion," they decided that Jews could be a great asset to Japan by bringing foreign capital (especially into their newly developing puppet state of Manchukuo in northeast China). Jewish influence could also help to improve world opinion, which had been souring after events such as the rape of Nanjing in 1937.

A few visionary young "experts" on Jewish matters, such as Norihiro Yasue (1886-1950), even went so far as to suggest that it would be useful to set up several areas called "Israel in Asia." These were envisioned as specially designed enclaves in Shanghai, Dalian, and Harbin. Although Yasue himself was demoted after the signing of Japan's alliance with Nazi Germany in 1940, a climate of interest in Jews lingered as the Walkin family landed in the port of Tsuruga and made its way to Kobe along with hundreds of other Polish refugees.

TANGERINES BOBBING IN THE SEA

Chaya Leah's journey to Japan comes across as a nightmare because of the fears and humiliation evoked by the Soviet police. A six-year-old Jewish child had no way of grasping all the other difficulties that beset the refugees' journey out of Stalinist Russia. Even when they finally reached Vladivostok, even while they were clutching one of the precious Sugihara visas, it was not clear that they would be able to get on a boat to Japan.

It is only recent research that has revealed the key role of Nei Saburo, Acting Consul in Vladivostok, who took it upon himself to facilitate the exit of Jews out of Russia to Japan. Like Chiune Sugihara, Nei had studied in Harbin, a Japanese-controlled city that had a considerable Jewish population. Even while other Japanese officials in the Foreign Ministry were beginning to question Sugihara's wisdom in granting so many transit visas in Kovno, Nei argued that if he did not honor these documents, the wider world may consider Japan "untrustworthy."[1]

This world had already condemned his country harshly for atrocities in China and Korea. Yet, Nei Saburo found a politically convincing rationale for facilitating Jewish entry into Japan. Even with Nei's goodwill, the problem of finding enough boats for hundreds of refugees remained. This problem is depicted in all its complexity in Akira Kitade's book *Visas for Life*. Based upon the records of the Japan Travel Bureau, Kitade explores all the details of journey

---

1 Yukata Taniuchi, *The Miracle Visas* (Jerusalem: Gefen Publishing House, 2001), 67.

that enabled families such as that of Chaya Leah Walkin to actually arrive upon the shores of Japan. Not a professional historian by training, Kitade follows the muse of his own interests, starting with the adventures of his own mentor at the Japan Travel Bureau. He then links that narrative to interviews with some of the Jews who traveled from Vladivostok to the small port of Tsuruga in the winter of 1940–41.

Unlike the Soviets' duplicitous views toward foreign currency, the Japan Travel Bureau was guided by sober and practical calculations. Working with the Thomas Cook agency, which was handling travel for the refugees, they came up with a fee of 183,600 yen for the transportation of 765 persons. The cost for each traveler came to 240 yen and the total received by the Japanese Travel Bureau by the end of October 1941 came to approximately 740,000 American dollars.[2] During the eleven months between July 1940 and May 1941, 4,664 refugees arrived in Japan. This figure included 2,498 German Jews and 2,166 refugees from Lithuania. After June 22, 1941, due to pressures from Nazi Germany, no more Jewish refugees were allowed to come into Japan.[3]

The journey to Tsuruga in the winter of 1940-41 had been especially difficult in turbulent weather. Each trip took three days, with two nights aboard such vessels as the *Amakusa-maru*, the old German-built ship that made most of the crossings that brought Jews from Vladivostok to Tsuruga. Tatsuo Osako, an assistant purser on the *Amakusa-maru*, remembered with fondness the refugees whom he had helped. In contrast to the terrible stories of extortion, rape and murder that pour forth from twenty-first-century refugees in the Middle East and Asia, Osako's recollections, as well as those of his Jewish passengers, center on small acts of kindness. Here, too, the *chesed* that Chaya Leah marveled at in Sugihara's case comes to the foreground in the tough passage to Tsuruga.

Even before landing on the shores of Japan, Tatsuo Osako was left with souvenirs and notes that expressed the Jewish refugee's warmth and gratitude to naval staff who did not speak German, Polish, or English. One of the Jewish young women who gave her photo to the Japanese captain signed her name in Polish; another wrote a few words of greeting in French.

Chaya Leah was too little to write messages and probably had no photograph to give away after the family's harrowing flight out of Poland. What

---

2 Akira Kitade, *Visas for Life and the Epic Journey: How the Sugihara Survivors Reached Japan* (Tokyo: Chobunsha, 2014), 21.
3 Ibid., 131.

the child missed on the boat to Tsuruga, an older woman embroidered with memory's golden threads. In her jottings for this book, Chaya Leah recalled the day of her landing in Japan as follows:

> We all ran out on the deck. The sun was shining. The air clean, the waters calm. Then, we noticed beautifully dressed women walking in wooden shoes—click click click. Their kimonos (a word I learned later) were so colorful. The harbor was so clean.
> The boat was still moving a little, and the women began throwing tangerines to us. This was a sign of welcome to us as foreigners.
> There were little tangerines bobbing all over in the sea. Somehow, we got them aboard the boat.

A little girl who had been terrified to relieve herself on the frozen tundra of Siberia glimpses an entirely different world here. Instead of soldiers with weapons, instead of the enforced silence on the train, she looked out upon a sea bobbing with tangerines and heard the gentle clopping of *geta* (Japanese shoes). This was the scene that greeted Chaya Leah in Japan, at least in memory's gaze.

Yet, even in this idyllic picture, a bit of the Walkin family's "truth" shines through. The child marveled at the fruit while her mother worriedly cried out:

> "Don't touch them! Don't eat them!"
> After all the harrowing times during our escape, she believed that they were trying to poison us. We were all going to die.
> The brave ones on our boat tried the tangerines, and nothing happened. Only then did my parents relent, and we ate some. I can still recall the taste of that juice, the softness of tangerine flesh.

Tzivia Walkin was a survivor of the escape from Poland, during which she had been convinced that the cart driver was going to murder her and her children. That kind of dread does not die easily. Arriving on the strange shores of an utterly alien land, after the horrors of Soviet Russia, she may be forgiven for fearing "poisoned" tangerines. Nothing in the Walkin family's previous journeys held any promise of welcome or the sweetness of fresh fruit.

Interestingly, fresh fruit also figures prominently in memories of the arrival of other Jewish refugees in Japan. Among the photographs surviving in the "Port of Humanity" Museum built by the Tsuruga municipality, images of

Japanese citizens handing fresh apples to the refugees take pride of place. This museum also collected oral histories from those who recall the arrival of the Jews. One woman from Tsuruga describes how her brother, who was 12 years old, went to the dock to welcome the refugees with apples:

> I was not allowed to go to the port as I was still in second grade so I did not see this myself. But my brother could not have taken out basketfuls of fruit on his own volition… I gather that our father, who used to frequent Vladivostok, must have known about the state of the poor refugees and sent my brother to distribute apples.[4]

In Kitade's book, such oral histories are juxtaposed with murderous attacks against Jews occurring in Europe at the same time. This author includes in his work a photograph of a little girl in a patched smock standing in the midst of Hungarian Jews who have just been transported to Auschwitz. She looks about Chaya Leah's age and faces the camera with frightened eyes while the kerchiefed women around her try to fathom the unbearable future that awaits them.

We know what happened to them. They were gassed. The little girl became nothing more than ashes. Chaya Leah lived. She was fortunate to be among the Jewish refugees whose lives were saved by the decency of one Japanese man—a decency augmented by the kindness and politeness of many other Japanese in Tsuruga and Kobe. Writing about the boy and the apples, Akira Kitade notes: "Although the boy gave away apples under his father's direction, I still feel very proud of his actions that exemplify the kindness of the Japanese people."[5]

Other images of Japanese, Jews, and apples are found in the Tsuruga museum as well. Beyond kindness, it also looks that Jews were buying and paying for apples.

In one photograph, recently arrived refugees appear eager and open faced, unlike Chaya Leah's mother, who would not let her children touch the tangerines. A Japanese merchant handing out the apples look positively happy to be involved in this exchange. The buyers sport broad smiles and bow their heads slightly in polite acknowledgment. Nothing like this positive encounter had happened to Jewish refugees in the many months that they had spent worrying about visas in Vilna or during the frigid train ride to Vladivostok.

---

4 Akira Kitade, *Visas for Life and the Epic Journey: How the Sugihara Survivors Reached Japan* (Tokyo: Chobunsha, 2014), 59.
5 Ibid., 70.

Samuel Iwry, like so many other survivors, notes the sense of relief palpable in Japan. Suddenly, Jews could wear clean shirts, take a bath, and could be refreshed in body and soul. From the Japanese sources, we also know that Tsuruga city officials decided to close the public Asahi bath house on certain days so that Jewish refugees could bathe. As one Tsuruga resident recalled:

> It must have been the spring of 1941 ... the Asahi bath house closed for a day to let the Jewish refugees use it for free. We felt uneasy to be in the tub where foreigners bathe, so we walked a long way to go to another bath house"[6]

The fact that ordinary Japanese considered their race especially pure (because they were direct descendants of the sun goddess Amaterasu) would probably strike Rabbi Walkin as naked idolatry. Ignorant of the religion of Shintoism, Chaya Leah and her family simply enjoyed bathing in hot water. This was a marvelous novelty after the grime and terror of leaving Europe. Finally, it was possible to be cleansed in a dignified fashion after the terrifying ordeal of the Siberian train and the tumultuous winter seas that carried Jewish refugees to Japan.

Chaya Leah's recollection of the tangerines and hot baths undergirds the ongoing need to express her gratitude to the Japanese people, not just to Chiune Sugihara. This distinctively Jewish commitment to gratitude was noted by the Japanese hosts themselves. As Yoshiko Saito, a pastor in western Tokyo, put it quite simply: "It seems that the Jewish people never forget a favor."[7]

The lingering fondness for the refugees in Japan may also be glimpsed in the Tsuruga museum's most concrete relic—a watch pawned long ago and never redeemed. Like Chaya Leah Small's family, Jews got off the boat with very few resources to start a new life. A little cash helped. But when money was in short supply, personal possessions became a means for survival. In one of the testimonies recorded for the Tsuruga museum, a young woman recalled being in high school when the Jews came through selling watches, rings, and more:

> My family was running a jewelry and watch dealership in front of the train station. Every time the ship would dock, a Jewish person with nothing in hand would show my father an empty wallet, gesture and eating motion, then ask him to buy his watch or ring saying "How much?" My father was

---

6   Ibid., 58.
7   Ibid., 147.

a college graduate so he could speak some English but maybe his accent was heavy. They wrote the words on paper. My father ended up buying a lot of rings and watches. The Jewish people would then take the money to the noodle shop in front of the station and have meals there.[8]

Chaya Leah's family would not have eaten at the noodle shop. Scrupulous about their observance of *kashrut* in the direst circumstances, they ate eat fruits, rice, and whatever else they had and shared with other Torah-observant travel companions. There was no hint of judgment in Chaya Leah's recollections about those who did use money to buy any kind of food in Japan. All refugees understood the need for possessions that could be traded for survival. With a little gold or silver, a Jew could cross a border, buy a meal.

Just how ingrained this understanding of tradeable goods was among Jewish refugees comes through in another Tsuruga testimony, which focuses on the silver candlesticks that the Jews had brought with them through Siberia. It seems that even Soviet officials allowed this minimum necessity for the observance of Shabbat to accompany those fleeing Stalin's secular "heaven." In Japan, many Jews needing money traded in their candlesticks. One antique dealer stashed all the candlesticks in a garage, keeping them wrapped in the foreign-language newspapers with which they had been originally packaged.

Later, going through a vault filled with junk, one candlestick broke. Inside it, the dealer found a gold chain. His daughter later recalled:

> After that, there was a quite a commotion in our family. Numerous candlesticks, big and small, were all broken by a hammer and they all exposed jewels, rings, necklaces, clocks, more jewelry. It was indeed treasure mountain. The porcelain candlesticks of various sizes, all contained these valuables inside and were sealed shut with wax at the bottom… Soon afterwards, the war became imminent… all was lost inside the vault that turned out to be flammable.[9]

Like Chaya Leah's vision of a sea bobbing with tangerines, this mountain of treasure looms larger in memory than it was in real life. Enlarged, it lends color and weight to Japanese recollections of the arrival of Jews in Tsuruga. As the

---

8 Ibid., 65–66.
9 Ibid., 67.

antique dealer quickly understood, refugees had no choice but to part with heirlooms that they had packed for survival.

It was harder for Japanese merchants to fathom the value of candlesticks for the spiritual survival of the Jews. According to Chaya Leah's recollection, German Jews were more likely to have prepared silver candelabra with wax bottoms since they knew that they were leaving Europe for good and thus were prepared to take valuables in a way that was hard to detect. By contrast, Polish Jews had been running in a hastier fashion. First, they had tried to escape the Soviet regime's hostility to religion; only later they became mindful of the full extent of the Nazi threat. Being more traditionally observant than modernized German Jews, their religious articles were not treated as vehicles for material survival.

The Walkin family's own silver candlesticks embody this tenacious attachment to the objects of Torah observance. They were a special gift from Rav Shmuel David to his young bride and were manufactured by the famous Dyckman Jewelers, a German firm that had a store in Warsaw as well as in Pinsk. Chaya Leah as a little girl remembered this treasured pair in her parents' homes in Kobe, Shanghai, and New York. Following up with Mr. Dyckman's brother in Manhattan, she discovered a wellspring of recollection:

> "Are you Shmuel David's daughter?"
> "Yes," I said.
> "Tell me about your father."
> "My grandfather did not live in Poland. He lived in Belarus. He lived in a town named Pinsk. He had a small store and traveled a lot. They sold silver. Your father always prided himself with the leichter he bought for his kallah. He talked about the leichter and the old friendship with my brother whenever we met."

The Walkin family candlesticks represented far more than capital to be used for survival. They were a link back to the world of Pinsk, to the careful craftsmanship that had adorned their Shabbat table back home and throughout their refuge in China and Japan. These precious objects could never be sold off for food. Rabbi Walkin and his family were probably as hungry as other refugees getting off the boat in Tsuruga. Nonetheless, the values that they carried within prevented them from eating at noodle shops on the streets of Japan. The food was not kosher. Fresh fruits and vegetables were preferred. Eventually, Chaya Leah recalls, pure rice was sanctioned, even when visiting the homes of Japanese schoolmates.

The treasured "leichters" from Pinsk continued to adorn each holiday and special occasion of the Walkin family after the war. They had pride of place at each engagement and wedding. They are there, visible, in Chaya Leah's own engagement photograph. The light pouring from these candlesticks embodied the vivifying illumination of Torah. This symbolism can also be seen on the cover of Yecheskel Leitner's *Operation Torah Rescue*, about the survival of the Mirrer Yeshiva during the Holocaust. In this photograph, two Chinese-style candlesticks shed a warm light upon the pages of a worn volume of the Talmud. Together, they convey a reverence for texts and Jewish temporality that had characterized the childhood of Chaya Leah Walkin, as well as the rest of her adult life.

AVRAHAM SETSUKO KOTSUJI—A GREAT FRIEND OF KOBE POLICE

The Japanese person who understood the most about Jewish refugees and sought to help them in their hour of need was neither a boy with apples nor an antique dealer. His name of was Setsuko Kotsuji (1899–1973) and he was Japan's most renowned Hebraist when Chaya Leah arrived in Kobe in early 1941. Kotsuji made it possible for Jews to stay in Japan with the visas that Sugihara had handed out in haste the summer before.

Residence Permit for Walkin family in Kobe, Japan. 1941.

When the Walkin family arrived from Tsuruga to Kobe, they had no idea how long they could stay. Their travel and living expenses were covered in part by the small Jewish community in Japan that had been coping with the influx of refugees since 1939. The resources of Kobe's more established Jews had been greatly strained by the unexpectedly large number of Polish arrivals. Sugihara visas had helped these refugees arrive in Japan. Now came the urgent problem of how to extend their stay until other options for survival emerged in an increasingly bewildering world. As one Japanese scholar, Jundai Yamada, put it—an urgent savior was needed to "anchor" the transit visas that had been granted in Lithuania. That rescuer turned out to be Setsuko Kotsuji.

One surviving document reveals the result of the kindness that took place in Japan through the actions of this one man. It is a residence permit card for the Walkin family, allowing them to remain in Kobe from March 25 to August 28, 1941. The card lists five persons: "Szmuel-David 46 male, Cyla 30 female, Chaia-Leja 6 female, Esther 5 female and Moisze-Joiel 2 male." These names are written with foreign letters, while everything else is in Japanese *kanji*. Bearing the seal of the governor of Hyogo Prefecture (in which Kobe was located), the document also states:

> Foreigners who wish to stay further after the expiration of the permitted period may apply to the governor of the prefecture in which they are living ten days before the expiration date.

What this creased piece of paper reveals is that the Walkin family was entitled to live in Japan although they had left Vilna with nothing more than a transit visa to Curacao. The residence certificate documents a highly improbable outcome since the Sugihara visas permitted only two weeks in Japan.

With Sugihara's help, Chaya Leah's family had managed to arrive in Japan. With self-sacrificing aid from Setsuko Kotsuji, they were able to stay long enough to craft the means for meaningful refuge, first in Kobe and later in Shanghai. Rav Shmuel David's friendship with this Japanese scholar lasted well into the 1960s. By that time, Kotsuji had converted to Judaism and had taken on the name Avraham. Late in life, he became a frequent guest in the Walkins' Brooklyn home.

The son of a long line of Shinto priests, Setsuko Kotsuji had began his journey toward the Jewish bible in the 1910s when, as a middle school student, he discovered in an antique shop a copy of the *Tanach* (the compendium of the five books of the Torah plus prophets, psalms, and so forth) translated into Japanese. Drawn to this text, he decided to study it in depth through graduate work in the United States. By 1937, he was a noted academic expert on the Hebrew language and grammar and went on to establish Tokyo University's department of Jewish studies. When Manchuria was conquered by Japan,

Professor Kotsuji's knowledge became even more useful in negotiations with the Jewish community of Harbin.

Although he considered himself a Christian at this point, the Hebrew-speaking academic had warm relations with the leader of the Manchurian Jewish community, Rabbi Moshe Aharon Kiskilov. Whenever Japanese policy planners needed someone to translate documents about the Jews, Setsuko Kotsuji was the expert they called upon.

After the formal signing of the Axis agreement on September 27, 1940, Japanese officials were being inundated with anti-Semitic materials produced in Japan and also by Japan's ally, Nazi Germany. It was in this poisonous climate that Setsuko Kotsuji chose to publish a book entitled *The True Character of the Jewish Nation* in which he criticized German myths and lies. During various public appeals in the tense months of 1941, Kotsuji declared:

> Divine Providence has brought thousands of unfortunate refugees to our shores, so that we could grant them a safe haven where they will find peace and tranquility. This is our mission in life. Let us not betray it.[10]

In a language calculated to appeal to Japanese nationalism and to the unique character of the descendants of Amaterasu, this professor of the Hebrew language sought to gain sympathy for the bedraggled Jews in Kobe.

By the spring of 1941, when more than a thousand Jewish refugees poured into Japan, Setsuko Kotsuji turned out to be the right man in the right place to make all the difference in their chances for survival. While Jewish relief agencies tried to help with daily needs such as food and housing, Kotsuji took it upon himself to negotiate the extension of their residence permits in Kobe. Local police, under pressure from the central government, were not inclined to allow so many Jews to remain in a city that was already suffering from food shortages due to the war in China and Korea.

The only possibility remaining was bribery. Kotsuji risked everything to try this avenue for the survival of the Jews. In his memoir entitled *From Tokyo to Jerusalem*, he describes a train journey to his wealthy brother-in-law who lived in Osaka. Large funds were needed for so many documents, and this man had considerable resources. It was not an easy meeting. A sense of urgency

---

10 Setsuzo Kotsuji, *From Tokyo to Jerusalem* (Jerusalem: distributed by Random House, 1964), 127.

compelled Kotsuji to ask in a way that his wife's brother might understand. The appeal was based on the Japanese concept of "face":

> I am trying to help some old friends, I said.
> In Manchuria my work was mostly with the Jewish people. They need me now, and I want to keep faith with them...
> You have said I should wear your clothes so as not to lose face. Now I need money so as not to lose face.
> "Is it important to you?" he asked.
> It is not for me, it is for humanity's sake. Look, you told me that once you lost a million yen overnight when the stock market fell. Money means nothing to you; it is only counters in a game. You can do something.[11]

Kotsuji's brother-in-law eventually agreed to a loan. With pockets bulging in cash, Japan's only Hebraist hurried back to Kobe and began a series of "conversations" with the police chief regarding doing something about all these refugees. Over luxurious meals hosted by this "good friend of the Kobe police," the visa extensions were agreed upon. Initially, police documents allowed only fifteen more days. Over time and with more cash, extensions became lengthier, as the Walkin residence document testifies.

Setsuko Kotsuji himself paid a high price for these acts of compassion. In addition to having to pay back his brother-in-law (a burden that left his wife and daughters in dire poverty), he also got in trouble with the military. By the end of 1942, the Japanese Bureau of Investigation began to give credence to German reports that Jewish subversives were planning to gain control of the world. Kotsuji was accused of aiding their infernal plot. While Chiune Sugihara continued to serve in relative luxury as a diplomat in Europe, Kotsuji was arrested and tortured by the domestic police. After being released from jail, he moved his family to Manchuria, where he continued to debunk anti-Semitic myths in essays and speeches about the Jews.

After the war, Kotsuji continued his correspondence with the Torah scholars whom he had befriended and helped in Kobe and in Harbin. He wrote them that he felt drawn more and more toward the faith of the Jews. In 1959, the sixty-year-old Setsuko Kotsuji converted to Judaism and took on the name Avraham ben Avraham. During a visit to Jerusalem, Avraham Kotsuji was

---

11 Ibid., 164.

hosted with great warmth by Rabbi Chaim Shmuelevitz, who had been the dean of the Mirrer Yeshiva in Kobe and in Shanghai. In a tiny, crowded apartment, the Japanese convert was toasted with the following words of tribute:

> My dear Reb Avraham. May you grow in Torah and Yiras Shamayim (awe of Heaven). May you become a true son of Avraham Avinu (Abraham our forefather) after whom you are named. We will never forget what you did for us when we were in Japan. Nor how you risked your life to save us. The merit of that *mesirus-nefesh* (self-sacrifice) is what stood in your stead and led you to seek shelter under the wings of the Shechina (Divine Presence) and to become a genuine member of the Nation you helped so much.[12]

Avraham Kotsuji died in 1974 in Brooklyn shortly after the Jewish High Holidays. A special committee of the Mirrer Yeshiva had raised funds to take care of all his needs. In keeping with his wishes, his body was brought for burial to the Mount of Rest (Har Ha Menuchot) in Jerusalem, where his interment was attended by a throng of communal leaders as well as yeshiva students.

NIPPON HAI—LONG LIVE JAPAN

Chaya Leah Walkin spent most of her time as a 6-year-old in Japan. Her parents chose to send her to a local school in Kobe where the young Jewish refugee learned to speak some Japanese, made a few friends, and picked up the games that children played. The setting of this singular time in her childhood left enduring impressions made more vivid by the contrast with the harsher environment of wartime Shanghai. Chaya Leah's jottings reveal a nostalgic appreciation for an exotic landscape that also nourished men such as Setsuko Kotsuji and Chiune Sugihara:

> In Japan, we lived on a hill in a beautiful wood house. Down the street from us lived more refugees. There was a little bridge in front of the door leading to the sidewalk that we crossed to get in or out of our home. Beautiful floors of little strips of fine bamboo, on which we sat to eat, and slept on them.
>
> No shoes were allowed in the house. We walked with socks on our feet that covered the toes—the four toes were in one part of the sock and the big toe in a separate part so that the socks fit the shoes.

---

12 D. Sofer, "The Japanese Convert," *Yated Neeman*, October 21, 2004.

> *In the back of the house was a room with a concrete floor to wash up. Cleanliness is a supreme virtue for the Japanese.*

Looking back, Chaya Leah recalls the wooden house, the little bridge in front of the entrance, the soft bamboo floor (more likely tatami mats with a covering woven out of soft rush straw called *igusa*). The Japanese shoes she first heard clapping upon arrival in Tsuruga now became linked to the *tabi* socks she was using inside the house. Above all, as with older survivors' recollections, it was the cleanliness of Japan that made the most enduring impression.

What is unusual in Chaya Leah's backward glance is the presence of Japanese "friends." Neighbors and fellow schoolchildren figure prominently in her recollections without any specific names, yet bathed in a positive light, which stands in sharp contrast to what she termed more generally the *unterwelt* (coarse shabbiness) of Shanghai:

> *Across the street were our friends, the Japanese family, and when they invited us over, we sat cross-legged on the floor.*
> *Going to the market, if you touched a fruit on display, you bought it.*
> *Good manners were also considered a mark of civilization by the Japanese and we took note of the constant bowing in welcome and farewell.*
> *Up the hill from our house was a Buddhist temple with a beautiful peaceful garden. I loved to go there.*
> *Across the street we had a Japanese family who had children our age and we played with them and went to school with them.*
> *I remember that every morning we got dressed to the nines (in our one and only dress) and crossed the little entrance bridge to wait for the Japanese children to come out. We would walk to school together.*
> *We wore our school bags backpack style and carried our books, paper, pencil.*
> *In school we studied Japanese, and I picked it up pretty fast.*
> *Oh how beautiful it was and how beautifully we were treated.*
> *Other memories are buried so deep I cannot haul them out. They must be really traumatic.*

Chaya Leah went from being a scared little girl being carted across the border from Poland to Lithuania, and then across all of Siberia, to being a student in a Japanese school in Kobe. Here, she carried a backpack like other kids. Here, there were good manners and kind neighbors. Even the Buddhist temple up the hill carried no negative connotations about idolatry for the eldest daughter of Rav Shmuel David Walkin. The peaceful garden was a welcome place of rest, like the entire country that seemed to welcome the Jewish refugees.

The Walkin family residence permit, extended though the help of Setsuko Kotsuji, gives the address of their home in Kobe. With the help my friend, Professor Yoshiko Samuels, I am able to map this address more concretely upon the Japanese landscape. "5 –chome 3 Kumachi-dori" is a neighborhood still visible today not far from the Shin-Kobe station for the bullet train and further north of Kasugonomichi. I gaze at the current map with wonder. The old Fukiai-ku neighborhood was merged with Itaku-ku and renamed Chuo-ku in 1980. It is still a residential area near the foot of a large hill. At the top stands the Ryushoji Temple, which made such an impression on the young Chaya Leah. Nearby stands the Kumauchi Shinto shrine, providing shade and a pleasant place for children and adults alike.

No such markers endure anywhere near the location of the house in which the Walkin family occupied their one room in Shanghai. Rapid development erased most of the geography inhabited by Jewish refugees in China. In Japan, by contrast, the clock ticked more slowly; thereby, I am able to follow more readily Chaya Leah's recollections of Shabbat strolls up the hill beyond their house in Kobe:

> *I do remember the hill. There was a garden with statues. I always thought it was a place for worship.*
> *I loved going there on Shabbat—it was so tranquil.*
> *I went to a Japanese school for Japanese children. A lot of the Jewish refugees and their children picked up the language. Chinese, by contrast, with all the different dialects, was very hard for us to learn. Even the people who had lived in Shanghai since the 1920s had trouble with the local language. The Japanese language, by contrast, had easier characters and only five vowels (called boin: a, i, u, e, o).*
> *I loved writing in Japanese. It was my first experience with Asian calligraphy.*

For the first time in her life, Chaya Leah was exposed to a milieu that was far from anything either Jewish or Polish. Instead of being unmoored by the cultural differences, the child was thrilled and eager to absorb the sounds, songs, and games of Japanese schoolmates. At the same time, Chaya Leah recalls her mother's remarks about certain habits that were unbecoming in Jewish eyes:

> *I do remember my mother commenting about the Japanese neighbors going out to do their "edger iseas" (relieving bodily needs) in the front of their homes.*

> But to me it was no big deal, as I did the same. I also remember my mother commenting about when the refugees went to market, they were like animals let loose in their loudness and general behavior. The Japanese looked at us in shock. Yet they accepted and tolerated us and hosted us with respect.

There is honesty in this recollection, which honors the child's need to relieve herself, much like Japanese neighbors. Rebbetzin Tzivia, who appreciated Japanese cleanliness and manners, conveyed to her young daughter an embarrassment at the behavior of fellow refugees. Without transgressing the Torah commandment to love one's fellow, she made sure that Chaya Leah understood what it means to act with dignity in all circumstances.

Having a single dress was not a problem. It was clean and provided pride in the wonderfully strange world of Chaya Leah's new school. In Kobe, unlike in Lukatch or Vilna, the six-year-old child could play with marvelously different classmates. For a brief sojourn, the refugee on the run could simply be a child. The haste and worry reflected in the collage in Chaya Leah's Chicago home centered upon the man in a black coat. In Japan, rope-tied suitcases and the anxious glance toward an uncertain future were put aside for a while. Instead, what Chaya Leah took from Kobe with her for the rest of her life was the children's rope-jumping song, which she passed down with delight to her own daughters:

> Our daughter Shanedy loved a rope game that I taught the children. It is a Japanese game. You tie rubber bands into a long rope. Then you put them around on your ankle and around the ankle of your friend. The third friend and put one foot under the first part of the rope and pulls it higher and higher. The song we sang as we jumped was:
> Jo se noh
> Yamahaka eh
> Taksah nakikeara a bodanoko eh
> Abou, abou, aboudanaka eh.
> Nippon Hai

What shines through in this song is the concrete memory of play. A little girl being allowed to be simply a child. The long rubber band, the ankles of two friends being tied together, two girls jumping together, while a third pulls the rope higher and higher to increase the challenge. The sheer fun of it shines through the memory of the foreign words that served to increase the joy.

Trying to trace the origins of Chaya Leah's rope-jumping song, Professor Masahiro Iwai (a noted ethnomusicologist at the University of Kobe) found that it was a mishmash of sounds that bore only a distant relationship to standard Japanese children's games. Nonetheless, it carried the flavor of a Jewish child's understanding of how native kids were playing and how she felt welcomed in their strange and colorful land. Professor Yoshiko Samuel summarized as follows her own feelings about Chaya Leah's song and Masahiro Iwai's findings:

> I feel rather emotional about the little girl who learned the song and kept it to this day. I can visualize her playing on the edge of a group of Japanese children, trying to find her new life in a strange land. My heart goes all out to her, and I continue to think about her as an elderly woman living in Chicago. "Nippon Hai" (Long live Japan) is not part of the song.
> The latter (*Nihon, or Nippon, teikoku banzai*) is a phrase that Sugihara wrote on the bottom of each visa he wrote for the Jewish people who sought his help in escaping their country. It has been speculated that he wrote the patriotic phrase to let the Japanese government know that, although he was issuing the visas in defiance of the government directive, he was still loyal to the country. It was, in other words, for self-protection.
> "*Yamahaka*" can mean "mountain graves," but if it is "Yamanaka," it can be the name of a well-known hot spring resort in the prefecture right next to the prefecture into which the refugee boats sailed.
> The melody generally called "Fanfare" is not found in Japanese folk-songs (*warabeuta*).
> "Nippon-kai" (The Sea of Japan) toward the end of the singing must have been the sea that they had sailed from Vladivostok to Tsuruga, Japan.
> Tsuruga is right on the shore of the Nippon-kai.[13]

This great effort to understand a little girl's jump-rope song speaks volumes about the Japanese-Jewish connection that endures so warmly in Chaya Leah's memory. The version of the song that Chaya Leah passed on to her daughters ends not with "Nippon kai" but consciously "Nippon Hai"—"Long live Japan." More than a wartime slogan or a self-protective phrase on Chiune Sugihara's

---

13 Professor Yoshiko Samuel, personal correspondence to the author, December 10, 2015.

official documents, these two words on the tongue of a Jewish child reflect gratitude for life gained during the Walkin family's sojourn in Kobe.

Before the attack on Pearl Harbor in December 1941, before the evacuation to Shanghai, Chaya Leah Walkin had been free to add "fanfare" and maybe even snippets of Yiddish to her song. In Japan, she had been free to get to know and befriend the "other"—a freedom that Chaya claims to this day by going out of her way to meet and delight in friends and acquaintances who are very different from herself:

> We were invited often to eat with Japanese children and to play with them. We would sit on the floor and there was a short, square table. The serving of little delicacies by the head of house was like a beautiful ceremony. We told them we could not eat anything, so they just made us rice. Papa said we were allowed to eat the rice.

For a child who would know bombings in Shanghai, who would pass terrifying cadavers on the streets while running to buy food for the family, the sojourn in Japan became an emblem of serenity and grace. Eating only rice was not a daunting prohibition. It simply allowed a Torah-observant little girl to sit on tatami mats with Japanese friends and observe the ritual of serving food on low, carefully arranged tables. Hospitality and kindness prevailed for a few months before the raw needs of survival became the norm in China. Chaya Leah understood the pleasure of ceremony that marks Jewish and Japanese culture alike.

MIR ZAYNEN ORIENTALN

What a six-year-old girl sensed in the home of Japanese neighbors, a venerable Jewish Rebbe put into words before Hirohito's top military officials. Rabbi Shimon Shlomo Kalish (1882–1954) was a noticeable figure among the Jewish refugees in Kobe. Known as the Amshenover Rebbe, he was not the only Chassidic leader among Torah scholars. But he was unique in gaining the respect and love of refugees who spanned the entire range of the religious spectrum. Rabbi Kalish had been among those who had encouraged and supported the exodus of yeshivas from Poland and then from Soviet Russia. He accompanied these students first to Kobe and later to Shanghai.

In Japan, the Amshenover Rebbe was looked upon for guidance and was increasingly delegated to serve as a spokesman for the embattled community of refugees. Even with Kotsuji's bribes and goodwill, the Jews felt pressure from Japanese officials as the alliance with Nazi Germany grew stronger. By the summer of 1941, a delegation was formed to travel to Tokyo to appeal to top Japanese brass in order to secure the ongoing safety of the refugees in Kobe. The delegation included Rabbi Moshe Shatskes (known before the war as the highly respected "Lomzhe Rov"), Leo Chanin (a prominent resident of Kobe), Rabbi Shlomo Shapiro (one of the younger Torah scholars who had a reputation as a linguist) and the Amshenover Rebbe. After a long train ride, the delegation met up with Professor Kotsuji in Tokyo.

A photograph (probably taken by Leo Chanin since he is not in it) shows the two elderly rabbis looking both dignified and worried. Setsuko Kotsuji in a white suit stands out among the black-suited men, not yet a member of their Orthodox Jewish faith. Shlomo Shapiro stands apart as well, aware of the great responsibility of conveying the words of venerated elders that will determine the fate of fellow Jews.

At the government offices, the Japanese delegation was taken into a windowless room. On one side of the table were four admirals in dress uniform. Heads shaven, arms folded stiffly, they sat motionless. Opening pleasantries were kept short. With the aid of a translator, they fired the most important question of the meeting:

> "What it the inherent evil of your people that our German friends hate you so much? ..."
>
> The Amshenover Rebbe turned to his own translator and he said: "*Mir zaynen orientaln* —Tell him the Germans hate us because we are Orientals. The Nazis hate the Jews because they know that we, like you, are Asians..."
>
> "What does this mean—you are Asians? We are Asians!"
>
> "Yes," the Rebbe agreed. "And you are on the list."
>
> "What list?"
>
> The Amshenover Rebbe smiled a smile so supremely serene, so totally out of keeping with the threatening atmosphere which the officers tried to create that, in spite of themselves, all four leaned forward, waiting for him to speak further.

> "My dear friends, I have just come from Europe. I have lived with the great hate that the Nazis have for others… Read what the Nazis write in original German. There, you will learn that you are also on their list of 'inferior people.' So are the gypsies, the blacks, the Slavs and the Japanese…. Consider what is the image of Hitler's master race. Always, always the so-called Aryans. Tall, broad-shouldered, blond, blue eyes. The reason they hate me, the reason they hate all of us is because we do not fit the image of the Aryan master race."[14]

By the end of this meeting, the Japanese admirals had softened their stance. They even asked the Jewish guests to share their religious views with some Shinto priests invited for this ceremonial occasion. After an extensive conversation, during which Rabbi Shatskes described the basic ideas and ceremonies of Judaism, one of the admirals reassured the rabbis:

> Go back to your people. Tell them they have nothing to fear. We Japanese will do our utmost to provide for your safety and peace. You have nothing to fear while in Japanese territory.[15]

Whether each word of this encounter was exactly as recalled later is not verifiable. What we do know from historical documents is that the harassment of the Jewish refugees in Kobe diminished for a little while until the last weeks of the summer of 1941. After that point in time, German pressure and war shortages made it impossible to keep so many Jews in Kobe. As a result, Chaya Leah Walkin and her family, along with most of the Mirrer Yeshiva and the Amshenover Rebbe, were shipped off to Japanese-occupied Shanghai, where promises of "safety" and "peace" were kept more or less as declared in the Tokyo meeting with the admirals.

The guiding principle for much of the remainder of the war had already been articulated in December 1940 by Foreign Minister Yosuke Matsuoka (1880–1946). This architect and supporter of the pact with Nazi Germany had reassured a group of Jewish businessmen as follows:

> I am the man responsible for the alliance with Hitler, but nowhere have I promised that we would carry out his anti-Semitic policies in Japan. This

---

14 Marvin Tokayer, *The Fugu Plan: The Untold Story of the Japanese and the Jews During World War II* (Jerusalem: Gefen Publishing House, 2004), 162–64.
15 Ibid., 186.

is not simply my personal opinion, it is the opinion of Japan and I have no compunction about announcing it to the world.[16]

Chaya Leah Walkin—walking to school with Japanese classmates, strolling in a Buddhist temple on Shabbat, partaking of rice in the home of Japanese neighbors—was a direct beneficiary of the "opinion" proclaimed by Matsuoka. Even as a child, she sensed that Kobe was a safe place. Here, being Jewish and remaining Torah observant was not a frightening challenge.

Older refugees, such as the yeshiva students who surrounded Chaya Leah's father, endured more difficulties than the little girl could imagine or understand. Uprooted from family, these soon-to-be-orphaned young men suffered physical and emotional deprivations. In one memoir of the Kobe refuge, Rabbi Ariyeh Leib Kramer, one of the Lubavitch young men, describes the weariness and food poisoning that was common among Jewish residents of Japan. The hot, humid weather was unfamiliar for boys who grew up in Poland and Russia. In one of the surviving photographs, Rabbi Kramer appears thin, tired, and dispirited amid fellow yeshiva students who are photographed dragging tattered suitcases on the streets of Kobe.

The same image of road weariness and uncertainty was on display in May 1941 at an exhibition held in the Osaka Asahi Kaikan Museum. The focus here was upon 22 photographs entitled "The Wandering Jews." Unlike Professor Kotsuji, who spoke Hebrew and was on friendly terms with the Torah-observant community, members of the avant-garde Tanpei Photography Club had been drawn to Kobe by a desire to capture the exotic look of yeshiva students. In this quaint Japanese city, one poet observed, Jews wore "tired looking clothes."[17]

The young men of the Mirrer Yeshiva looked less weary in one of the photographs preserved from the Tanpei exhibit. These students are wearing clean shirts, pressed suits, and one young man is even sporting a fashionable vest. Most are wearing fashionable European hats, a few at a jaunty angle, seemingly glad to be photographed. Two little children, the age of Chaya Leah's younger siblings Esther and Moshe, are playing at the edge of this image. They are also wearing Western-style clothes. One little girl facing the camera is sucking her finger. She is the only figure in this portrait of "'well-being" who reveals her bewilderment openly.

---

16 Daniel Kapner and Stephen Levine, "Jews of Japan," *Jerusalem Center for Public Affairs* (March 1, 2000), 2.

17 Susan Bachrach and Anita Kassof, *Flight and Rescue* (Washington, DC: The United States Holocaust Museum, 2000).

Another photograph from the same period shows the yeshiva students actually studying Talmud in Kobe. In the center is Avraham Blumenkrantz, one of the young men who went on to make significant contributions to Torah scholarship after the war. Here, we see the inner world of Jewish refugees. The table is a makeshift bench. The young men sit on plain planks of wood in deep concentration. One is wearing a 3-piece suit and hat, not simply because he had it. But because it was—and remains—a custom to honor Torah study with clean and dignified clothing. Next to Blumenkrantz, a student in far more modest clothing and cap is fully focused on the folio in front of him. To the right, a man without a hat holds his chin in concentration.

The various volumes in front of these young men reveal the effort it took to carry Torah sources from Poland and Lithuania to Japan. On this makeshift table in Kobe can be seen the tools that enabled Jewish refugees like Chaya Leah's father to craft a soul-sustaining refuge out of their predicament as refugees. In the metaphorical "woods" of geographical and cultural dislocation, they created a sheltering shade out of Torah study. This became the "sweet fruit" savored in *Shir Ha'Shirim*. For this nourishment, the Jews were not dependent upon the goodwill of Japanese or, later, Chinese authorities. This gift came from within their own tradition.

Among the young men savoring the joys of study in Kobe was also Rabbi Walkin's cousin, Boruch Sorotzkin (1917–79). A descendant from the Walkin family through his mother's side, Rabbi Sorotzkin carried with him to Japan a strong sense of responsibility for furthering Torah learning on foreign soil. His father, Rabbi Zalman Sorotzkin, had been a well-known community leader in the Grodno area. Sending off his newly married son with an older cousin to Vilna and beyond must have been a difficult decision. Groomed for leadership, Boruch Sorotzkin managed to get one of the few precious visas directly from Japan to the United Sates.

Shortly after arriving on American shores, he went on to become one of the leaders of the Teltz Yeshiva in Cleveland, one of the distinguished Torah institutions to carry on the European tradition of Talmudic scholarship, just as the Bais Aharon had envisioned during his prescient visit to United States. Where others only saw a world mired in materialism and irreligiosity, the Pinsker Rav had dared to imagine flourishing centers of Torah learning, just like the one set up in Cleveland by Rabbi Sorotzkin, the refugee from Kobe.

One of the pressing religious questions that affected the entire community in Japan centered on how to observe Shabbat and the high holidays given some uncertainty about the exact location of the International Date Line. Debates about this aspect of Torah law have challenged scholars worldwide. Among the refugees in Japan, this was a passionate subject with dramatic consequences for everyday life. The majority opinion held that the calendar and the days of the week as observed in Japan were correct and that one could satisfy the laws of Shabbat observance on the local Saturday. A minority opinion argued that, due to the unclear location of the date line, Shabbat should be observed on the local Sunday.

The Mirrer Yeshiva was advised to keep Shabbat on the local Sunday while Lubavitch Yeshiva students kept Shabbat on the local Saturday. Due to these complex debates, most Torah-observant Jews tried not to violate Shabbat prohibitions both on Saturday and Sunday. Shabbat Torah readings went on both days, often using the personal Torah scroll that the Amshenover Rebbe had carried to Japan and China.

As the High Holidays of 1941 drew closer, the debate became more acute and many feared the prospect of a two-day fast for Yom Kippur. Even as a small child, Chaya Leah sensed the tension rising before October 1—the date on which Yom Kippur was to be celebrated in Japan:

> Picture Kobe. Because of the time zones, when we were in Kobe around Rosh Hashanah time, we did not know for sure when Yom Kippur fell.
>
> There is a photograph that shows Rabbi Neiman and several other rabbanim going over the books to figure out when the Yom Kippur fast starts. Rabbi Shaya Shimanowitz was not comfortable with the complex discussions about time zones, so he fasted for two days.

Rabbi Yeshaya Shimanowitz (1908–98) was twenty-six years older than Chaya Leah Walkin. He was also a close friend of the Walkin family in Kobe as well as in Shanghai. One of the favorite disciples of Rav Aahron Kotler, he was able to take on restrictions that were far too daunting for children or even for a family man such as Rav Shmuel David Walkin.

As a result, what prevailed in Kobe, as well as in Chin, was mutual respect and understanding. Everyone agreed that there were different ways to interpret Torah law. What mattered most was the effort to keep learning the various ways in which Jewish values were a guide for daily life. This challenge could not be postponed or avoided despite the difficulties of travel, exile, poverty, and war.

In the end, the religious dilemmas of Kobe were solved not by Talmudic inquiry but by forcible transportation of the Jewish refugees out of Japan to Shanghai. Soon after the Tokyo meeting attended by the Amshenover Rebbe and Professor Kotsuji, reassurances about the extent of Jewish safety in Japan began to become less credible. In July 1941, Japanese forces occupied French Indochina. In retaliation, the United States government imposed an oil embargo and froze all Japanese assets. Money from Jewish aid organizations could not be accessed. Due to shrinking resources and increasing shortages for the native population, the Japanese government instructed all foreigners to leave Japan.

The yeshiva students who had just savored a few months of regularized study with secure housing and food faced the prospect of dislocation with dread. Yet, as with the flight from Vilna, the Mirrer Yeshiva was among the first to mobilize for departure. By the end of September, most of the students and faculty were in Shanghai, celebrating only one day of Yom Kippur. By the end of October, most of the stateless Polish refugees had been forced to relocate to Shanghai.

Leaving Japan was not easy, especially with incoming news about the shabbiness and dangers that awaited the refugees in Shanghai. The dejected look of the Jews forced to move once again is amply evident in a photograph published in the August 21 edition of *Osaka Mainichi & Tokyo Nichi*. Labeled "Jewish Refugees Leave Kobe for Shanghai," the faded newspaper reveals a line of young men carrying tattered suitcases and even more travel-worn hat boxes. Some of the yeshiva students are wearing long black coats, some short Western jackets. Tired, they also carry a firm look of determination: They will go on, endure, learn, survive. And, beyond their wildest dreams, they will reestablish the foundations for Torah learning after the war.

Looking back, Chaya Leah is aware of how memory had glazed over her nine months in Japan. She even wonders whether recollection had polished reality a bit too brightly:

> The Japanese at that time gave us so much respect. How beautiful it was and how beautifully we were treated. I remember all the pleasant things and other memories are buried so deep I cannot haul them out...

This glowing remembrance is echoed in almost all the memoirs recorded by Jewish refugees in Japan. Each found solace in the orderly cleanliness of

Japanese daily life. Their ritualized encounters with Japanese officials left them with a sense of gratitude. Respect prevailed and was further nourished by fond memories of the help extended by Chiune Sugihara to Jewish refugees during the summer of 1940.

In Kovno, stateless Jews had been beggars at the gates of the Japanese consulate. On the train through Siberia, they had been terrified of being dragged off to labor camps in the frozen tundra. On the boat to Tsuruga, they were still running, still looking for safe landing. In Kobe, with residence permits secured and extended through Kotsuji's bribes, they finally felt fully human. Professor Kotsuji spoke not only their "language" but he seemed to understand the deeper Jewish commitment to *hakarat ha tov*—gratitude for unearned kindness.

When exactly Setsuko Kotsuji started his own studies of *Shir Ha'Shirim* is not clear. What we do know is that he understood that the Jewish quest for refuge was both physical and spiritual. Although he could not single-handedly ensure their extended stay in Japan after October 1941, Kotsuji continued his correspondence with the Torah scholars whom he had befriended in Kobe. He was himself like an apple tree in the woods—a man who stood out by virtue of his compassion.

Other Japanese citizens came with baskets of apples to give and sell to Jewish refuges. Setsuko Kotsuji brought his heart and mind, and that gift continued after the forced transfer to Shanghai.

For a little less than a year in Japan, the Walkin family—like other Jewish refugees—had found comforting shade and sweet fruit, to use the metaphors of *Shir Ha'Shirim*. Thus heartened, they journeyed on to face the raw challenge of survival in war-torn China. Arriving into a Japanese-occupied city shortly before the attack on Pearl Harbor made the transition both rougher and also oddly familiar.

CHAPTER 4

TENDER KIDS BESIDE THE SHEPHERDS' TENTS:

Starting Anew in Shanghai

If you do not know...
Follow the footsteps of the flock,
Graze your tender kids
Beside the shepherds' tents.

Shir Ha'Shirim 1:8

By the end of 1941, there was no doubt about who controlled East Asia, including Shanghai—the port of last refuge for Jews fleeing the Nazi death machine. The Japanese expression *Dai-tō-a Kyōeiken* (Greater East Asia Co-Prosperity Sphere) might not have been familiar to Rav Shmuel David Walkin and his fellow Torah scholars who were starting new lives in China after the Jewish High Holidays. Nor was it a term familiar to more than 15,000 German Jews who managed to escape Hitler's clutches and were now crowding into the alleys of Shanghai. Yet, it was this Japanese ideal that dictated policy during the war years. With the aid of this propaganda slogan, Emperor Hirohito's regime carried out an occupation that was brutal for the vast majority of Chinese, Japanese, Korean, Vietnamese, and Burmese citizens while at the same time enabling Jewish refugees in Shanghai to survive against all the odds stacked against them in a Europe left behind.

The Japanese war machine in East Asian rolled on with great success after the Jews from Kobe were shipped to China. Shortly after the attack on Pearl Harbor, Hong Kong fell easily on December 18, 1941. By the middle of 1942, central China was firmly under the Japanese occupation while the Nationalist Government (KMT) of Jiang Kai-shek fled inward into Siquan province to establish there the wartime capital in Chongqing. The Chinese Communists (now allied with the KMT in the Second United Front) were fighting behind the Japanese lines in north China. Mao Zedong wielded the reigns of power from the caves of Yenan in Shanxi province unaware of the Jewish refugees congregating in Japanese-controlled Shanghai.

With the occupation of Burma was completed by May 1942, there were few public voices in Japanese-controlled territories to question the propaganda blitz advocating "Asia for the Asiatics." Perhaps the Amshenover Rebbe had an early inkling of how this narrative would play out for his fellow Jewish refugees when he told Japanese officials in Tokyo in the summer of 1941: "*Mir zaynen orientaln.*" Being an "oriental" was a beneficial identity in a Japanese empire that had tried to mask its conquests in the language of liberation from Western control.

The United States having joined the war after the attack on Pearl Harbor concentrated its efforts in 1942–43 on the island-hopping policy, trying to nibble away at Japanese dominion through attacks on distant locations such as Guadalcanal. America's alliance with the Nationalist government in China was being managed by the war-seasoned general Joseph Stillwell, who concentrated on getting supplies into southwest China across the Burma Hump without much concern for Jews like Rabbi Walkin and his fellow Polish refugees. They were a small, negligible factor in a strategic battle that Stillwell aimed to win on the Chinese mainland.

Unlike General Stilwell, the Nationalist (KMT) government had taken an interest in the Jewish problem during the years right before Pearl Harbor. Sun Yat-sen's own son, Sun Ke (who was serving as President of the Nationalist Government's Legislative Yuan) had proposed in February 1939 that China adopt a policy of resettling Jewish refugees in southwest China. Unlike the Japanese Fugu Plan, which aimed to use the resources of wealthy Jews to build up the puppet state of Manchukuo, Sun's plan seemed motivated by a genuine concern for the Nazi persecution of the Jews. By the winter of 1941–42, however, southwest China was also in the shadow of the Greater East Asia Co-Prosperity Sphere, with the Nationalist government barely surviving repeated assaults on Chongqing.

The words of *Shir Ha'Shirim* help us enter this bewildering time with an extra measure of empathy. In a world of diminishing options, the shepherdess is told to follow in the footsteps of the flock. In effect, she must find security where the winds of fate take her. Instead of direct reassurance and guidance, her beloved sends the tender kids toward the tents of other shepherds. On this very precarious path, she is to find her strength, refine her goals. And she does,

much like Chaya Leah Walkin who felt that a benevolent, even if unseen, hand was guiding the family during the darkest hours of the war in Shanghai.

The most unexpected "tent" was provided by the puppet regime of Wang Jingwei (1883–1944). A close ally of Sun Yat-sen, Wang had broken with the Nationalist government in March 1940 in order to set up the "Republic of China" known in Chinese as *Zhōnghuá Mínguó* and in Japanese as *Chūka Minkoku*. It was this Japanese-controlled entity that placed its large seal upon a key document that survived the war: Chaya Leah's own residence permit dated April 25, 1944.

In this very month, on the other side of the world, the first group of Greek Jews were being transported to Auschwitz-Birkenau. In April 1944 as well, Japan carried out one of its most vicious attacks on Chinese positions in Henan while the American forces started bombing German-occupied Normandy. Although Wang Jingwei's collaborationist government was disbanded after the surrender of Japan in August 1945, one year earlier, it was still able to shelter "tender kids" such as Chaya Leah Walkin.

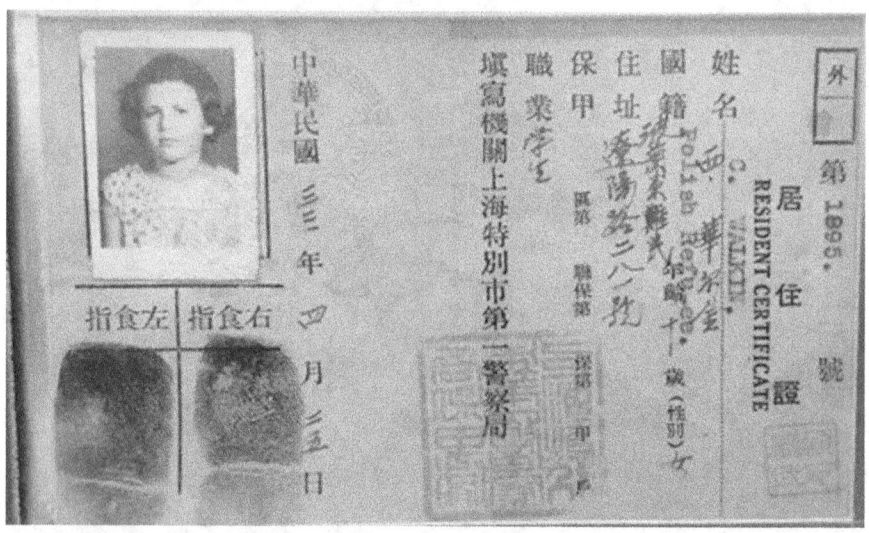

Chaya's Shanghai ID

Chaya Leah's document provides a revealing snapshot of Jewish survival in Japanese-occupied Shanghai. It has an official number—1895—suggesting that officials of Wang Jingwei's Republic of China aimed to keep a clear record of the foreigners swelling the population of an already congested city. There are six English words on the yellowing page amid row upon row of Chinese characters. "RESIDENCE PERMIT" is printed in all capital letters along with

"C. Walkin" identifying the Jewish girl whose photograph is appended to the upper left corner. In the row indicating "nationality" appears the most telling identification of Chaya Leah in English as a "Polish refugee."

This appellation is also translated into Chinese as 波蘭難民 (*Bolan nanmin*). *Nanmin* means, literally, a people enduring hardship, which is a far more truthful description of Chaya Leah's people than the more passive implication of statelessness carried by the term "refugee." Clearly, the local Shanghai government knew about the predicament of families such as the Walkins even if it could not provide aid or fathom the extent of their self-supporting resources, both material and spiritual.

In this residence permit, the girl's age is recorded as eleven. The image above the enlarged fingerprints shows a child with short hair, a summer dress, and a firm frontal gaze. She neither wants to be photographed nor resists the camera's eye. She seems to know what is required of her. The Shanghai Municipality's document also records in Chinese the family's address: 281 Liaoyang Road. Liao—遼 in Chinese—means vast, extensive, hard to reach, not unlike the place of refuge sought by the beleaguered Walkin family, which ended up cramming its hopes into one room in the crowded dwelling that was Chaya Leah's home during the war years. The second character of Chaya Leah's address is *yang*—陽—an ancient character suggesting brightness and vigor. Against all odds, this Chinese ideograph captures the vitality of the small, Torah-observant community that congregated in Rav Shmuel David Walkin's living quarters during the harshest years of the war.

"UNTERWELT"

Suggestive Chinese characters and official stamps dating from April 1944 remain mute, however, about the shock that greeted Jewish refugees upon their arrival in Shanghai from Kobe. In Japan, Chaya Leah's life had been contained in a clean house surrounded by kind neighbors, interesting schoolmates, and the park up the hill, which added to the peace of a Shabbat stroll. In China, by contrast, war spilled over into daily life and the smells and sounds of poverty assaulted the child's eyes and ears. Looking back, Chaya Leah still shudders from the bewildering cacophony of Shanghai:

> In Shanghai, there were so many cultures and so many languages. There were many Indians, Sephardic, Ashkenazi, all sorts of Chinese, British, French—it contained a multitude of cultures and ethnics.

> It was a booming city where anything goes and anyone can come in—no questions asked. In Shanghai, you always had to watch your back. In Shanghai, you could not trust anyone. It was an "underwelt"—a corrupt country. The contrast between Japan and Shanghai was immeasurable.

In this fragment, an older woman seeks to make sense out of the child's bewilderment. The daughter of a woman who grew up in the home of the Chofetz Chaim, Chaya Leah Walkin had been groomed for exemplary behavior even in the darkest hours while the family was fleeing Poland and Soviet Russia. Dressed with great care even in times of great material scarcity, this little girl landed in 1941 into a world in which none of the rules of Jewish life applied.

The very cacophony of cultures and languages became an ocean that nearly drowned Jewish refugees while also invigorating them. In the words of Taras Grescoe's recent novel, *Shanghai Grand*, this corner of China was a unique place where "the ambitious, the wily and the desperate could escape."[1] Escape was one thing. Comprehension demanded an altogether different skill, which the young Chaya Leah lacked at first.

Looking back, one Yiddish term from back home—*unterwelt*—sufficed to describe the Shanghai that desperate Jews encountered in 1941 and that they would leave strengthened and transformed. Describing the criminality that is the hallmark of every large city, the *unterwelt* in China also suggested a cultural mix that ended up being an enlivening environment for a Jewish girl whose world had already began to expand in Kobe.

But first came the shock, the dismay, the disorientation. Chaya Leah's sense of what lay beneath the world that she was cast into in the fall of 1941 was shared by older Jews arriving from Japan. Actress Shoshana Kahan, for example, was 46 years old in October 1941 when she arrived from Kobe to Shanghai. An established performer on the Yiddish stage, Kahan was both older and more secular than Chaya Leah Walkin. Yet, she would have understood perfectly the use of the term *unterwelt*—not because it was Yiddish but because it captured her own feelings as she landed in Shanghai.

Shoshana Kahan's diaries convey the dread of seeing one's name on the list for evacuation from Japan to China. Disembarking in Shanghai on

---

[1] Taras Grescoe, *Shanghai Grand: Forbidden Love and International Intrigue on the Eve of the Second World War* (New York: St. Martin's Press, 2016), 2.

Tender Kids Beside the Shepherds' Tents: Starting Anew in Shanghai • CHAPTER 4

October 23, the Polish-born actress bemoaned the great difference between China and the world left behind in Kobe:

> What a disgusting city Shanghai is... Now I understand why everyone fought with all their might to stay in Japan... Now I understand the terrible letters we received from those who had the misfortune to be sent here. A dirty and disgusting city...
>
> The Japanese work diligently and quietly, the Chinese slowly and very noisily. You never hear his (the Chinese) steps because he wears soft slippers and straw sandals, but you can always hear his yelling. One Chinese wants to deprive another of his income... Everybody grabbed a piece of (our) luggage and I was simply scared.[2]

As a child, even if the oldest among her siblings, Chaya Leah did not have to negotiate the transport of the family luggage at the Shanghai port. It is unlikely that the Walkin family had been welcomed with flowers, as had been the famous actress.

Shoshana Kahan was a star of the Jewish stage while Chaya Leah was the sheltered daughter of a rabbinical family. Yet, they reacted similarly to the bewildering new world of Shanghai. Tsuruga and Kobe had been different, unfamiliar. But a sense of ordered civility had prevailed in Japan. This was shattered in Shanghai.

Kahan's contempt-filled generalizations about Chinese laborers, however, were not likely to find their way into the lexicon of Chaya Leah Walkin. Rav Walkin's daughter had been taught to respect all of God's creations; this lesson endured even in the *unterwelt* of Shanghai. To be sure, the child heard and saw a crushing variety of sounds, smells, and customs. But she was also protected by her youth and upbringing. Chaya Leah's parents and their friends provided the first line of defense. They were the ones who had to find the words to articulate Jewish sorrows on China's war-torn terrain.

One of Rav Shmuel David's young friends, Simcha Elberg (1915–95) was one of the Polish refugees who put into verse the pain of arrival in China. Being 26 years old and a student in the Mirrer Yeshiva, Elberg was known to Chaya Leah as a friend and frequent guest of the Walkin family. After the refuge in Shanghai, Rabbi Elberg and his wife Maritza would become mentors to Chaya Leah when she became a young bride. In China, however, the little girl only

---

2 Eber, *Voices from Shanghai*, 108.

knew the yeshiva student as one of many who came to per parents' home on Liaoyang Road for comfort and advice.

In 1941, Chaya Leah was too young to read Yiddish-language journals such as *Undzer Lebn* (Our Life) and *Dos Vort* (The Word)—both geared to the Torah community in Shanghai. She had no way to understand the poem penned by Simcha Elberg in the month of Elul, right before the high holidays, which marked the Mirrer Yeshiva's arrival in Shanghai. Entitled "Three Countries Spit Me Out," this work did not dwell on the dirt and cacophony of Shanghai. Instead, in the spirit of Elul reflections, the poem looks back at all the other places that had spewed out the Jews who landed in China.

Elberg's poem is framed around the theme of shepherds, much like *Shir Ha'Shirim*. But his darker verses draw inspiration from Jeremiah's words (23:2–4): "Thus says Lord God of Yisrael against the shepherds that fed my people: You have scattered my flock, and driven them away, and have not taken care of them." Yes, Chiune Sugihara had been one of those who "fed" the Jewish people along the way. Yes, Setsuko Kotsuji managed to soften the hearts of Japanese police with his bribes. But in the fall of 1941, Shanghai did not appear to be a safe haven for the tender kids who had been run ragged by narrow escapes. As a result, Simcha Elberg's poem is a cry directed at a heartless world:

> Three countries spat me out
> as a dead body
> by stormy seas.
>
> My home, Poland,
> Locked in a ghetto, entombed
> I don't know who still prays "Rakhamim" in his need,
> who whispers "Sh'ma Yisrael" quietly
> praying for his death.
>
> My stepmother Lithuania…
> On a day of snow
> I escaped in fright…
> In Japan, I made ink from the seas,
> from heaven a white sheet of paper,
> even the wind did groan
> when I wrote: send me a visa!

Tender Kids Beside the Shepherds' Tents: Starting Anew in Shanghai • CHAPTER 4 | 87

> On a humid day,
> when the Japanese tie up their nose
> and step with wooden feet,
> Japan spat me out
> into Shanghai.³

Without self-pity, like Chaya Leah's description of the *unterwelt*, Simcha Elberg's poem simply describes the background for the forced wanderings of his fellow Jews. News of the Warsaw ghetto seemed to have already reached Shanghai by the fall of 1941 even though mourning for parents and siblings did not begin in earnest until after the war. What was apparent during the high holidays in China was that there was no mercy or hope left in Poland, or in Lithuania. As a result, two weeks before Rosh Hashanah, one young man who had travelled with the Mirrer Yeshiva stopped to take account of the cruelty that had brought his Jewish brethren to bedraggled Shanghai.

INSIDE NUMBER 281 ON THE STREET OF EXPANSIVE VIGOR

The streets of Shanghai are not unfamiliar to me. I started to walk them in the 1970s when I lived in China as part of the first group of American exchange scholars to arrive on the eve of the reestablishment of China's diplomatic relations with the United States. Back then, it was not yet the city of commerce and expats that it is now and what it has also been before the Second World War. I have also studied and written about wartime Shanghai, known in Chinese intellectual circles as *gudao*—孤島—the "orphaned island."

This was a place of refuge in the midst of the war with Japan, where one could eke out a paltry living and still savor cultural creativity if one chose not to risk the journey into the hinterland of Siquan (the KMT wartime capital) or to Yenan (the communist-held hamlet behind the Japanese lines in the northwest). I had even mapped in my mind's eye the various compounds of Jewish refugees from Germany—those crowded rooms tucked inside the alleys of the old Chinese city that bore the ironic title of *heim* (home).

None of these explorations prepared me for Chaya Leah's emotional invitation to enter her own wartime home on 281 Liaoyang Road (see Figure 1).

By the time I received a lengthy email from her on this subject on January 26, 2016, the street name had been simplified. Today, characters have little connection to the gracious ideographs that had still been in use in the 1940s.

---

3   Ibid., 59–60.

Liao (遼) once connoted expansive exaltation. By 2016, it had been shrunken to the image of a running child—辽. Mirroring the fate of the houses on Chaya's old street, this character, too, has been torn down. Gone is the rich symbolism of the traditional character that called to mind grasses burning over a sacrificial fire. That despoiled illumination is also the fate of the second character in Chaya Leah's Chinese address: 陽, *Yang*, which once suggested an energizing illumination. Today's 阳 retains the sun but not the fan of rays below it. As so much of China's public history, it has been stripped down to an easily communicable concept. It has lost the vibrancy that long ago had colored the imagination of the Daoist classics.

No one walking around today on the terrain around 281 Liaoyang Road could possibly imagine that this area had an added poetic name in the 1930s and 1940s: *Yue Hua Xiang*—月华巷— Alley of the Flourishing Moon. Nothing but new office buildings and a few dilapidated workers' huts dot the shifting landscape today. In a 2010 essay about a few buildings remaining around the Liaoyang neighborhood, Paul French described with pathos the old block of houses that had been built here around 1925. Bemoaning the fate of a neighborhood rapidly becoming a slum, French recalled homes such as the one that the Walkin family moved into in 1941:

> Most buildings had been in good shape. However, large-scale destruction is going on around them and their future remains unclear. The rooms were actually light and airy; the roof was in good condition. These properties

Figure 1. Map showing location of Chaya Leah's wartime home in Shanghai on 281 Liaoyang Road.2

could easily have been refurbished to the highest standards for the families living in them. However, their fate remains unclear and while families have worked to maintain the properties they are now rather losing heart when they see wastelands appearing all around them.⁴

In the conclusion of this rather mournful account, the author reflects upon the ceaseless process that keeps creating slums in Shanghai from the 1920s to the present. In his view, Mark Twain's words are especially apt for this corner of China in which "history doesn't repeat itself, but it does rhyme."⁵

Some of this rhyme can be heard in Chaya Leah's recollections of the Liaoyang neighborhood as well. Having visited the ravaged sight a few years ago, she is aware of Shanghai's massive building frenzy, which has decimated history and landscape alike. Precisely because of this, her email of January 2016 extended to me an intimate invitation to savor the sounds and sights of her childhood. It asked me to come along as a friend, not as the writer of this book:

> Hold my hand Verishka, hold my hand tight and we will go home, into my house. As we walk down the street to get into our gated courtyard, the noise will be overwhelming. It is market day, and all the merchants are on the street selling their wares, and fruits and vegetables. It is bumper to bumper people; it is noisy as can be. The sounds of haggling, the negotiations, the watchfulness for thieves stealing.
>
> Hold my hand Vera. Block out the noise and listen to the chickadees in the cages.
>
> I want to buy one for a pet, but that is an extravagance, and who can afford it and they are so noisy, we will be up all night with the noise, but they will scare away the mosquitoes.

I like being called "Verishka." It calls to mind my own childhood in Romania, where Yiddish diminutives were not far from the tongue of neighbors who had survived the *Shoah*. I also treasure the dense details of this invitation.

Before I received this email from Chaya Leah, I had already drafted the chapter about her home on Liaoyang Road. I had already documented the various occupants who had shared the Walkins' house and how they had enriched each other's lives beyond the fear and poverty that was the common lot of Jewish refugees.

---

4 Paul French, *The Old Shanghai A to Z* (Hong Kong: Hong Kong University Press, 2010), 27.
5 Ibid.

What was startling in this invitation was Chaya Leah's valiantly determined effort to reenter a childhood framed by war and dislocation. Here was the voice of the little girl longing for a caged chickadee, a precocious six-year-old aware of the family's limited means and the fear of disease-causing mosquitos, which troubled the sleep of parents and young siblings alike. The child who learned in time how to haggle with the vendors on the street took me along to explore an inner landscape that had been lying dormant for decades.

When Chaya Leah first started to write about her childhood in China, she relied on her expertise as a real-estate agent to muffle some of the emotional echoes that surfaced in the "Hold my hand, Verishka" email. I quote from these jottings because they also convey the effort to come close to the past while also maintaining some emotional distance from the trauma of the refugee experience that had shaped the woman who became a pillar of the Jewish community of Chicago after the war:

> On a beautiful summer day, I went to see a showcase house in Lake Forest, Illinois, an upscale suburb of Chicago. The house was built for a Russian princess. Rumors have it that she was a Rachmaninoff who married into the Armour family and hired the famed architect David Adler to build this estate. Wandering around the grounds, I had a feeling of déjà vu. A familiarity hit me. My home in China was so similar. I have never seen anything like this before. It was an upscale incarnation of what I remember.

The entry point here is a breezy summer day, nothing like the scorching humidity of Shanghai that Chaya Leah recalls in other jottings. In the palatial surroundings of a Georgian-style home in the suburbs of Chicago, the war years in China can be called to mind more safely. The Walkins' home appears here as a scaled-down version of a place built for a Russian princess:

> In Shanghai, we lived in a single-family home with servant quarters and a coach house. It was gated.
> There was a large front yard and a large backyard. The air raid shelter was located there after we moved in. The first floor had a living room, dining room, kitchen, and a half bath. The second floor had four bedrooms and I think only one bathroom. The attic was large and was used as a ballroom.
> The servant quarters were in the same Georgian style as the rest of the house, but smaller. The coach house was on a level of its own to accommodate both a stable or one car.

Tender Kids Beside the Shepherds' Tents: Starting Anew in Shanghai • CHAPTER 4 | 91

Using her eyes as a real estate agent, Chaya Leah paints the house on Liaoyang Road as it might have appeared to a prospective buyer, not the Jewish families who crowded in there in 1941, grateful to be able to rent a space that was indeed palatial compared to the more impoverished German refugees sequestered in the claustrophobic rooms of Hongkew. The house on Liaoyang Road was a short walk from the *heims* of secular Jews from Berlin and Vienna who were despoiled of all of their expectations about culture and civilization. For Chaya Leah, by contrast, the childhood home in Shanghai had an expansive quality that echoes the "airy rooms" described in Paul French's writings:

> Our family had the living room on the first floor. In our room, there was not much furniture. We had one bed. One sofa, one table, and several chairs. We also had an armoire. My infant brother slept in the drawer of the armoire. My sister and I slept on the floor. Our bedroom, to the best of my recollection, may have been a sun parlor off the living room or a small extension of the living room. Or maybe even a separation.

In the mind's eye, one bed, one table, and one armoire suffices to bring back a sense of well-being that Chaya associated with her home on Liaoyang Road. The brother who slept in the drawer was not born until the end of the war, in September 1945. Chronological details are blurred here. They matter little compared to the marvel of the makeshift stove that enabled the Rav Shmuel David's family to cook their own meals:

> A treasure! There was only one kitchen for about 14 families and only one stove for all the inhabitants. We had our own stove made out of a used metal oilcan covered with clay. The grill was put inside. Fuel was a mixture of coal dust, cinders, ashes, straw, and sand. Cooking took all day. But I don't remember being hungry.

This tin can fed by coal dust comes up again and again in Chaya Leah's recollections. While witnessing the dirty, long process of cooking on this "treasure," the woman looking back wants me to understand that hunger, like the hunger that had plagued German refugees and the poor Chinese residents of war-torn Shanghai, had not haunted her family.

In the email consciously and personally inviting me back into her memories of the house at 281 Liaoyang Road, Chaya Leah provided even more details about what made her home life more spacious than the *heims* of the German refugees. What comes across from these fragments is the sense of community informed by the Torah values that prevailed in this shared dwelling. Chaya Leah, as the oldest among the children in the compound, shouldered more responsibility but also took pride in shaping the experience of younger children less prepared to cope with the fears of war in the strange setting of the *unterwelt*:

> *A couple more steps, Verishka, and so I will take you to the backyard. There is a little patio—that's where I clean the chickens, and a small yard.*
> *There are no flowers, but the small stones that you see are coal that we made and use for our stove.*
> *You know, Vera, we do not need anyone; we have a little community at 281 Liaoyang Road.*
> *Of all the children I am the oldest, so I make up games, and play with them, and help out the mothers when I am not in school.*

Here, pride in the community created by the refugees is as real as the child's distaste for plucking chickens on the gritty "patio." Again, the precious stove holds center stage because it allowed the Walkin family to cook the food that became the most concrete form of mutual aid among Jewish families who had shared the journey of the Mirrer Yeshiva from Vilna through Kobe to Shanghai.

At the same time, Chaya Leah's recollections do not gloss over the very different ways of coping with scarcity that had prevailed inside the compound at 281 Liaoyang Road:

> *Verishka, come up with me to the second floor and I will introduce you to my friends. They are younger than us but they make good playmates.*
> *Rabbi Naiman was and is a Brisker, the stories he would tell us about the Brisker Rov, we really did not pay attention. Now we are sorry—he loved to talk and tell stories, he was a big lamdan (skilled student of Torah texts).*
> *Chaikie, his wife was a powerful, no-nonsense woman.*
> *There are four girls in the family, and she feeds them in a snap. Come with me and see.*
> *Reb Naiman lines them up. On the table, the horrific food that we do not want to eat and carry on about at home, while our mother and father are begging us to eat and are trying to bribe us if we will finish.*
> *This is not Rebbetzin Chaikie's style. Yes, like in the military, she lines them up in a straight row on the table, pulls their head back by their ponytails (Schup)*

Tender Kids Beside the Shepherds' Tents: Starting Anew in Shanghai • CHAPTER 4 | 93

> *with such force that they open their mouths. She shoves in a spoonful of food and, voilà, down it goes. It does not take her long to feed them.*

The honesty of this recollection is striking. Published essays and obituaries about Rabbi Yaakov Naiman (1909–2009) emphasize his moral leadership in the Mirrer Yeshiva's journey out of Europe as well as his role in rebuilding Torah learning in Chicago and on Long Island after the war. This modest yet formidable scholar (*lamdan*) was shaped by the critical method of Talmudic scholarship pioneered by the Brisker Rov (Yitshok Zev Soloveitchik, 1886–1959).

Reb Naiman's tales about his mentor did not hold Chaya Leah's attention during the war as much as the process of feeding little girls. The pulling of ponytails, the urgent and efficient way of nourishing children, stands in harsh contrast here to the smaller Walkin family, where parents took time to beg and bribe Chaya Leah and her two younger siblings to swallow the "horrific food."

A similarly honest glimpse of life in the Liaoyang house comes across in Chaya Leah's recollection of Rabbi Yeshaya Dov Meir Shimanowitz, another neighbor in war-torn China:

> *Come Vera, hold my hand. Let's go to the back of the house. Shimanowitz.*
> *Reb. Shaya Shimanowitz was strong. He fasted for 2 days when he was not sure about the date line. He was physically strong and religiously strong.*
> *Mrs. Shimanowitz is someone you did not mess with. When the milkman came into the courtyard to sell milk and butter, if there was not enough merchandise and she wanted it, everyone backed off.*
> *She was tall, gorgeous, and strong.*
> *No nonsense.*
> *Mushka, her oldest daughter, is my friend. Their son Berele is Moishe's friend.*
> *Vera, you must remember him.*

I never met Rabbi Shimanowitz, but now I am urged to remember him. To be sure, his strenuous efforts to fast for two days during Yom Kippur in Japan are well known in the memoir literature surrounding the Mirrer Yeshiva community. None of those works, however, brings to life his wife, the "no-nonsense" woman who pushed everyone aside in order to get scarce items such as butter and milk for her family in Shanghai. Chaya Leah, the child, was more than a friend of Mushka Shimanowitz. She was a conscious witness to the gritty realities and disparate personalities that comprised the community on the street of Expansive Vigor.

Unadorned details continue to pour forth as Chaya Leah takes me through her family's residence to the bathroom and the shared kitchen used by all the refugees. She acknowledges that the Walkin family had the biggest room in the house and that they were reluctant to use the communal "facilities" because they were often crowded and dirty. In a passage that is at once truthful and also colored by a child's naïveté, she writes:

> Our home has a private corner, and the amah *that comes in every day cleans it very well.*
> *We like her a lot. She is so gentle and kind.*

Here, I am introduced for the first time to the Chinese woman who played a significant role in Chaya Leah's wartime childhood. Not surprisingly, she is a servant. She comes each day to clean the private corner where the Walkin family members relieve themselves with a bit more dignity than many other refugees. For Chaya Leah, the "we" includes her siblings. She is the oldest and therefore speaks for them as well when describing the servant as gentle and kind. Simplistic at first, these qualities gain depth as I enter more deeply in a world in which refugee adults had little choice but to become tough, and even harsh, in order to procure the basic necessities of everyday life.

HER WAGES? A MEAL

The *amah* features prominently in most Westerners' writings about childhood in China. It was not only wartime poverty that led young country girls to seek menial employment in the houses of foreigners with ampler means. For over a century before the Walkins took up residence on Liaoyang Road, Chinese women had been cleaning house, washing laundry, and shouldering much of the childcare in foreign as well as wealthy native families. The common Chinese term for this all-purpose helper is derived from the Portuguese *a-ma*, meaning "mother." Chaya Leah's *amah* was no substitute for Rebbetzin Walkin. She was merely a servant, yet she brought a distinctive measure of grace and dignity in a world sorely lacking in such niceties.

A single torn photograph of this key figure remains in Chaya Leah's possession. It shows a Chinese woman dressed in black peasant garb surrounded by the three Walkin children, while Chaya Leah's mother is standing tallest in the back. The serious-faced young *amah* is holding Moshe on her lap. The young boy appears at ease in white short pants and shirt, his light hair covered by a *yarmulke*, the expected head covering for males in a Torah-observant community. Chaya Leah, her sister Esther, and Rebbetzin Walkin are all dressed in white. Large bows, like giant butterflies, adorn the girls' hair while their mother appears quite stylish in a well-cut suit. The season appears to be summer since Westerners traditionally preferred light-colored clothes in the heat and humidity of Shanghai. A working woman from the countryside, Chaya's *amah* is strikingly different in their midst. She is seated, central, a source of support, and also clearly the "other."

In "Love Without Boundaries," the Chinese-sponsored painting exhibition of Jewish life in Shanghai, the "Chinese nanny" figures prominently as well. Here, however, there is an official discourse about "friendship" suggesting that refugees and locals were closer than actual servitude implied. In one key image, a predictably vulnerable little blonde girl stands beside her *amah* as if the sad-eyed Chinese woman was truly her guardian and protector. The street scene behind them is orderly and clean, nothing like the cacophonous alleys evoked by Chaya Leah's jottings. The central figure here, too, is dressed in peasant pants and jacket and she faces the viewer with an unassuaged longing for recognition by posterity. The accompanying text drives this message home in unequivocal terms:

> The Jews and Chinese forged a long-lasting friendship during their time in Shanghai. In that period, Chinese children were seen playing with Jewish children and in fact most Jewish children were looked after by Chinese nannies. Jews is a race who demonstrated abundance of emotions and gratitude. As the years passed by, the little girl in the painting once returned to China in search of her nanny, wishing to express her attitude, but it was regretful that she could not remember her nanny's name.[6]

This supposed "friendship" between Chinese and Jews has been challenged by many survivors of the refuge in Shanghai, most notably Lotte Lustig Marcus. In her memoirs, she documents the scarcity of contact between Jewish refugees and local residents of Shanghai. Even Chaya Leah, who describes the *amah* as gentle and kind, knows better than to call her a "friend." Chinese authorities loved the torn photograph when she returned for a visit in 2007. It seemed as

---

6 Mira Altman, "From Shanghai to the ICC Jerusalem," *The Jerusalem Post*, May 20, 2015.

if she was just like the girl in the painting, longing to express gratitude to kind locals who protected and befriended the Jews.

In reality, Chaya Leah knew that it was the Japanese occupation of Shanghai that aided her family's survival. She also recalls only too well that the *amah* was more servant than nanny:

> Our amah *took care of us, did the laundry, helped with watching us, and kept us close to her. She only spoke Chinese, yet we communicated with her with our hands. She watched us in the yard, played with us. She made us dolls out of wood and rags. And we laughed a lot when we played ball.*
> *Her wages?*
> *A meal.*
> *I don't know if she had family, but this is how she survived. To be able to get a meal, you lived one day at a time.*
> *I think most of the Chinese in the ghetto had no plans for a future. They just struggled to live, to survive. If you were a proprietor, if you had a rickshaw, if you had a skill to read or to write you had some future…*
> *Life in Shanghai for the poor Chinese was so hard, so meaningless, hopeless, a total void.*
> *We gave our* amah *a glimpse of the meaning of living.*
> *Our nanny was a German Jew who took care of my brother.*
> *Her wages? Also the daily meal.*

Clearly, there was a hierarchy of status between the *amah* and the nanny. Although Moshe, the young boy, is sitting in the Chinese girl's lap in the torn photograph, his personal care was entrusted to a fellow Jewish refugee. Like the native country girl, the German nanny also worked for her meals, since the Walkins were one of the few families able to share their meager food with others.

In contrast to the glossy painting of "friendship," Chaya Leah's portrayal is honest about the lack of communication between Chinese and Jews. Hand gestures and hastily crafted toys, however, sufficed to win the hearts of children seeking some fun in the midst of war. What the Walkin family's oldest child recalls most vividly is the hopelessness of Chinese lives around Liaoyang Road. The meal provided for the Chinese servant was "a taste of living" that went beyond raw survival. It was meant to extricate both the *amah* and the German nanny from the indignity of hunger and despair.

When Chaya Leah herself looks at the photograph of the *amah* and the Walkin children, she does not see "friendship." Instead, she is eloquent in acknowledging the Chinese woman's role in maintaining the Jewish dignity so precious to Rebbetzin Walkin. "*Malbushim Kovod*"— "robe yourself like royalty"—was Chaya Leah's mother's refrain before the war as well as during the harshest years in China. It was in fulfilling this mandate that the Chinese servant became such a precious partner:

> Picture the children with our amah. We posed in our Shabbos/Yom Tov clothes. We only had two outfits, one for the weekday and one for Shabbos and the chagim.
> The bows had to be perfect, the shoes had to be clean, the socks had to be just right, the dress was ironed, but would wrinkle almost immediately.
> Malbushim Kovod! Malbushim Kovod!
> When we hung the laundry outside to dry, someone had to always watch the laundry for fear of theft.
> She was young and so gentle. She loved to tie our bows in back of our dresses and always hovered around us that we should go out looking neat and clean.

Laundering in Shanghai was thus not merely a matter of hygiene or of maintaining an image of a superior Westerner. In the Walkin household, it was an essential part of praising the divine image in man, of keeping Shabbat special, of honoring the holidays by a certain dignified demeanor. All this was supposed to be reflected in the clothing that the *amah* maintained with great effort.

MALBUSHIM KOVOD

Chaya Leah's evocation of the Chinese woman's services honors both the person and the tasks that were part of living in a Jewish manner in China. The painstaking process of keeping clothes neat in Shanghai—of making them worthy of being called *Malbushim Kovod*—is something that impacted Chaya Leah for the rest of her life. Following in the footsteps of her beloved *amah* as well as taking Rebbetzin Walkin's dictum to heart, Chaya Leah became a fixer of garments as well:

> Looking back at our family photographs from Shanghai, I see the care that was taken to preserve the life of each and every garment.

> Later, I remember being in school in America, and if anything was torn, a safety pin came to the rescue. But my mother's way was different. I remember her always with a needle and thread in hand, fixing things.
> I also do not use safety pins. I have such an aversion. Instead, you can find me with needle and thread fixing clothes like my mother. I am always checking to see if the hem is not torn, if there are any splits, buttons missing. I also know how to darn socks. My children laugh at me. In our throwaway society, the joy of fixing something useable is a lost treasure.

Perhaps other refugee children who endured hardship and scarcity in China also developed an aversion to the throwaway society they encountered after the war. But for Chaya Leah, as for her mother, clothes were never merely garments to cover human nakedness with some style. *Malbushim Kovod* required a consciousness of the purpose of human existence. The glory of one's divine purpose had to be reflected in one's personal demeanor. That required a huge amount of effort, as Chaya Leah learned by observing and appreciating her *amah* in Shanghai.

The most concrete delight for a little girl during the Jewish holidays in China comes across when Chaya Leah recalls the rare event of getting new clothes. Shoes were even harder to get and spurred an intense longing in a child already used to the scarcities that molded the life of refugees:

> Every year, we would get either a new dress or a new pair of shoes. For the dress, we would go to the dressmaker and a shoemaker down the street made the shoes for us. Here in Shanghai was a Jewish man making shoes. For clothing, we were able to use hand-me-downs, but shoes were not easy.
> You could not buy ready-made shoes—they had to be made to order.
> For one Pesach, my mother said I could have a new pair of shoes. I wanted a sandal, and I wanted it to be with red, white and blue stripes. I dreamed of the shoes, every day, and could not wait for Pesach to come so that I can wear the shoes.
> When I finally got them, I slept with them tight to my chest, rubbed the shiny leather, opened and closed the strap, my most prized possession. The day I put them on I wanted to walk barefooted so that I would not ruin them. To this day, I have a shoe fetish.

There is a striking honesty in this recollection that allows us to glimpse the childish origins of a woman's obsession with footwear many years after the holidays that the Walkin family celebrated with such care in Shanghai.

To be sure, many other refugee children did not even have one pair of new shoes a year. Chaya Leah herself accepted the fact that "new" clothes most often came from a previous user. She also voices here a retrospective acknowledgment of a fellow Jewish refugee who made ends meet for his family by crafting fancies such as Chaya Leah's shiny, colorful sandals. Yet, it is the child who went to bed hugging her shoes and wanting to walk barefoot rather than ruin them who lingers most vividly in mind.

To enter the Walkin family's life on Liaoyang Road thus requires a suspension of generalizations about Westerners and their Chinese servants, about the more impoverished German refugees and the slightly better off Torah-observant Jews who came along with the Walkin family from Kobe to Shanghai.

Without knowing the *amah's* name or her place of origin, Chaya Leah's recollections convey the predicament of poverty and displacement that bound the provincial native in dark clothes to the Jewish children and their mother sporting white Shabbos clothes. The *amah* and the nameless shoemaker are recalled as appreciated helpers—wordless witnesses—to an effort to survive the *unterwelt* with dignity and a moral conscience guided by the light of religious observance.

Guiding "tender kids" along unknown paths, in the words of *Shir Ha'Shirim*, was no light matter. The tents of the shepherds were set up in strange territory, made even more daunting in China during the war. Rebbetzin Walkin made every effort to follow the ethical norms from back home while adjusting to the harsh realities of life as a refugee on Liaoyang Road. From back in Radin, she carried more than a motto about *Malbushim Kovod*. She also learned how to express respect for non-Jewish helpers who enabled her to raise children in keeping with Torah traditions:

> Back in Radin, there was always a *shiksel* (a young non-Jewish girl) in my maternal grandfather's home. My mother grew up with the respect for such a worker, and this carried over to Shanghai.
> Mother always served the maid herself. She always served the maid first and then she ate. There was always a glass of water ready for her. My mother made sure that the maid was dressed properly. If she did not have clothes, she would give her her own clothes.
> Mother would also make sure to tell the maid to rest when she was working too hard. My husband would often quip: "If I should be reincarnated, I would like to come back as your mother's maid."

Building on lessons learned in the home of the Chofetz Chaim and that of her own parents, Rebbetzin Walkin gave the young *amah* in Shanghai more than a daily meal. She exuded respect and her children, in turn, learned to show appreciation for the small kindnesses of the Chinese servant. The dolls she made, the ball games she played, the songs she sang to the children were all "extra." Unpaid, unasked for, these tokens of kindness speak of a special human connection that has not been forgotten.

Chaya Leah's claim that "we gave our *amah* a glimpse of the meaning of living" reflects more than the patronizing attitude of a Westerner looking back at a Chinese native rescued temporarily from utter poverty. It also captures a seasoned woman's effort to imagine what lies within the mind of a Chinese girl dressed in black holding Moshe on her lap. Payment in meals to the *amah* and to the German nanny were in keeping with the famous dictum in *Pirkei Avot* 3:21: *Ein kemach, ein Torah.* Without flour (basic food), there is no Torah. Material sustenance comes first. This is the lesson that the Walkin family managed to share with a poor Chinese woman as well as a German-Jewish refugee.

Once there was food, then one could worry about the finer points involved in serving God. Therefore, *Kovod* was not only something material that the Walkin children were robed with. It was a cardinal value that was to be carried over also to the way in which one gave food to those who helped out the family. Jewish or non-Jewish, members of the household had to be treated with respect. This basic *Kovod* did not need translation into Chinese or into the language of *Shir Ha'Shirim*. It was simply how things were done.

Many decades after Shanghai, when Chaya Leah's husband Rabbi Small quipped about the good fortune of a Walkin maid, he was merely emphasizing the lessons learned in the "shepherd's tents." These had become the family norm. They represented Torah values translated in action. The *amah's* "glimpse of the meaning of living" had come to be a guiding light in Rebbetzin Chaya Leah Small's own life: There is no greater honor than honoring others.

HONEYPOTS AND THE CHINESE WATCHMAN

Looking back upon survival in Shanghai, the larger lessons Chaya Leah carried with her are embedded in the emotions of everyday life on the street of Expansive Vigor. I follow her footsteps and marvel at the child who helped to maintain her family's traditions while confronting the stench of despair in wartime China. Walking toward the gated courtyard, Chaya Leah's email already asked me to block out the noise of haggling vendors in order to hear the caged chickadees she loved but could not buy. What follows is a more gruesome sight that the child learned to accept, though it defied the core Jewish belief that all humanity is created in the divine image:

> Hold my hand, little Vera.
> We will walk on the side of the street that the gate is on. The shoemaker is there and his tiny little closet is his store.
> Don't be afraid of the man in rags lying against the bricks in the corner of a house—he is probably dead and will be picked up in a wagon in the morning to be dumped in the mass field or is sleeping.
> Just walk around him and ignore all the flies on his body and all the wounds oozing.
> Take a look across the street, our hot water man, we almost go every day for water—hot water, that is. His cauldron takes up half his store. We don't often buy hot water. Every groshen is carefully watched.

The sight of dead bodies accosted Chaya Leah every day. Older Jewish refugees also commented on this shocking reality in Shanghai that defied the moral imagination yet was part of China's predicament during the war. The child, however, had to learn how to walk around cadavers in rags every day. By making me "little Vera," Chaya Leah herself is able to call up old nightmares and thereby guide me forward to the shoemaker and the hot water man.

The dead have no voice here, even decades later. Yet, their presence lingers in the child's mind augmented by the stench of human refuse:

> Every morning there were two rituals: one was to pick up the waste in the honey pots and the other was to pick up the dead bodies. They were simply left on the sidewalk for the pickup. You could see the cart, pulled by a coolie, filled with dead bodies, one on top of the other, hands hanging out, feet dangling. One on top of the other. Completely open, not even covered with a sheet or tarp. It looked so horrific. I am sure the carts were covered with flies, but I always kept my eyes closed. I was too scared to look and too scared to talk. Not verbalizing this fear left its mark and trauma.

Looking back, Chaya Leah still tries to avert her eyes from the flies covering the piles of corpses picked up each morning, along with the human feces used to fertilize the fields beyond the Shanghai municipality. The child refugee in

China had not yet seen images of Jewish bodies piled up upon each other at the Auschwitz-Birkenau extermination camps. But this everyday sight in China served to deepen the trauma that lingers wordlessly in so many survivors of the *Shoah*.

Unvoiced, the impact of the dead left lying in the streets of Shanghai lingers on as a dark shadow. Nonetheless, Chaya urges me on. The girl who had hoped for new shoes around the holidays was sent out to get hot water before each Shabbos. Despite the huge cost and the corpses on Liaoyang Road, Chaya Leah wants me to meet the vendors who loomed larger in her daily life.

What becomes clear to me as I follow Chaya Leah is that a feeling of protection lingered over the harshest encounters in Shanghai. The gated courtyard, the familiar neighbors who were part of the yeshiva community literally sheltered this child and her younger friends. In addition, there were Chinese protectors. The young *amah* was one of them. The Chinese watchman and his wife were also key to Chaya Leah's sense of well-being:

> A couple more steps, Verishka, and you will enter our world.
> At the entrance of the open gate is our watchman. His wife is fat, and sits on a stool by the entrance—she cannot move around well as her feet were bound as a child, and her husband helps her around.
> I think she is not well, and she is so immobile, but she laughs as we play and smiles all the time. She somehow will look out for you and me, so I am always very friendly to her.
> You and I will make sure to say hello to her, but she does not understand a word we will say to her.

Clearly, the Walkin children and their friends were guarded by the Chinese watchman. A fixture of any well-to-do Shanghai compound, he was an especially endearing figure for the refugees who had so little protection in a heartless world.

Chaya Leah takes time to notice and to greet the wordless wife as well. This is the child's most intimate encounter with China's tradition of foot binding. By the winter of 1941–42, campaigns against this brutal infliction upon young girls had succeeded among Chinese intellectuals and urban dwellers. Started initially by Christian missionaries in the late nineteenth century, anti-foot-binding activism had rallied Chinese revolutionaries both in the Nationalist and Communist camps.

Chaya Leah's watchman and his wife, however, were most likely from the countryside. Lucky to find employment in the city in time of war, they made do with a small salary and the hut that simultaneously served as the compound gate. The daughter of Jewish refugees knew nothing about the politics of the anti-foot-binding campaign. But she took time to notice the gentle ways of the watchman who cared for his heavy-set, hobbling wife. Being childless, as Chaya Leah learned over the war years, the Chinese couple at the gate took an extra interest in the Jewish children who went in and out of the gate:

> *The watchman and his wife had no children, so she adopted all the little ones in the complex. The two of them were always there for us. If we had a fight or misbehaved, they would step in. We did not speak Chinese and they did not speak Yiddish or German, but somehow we communicated with our hands and eyes and unspoken words.*

Although Shanghai was synonymous with a cacophony of languages, Chaya Leah managed to feel safe without words. Chaya Leah is direct in allowing us to see the difference between the Walkins' gated home and the hut shared by the watchman and his wife. Even if the gate was embedded in a pockmarked cement wall, it symbolized some safety in the larger *unterwelt*.

In this recollection, as in Chaya Leah's description of the *amah*, the mind's eye lingers on unexpected details: the watchman's concern that the children not stray beyond the gate, his wife's bound feet. Each child was probably admonished again and again not to go beyond the gate. Chaya Leah was explicitly told not to play in the front of the house. What made an even greater impression than these warnings was the childless couple's pleasure in watching the little Jewish children at play. The memory of "the two of them always being there for us" is vague in its generalized affection. Yet, one senses both warmth and reassurance despite the vague words.

Looking back, Chaya Leah's recollections honor a poor Chinese man and his tradition-bound wife because they managed some communication with Jewish children. The Yiddish and German languages were "inside" tongues. They framed family life as it unfolded indoors. The watchman and his wife were presences outside. They guarded more than possessions and the children. This poor Chinese couple seemed to have held the keys to a more primal human communication. Defying the language barrier, Chaya Leah could make herself heard. She felt herself understood. This was a gift whose magnitude would grow over the years.

SHOPPING, SHABBOS, AND A TAPEWORM

Though guarded and protected, Chaya Leah encountered Shanghai's hubbub nonetheless while helping to shop and prepare food for Shabbos. Unlike the German-Jewish refugees who depended on soup kitchens for their daily nourishment, the Walkin family was able to cook its own food and share it with others. American aid organizations like the American Jewish Joint Distribution Committee had been hampered in getting funds to Shanghai after the United States joined the war against Japan. The Vaad ha-Hatzala organization, by contrast, was determined to help the Torah leadership rescued from Poland even if it meant circumventing rules and regulations about fundraising.

Rabbi Avraham Kalmanowitz (1891–1964) had no hesitation about riding in a car on the holy day of Shabbat to solicit money for the Jewish refugees in China. His organization defied US regulations and managed to send funds through South America and Europe to families such as that of Rav Shmuel David Walkin in Shanghai. Chaya Leah's awareness of these complexities was very limited. Many years later, as she recalled delivering *lockshen* (noodles) to and from other refugees, she came to realize that being a child had been helpful in processing foreign funds during the war years in Shanghai.

What was amply apparent to the six-year-old girl who lived on Liaoyang Road was that food was scarce and needed to be handled with special care in order to meet the needs of observant Jews such as her parents. As the oldest child, she was entrusted with much of the shopping. This was a challenge and a thrill that expanded her world beyond the protected courtyard:

> The milkman would come on an irregular basis, and all the women and children and residents would come to greet the amazing peddler or entrepreneur. We would buy the little bit of milk or butter. Some people who could not afford anything just looked on.
>
> I used to love to go to greet all the salesmen and see all the excitement. There were many fights and the disappointments. For us children, all this was a special treat and event.
>
> I do not remember much about mealtime as a routine. I know how we hated the breakfast that was forced down our throats to give us strength, usually one small item for dinner. We were not hungry, but not full. Water was free so we had lots of soups and anything that we could get was put into the soup.

> *Rice was cheap, but full of bugs, so we would use a cup, then we put the rice in a bowl of water and watch all the bugs come to the top. The cleaning of the rice had to be done several times till we were sure there were no more bugs. Nothing in Shanghai could be eaten raw—everything had to be cooked.*

The Walkin family was privileged to have milk and butter brought to them. German refugees living in their more crowded *heims* had to go out and fight for these precious goods.

Even as Chaya Leah was aware of the gnawing needs of German Jews such as the family's nanny, she was also delighted by being part of the crush of people that greeted vendors on Liaoyang Road. For the Walkins and their rabbinical colleagues, the Torah prohibition against eating insects took on more dramatic, more vivid proportions in Shanghai. Other refugees whose hunger was more acute could dispense with checking every grain of rice. They, too, however, shared the understanding that one had to boil every vegetable for the sake of survival.

Even with all the checking of food, children were at risk of infection. The most common and dangerous threat was the intestinal tapeworm. Chaya Leah witnessed her brother fall prey to this disease. With a child's keen interest, she was allowed to look inside the euphemistically named "honey pot":

> *My brother had been eating but looked malnourished. He was skinny as a rail. Of course, we knew something was devouring from the inside everything that he ate. All the remedies did not help get rid of the tapeworm.*
> *Then, we heard that bananas were the new solution. How do you get bananas in wartime Shanghai? Who could possibly afford this luxury? Yet, a child was wasting away. We had to do something.*
> *My father was the kind of man who did not know the expression "it cannot be done."*
> *One day, a banana appears on our table. The sight of this golden yellow fruit was a wonder to us. We could only look, not touch. My mother gently peeled the banana and slowly fed it my brother.*
> *We knew we should not ask for this precious medicine that might save our brother.*
> *But the aroma was too tempting. The desire to taste this rare treat was too strong. So, ingeniously, my sister and I took the peel and whatever was left on it and licked the treasure. Bananas are still my favorite fruit, and the taste remains tantalizing.*

> But in Shanghai, it had a higher purpose. It got rid of the tapeworm. Many weeks later, after trials and tribulations, my brother eliminated the tapeworm. It was at least 8 inches long and ghostly white. My mother kept that tapeworm for several days in the honey pot so that everyone had a chance to view the efficacy of bananas in times of duress.

The vivid taste of banana peels and the sight of the lengthy tapeworm in the chamber pot linger from childhood in the older woman's mind. It is also clear that Rabbi Walkin went to great lengths to procure this one rare fruit for the boy who was ill. Though immersed in Torah study much of the time, like other members of the yeshiva community, the responsibilities of taking care of one's family came first. His "can do" attitude was passed on to his eldest child, a daughter whose fierce will and resourcefulness was tested again and again, in Shanghai as well as in later years.

Chaya Leah learned early that certain foods, such as bananas, were too expensive and could not be had at all. She learned to make do with the one-pot meal most days. It was this food that was shared with the family servants as well. It was simple, it was kosher, and it was deemed enough.

Like the biblical Jews who traveled in the desert who made do with manna day in and day out, this Jewish child was trained early on to accept with gratitude what was, as it was. In their wanderings through the desert, some Jews had complained about the manna because it was always the same—day in and day out. For Chaya Leah and her family, knowing fully well the predicament of scarcity among Jewish refugees in Shanghai, the one-pot meal was ample enough.

Shabbat, however, demanded more honor, more preparation, more expenditure of time and money. Refugees for whom the seventh day of the week was just another workday looked with angry disapproval at the huge effort that observant families like Chaya Leah's made to obtain chicken and other delicacies. Reading a child's recollection of Shabbos preparation does not diminish this roar of resentment, but it does allow us to glimpse from within what it took to *shamor ve zachor*—to keep and to remember—the holiness of the seventh day in Shanghai:

> The greatest luxury we had in Shanghai was "le kovod Yom Tov"—"in honor of the holy days" was chicken.
> My mother would give me instructions: "My child, get a chicken that is fat."
> "How do I know how to tell if it is fat?"

> "Just feel under her belly and you will know."
> I went to the chicken seller who had a small store in the front of his house. In the back were the living quarters, again one room.
> I would pick the one after groping several and then go to the shochet to slaughter the chicken.
> The shochet was in back of a small café. He took the chicken from me, then went into the alley and slaughtered the chicken, spilling the blood on the ashes in the alley. Walking back, the chicken was still squawking and blood was dripping on the sidewalk. I remember being so sad carrying the chicken home. I thought it was still alive.

The child who had walked past corpses, who had seen the ghostly tapeworm in the honey pot, had not been schooled out of her affection for living creatures. Sent to shop for the honor of various holy days that were scrupulously observed in China, she had to learn how to feel for the fat of a precious chicken.

She had to swallow her qualms and carry the tied up fowl to yet another refugee, a *shochet* trained in the laws of ritual slaughter. Chaya Leah does not mention here the name Rabbi Chaim Plotkin, the *shochet* from Lublin who supervised the small store behind the café. Older refugees from the yeshiva community recall how this one man worked tirelessly to make sure that there was no possibility that a customer, even an easily fooled youngster such as Chaya Leah, would bring home non-kosher meat.

As a child during the war, Chaya Leah had only the vaguest sense of how hard her father and the Amshenover Rebbe had worked to spread the observance of *kashrut* in Shanghai. They even managed to bring a second helper for Reb Chaim, the *shochet*, in the person of Rabbi Yosef Rosenberg from the city of Zembrava, Poland. These rabbis were all refugees, like Chaya Leah's family. But *kashrut* and Shabbat observance were non-negotiable foundations of their life, whether in Poland, Japan, or in China.[7]

Having brought the kosher chicken home from the *shochet* was not the end of Chaya Leah's contribution to the observance of holy days in Shanghai. As if carrying the bloody carcass was not enough, the child was also expected to participate in *flickening*—the slow, unpleasant task of removing the feathers:

> It was a messy job, and the feathers would fly all over the yard. Near the neck, the feathers were saturated with blood. I would clean the chicken on the concrete in our backyard.

---

7   David Mandelbaum and Yechiel Benzion Fishoff, *From Lublin to Shanghai: The Miraculous Exile of Yeshivas Chachmei Lublin* (New York: Mesorah Publications, Ltd, 2012), 274.

> *Job done. Now, came the other steps: Cut up the chicken, remove the gut, and then kasher it. First, it had to be soaked in water for half an hour. Then salted on a board for one hour.*
>
> *This chicken one was shared between two families. Half each. The liver was cut in half, the pupick (stomach) was cut in half. If there were eggs, we would share, half and half. But if there were an uneven number of eggs, I would keep the extra one. Nothing, but nothing, tasted as good as eggs cooked in the chicken soup.*

The Shabbos chicken was not a private affair for the Walkin family. It was scrupulously shared by at least 2 families, with only an extra egg being Chaya Leah's personal reward for enduring the gruesome process of buying and preparing kosher meat *"le kovod Yom Tov."* When fowl was not available, Chaya Leah would be sent out to buy fish. There was no need to palpate for fat here. The shopkeeper would just follow the child's pointing finger and catch the one that she chose:

> *Then, the proprietor would hit the fish on the head several times, put it in a bag and off I went. Cleaning the fish was easier, just remove the scales. We used the whole fish. We discarded only the gut and the eyes. Every part was used. The bones were used to make a dairy soup with potatoes, onions, and carrots.*
>
> *I hated it, but you eat when you are hungry.*

Here, a child is being trained for adult responsibilities. Chaya Leah's family had been on the run since she was less than five years old. Later, after the war, Chaya Leah readily assumed responsibility for younger siblings when her mother became an invalid in New York. Looking back, it is clear that the half-decade spent in Shanghai prepared the little girl to serve as her family's liaison with the bewildering outside world. This short childhood also reinforced for Chaya Leah the need to maintain Jewish traditions, no matter the cost or the effort that they entailed.

Chicken and fish had been two key provisions in honoring Shabbat in Shanghai. Wine was another. Because the *kashrut* expectations for wine were complex and stringent, Rebbetzin Walkin took it upon herself to make wine. As with much else, little Chaya Leah was expected to help and actually do the harder tasks involved in its preparation:

> *My mother used to make wine for Shabbos and Pesach. One night, a jar of fermenting grapes shattered to pieces. Waking up to the sticky, sugary syrup*

was not exactly fun. Cleaning up with no running water was also hard, but all that did not stop my family from making wine again and again for the Chagim (holidays).

Cleaning up shards of glass was hard enough. What Chaya Leah recalls even more vividly in the preparation for the holidays was the long, arduous process of cooking itself. Even after buying the chicken and fish, and helping to clean these and the sticky floor, the child was not done.

She was still left with the task of *fochening*—fanning the flames of the makeshift family stove. This contraption appears most frequently in Chaya Leah's recollections and it is attributed to one of the yeshiva students who tried to make a living by peddling cooking oil to fellow refugees. One day, having an empty can left, this Yoselle Eisenstein (who came from Poland and married a German refugee in Shanghai) brought the precious gift of an empty can as a gift to Rebbetzin Walkin:

> We removed the top of the can, covered the inside with mud, and put wiring on top. When it dried, we used the coal that we made out of manure to heat the stove. I remember my mother making merlekh (carrots) on that stove. We had to keep on fanning all the time to keep the flame going. My mother's refrain lingers in my mind: "Meine kinde helf mir fochening"—"My child, help me stoke the fire."

Honoring Shabbat was thus a difficult, whole-family affair. Rebbetzin Walkin was the supervisor, like the *shochet* in the little store near the café. She was responsible for making sure that Rabbi Walkin maintained the high standards of *kashrut* he had learned in the home of Bais Aharon.

Long before news of her grandfather's death reached Shanghai, Chaya had already learned that there was to be no hesitation in coming to aid her mother's *fochening*. Stoking a small fire was a big job and it grew ever larger, especially in contrast to the deadly fires that were consuming Jewish bodies in the world that the Walkin family had left behind.

FAR VOS LAYT DAYN FOLK YISROEL?—WHY DOES YOUR NATION ISRAEL SUFFER?

Portentious questions about the fate of the Jewish people hovered over the life of the child. She understood more with her heart and eyes than could have been expressed by words. It was through the small details of life in Shanghai that Chaya Leah experienced the tribulations of refugee life. By lingering alongside the little girl and her daily routines, I managed to glimpse a broader canvas.

Inside the family compound on Liaoyang Road, Jewish families made do with whatever they could get, sharing what little they had. Beyond the gate lay a different world from which the necessities for survival had to be procured. In China during the war, Chaya Leah learned to reflect more deeply upon life's vicissitudes than if she had grown up in Lukatch as the treasured oldest child of the town rabbi. If they had stayed, however, the family would have been murdered.

In Shanghai, beyond the challenges of shopping and averting one's eyes from the deadly stench of daily life, the weather itself was hard to bear. Bone-chilling winters and humid summer were the price for life at a time when the familiar world back in Poland grew increasingly murderous:

> Winters were bitter cold, but summers were unbearable. The heat, the humidity, the stench. People walked around with wet towels to cool off.
>
> The horrific tropical weather and low resistance due to poor and inadequate nutrition made us more vulnerable to the rampant diseases of dysentery, malaria, typhoid, and cholera.
>
> We were the lucky ones—we had running water, water closets that worked, and decent electricity. Yet, with all these "luxuries," it was still impossible to accommodate the needs of all the people living in this one house.
>
> My parents had a *shisel*, a large pot we used as a bathtub. You could sit in it, but your legs had to be crossed or under your bottom. Hot water was sold across the street. The proprietor would sell a cup full of water for a token stick. I remember my sister Esther taking a bath, and I kept running back and forth to get more water. We never had enough money to fill that shisel to the top, but a little water would do.
>
> During the summer time, it was not so bad. But in the winter cold, we would sit in the tub and shiver.

At a time when children her age were being gassed in Auschwitz, Chaya Leah Walkin was running to buy hot water for her younger sister's bath. The *shisel* used for bathing was more than a cramped tin tub. It was yet another instrument for maintaining *kovod*—dignity—in difficult times.

The shortage of hot water was something that Chaya and her family coped with rather easily in Shanghai. To be sure, memories of better times—

especially in Kobe—became ever more precious as war in China brought grime and despair closer to the compound in Liaoyang Road. Life in Japan brightened in memory with every passing day of corpses and honey pots. A simple local fire on Liaoyang Road sharpened for Chaya Leah the contrast between Kobe and Shanghai:

> I remember we had a fire in one of the houses on the row we lived on in Japan. To me, it looked like it would take minutes for everything to go up in smoke, everything was built of wood and paper. The fire was put out in a civil way.
> We also had a fire in Shanghai on Liaoyang Road, which was a fiasco. The fire department came, but the water hoses were all torn. So they were trying to put out the fire and water was leaking out all over—everyone was yelling at each other. The pails also had holes.
> It was like a zoo. I have never forgotten that fiasco. It took a while for the fire to be put out, but no one was hurt. On Liaoyang Road, we also had an outdoor pump for water, so the residents were filling up their pails with water and helping to put out the fire. Drop by drop.

The yelling, the communal effort to deal with the danger drop by drop recalls Shoshanna Kahan's more detailed distaste for Chinese inefficacy. In Japan, houses had been more vulnerable than the solid structures on the street of Expansive Vigor. Life in Kobe seemed at once more civil and more fragile. In Shanghai, Chaya Leah experienced the bewildering cacophony of a war weary, impoverished population.

As the oldest sibling, she had more responsibilities in China than in Japan. On Liaoyang Road, Chaya Leah was allowed to stay up later than her younger sister and brother. It was at night, when various yeshiva students would gather in the Walkins' "salon," that Chaya Leah learned the darker nuances of Jewish survival in China. This one room became the place where many other refugees came to reminisce about the worlds left behind.

One of the most poignant moments in Chaya Leah's recollections came when she started to hum the words to a Yiddish song that had been on the lips of the young men surrounding her father in Shanghai. Without yet knowing the atrocious fate of their parents, these yeshiva students looked upon Rabbi Walkin as their own parent even as they sang:

> Far vos layt dayn folk Yisroel?
> Azoy fil tsoros un payn
> Du host dokh undz tsugezogt a mol

> Az mir zaynen dayn eyntsig folk dayns
> Tsi iz den vaser undzer blut?
> Tsi zaynen undzere trern
> Tzi vayl mir hobn dem nomen Yid
> Darfn mir azoy fil tsoros layden?
>
> Why does your nation Israel suffer?
> so much hardship, so much pain?
> Did you not promise us once
> that we are your favored nation?
> Is our blood water?
> Our tears endless?
> Because we are called Jew
> Do we merit to suffer so?

The little girl hummed along with young men who did not yet know that they were orphans, their parents and siblings killed like the entire family of Benny Fishoff.

The Yiddish song that Chaya Leah recalls is in the form of questions addressed to the Master of the Universe. Like the famous Kaddish of Rabbi Levi-Yitzhok from Berdichev, this is an interrogation of the God who chose the Jewish people and continues to sustain them. Rabbi Levi-Yitzhok's Kaddish starts with a chattier tone than the song from Shanghai. Then, it becomes more challenging as it calls for a *"din Toirah"*—a Torah law case, bringing the divine into the courtroom of human history.

The Berdichever Rebbe's Kaddish addressed the same dilemma: Why are the Jewish people condemned to suffer so? Although Chaya Leah's childhood in Shanghai was protected by the *amah* and the watchman, although she enjoyed the sounds of shopping and the glow that surrounded Shabbat and the holidays, she joined in the song of the orphaned yeshiva students as if it were her own.

The Yiddish words convey the cry of the tender kid left in the care of careless shepherds. They call out to the Shepherd of shepherds, who was accompanying them in the darkest hours of refuge in Shanghai. The child, like rabbi Simcha Elberg, knows instinctively what it is like to be forlorn and forsaken. Even with loving parents around, Chaya knew she was part of *dein folk Yisroel*—"your nation, Israel."

CHAPTER 5

IN THE CROOK OF THE ROCK:

Expanding the Meaning of Survival

> *My dove in the crook of the rock*
> *In the hiding place of the steep*
> *Show me your visage*
> *Let me hear your voice.*
>
> Shir Ha'Shirim 2:14

News of the devastating war against the Jews trickled into the Liaoyang Road compound slowly. Its losses did not become fully apparent until the end of the war in late 1945. Nonetheless, the madness of hatred and wanton cruelty was palpable in China as well as across Europe. By the winter and spring of 1942, as Chaya turned eight years old in Shanghai, the Wansee Conference (which took place on January 20, 1942) already spelled out a plan that led to the murder of more than one million Jewish children. Mass genocide gained momentum with the establishment of the Auschwitz-Birkenau concentration camp on March 1, 1942.

In China, already suffering from the brutal Japanese occupation, mass devastation took on the added dimension of famine. Between 1942 and 1943, close to three million people died in western Henan province alone due to natural disasters compounded by the politics of war being waged by the regime of Jiang Kai-shek. American photographer and correspondent Theodore White described the disaster with urgency and compassion. Photographs of skeletal Chinese children augmented his report:

> In the mountain districts there were uglier tales of refugees caught on lonely roads and killed for their flesh. How much of this was just gruesome

legend and how much truth we could not judge. But we heard the same tales too frequently, in too widely scattered places, to ignore the fact that in Honan human beings were eating their own kind."[1]

News of the kind that Theodore White was seeking to convey did not fall upon receptive ears, not in China, not in Europe, and not in the United States. Even today, the history of this famine is being denied on the Chinese mainland because it echoes the politically induced disaster that led to the unnatural death of more than ten million people during the Maoist "Great Leap Forward" of 1959–60.

Calling to mind these atrocities, however, is important if one wants to fathom the meanings of the refuge crafted by the Jewish community of Shanghai during the war. This community was in no position to alleviate the plight of starving Chinese. Jews could not even provide aid to family and friends being herded into the concentration camps and into the ovens of Auschwitz-Birkenau. What they could do—and did—was to dignify daily life in China with the values they carried forward from home.

Beyond the community on Liaoyang Road, the world was hurtling toward more and more devastation. A willful deafness to human suffering grew more acute, as George Orwell noted in an essay written in 1943, after his return from Spanish Civil War. In this work, Orwell linked China's suffering to that of the Jews with forceful irony and indignation:

> Recently I noticed that the very people who swallowed any and every horror story about the Japanese in Nanking refused to believe exactly the same stories about Hong Kong in 1942... The raping and butchering of Chinese cities, the tortures in the cellars of the Gestapo, the elderly professors flung into cesspools, the machine-gunning down of refugees along Spanish roads—they all happened, and they did not happen any less because the *Daily Telegraph* suddenly took notice of them five years too late.[2]

Not taking notice in time thus appeared to be a large-scale malady as Chaya Leah Walkin began her schooling in Shanghai. Yet, it was in the midst of this

---

1 Theodore White, "The desperate urgency of flight," *Time* 40, no. 17 (October 26, 1942), 38.
2 George Orwell, "Looking back at the Spanish Civil War," in *Collected Essays and Journalism 1940-1943* (London: Secker & Warburg, 1961), 61.

moral deafness that the Shanghai refugees discovered the purpose of their survival as Jews.

To use the words of *Shir Ha'Shirim,* they embraced the predicament of the vulnerable dove hidden inside a steep cliff. Chaya Leah and her family managed to display the best of their spiritual resources during the war years in China. They knew that the honor of their cherished traditions was at stake in the *unterwelt* of Shanghai. Chaya Chaya, though still a child, understood this challenge. Looking back, the harshest years of the war appear as a formative—and indeed exhilarating—time because they provided testimony for survival with dignity. The "dove" was tested, and she sang. Instead of the Sea of Reeds and the Egyptian chariots, Jewish refugees in China had faced scarcity, disease, and the dread of daily bombings. With all that, they had embraced the continuing study of Torah as a constant, non-negotiable obligation and managed to build an enduring sense of community in the midst of a rapacious world.

Two contrasting photographs from 1943 bring the uniqueness of Jewish refuge in Shanghai into sharper focus. One is the iconic image dated, May 1943, which shows a little Jewish boy in tall socks, cap and coat, marching with his hands up in the air as Nazi soldiers point their guns at him. A woman, maybe the boy's mother, glances distraughtly backward toward the menace that will end their lives one way or another. This photograph comes from a report sent to Heinrich Himmler just as the Warsaw Uprising during Passover 1943 was being crushed by Nazi troops. Jürgen Stroop, the SS General who wrote the lengthy report, had labeled the photo of the child as follows: "Forcibly pulled out of the dug-outs."[3] These words reveal the terrible fate of the dove wrenched out of the crook of the rock. She had no chance to hide. In such a defenseless world, terror of the Nazis spread starkly upon a child's face.

In Shanghai, around the same time, someone snapped a picture of the Walkin siblings and Berele Shimanowitz in the backyard of the Liaoyang Road compound. Four smiling Jewish children stand in casual summer clothes. Chaya Leah and her sister Esther are dressed in short shorts and hold up parasols, one sign of the scorching heat setting this world apart from a murderously chilly Warsaw. The two little boys in this photograph are only slightly younger than the child with tall socks, cap, and hands up in the air. These boys, however, are wearing flimsy undershirts and are completely at ease. No fear of vulnerability here. They face the trusted adult snapping the photograph with practiced smiles.

---

3   Jean-Michel Frodon, *Cinema et la Shoah* (Paris: Cahiers du cinéma, 2007), 143.

These children have a future. The boy in Warsaw is marked for death. Chaya Leah and her family, augmented by a new brother born in 1945, made it to America. There, it became clear that they had done far more than survive the war. They now carried with them from China the "visage" and "the song" crafted during their time in the cleft of the rock. Each of the children caught in the snapshot on Liaoyang Road contributed to the rebuilding of Torah learning after the war. In Shanghai, these four children had been firmly embedded in a protective community that made every effort to celebrate the unfolding of the Jewish holidays while broadening the circle of friendship and mutual aid among fellow refugees.

I GREW UP AMONG GEDOLIM

Michael Blumenthal (former Secretary of the Treasury under President Carter) has also written about the formative impact of the Shanghai interlude upon his life as a young Jewish refugee. The friendships that he formed in China endured after the war. Lessons in endurance and community building experienced in the early 1940s continue to shape his sense of responsibility and engagement with the Jewish Holocaust Museum in Berlin today.

For Blumenthal, as for Chaya Leah Walkin, the deprivations and challenges of survival in Shanghai became a springboard toward a larger concern with the meanings of the *Shoah* as it affects Jews and non-Jews alike. Chaya Leah's own commitment to Holocaust education is manifest in the great effort that she expends in order to maintain friendships begun in China. Seeking out survivors who are in good or ill health, reminiscing about the morsels of daily life in Shanghai, has become a near full-time job for Chaya Leah. There is no idle pleasure in this memory work.

Instead, Chaya Leah is seeking to maintain and expand a framework of homage to the Torah giants whom she was privileged to meet and know as a child. As she put to me in an email on December 30, 2015:

> Vera, we rubbed shoulders with the gedolim of that era. I want my family and the world to know how normal and down to earth they all were.
> How they loved each and every Yid. When they paskenned, it was with heart, understanding, and compassion. They listened and heard that which was not even said. It was such a special and holy generation.

To be sure, Chaya Leah's lineage gave her a front row seat among the *gedolim*—the scholars of her generation. Her grandfather's name is still revered in the yeshiva world even today. Her mother's childhood in the home of the Chofetz Chaim brought glory even after the war. Chaya Leah's own father played such a prominent role in the refugee community in Shanghai that the Mirrer Rosh Yeshiva, Rabbi Chaim Leib Shmuelevitz (1902–79) fondly referred to him as *"meine bruder"* and *"Rosh ha Golah."*

Being called a "beloved brother" by this prominent Torah authority was just one sign of the respect that Rav Shmuel David Walkin had earned among the many scholars who had taken refuge in China and Japan. The honorific *"Rosh ha Golah"* harkened back to the position of exilarch held by the most accomplished and caring leaders of the exiled community in Babylonia many centuries before Rav Shmuel David offered advice and solace to younger refugees in China.

Greatness, as Chaya Leah's email makes clear, reflects something more important than status and accolades. *Gedolim* refers here to leaders who had an unusually keen sense of responsibility for the welfare of fellow Jews. "Every Yid," as Chaya Leah puts it, even the most ordinary person, is deemed worthy of compassion. When called upon to *pasken*, to make judgments about the applicability of Torah laws to daily life, these scholars did not hesitate to take into consideration the particular needs of the person who came to seek their advice. Far from imposing abstract values and heartless stringencies upon less observant Jews, they were determined to reach out and meet every Jew in whatever circumstances the war had flung into his or her face.

Chaya Leah's effort to convey life among the *gedolim* is not about dropping names. It is a reminder of the deep humanity of the men and women who became famous Jewish leaders after the war. If one were to look at garb and prominence alone, one would miss what Chaya Leah witnessed so intimately in China as well as after the war among the survivors of the Shanghai refuge—that the circle of prominent rabbinical figures around her family were simply "normal" (not extreme religious fanatics) and eminently "down to earth" (conversant with the ways of the world beyond the yeshiva walls).

Most importantly, in Chaya Leah's view, was the fact that the *gedolim* she knew in China loved each and every Jew as he or she was. This quality became essential in Chaya Leah's life too. She is not one to make judgments against those who are different, less religious, or come from other worlds of social and political engagement.

Although Chaya Leah herself did not *"pasken"* on matters of communal law, her father and his fellow scholars did. What lingers from that "special and holy generation" is not only a vast body of writings but a capacity for understanding with the heart and not just the head.

Rav Walkin and yeshiva students.

As a little girl in Shanghai, Chaya Leah was in the room with the *gedolim* and was keen enough to note how they paid attention even to what remained unsaid. Grief, fear, and loneliness were as much a matter of concern as the solid books of the Talmud that occupied her father's hands day and night. This compassion became evident as we spoke about the photograph in the United States Holocaust which is entitled "A group of Jewish refugee yeshiva students in Shanghai gather around Rabbi Samuel Walkin, the former rebbe of Lukatz Kreuz (near Poznan)." This long title was given most likely by a curator seeking to locate the place, if not the exact time, that the photograph was taken.

The lengthy title suits the dense memories contained in this one image. Rabbi Walkin is in the center. He looks small and yet appears different from the other men. He has the longest beard and the least amount of hair among the younger men. Most of the younger yeshiva students are in open-necked shirts. The site of the gathering is identified in the archives as the "Refugee Settlement, Mir" known also as "Yeshiva/Cheder/Beit Midrash." Chaya Leah's father is given his full title as Rebbe of Lukatz, the Polish city that was near the Walkin residence before the war. The "Rebbe" in this photograph (a title of respect not limited to Chassidic masters) is posing in the center, formally garbed amid younger men with their shirt sleeves rolled up.

Most of the figures in the photograph are smiling for the camera while they also share a look of weariness. War has caught up with them. Their companionship provides some solace, but these are also refugees—stateless Jews trying to continue their studies of the Torah during the war. When Chaya Leah and I first looked at this photograph at her home in Chicago, she immediately was drawn to a dark-bearded young man who stands right behind her father. She tells me that even as a little girl she knew he was different, that there was something tragic about him. A little girl, exposed to the *gedolim*, she had also learned early on to pay attention to what was not being said.

Certainly, the young man's eyes bespeak some nameless grief. She remembered his last name, Kamien. I was struck by the depth of her empathy even after so many decades had passed. I asked her to think more about this *bocher*. After a meeting with another Shanghai survivor, Chaya wrote me:

> I am going to jump to Kamien. He was tall and handsome, dark eyes, jet-black hair, and a jet-black beard. In Vilna, he had papers to leave on April 11, 1940.
> Rumors had it that he was engaged and was meeting his bride. As per Benny Fishoff, on April 7, Vilna was invaded, Kamien was standing and davening Shmona Esrei. Standing and davening, for an unusually long time.
> Benny went over to him and shook him and he realized that something was wrong. Kamien's blank stare, blank-eyed, shock.
> Panic.
> Kamien was never the same after that.

One photograph, one man, and Chaya Leah's inheritance from the *gedolim* becomes clear. A seven-year-old girl already sensed a young man's disturbed state of mind. Later, she sent me another document identifying the yeshiva student as Moshe Abba Kamien, born in Makaw, Poland. The certificate was initiated by a Chicago-based cousin who sought to bring the distressed young man from Kobe to the United States by providing the required financial guarantee. The document, alas, was of no use during the short months that the yeshiva community was in Japan. Kamien did not make it to the United States—instead, spending the war years in China.

There, the look of despair and trauma deepened. Like other refugees, he was marked by the wound of historical trauma. But his scars showed up more openly than those of others. What Chaya Leah remembered many years later is that Moshe Abba Kamien's face wore his grief more nakedly than fellow survivors. Kamien had lost the bride of his youth. Every young man around the Lukatz Rebbe had suffered similar losses. Rav Shmuel David Walkin himself found out after the war the tragic fate that befell most of his siblings. But for one moment in the photograph, only Kamien's eye showed the panic and the shock.

This remnant of the war was donated to the United States Holocaust Museum by Rabbi Yaakov Yehuda Ederman, who had been one of the young men of the Mirrer Yeshiva who frequented the home of Rabbi Walkin. As a young *bocher* back in Poland, Ederman was the force behind procuring passports for the entire yeshiva. Before the Sugihara visas could be applied for, official documents had to be acquired stating one's place of origin. While older rabbis debated the advisability of leaving old centers of learning behind in Europe, this young man approached the representative of the Polish government in exile in Kovno and obtained 300 passports for the entire Mirrer yeshiva.

Ederman traveled with his fellow students and teachers through Soviet Russia and Kobe to Shanghai. In China, among the heart-sore refugees, Yankele (as he was known affectionately) provided the balm of song and music. His voice accompanied most of refugee gatherings in China and delighted Chaya Leah whenever she was present for one of his performances:

> *Who can forget Yankele Ederman's chazoniche talent?*
> *It was Yankele who found out about Sempo Sugihara, who served as the Vice Consul for the Empire of Japan in Lithuania*
> *Who can forget, the heart and pain in every song?*
> *The hope, the longing, and the loneliness.*
> *But there was music in the house, and joy, and friendship, and sharing. A powerful bonding with every type of Jew.*

A well-known cantor after the war in Brooklyn, Yaakov Ederman is recalled here for the solace that his singing provided the refugee community. In his lilting voice, fellow Jews heard the accents of home undiminished by the pain of flight—an escape that the young Ederman himself had helped to facilitate. After the precious passports and Sugihara visas, he also found a way to express the hope and the pain present in Jewish hearts during the war years in China.

Chaya Leah's search for the "taste" of the Shanghai life among the *gedolim* comes back again and again to the unique atmosphere of her own family. It is not arrogance that colors these recollections. Rather, she aims to express the appreciation felt also by many of the young men who passed through the one-room "salon" on Liaoyang Road:

> "Once you walked into the Walkin home you never left."
> This was a comment made to me when I asked a bocher how he met my family.
> He continued:
> "It was in Shanghai—they did not have much when
> I came to visit. They shared the little they had.
> They made me feel so welcome and wanted.
> They wanted to help in any way they could.
> Their welcome, their warmth!
> They made me feel as if I was the only one in their lives."

One could read this as a dutiful, loving daughter's quest to voice through the words of a guest an homage to her parents' generosity of spirit. But there is more to this than one nostalgic young man's view of solace in the Walkin household.

Sharing food with the *amah*, the nanny, and neighbors had been what Rav Shmuel David and his wife did naturally in China day in and day out. What is being recalled here is not merely physical nourishment. It is the warmth of the hosts that kept orphaned young men coming back repeatedly. Chaya is not placing words into the *bocher's* mouth. These recollections bear witness to a fragile and precious sense of respite among the refugees.

This kind of psychological support was crucial in supplementing the meager material aid trickling into Shanghai from abroad. The other key figure often mentioned for his many-sided help to the refugee community is Rabbi Meir Ashkenazi (1892–1954), the chief rabbi of Shanghai at the time that the Polish yeshiva students arrived bedraggled and stateless from Japan. Having been chosen as the personal representative of the previous Lubavitcher Rebbe, Rav Ashkenazi was supposed to minister to the spiritual needs of the Russian Jews, most of whom had fled to China after the outbreak of the Bolshevik revolution in the 1920s. With the huge influx of Austrian and German refugees arriving in 1938–39, augmented by the Polish rabbis and their students and families coming from Kobe in 1941, Rabbi Ashkenazi became the central fulcrum for material as well as religious aid to the entire Jewish community.

He took over the Ohel Moshe synagogue in the Hongkew area. It was to this address that Chaya Leah went to *kasher* dishes for Pesach, it was there that most weddings took place with Rabbi Ashkenazi officiating. Today, the legacy of Rav Meir Ashkenazi is memorialized in the Shanghai Jewish Refugee Museum located inside the old Ohel Moshe synagogue.

Chaya Leah knew Rabbi Ashkenazi as a child and was aware of his special kindness and openness to all the sorrows that enveloped the refugee community. As a girl growing up in Shanghai, she was particularly moved by the hospitality he extended to a young woman a decade older than herself: Rishel Friedman, who was born in 1923 to a distinguished family of rabbinical lineage from Germany and Lithuania. In 1941, at the age of 17, Rishel had become engaged to a promising young scholar, Shneur Kotler. The groom was the son of Rav Aharon Kotler, who was active in raising rescue funds for the Mirrer Yeshiva during the war.

Alone, without her parents or her groom, the young bride made her way through Poland and Soviet Russia to Kobe, and then to Shanghai. In China, Rishel (orphaned by the *Shoah* and still unmarried) was taken in by Rabbi Ashkenazi and his wife. Rishel, in turn, took Rav Shmuel David's daughter under her wing, calling her simply "*Chayale, mayn kind.*" Yiddish was the language of affection among the refugees in China, and remains the language of memory for Chaya Leah, who recalls Rishel with the fondness of a younger sibling still moved by the older girl's trials and tribulations during the China years.

The young woman who was the beneficiary of Rabbi Ashkenazi's care and Chaya Leah's affection got very sick in Shanghai. Infected with tuberculosis, Rishel lost use of one of her lungs while the other became seriously compromised as well. Her knees and feet developed dangerous ulcers. As Chaya Leah and other refugees recall, Rishel's prognosis was very grim. Even if she survived, the doctors warned, she would be unable to have children.

Rabbi Ashkenazi was among the few people around Rishel who argued that she should proceed with the marriage as previously agreed upon before the war, no matter what. This presented Rav Aharon Kotler with a serious dilemma: should he allow the marriage of his son to a woman who was incapable of producing prodigy? Even as a little girl, Chaya Leah was aware of these rumblings in Shanghai:

> *Everyone was trying to talk Reb Aron out of the Shidduch.*
> *His answer: "I will not cause pain to an orphan.*
> *I will not cause her pain."*
> *It is called Emunas Hashem (faith in God).*

While the actual deliberations turned out to be more complex than Chaya recalls, what lingers in the mind's eye is the reluctance to inflict pain upon an orphaned and sick young woman. As other documentation shows, communication between Rav Kotler and Rav Ashkenazi continued about the Rishel's engagement. It appears that the two rabbis disagreed on this matter more than Rav Walkin's young daughter understood in China. Rav Kotler held out against the marriage far longer than Chaya Leah recalled. What matters to her in retrospect is the fact that Rishel's illness brought out a spiritual quality, which she calls "*Emunas Hashem.*" This act of faith overrides Torah law that does allow for breaking a marriage agreement if childlessness is an obvious likelihood.

In the Shanghai refugee community, however, the fate of a sick orphan could not be judged on the merits of Torah law alone. As a result, Rav Ashkenazi argued Rishel's case with Rav Kotler in America and prevailed. The marriage took place and Rishel went on to defy all the doctors' gloomy predictions. A higher truth prevailed, and Chaya Leah sensed that, even as a child basking in the friendship of the older girl.

A 2015 obituary for Rebbetzin Rishel Kotler quotes her eminent father-in-law's words in even more detail than Chaya Leah had recalled from their shared days in Shanghai. According to this account, when Rav Kotler got the news of Rishel's illness in Shanghai, he had declared: "*Ikh vil nisht tchepenen a yosems shidduch.*"[4] "I will not tamper with an orphan's marriage arrangement…let's proceed with the marriage agreement. "*Tchepenen*" in this quote means more than "tamper with." The great leader of the Torah community in the United States is portrayed as refusing to wear down the remaining self-respect of an orphan caught by the winds of war in China.

Despite all her ailments, Rishel was married on January 1949 in Lakewood, New Jersey, where her father-in-law had started building the Yeshiva Ha Gevoha, the largest center of Torah learning in America. She not only lived to have children but she also became an active builder of the renewed Lakewood community. Having turned 92 years old at the time of her death, Rishel Kotler "outlived everyone—her doctors, her husband and most of the people who were around at that time."[5]

SILAS'S FOLLY

The miracle of Rishel Kotler's lengthy life despite a grim prognosis is but one of many that shaped Chaya Leah's view of life in Shanghai. More public, and

---

4 Yair Hoffman, "Rebbetzin Rishel Kotler." *The 5 Towns Jewish Times.* July 22, 2015.
5 Ibid.

perhaps more dramatic, was the survival of the Mirrer Yeshiva itself during the war. Much has been written about this institution and how it managed to thrive during the war years in China. The *bochrim* and their rabbis look back at the Mirrer experience in China as a sign of Divine providence and protection. Rabbi Shmuelevitz went as far as to suggest that every day there were more miracles in Shanghai than during the entire Purim narrative, which centers on the salvation of the Jews from the ancient Persian empire.[6]

Listening to Chaya Leah, one comes to sees the China refuge as both divine and supremely human. It was in China that devotion to Torah learning was displayed in all its glory. Rav Walkin, his family, and his friends spared no effort to affirm the importance of Jewish values on a terrain far, far removed from their native ground. This was a striking example of what academic scholars term "agency"—the capacity of an actor to defy circumstantial factors in order to display one's consciousness and thereby effect a concrete transformation in the environment itself.[7]

Simply put, Jewish refugees in Chaya Leah's circle were both changed by China and also changed the world they found there upon arrival from Kobe. In wartime Shanghai, they testified to the truth of an axiom first articulated in the Jerusalem Talmud: *Divrei Torah aniim be'mekomam ve'ashirim be'makom acher*—"Words of Torah are impoverished on native ground and grow enriched in a strange place."[8] In the case of the Walkin family, words of Torah had already been precious back in Pinsk and Radin, where the source springs of wisdom had been constantly irrigated by exemplars such as the Bais Aharon and the Chofetz Chaim. And yet, carrying all that knowledge to China was a challenge that could not have been imagined before 1941. Only in Shanghai during the war did the life-sustaining value of Torah learning become fully apparent, especially since there seemed to be little need or place for it before the Jewish refugees arrived.

The famous photograph of more than two hundred young men of the Mirrer Yeshiva standing and learning Torah in Shanghai brings the ancient maxim from Talmud Yerushalmi to life in a vivid fashion. Here was a strange and unexpected setting: the Beth Aharon synagogue built in 1927 by Silas Hardoon (1851–1931), a thoroughly assimilated business tycoon, in memory

---

6   Chayim Shmuelevitz, *Pirkei Chayim* [Chapters of a Life] (Jerusalem: Yeshivat Mir, 1989), 68.
7   Michael Silberstein and Anthony Chemero, "Dynamics, Agency and Intentional Action," 2011, accessed November 4, 2017, https://www.semanticscholar.org/paper/Dynamics-Agency-and-Intentional-Action-Silberstein-Chemero/7cb6c46b9c5e464bfe60f5a59af982f7e82d2d1f
8   Yerushalmi, Rosh Hashanah, perek 3, halacha 5.

of his father, Aharon. Silas Hardoon himself had no interest in Talmudic scholarship and had died before the war, never imagining that his momentary tribute to his father's Jewish tradition would shelter and enliven Torah learning during the European Holocaust.

As a child, Chaya Leah understood little about the financial and political complexities that enabled the Mirrer Yeshiva to survive. She was an innocent runner of "*lokshen*" to and from the black market, without realizing that this was currency, not food. Looking at the girl who had empathized with the orphaned *bochrim*, who sensed their hidden and not so hidden ailments and grief, she too marvels at the Mirrer Yeshiva photograph. In her eyes, the survival of this singular institution of higher Jewish learning is a concrete testament to a complex tapestry that providence weaves out of the folly of men:

> *The master plan is executed when we do something that is not the norm. We wonder what prompted us to do it. But there is a reason for everything.*
> *Silas Hardoon, who was brought in from Iraq by the Sassoon family to help manage their real estate business, succeeded beyond belief on his own. His personal real estate business grew into a huge enterprise. The Kadoories and the Sassoons built synagogues in Shanghai and Hong Kong in memory of their parents.*
> *The story goes that Silas Hardoon's father appeared to him in a dream and he asked him to build a shul. Silas does not build the shul in the center of town, but way out from the reasonable and accessible location for the public. The shul had two hundred and fifty seats, a huge kitchen, and dining hall.*
> *But the shul was empty for years.*

Chaya Leah's recollection draws upon some of the memoirs written by friends of Rav Shmuel David from the Shanghai years. The details about the number of seats and the two kosher kitchens inside the Beth Aharon Synagogue can be found in other accounts by some of the young men who were in the photograph. The history of the "Baghdadi Jews"—the highly Anglicized elite that accompanied British imperialism into China—is recorded more fully by scholars such as Maisie Meyer, among others. What is striking in Chaya Leah's backward glance is the effort to make sense out of the unexpected turn of events in Shanghai. What she senses as "the master plan" appeared to the child in odd, strange fragments:

> *Silas's folly.*
> *When the Mirrer Yeshiva came to Shanghai, they occupied the shul, which became a beth medrash. There were exactly 252 seats, and exactly 252-yeshiva*

> bochrim. The kitchens were used to feed the needy.
> Is this Silas's folly or is it Yad Hashem?

There is a quality of the fabulous in this recollection, as in the writings of other impoverished refugees who encountered the grandiose wealth of the Sephardi families in Shanghai. One can almost see the little girl in awe of tales told around the family table about the palaces of the wealthy magnates, which her own father visited more than once in an effort to raise funds to help support the Polish Jews.

But there is more here than dazzling riches, and a case of inadvertent generosity that helped to save the entire Mirrer Yeshiva. Chaya Leah, looking back, is asking a profound question. Instead of simply asserting that it was Divine Providence that accomplished the Mirrer "miracle," she tries to fathom more deeply the source and consequences of human action. Like the Sugihara visas, this salvation too depended on doing something that was not the norm. In Chaya Leah's view, it is through human actions that providence is revealed most concretely and most interestingly.

Silas Aaron Hardoon, as Chaya Leah knew even as a little girl, was the least likely benefactor of Torah learning Jews. He, along with his Eurasian wife, Luo Jialing, inhabited the extravagantly posh Aili Garden estate where Buddhist priests and Chinese generals were more likely to visit than any Polish rabbi. Hardoon's philanthropy also extended to children of all races. He and Luo adopted some eleven foreign children, some of them Jewish, who had been abandoned by impoverished Russian families when they fled the Bolshevik Revolution in 1917. Orphans from displaced Chinese families went on to take Luo Jialing's last name. At the time of his death in 1931, Silas Hardoon was reputed to be the richest individual foreigner in East Asia. He owned valuable land along Nanking Road, Shanghai's fashionable commercial thoroughfare, a shopping area comparable to London's Oxford Street and New York's Fifth Avenue.

Hardoon's funeral rites were orchestrated by Buddhist and Daoist clergy. So where did the "miracle" that helped the Mirrer Yeshiva come from? Most biographies speak of a dream that the Baghdad-born magnate had of his parents. Having strayed far from his religious roots, he wanted to do something to appease his ancestors—a thoroughly Chinese and also Jewish act of filial piety. Silas Hardoon commissioned the spacious Beth Aharon synagogue during the last decade of his life and there is no evidence that he ever made any use of this space for Jewish worship. Yet, fourteen years after its completion, when the Mirrer Yeshiva arrived from Kobe, Rabbi Ashkenazi managed to secure the Beth Aharon structure for their learning. Its large, gracious interior became a Beit Midrash—hall of study where words of Torah became more precious because of the strangeness of China and the war roiling loudly outside.

Chaya Leah's question stands: was it folly or Yad Hashem—God's hand in human affairs? Without the need to reference academic theories of agency, her answer is clearly both. We have few means to understand the purpose of our own actions. A glimmer of their significance appears only in retrospect and only when the predictable pattern of events takes an unexpected turn. The fact that Silas Hardoon and Luo Jialing adopted stray children and created a school for them in their ample mansions made "sense." Building a religious structure suited for Jewish orthodox worship did not.

Both as a child and as an experienced Rebbetzin, Chaya does not jump to religious conclusions readily. She remains mindful of the marvels of rescue that marked her family's life and that of the Jewish people. But there is no presumption here—only gratitude and a willingness to allow the retrospective gaze to weave a fabric of meaning out of the unlikely occurrences that dotted life in Shanghai, and beyond.

THE SECRET OF THE JEW'S ETERNITY

Actions that broke the pattern of expectations did not "befall" the community of Torah-observant refugees like manna in the desert. Even as they acknowledged the great help that came through the hands of Chiune Sugihara, Avraham Kotsuji, and Silas Hardoon, it was their own determination to persevere in learning that added meaning to survival. This commitment may be the greatest "miracle" of all—and it was an amply human and most difficult task to accomplish in Shanghai during the war.

Chaya Leah pays tribute to this effort in recounting her own father's Torah studies in Shanghai. Although he was older than most of the single young men who stood so proudly next to their *shtenders* (podiums) in the Beth Aharon Beit Midrash, he was, as his daughter put it: "never without a *sefer* in his hand." Burdened with the responsibility of providing for his family, Rabbi Shmuel David Walkin nonetheless maintained a rigorous schedule of study. Furthermore, he went to great lengths to reprint one of his father's commentaries on the Talmud.

Written under duress and imprisonment in Soviet Russia, Rav Aharon Walkin's work gained yet another life among the refugees in China. Chaya Leah tells the story of this publication with a daughter's appreciation for what was truly at stake in Jewish survival during the war:

My father published my grandfather's sefer, Metzach Aharon in Shanghai. The Pinsker Rov published twenty-three books as responsa to the Talmud. His works are studied and used in the yeshivas of today.

Our grandfather's sefer was published in Shanghai to be used by the bochrim of the yeshiva. We did not have enough money for much, but we spent our money on bare necessities to nourish our body and to nourish our souls.

The seforim were our souls. The Torah our guide to living, a blueprint for life. We shared our food to nourish the body. We shared our seforim to nourish the soul. Simple. We made life simple and meaningful. That was the key to our survival. Achdus. A community. A group of friends with the same goals. One helping another. One loving the other unconditionally.

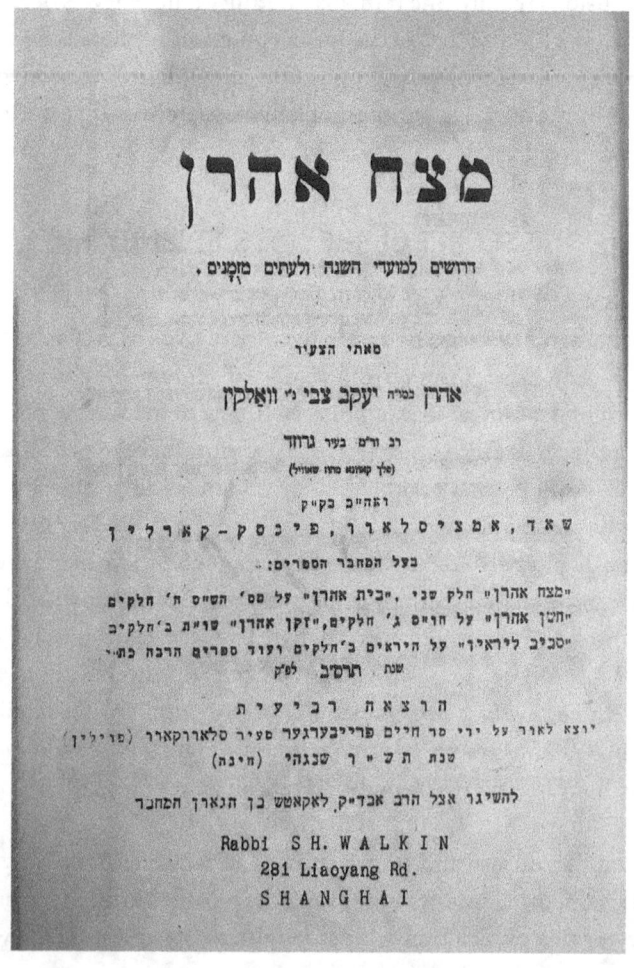

Metzach Aharon, writings by Rav Aharon Walkin, the Pinkser Rav reprinted in Shanghai during the war by his son, Shmuel David Walkin.

Here, we have the crystallized essence of what survival meant in Shanghai for Chaya Leah and her family. Unlike the more numerous and more impoverished German refugees, they had not come to Shanghai with *Kultur*—with a worldly sense of personal accomplishment and entitlement. Reduced to penury, many intellectuals from Berlin and Vienna had to sell their books in China simply to eke out a living in the crowded *heims*. They had to fight each other for food and jobs. By contrast, the Polish refugees came as a community and maintained a strong sense of religious solidarity. The books they carried and reprinted with great effort were not for personal enlightenment and social prestige. The *seforim* represented a gateway into the *mesorah*—a lineage of learning in which one's own name mattered less than what was conveyed forward in time by generations of previous scholars and teachers.

Rabbi Shmuel David Walkin, mindful of his father's importance in the world of Talmudic scholarship, chose to use the limited material resources in Shanghai in order to keep his commentaries alive in the refugee world. Long before he heard about his father's death, *Metzach Aharon* had to be printed in China. The title of the book calls to mind not only the first name of its author but also Aharon, the Kohen Gadol, the high priest who wore a special plate of gold upon his forehead—his *metzach*. Upon this plate were engraved the words that took on new meaning as Torah study deepened in Shanghai: *Kodesh l'Hashem*—'Holy to God.'

This was a mission statement not only for one individual but for an entire people. Upon Aharon's forehead lay the burden of keeping holiness alive for the entire nation of Israel. *Metzach Aharon*, as stated in the book of Exodus, was to be an eternal testament of Jewish sanctity. Translating that testament into action was the daily challenge faced by Rav Walkin and his fellow refugees during the war years in China.

The cover page of the volume printed in Shanghai lists the Bais Aharon's other works and gives the date of publication of this particular edition as 1944. This was the year during which the fires of the Holocaust continued to rage across Europe. In March 1944, Germany occupied Hungary. By May, the Nazi regime (aided by local fascists) started the deportation of 440,000 Hungarian Jews to Auschwitz, my grandparents among them. Shanghai, by contrast, was a place where Jews found both life and purpose. As Chaya points out, here the soul was nourished and consciously involved in creating meaning out of sheer survival. Rabbi Shmuel David Walkin was furthering Torah education at his own expense. His own name and address—281 Liaoyang Road—is given at the bottom of the frontispiece. The book was available to all who needed it.

Metzach Aharon was far from the only book published in Shanghai during the Holocaust. According to a list compiled by a London antiquarian firm, there were over one hundred volumes of Hebrew-language texts that were printed in Shanghai and survived from the period between 1941 and 1946. These volumes range from tractates of the Talmud through Mishnah, studies of Mussar (Jewish ethics), and Chassidut (such as the "Tanya") and much more. No area of Jewish learning was too distant during the darkest hours of the war. If Jews could learn, then learn they must. That was the article of faith in Chaya Leah's community.

A list of books, however, does not capture the soul-nourishing exaltation experienced by those who finally had access to sacred texts in China. David Mandelbaum, author of *From Lublin to Shanghai*, describes the wonder of discovering one of the commentaries of the Gerrer Rebbe, the Sfat Emet (1847–1905), on the Mishnah of *Seder Kedoshim*. It was the winter of 1943, when two bedraggled refugees found themselves in a large university library in the northwest city of Harbin. Here, they glimpsed the unexpected text that made the world of Torah left behind even more precious in their eyes:

> How did the holy *sefer* reach this far flung place? Who would have expected to find a volume of Sfas Emes in China? Wishing to spare the *sefer* disgrace, they placed it into one of their bags and slipped away from the university with their find.[9]

Stealing a book from the university may not have been the most ethical action at that time and place, but even in this theft, one senses the fierce need to accord respect to the work of Jewish sages. This *sefer*, once ferreted back to Shanghai, was reprinted with the permission of the Gerrer Rebbe. In the midst of all the refugee worries about daily survival in Shanghai during the *Shoah*, a telegram came through authorizing the rebbe's followers to republish this book.

By far the most public celebration of Torah scholarship took place in Shanghai on May 5, 1942. The day was *Lag B'Omer*, recalling the passing of Rabbi Shimon bar Yochai (a sage who lived in the second century CE). In Europe, the mass murder of the Jews had begun in earnest. In one Belarus hamlet called Dokshitz, the Nazis chose this holiday for taking large numbers of Jews to a nearby ravine and killed them all. In Shanghai, by contrast,

---

9 David Mandelbaum and Yechiel Benzion Fishoff, *From Lublin to Shanghai: The Miraculous Exile of Yeshivas Chachmei Lublin* (New York: Mesorah Publications, Ltd, 2012), 187.

a large celebration was organized in honor of the first reprinting of 250 copies of *Masechet Gittin*—the tractate of the Babylonian Talmud that the yeshiva students had been studying at the time.

Among those making special remarks at the gathering in the Russian-Jewish Club were Rabbi Meir Ashkenazi, Rabbi Chaim Shmuelevitz, and Rabbi Shimon Shlomo Kalish, the Amshenover Rebbe. Such an event had been literally inconceivable a year before. Kobe had been a temporary stopover. It was the prolonged duress in Shanghai that unveiled both the great need and great enthusiasm for Torah scholarship among the refugees.

Here, in the middle of the worst war that had befallen world Jewry, rabbis and their students began dancing because of the reprinting of an ancient text. As one Polish journalist noted:

> One who did not witness the Amshenover Rebbe and Yeshiva students dance at receiving this marvelous gift, has never seen true Jewish joy or felt the secret of the Jew's eternity.[10]

Like Mark Twain in his famous 1899 essay in *Harper's Magazine* entitled "Concerning the Jews," this journalist was also seeking the source of Jewish endurance. Mark Twain phrased his question as sharply as Chaya Leah's inquiry into Silas's folly: "All things are mortal but the Jew; all other forces pass, but he remains. What is the secret of his immortality?"[11]

In Shanghai, as Chaya Leah recalled so poignantly, the answer was *seforim*. The Amshenover Rebbe, like Rabbi Walkin and the leaders of the Mirrer Yeshiva, was treated with the respect given to a Torah scroll. Each person who embodied and passed on the legacy of learning had a share in *Metzach Aharon*—each had earned the title "Holy to God." A tireless commitment to conveying the teachings of Jewish tradition made each teacher and each book an active force in shaping meaningful survival in China.

Another fount of continual inspiration for the Torah community in wartime was the rhythm of the holidays. In additional to the weekly preparations for Shabbos, which included the effort to buy and defeather a chicken, there were the ceaseless preparations to be carried out in honor of Passover and Sukkot. In many of the memoirs penned by the yeshiva community, preparations for Pesach are mentioned because they were so daunting under difficult circumstances.

---

10 David Kranzler, *Japanese, Nazis & Jews: The Jewish Refugee Community of Shanghai, 1938–1945* (New York: Yeshiva University Press, 1976), 434.
11 Mark Twain, "Concerning the Jews," *Harper's Magazine* (June–November, 1899), 67.

As with Torah learning, the effort to continue the rigorous observances that had been maintained back in Poland and Lithuanian cost more in Shanghai—both in time and money. Yet, in the circle of Rabbi Walkin and his family, there would be no compromise. As Chaya Leah recalls, one of the most time-consuming efforts centered around making their few cooking utensils fit for Passover use:

> *We had one soup pot and a fendele, a small frying pan, and also the shishel (little pot), which was used for almost everything. Several pieces of silverware. None of them matched. One sharp knife, bare minimum. When the pot would get a hole in it, there was a Chinese man or a Jewish man who walked up and down the streets hawking this business. They filled the hole with tin or steel. We fixed everything that was broken. Nothing was ever thrown out even when we were ready to change the chometz items and make everything pesachdik. In the front yard of the Ohel Moishe, there was a huge cauldron with hot water. We tied up our flatware with string. We also tied up our pot with string, then we climbed up on a chair and dropped the utensils into the hot water. When ready, we pulled out the string. Voila! We had our Pesach-koshered pots. Many times, the string got loose and pots or silverware fell to the bottom. Then came the panic that these valuable possessions might be lost.*

Clearly, the Walkin family was not alone in trying to make a few utensils usable for Passover. The fact the Rabbi Ashkenazi organized the large pot of hot water in the courtyard of Ohel Moshe suggests that there were many other Jews seeking to keep this daunting holiday in wartime China. Those who could not make their own utensils kosher made use of the soup kitchens that provided matza and Passover food.

Chaya Leah's recollection of the panic that struck when the koshering string broke betrays the child's fear of not measuring up to adult responsibility. It is also a statement of plain fact about the few dishes the family could use. Looking back at the scarcity of kitchen utensils, Chaya Leah allowed herself a certain irony that places poverty in a more gilded context:

> *Thinking about our luxurious kitchen and dinner utensils, I remember when a few Jewish soldiers of the American military came to visit in China, and my mother was showing off her pot with all the patches and some of the silverware. She innocently asked them:*
> "Do you have such items in America?"
> "No," they answered.

Chaya Leah's humorous and self-conscious look back at koshering dishes for Pesach does not diminish the hard work involved.

Clearly, the community had a central focal point: the giant pot in the courtyard of Rav Ashkenazi's shul. The fragile string holding up a small possession can be seen as a symbol of the effort involved in preparing for dignity of the holiday. One can picture the child on the chair peering into the boiling water, feeling responsible for each fork and knife. Mrs. Walkin's much-patched pot was not an object of pride. It was necessity that endowed these daily objects with their value, not unlike the books reprinted at considerable cost.

Maintaining a traditional Jewish life in wartime China was a most important calling for Chaya Leah and her family. Two pieces of Chinese cloth speak volumes about the ways that the Walkin family and their friends scrambled to find local items in order to make Passover special. The commitment was not only to the observance of Torah commandments (such as not eating leavened bread) but also to *hiddur mitzvah*—to beautifying observance in the best way possible given one's strained circumstances. These bits of local art, as Chaya Leah recalls, had been used to wrap up the special part of the matza that concludes the Seder:

> *The two little rags framed in the master bedroom were a gift to me in a suitcase that came from Europe to Shanghai and then to America. They were used for the afikomen. It was wrapped in those little shmatkeles.*

These two bits of cloths, these *shmatkeles*, brought honor to the Seder table in Shanghai and now grace Chaya Leah's home in Chicago. Even in China, the design on these fragments of fabric would be considered special: two decorative urns and two pagodas framed by pine trees and blue cliffs draw our attention to aesthetic details.

To be sure, these *shmatkeles* were not expensive silk or hand-painted works of art. They were made of simple local cotton. But they were special because they had been bought locally to augment the beauty of the Passover table. They beckon one to enter another world, one in which Chinese art helped to enrich Jewish observance of the Torah. Like so many of Chaya Leah's more recently acquired, more expensive Chinese vases, jars, cabinets, and jewelry boxes, the two pieces of cloth convey a longing to adorn what is most precious in Jewish tradition with what is most elegant in an Asian idiom.

In addition to playing her part in Pesach preparations, Chaya Leah also recalls Purim at the Hardoon synagogue and Sukkot when children marched with flags and apples as they once did in Radin and Pinsk. These Jewish holidays brought together different parts of the Jewish community in Shanghai. There were at least three different communities joining forces during these celebrations.[12] Samuel Iwry called them the "*drei kehilos*" in an essay penned in Shanghai during the war years. In this work, the future expert on the Dead Sea Scrolls paints in vivid colors the cultural differences between the wealthy Sephardim, the impoverished, more secular German refugees and the Torah-observant rabbis and their students from Poland, Russia, and Lithuania.

One of the reasons that these disparate *kehilos* did not sever their ties to each other was that Rav Ashkenazi was a benefactor who was able to draw support from all three. With his tact and effective fundraising, he could paper over some of the differences that divided fellow Jews in Shanghai. In survivors' memoirs of the war years in China, this one rabbi appears again and again as the key figure in creating the "crook of the rock" that sheltered the vulnerable "dove."

Rav Ashkenazi had been sent to China before the need for refuge even emerged in the Jewish world. Once the stateless Jews poured into Shanghai, he embraced the responsibility of providing each community with some of their needs. If they were able to flourish at all (and they all did, differently) their "songs" were enabled by the sheltering he provided.

TZELEM ELOKIM

Chaya Leah's recollections honor Rav Ashkenazi's unifying influence, especially in bringing together refugees during Purim and Sukkot. These holidays of joy softened the cultural divide somewhat. For Chaya Leah, as a child, what lingers in the mind is not only the communal delight. There is also a thread of darkness that colors her description of these holidays during the war years. Looking back, a little girl who reached early adolescence in Shanghai recalls witnessing the death of one of the yeshiva students right before the holiday of Sukkot:

> One Succoth, we put up our own temporary Sukkah next to the watchman's home. We were so proud with all the junk that the bochrim had collected. It was a feat to be able to build a Sukkah in wartime Shanghai.
> One of the bochrim suggested that we put in a light. He went off to find an electric wire. I do not remember what happened exactly. But there was an accident, and he was electrocuted.

---

12 Iwry, *To Wear the Dust of War*, 167.

> *The shock and pain was felt by all. I remember going to his levaya (burial). He was covered in a cloth and put on a cart. The bochrim pulled the cart to the cemetery, and many refugees followed the procession crying.*

The memory of this one death remains firmly in the mind for the eldest daughter of Rav Shmuel David Walkin. To be sure, Chaya Leah knew that many other Jews died in China of hunger and disease. But this one death left a deeper impact.

There is a list of 1432 recorded deaths of Jewish refugees in Shanghai between January 1940 and December 1945 still extant at Yad Hashem—the Holocaust Memorial Authority in Jerusalem. On that list, German names dominate by far. Yet, for Chaya Leah, it was the electrocution of one Polish yeshiva student that became a memorable event. This death took place in her family's courtyard. No sooner was the precious mitzvah of putting up a Sukkah actualized in wartime China, one young man ended up paying for its illumination with his life. Electrocution must have been a grim sight for the young school girl. Equally unforgettable was the honor accorded to the funeral by the local people:

> *Chinese were standing on the side of the road watching with respect. Our watchman followed the procession since the tragedy had happened right near his home. His wife was sitting by the entrance as usual, crying. At the age of ten, this was my first exposure to a funeral and the pain of loss.*

Here, a ten-year-old girl who had already seen dead bodies on the streets of Shanghai allows herself to feel the grief in a fresh manner. This was not just one more casualty of China's poverty. The young man had most likely been invited in for tea by the Walkin family. He was trying in his way to add the luster of electricity to the commandment of dwelling in booths, even in a place and time where permanent dwellings were not much better than the huts had been used by Jews in the desert after the exodus from Egypt.

The *bocher*, who knew Torah sources well, seems to have been less well versed about the laws of electricity. It must have been terrifying for the little girl to see him fall, to see the shock on adult faces. Being allowed to go to the *levaya*, the burial, must have been a privilege of sorts. The child became part of the grown-up community of mourners. From that vantage point, her eyes followed the other yeshiva students carrying their compatriot to the Jewish cemetery of Shanghai.

Some of these places for burial in China had been established before the refugees arrived in the late 1930s. Russian Jews who had fled the pogroms of the late nineteenth and early twentieth century established in Shanghai a *Chevra Kadisha* (Sacred Burial Society), which maintained two cemeteries, the oldest being on Baikal Road. In 1940, the *Judische Gemeinde* (Communal Association of Central European Jews) established their own cemetery on Columbia Road. Another cemetery on Point Road was established in the late 1930s to accommodate the large increase in deaths among Jewish refugees.

Lists of the dead, such as the one at Yad Vashem, cannot convey what the child's eyes glimpsed on Liaoyang Road. In addition to the shocked grief of the adults, Chaya Leah recalls the respect of the Chinese watchman and the tears of his wife. They had been close by when the electrocution happened. Without fully grasping the dark shadow that now engulfed the holiday of Sukkot (also called *z'man simchateinu*—the season of our rejoicing), they empathized with the grieving Jews. This basic humanity became increasingly important to Chaya over time, long after leaving Shanghai. Being an unfeeling bystander was not her way, nor that of the Walkin family, nor that of the Chinese watchman and his wife. A core value bound them all—one that Torah Jews call respect for *tzelem elokim*, the image of God in man.

The biblical narrative of creation was familiar to the Jewish refugees in China. *Tzelem elokim* was a difficult concept to fathom, and it was even harder to pay homage to in the horrifying, nearly inhuman circumstances of the refugees' ordinary lives. Both Sigmund Tobias and Samuel Iwry write about their loss of faith in the godly image on the streets of Shanghai. For Tobias, it was the relentless brutality and poverty of daily life that corroded any notion of the inner sacredness of man. Samuel Iwry writes that he began to doubt his faith as soon as news of the *Shoah* began to seep into the already violent world of Shanghai. If men could do such awful things to their fellow beings, why bother holding on to sentimental assertions about *tzelem elokim*? It had been trampled into nonexistence and there was no point in creating a glow of affection around this mud-encrusted image.

In Chaya Leah's world, by contrast, there was a conscious effort to both maintain and honor the image of God in man. The simple yet honorable burial of one yeshiva student, of course, could not erase the cruelties perpetrated upon so many human beings, both Chinese and Jews. Yet, one moment in time did make a difference. Placing the body of one young Torah scholar into the soil of war-torn China remained as a marker of what is possible even under great duress. The effort to make sure that the burial took place according to Jewish values represents a conscious commitment to keep the idea of *tzelem elokim* alive for all those accompanying the cortege.

Another example of the effort comes across in a directive to the yeshiva students by Rabbi Yechezkiel Levenstein (1875–1974). Born in Warsaw, he had studied in the great yeshivas before the *Shoah*, including in Radin under the Chofetz Chaim. In Shanghai, among the refugees, Rav Levenstein was considered the foremost *mashgiach ruchani* (spiritual mentor/supervisor/counselor) for the Mirrer students. In order to keep alive *tzelem elokim* in his pupils' minds, he forbade them from riding rickshaws. To be carried on the backs of other men was, in his view, a way to demean both the Jewish rider and the Chinese coolie.[13] This sensitivity may have also been the reason that Chaya Leah's family did not allow her to ride rickshaws as well.

While almost every refugee in China, including some Mirrer students, had a photograph taken alongside a rickshaw, the exoticism of the experience was clearly frowned upon in the Torah community. There was something higher at stake, even in China—*especially* in China—that must not be desecrated. Chaya Leah came to understand this even without sitting in the same study hall as her father and the yeshiva students. Her family's values and behavior set a high standard. This carefully cultivated awareness of the sacred image embedded in each and every human being is something that Chaya Leah continued to impart to her children and grandchildren after the war. It was one of the hard-won gifts carried from Shanghai to Chicago.

A PAINTED POT WITH FLOWERS

It was, however, not the only gift. The commitment to see and honor *tzelem elokim* also thrived in Chaya Leah's world through friendships that crossed religious and cultural boundaries. Even though the child's everyday world was framed by the rabbis and their families on Liaoyang Road, this was not the only reality that Chaya Leah cherished. Among the visitors and friends invited into the Walkin home were also secular German refugees. In addition to the nanny who worked for her meals, Chaya Leah was especially moved by one painter, Max Heimann. Born in 1909, Heimann had attended the Academy of Fine Arts in Berlin. Upon graduating from this distinguished school, he became head of the Art Department of two different high schools until he was forced to leave Germany in 1939. Max Heinmann's next eight years were spent in Shanghai, where he gained a reputation as a portrait painter, receiving many commissions from the foreign residents—including Rav Shmuel David Walkin.

---

13 Mandelbaum, *From Lublin to Shanghai*, 245.

Chaya Leah was twenty-five years younger than Max Heimann, who lived next door on the Street of Exuberant Vigor. The fascination of the child for the artist was augmented by an early interest in painting. Although Chaya Leah did not pick up a brush until many decades after Shanghai, her recollection of the artist beckons me to accompany her beyond the learning-laden landscape of childhood in Shanghai:

> Vera, you know where I really want to take you? Let's go to the house next door. On the second floor, in a tiny room lives an artist, his wife, and sister-in-law. They have no children. All day he sits and paints. I don't know if he is good or not but it is so nice to see what he creates. I can watch him for hours, sit there quietly and watch. Vera, we will sit on the floor and watch him create beauty. Someday I, too, will want to paint.
> I will go to school and study hard.
> I will.
> Vera, we will ask him to make us a flower. He will, and his wife will smile and tell us to take good care of it. She will love us for coming.
> The buildings where they live have all German Jews and there are no children there.

I follow Chaya Leah's trail into the studio of Max Heimann because I am deeply taken by the gift of the flower painting she evokes here. The same child who greeted vendors in her family's courtyard and shouldered the responsibility of making dishes kosher for Passover found a soul reprieve among the German refugees next door. Here, she found time and space to simply sit still, to watch beauty created one canvas at a time. Just as the brutality of war increased in China, Chaya's appreciation of art deepened.

Looking back, she sees with the clarity and empathy of age that the presence of a well-behaved religious child in the home of childless German refugees was experienced as a momentary blessing. Max Heinmann's wife is imagined retrospectively as a loving woman who more than tolerates a little girl's presence in her husband's studio. Beyond all these imaginings and recollections stands the gift of art itself: a small painting of flowers in a tin pot. It is not a large canvas and it does not immediately command attention when I enter Chaya Leah's gracious dining room in Chicago. Yet, once I know its provenance, my eyes will not leave the vibrantly reddish painting honored here with a fine, simple black frame.

Max Heimann's skill comes through in a simple composition: a metal pot with zinnias, most them orange and red. The dish could well pass for one of Rebbetzin Walkin's patched cooking utensils made to glisten through the careful use of light and shadows. The flowers arching out of the tin are not the expensive kind, like roses or peonies. They are blossoms of the field, perhaps a nod to a countryside left behind or still greening in the German refugee's memory as he faces war in Shanghai.

They are common zinnias stretching their stems in all directions, filling the canvas, one even bending down like a Chinese dragon's head. This rhythmic evocation in red, green, silver, and gold added a touch of nonutilitarian beauty to the Walkins' one- room home on Liaoyang Road. With the aid of this one painting, I am able to picture the "crook of the rock" in more vivid colors than before. Refuge in China was not always, or even primarily, bleak. There were "doves" to be seen and heard in the least likely places.

This extra dimension of art beyond familiar books and old-world words was deemed by Chaya Leah's parents to foster a sensitivity to *tzelem elokim* as well. Even as a child, Chaya Leah understood that something beautiful could humanize the heart, could peel away some of the coarseness so amply evident on the streets of Shanghai. Yonia Fain was another artist who moved in and out of the Walkin circle. Born in 1913, Fain came from a family that had fled from the Bolshevik revolution by moving to Vilna in 1924. Having developed his artistic skills in Paris and in Poland, Yonia Fain also escaped from the Nazi threat with the aid of a Sugihara visa, much like Chaya Leah and her family.

In Shanghai, Fain also made ends meet by painting portraits of the Polish refugees. From May 31 to June 15, 1942, during the same period of time that Masechet Gittin was being reprinted and celebrated in the Yeshiva community, Fain had a solo exhibition at the Russian Jewish club in Shanghai. The dancing *bochrim* might have even noticed his finely crafted pencil drawings on the wall. Without the lush colors and classical depth of Max Heinmann's gift to the Walkin family, Fain's art nonetheless testifies to the survival of the human spirit: "They did not destroy us. People risked their lives to live their values and engage in humane acts. This was a triumph in the face of evil." (Fain testimony, Yad Vashem).

As a young child in Shanghai, Chaya Leah sensed this triumph of the spirit in the studio next door on Liaoyang Road. Here, beauty continued to be created despite deprivations and uncertainty. As a married woman, Chaya Leah would try her own hand at painting, creating images that added color and light to a home built on old values and new hopes. This became her way of continuing the nourishment of the human spirit that refugee artists such as Heimann and Fain had already captured in Shanghai.

Drawing of Rabbi Shmuel David Walkin

At the request of Benny Fishoff, a German painter named Ernst Handel did a portrait of Rabbi Shmuel David Walkin during the war. Born in Vienna, Handel, too, had escaped to Shanghai by 1939. While there, he made his living taking commissions from fellow refugees. Although his post-war paintings of the cable cars in San Francisco have gained more fame, one small sketch from China tells a deeper story.

This portrait of Rav Shmuel David Walkin in pencil captures the focused effort required to keep on learning Torah in Shanghai. Multiple dense strokes bring to life the bearded figure bent upon a book, his large brow furrowed in concentration. Here, too, a golden light surrounds the central subject, much like the zinnias in Chaya Leah's Chicago dining room. In both of these works of art, what matters is not what the painting is about. Instead, what shines through is the determination to glimpse and to create beauty during the most inimical times.

Secular German artists such as Handel and Heimann did not follow the religious codes that guided Rav Shmuel David Walkin and his family. Yet, their training in art sufficed to evoke with vivid sensitivity the gravitas of Jewish life even in wartime China.

HEILIGE CHOLENT

David Bloch, another refugee artist in Shanghai, used a less luscious palette to evoke the search for *tzelem elokim* in a world in which there seemed to be none. Born in 1905 in Bavaria, Bloch had been interned in Dachau after Kristallnacht. Miraculously released, this German artist also made his way to Shanghai in May 1940, much like Chaya Leah's neighbors on Liaoyang Road. In China, David Bloch paid close attention to the hardship endured by fellow refugees through numerous photographs and sketches. One of Bloch's most famous works shows a displaced person named "D.P.NOBODY" sitting over a suitcase marked simply "ANYWHERE." This black-and-white drawing captures the despair of being spewed out of all the nations of Europe, a predicament also evoked powerfully in the Eisenberg poem.

The face of this refugee is hidden, unlike that of Rabbi Walkin, which is clearly open and focused upon a book of Jewish learning. Yet, the bent back of the nameless Jew, like the bearded rabbi, conveys a call to conscience addressed to an unfeeling world—here is a man worth taking seriously, worth protecting if only one could rouse the heart of the world enough to care.

Back in Germany, another older artist named Felix Nussbaum created yet another kind of testimony to the human spirit. Born in 1909, he was unable to escape the Nazi atrocities like David Bloch, Max Heimann, and Ernst Handel. Arrested in Belgium as a "hostile alien," Nussbaum was eventually deported to

Auschwitz and killed along with his parents and wife in 1944. The paintings he left behind, however, speak volumes about terror and hope alike.

One of his moving images is entitled simply "Fear," which shows the artist trying to protect a young woman who eventually became his wife. Worried eyes and veined hands encircle the face of a bride trapped beneath a darkened street lamp. Even more than Chaya Leah's flower painting or the portrait of Rav Walkin learning Torah in Shanghai, this image begs for some acknowledgment of the Godliness in man despite the daily brutality of death.

This kind of terror was not the common predicament of Jewish refugees in Shanghai. They endured hardships, to be sure. But these were bearable and could even be gilded by the grace of an artist's brush. What could not be papered over, however, was a feeling of resentment that some Jewish refugees lived better than others. The flames of this acrimony between secular German refugees and the community of rabbis and students from Poland and Lithuania have been fanned by the scholarly literature after the war.

Ephraim Zuroff's work has garnered the most attention in this contestation. In one public discussion of the yeshiva students' regimen in China, Zuroff exclaimed: "Why did they not close their Gemaros in Shanghai?"[14] The very text that appears so enlivening in Ernst Handel's sketch of Rav Shmuel David Walkin is deemed by Zuroff to be a screen against the pain of others. Immersed in traditional Jewish learning, the yeshiva community is described by him as "selfish" and "particularistic."

Chaya Leah's recollections do not diminish the gulf in living standards between the more unified yeshiva community and that of the more divided and more impoverished German refugees. She knew only too well that her family's one-room home and private oil-can "stove" afforded them more comfort than was possible in crowded *heims* of the Hongkew ghetto. Even as child, she senses that chicken for Shabbos was almost unheard among the secular German Jews. The gulf was real but not as unbridgeable and as unfeeling as Zuroff implies.

Reports of the meals served to the yeshiva students led some nonreligious parents such as those of Sigmund Tobias to send their sons to be educated by the refugee rabbis. In addition to another meal a day, the boys got a glimpse of the values and learning that lay behind the tomes depicted in Handel's painting. Chaya Leah's family did not view German Jews as less human than the yeshiva *bochers* who came for solace and sustenance in their home on Liaoyang Road.

---

14 Jonathan Rosenblum, "Anatomy of a Slander," *The Jewish Observer*, August, 2005.

Indeed, the *bochrim* were entrusted with the special mission of carrying on Torah traditions that were deemed to be the foundations of communal and family life for all Jews. But this calling did not dull their sense of responsibility for fellow Jews. In fact, it was supposed to make them more keenly aware of the pain of others. Thus, during the time of the greatest food shortages in Shanghai (from late 1942 to early 1944), Rabbi Walkin and the Amshenover Rebbe took the lead in opening a soup kitchen for German and Polish refugees alike.[15]

Both communities were hungry. Both needed help. Rav Walkin and the Rebbe worked hard to make sure that the food was kosher and especially available on Shabbat. This brought a measure of shared benefit for secular and religious Jews alike. Chaya Leah recalls one of her mother's stories about eating a Shabbos meal along side nonobservant refugees as follows:

> Food conditions were dire in Shanghai and we did use soup kitchens too.
> One Shabbos, we were sitting at the table when we overheard a German couple.
> The wife prompted her husband saying:
> "Hans, setzenauf deine Kippa. Der heilige cholent wird nun serviert jetzt."
> (Hans, put on your head covering. The holy stew is being served to us soon.)

This talk of a "holy" Shabbos cholent may have been ironical. Putting on a head covering—a kippa—in this soup kitchen may have been simply a gesture of acquiescence to the expectations of the rabbis who both provided and served the kosher food in war-torn China.

Yet, one senses something more in Chaya Leah's recollection. The German couple was sitting nearby. Like the Walkin family, they were hungry. Maybe they did not observe all the stringencies of the Shabbat as Rav Shmuel David did. But they were all Jews sharing a special day during which food was meant to nourish body and soul alike.

Dr. Robert Reuven Sokal was eight years older than Chaya Leah in Shanghai. Although they never met in China, the bond between Chaya Leah and Sokal's son in New York runs very deep. Born in Vienna in 1926, Robert Sokal attended St. John's College in Shanghai and became a noted biologist in the United States after the war. He raised two children literate in Jewish tradition and learning with a Chinese wife. She chose to embrace the faith of a German refugee who had little Torah exposure before his arrival in Shanghai.

---

15 Mandelbaum, *From Lublin to Shanghai*, 214.

During interviews, Dr. Sokal had emphasized positive memories of his encounters with religious youths in Shanghai:

> There for the first time I learned to speak Yiddish, there I learned about Zionism, there I learned about Torah observances for the first time.[16]

The boundaries between Chaya Leah's world and that of Robert (Reuven) Sokal were not as firm and as high as some would depict them after the war. There was affection, respect, and sheer material need that brought together Torah-observant rabbis (and their families) with the more secular German refugees. There were also love affairs that blended these separate worlds.

One memory that Chaya Leah recalls with extraordinary sensitivity to the feelings of German Jews is that Hilda, whom the children of the Walkin family kept calling "the *Daitshke*—the German lady." This young woman married Yosele Eisenstein, one of the boys who was a religious Polish refugee. In an email entitled "That scarlet word" Chaya Leah acknowledges that in her Shanghai childhood, a Yiddish diminutive for Yosele's bride had caused enduring pain:

> *Hilda never got over the fact that we children called her Daitshke. So many years and she still feels the same. I think what must have happened is that we were so excited to meet her and Yosele, that as we saw her coming, not knowing her name, we knew she was a daitcheke, so we announced it as a welcoming gesture.*
> *I remember often when we had guests we would anxiously wait outside and then ran into the house with the news of the arrival of our guest.*
> *Listening to Hilda's tapes remembering Shanghai, I can tell her pain is deep…*

Here, a little girl who grew up in Shanghai is making retrospective amends to the young woman who felt labeled and reduced somehow when coming to the home of religious Polish refugees.

Children everywhere learn to note and name differences between themselves and others. In Shanghai, where the mélange of different Jews was palpable, the Walkin siblings understood that Yosele's bride was German, like the painter next door. They had not meant to demean Hilda, but clearly she felt

---

16 Vera Schwarcz, *Bridge Across Brsokomoen Time: Chinese and Jewish Cultural Memory* (New Haven, CT: Yale University Press, 1999), 184.

aggrieved at the very moment that she was being drawn deeper into the Torah community of her groom.

Being sheltered in the crook of the rock was, thus, no simple affair. Yes, there was a sense of protection and even exuberant affirmation of Torah and culture during the war years in Shanghai. At the same time, there were serious and often painful differences among the Jewish refugees who crowded together around the impoverished area of Hongkew. Some families were marginally better off than others, and that tiny margin loomed large in the perception of those who had to make do with less. Even among the children, there were different ways to show one's visage, sing one's song.

Chaya Leah's recollections invite one into the disparate worlds in which her father managed to publish the *Metzach Aharon* while the childless German couple next door barely eked out a living. Yet, the painting of the flower pot and the sketch of Rav Walkin bent in concentration over an ancient text suggest a crossing of boundaries and a willingness to build up Jewish life despite the hardships of exile and war. More than that, they reveal how it is possible to live creatively upon a soil that appeared at first so inimical to the refugees' survival as Jews.

CHAPTER 6

THE VINE HAS BUDDED:

Schooling, Bombings and Beyond

> *I went down to the walnut grove*
> *To see the new green by the brook*
> *To see if the vine has budded,*
> *If pomegranates were in flower.*
>
> Shir Ha'Shirim 6: 11

1943, the year in which Chaya Leah Walkin turned nine years old in Shanghai, was not a good year for the larger Jewish community that lay beyond the protected courtyard on Liaoyang Road. The Warsaw Uprising was brutally crushed by the Nazis during the same Passover season in which Chaya Leah was learning how to kasher household utensils in the cauldron of hot water in Shanghai. The deadly famine in China showed no signs of diminishing as winter turned to spring.

In Washington, DC, politicians debated the course of the war while turning a deaf ear to news of the extermination camps being set up in Europe. Debates in Congress focused on the repeal of the Chinese Exclusion Act of 1882, which had limited the number of Chinese laborers coming into the United States. As part of America's deepening alliance with the Nationalist regime of Jiang Kai-shek, this legislation was overturned in May 1943, along with the unequal treaties forced upon imperial China during the second half of the nineteenth century. The United States was focused upon war with Japan, not the rescue of persecuted Jews.

Rabbi Stephen Wise (1874–1949), a key advisor to Franklin Delano Roosevelt, was fully aware of the plan that spelled certain death for his coreligionists in Auschwitz-Birkenau and other extermination camps in Europe. Nonetheless, Wise supported American policies preventing aid to those trapped in occupied countries—which included the Japanese-occupied territories such as Shanghai. Rabbi Wise's famous (and some would argue infamous) "Dear Boss" letter addressed to FDR in December 1942 sought to bring the plight of the Jews to the president's attention in an understated tone full of concern for larger issues: "I do not want to add an atom to the awful burden which you are bearing with magic, and I believe heaven-inspired strength at this time. But you know that the most overwhelming disaster of Jewish history has befallen Jews in the form of the Hitler massacres."[1] Clearly, Wise understood the magnitude of the threat yet chose to place his faith in FDR's magic—which delivered no salvation for the Jews.

Outraged by the lack of response from the US government, the leaders of the Orthodox Jewish community organized the only public protest against the Holocaust to take place in Washington, DC during the war. On October 6, 1943, three days before Yom Kippur, Rabbi Kalmanowitz and 400 other rabbis walked from Union Station to the Capital and then to the White House. In addition to Psalms, the Rabbis recited Kaddish for their murdered brethren in Europe and sang the Star Spangled banner.

FDR and his close advisors refused to meet with the delegation. Stephen Wise, who had fiercely opposed this public demonstration, refused to give any credence to the bearded men with their covered heads. He reacted with anger, as if too much visual evidence for the old-fashioned values of Torah Jewry had spilled into the modern capital of a nation at war.

In China, at the same time, life for Jewish refugees also took a turn for the worse. Pressured by their Nazi allies since November 1942, Japanese authorities felt compelled to do something about the large number of "enemies" of the Reich who had found shelter in the alleys of Shanghai. The result was the February 18 declaration outlining a "Restricted Sector for Stateless Refugees," known in Japanese as *mukokuseki nanmin gentei chiku*. All those Jews who arrived after 1937 were given three months to move their residences and business into the tightly controlled area of the old Chinese city known as Hongkew.

Most of the German refugees were already cramped into this impoverished section, which was both the cheapest and dirtiest part of Shanghai. Nonetheless, their predicament worsened as many more Jews were forced

---

1   Young, Dwight, ed. "Stephen S. Wise to Franklin D. Roosevelt," in *Dear Mr. President: Letters to the Oval Office from the Files of the National Archives*, ed. Dwight Young, 70–71 (Washington, DC: National Geographic).

to relocate into this neighborhood. Food shortages became ever more acute and the terror of being monitored by Japanese authorities also increased over time. While there was never barbed wire around the so-called Hongkew "ghetto" (as later Chinese paintings would suggest), the area bounded by Yangtze Poo Road, Chow Foong Road, and Point Road became a hellish place for Jews who had managed to avoid certain death in the Europe they left behind.

Liaoyang Road did not become part of the "Designated Area for Stateless Refugees." As a result, the Walkin family continued life in their one-room home, along with the neighbors and friends who surrounded them at number 281 on the Street of Expansive Vigor. Nonetheless, the deprivations and fears of fellow refugees became their daily fare as well. Their names appeared on the same list as that of thousands of other Jews who lived a few streets away in the congested alleys of Hongkew. One such record survived the war, which lists Chaya Leah and her kin as numbers 8875, 8876, 8877, 8878, and 8879. This list contained the family name, the locality, and year in which the stateless person was born and place of origin before arrival in Shanghai. The order of listing was from youngest to oldest; thus, "Wolkin Mojzesz" was listed first as having been born in 1938 in Lakowcze. Esther came next, born in 1935 in Troki. Chaja Leah—number 8877—was listed as born in 1934 in Pinsk. Cyla Wolkin's number was 8878 and the record indicates that she was born in 1913 in Troki. Szmul Dawid Wolkin, number 8879, was listed as having been born in 1900 in town of Gruzd.

We may never know who decided on the spelling of the place of origin and the names of the stateless refugees listed along with Chaya Leah's family. What is amply apparent in this fragment of history is that there were many different kinds of Jews lumped together by the authorities in Shanghai and that their very multiplicity afforded some breathing room in the most difficult of times. Homogeneity was neither conceivable nor enforceable in Japanese-occupied Shanghai despite the February 18 declaration outlining a single area for all stateless refugees who sought to escape from the Nazi war machine.

Each family, each person, contained seeds of hope. Each embodied some potential for flourishing that went far beyond the sequence of names attached to 8875, 8876, 8877, 8878, and 8879. Unlike the numbers burned into the flesh of Jews in the concentration camps, this record marked one for life. Using the words of *Shir Ha'Shirim*, one can imagine even such a listing of refugees as a walnut grove by a newly greening brook—a manifesto of potential flourishing despite surrounding circumstances.

The Vine has Budded: Schooling, Bombings and Beyond • CHAPTER 6

Initial Bais Yaakov group in Shanghai, Chaya Leah Walkin second from the right in front row, ca. 1943.

In the imagery of Solomon's poem, this season is not quite ripe for fulsome growth. Nonetheless, the beloved casts an eager glance upon each grapevine and each pomegranate tree. Chaya Leah Walkin turning nine years old in China during the *Shoah* was one such "vine." Despite all the deprivations of war, she went to school and survived bombings and the harsh restrictions imposed upon the Jews in the Hongkew ghetto. She came more and more alive, budding into a teenager, as verdant in her promise as the landscape of a walnut grove.

One photograph stands out in all of Chaya Leah's recollections as a concrete reminder of vibrant growth in Shanghai during the war. It shows the largest collection of friends and neighbors in Shanghai. Twenty-one adults and children are lined up in front of the bomb shelter in the front yard of 281 Liaoyang Road:

> My favorite picture is the shelter.
> You see the rites of life: We are all alive in this picture, standing in front of our shelter. This was to be our final resting place, to be used as the bombs fell.
> We built our own graves, no carts carrying off the bodies.

> We see mothers holding new babies, the future.
> We see pregnant women—the hope of a future.
> We see children, babies, and teens—life.
> We see the Orthodox Jews and we see the Austrian and German Jews together.
> All the people are from the complex.
> Unity, achdus.

In Chaya Leah's recollection, life towers over death—just like the children in the photograph who are standing behind the adults. They embody a ray of hope against the despair of war. Chaya is the tallest among the children while Rebbetzin Walkin appears in the very center of the adults. Rav Shmuel David Walkin, with the longest graying beard, stands at the far left wearing a striped robe.

The memory of unity is crucial for Chaya Leah as she brings the photograph to life. Here is a clear image of a greening brook despite the hardships and enmities of war. Among the six women, two are German refugees sporting an upward coiffed hairdo. The three rebbetzins in the photograph all have covered their hair. One is holding a toddler and two are pregnant, including Tzivia Walkin.

Here is visual evidence for the budding vine. This flourishing of life underscores the real meaning of refuge in Shanghai, along with the eight children standing on the top of the shelter. These offspring, like the women's bellies, testify to a herculean determination to bring new life into the world despite the difficulties encountered in Shanghai.

But there was more to this portrait of rounded bellies than a dutiful observance of Torah laws. It represents an affirmation of the expanded definition of "survival" that came to include the intentional flourishing of Jewish life during and after the war. These families also suffered shortages of food, though not quite as severe as that of the German refugees. In addition to slightly better nourishment, Chaya Leah's neighbors benefited from a collective support network. They were like a ripening pomegranate seeded with hope for a future that was still unfathomable during the hardships they shared in Shanghai.

Yet, this future had to be grasped nonetheless. Bearing children, educating them in both Torah and secular subjects, was a high priority for parents who were determined to see the "ripening of vines" along the Whampoo River. Their efforts and faith call to mind the greening brook celebrated so eloquently in the verses of *Shir Ha'Shirim*.

The King's English in Shanghai

Chaya Leah's education during the war in China benefited from visionary efforts started even before disaster struck the Jewish communities of Europe. In Kobe, she was one of the few foreign children sent to a Japanese school. It was a temporary solution for refugees who sensed that their time in Japan was going to be limited indeed. Even though the six-year-old child was too young to fully understand that this was a temporary respite, Chaya Leah's retrospective delight in educational morsels garnered in Kobe reveals that she understood the preciousness of this moment in time.

Refuge in Shanghai, by contrast, lasted during the entire war with all of its uncertainties and daily dangers. The little girl who neared adolescence during the five years that the Walkin family lived on Liaoyang Road knew that schooling in Shanghai was meant to build enduring skills. Not surprisingly, attending classes became a matter of routine expectations in which learning Chinese had no place at all. Furthermore, Chaya Leah was but one among hundreds of Jewish children who had to be educated in wartime China. With the aid of existing institutions and new philanthropic enterprises, Chaya Leah Walkin not only survived but also came to learn what she called "the King's English."

Her first experience with schooling after Japan was in the Shanghai Jewish School, which had been established in the early twentieth century by the small Ashkenazi community of Russian Jews. By 1932, the school was moved from the crowded area on Dixwell Road next to the newly established Ohel Rachel synagogue. This was a gracious structure completed in 1921 by Sir Jacob Elias Sassoon in memory of his wife Rachel. Like the more posh Beit Aharon (which became the Beit Midrash of the Mirrer Yeshiva), Ohel Rachel served the Sephardi community and the larger Jewish public as well.

Chaya Leah Walkin arrived in 1941 to an institution that was once considered the best educational stepping stone for Jewish children in Shanghai. It had originally been designed as a very modern building with a well-equipped laboratory. By the time Chaya Leah was enrolled, however, the rapid expansion of the refugee population had overwhelmed Shanghai Jewish School (SJS) both with the numbers as well as the health issues of its students.

Horace Kadoorie (1902–95), one the most renowned members of the Sephardi community, visited the SJS in February 1937, even before the mass arrival of German and Polish refugees. This budding industrialist with a strong social conscience was appalled when he found that the children were malnourished and plagued by tuberculosis as well as having almost no opportunities for employment after graduation. To remedy the disaster, the Sephardi businessman first started a "Jewish Children's Fresh Air Camp," which developed into a new school closer to the Hongkew area.

By 1943, there were some seven hundred Jewish children studying in the Kadoorie School, with Chaya Leah Walkin among them. In one of the surviving photographs from this educational institution (also known as the Shanghai Jewish Youth Association School), we see a classroom of children of mixed ages (Figure 2). The desks are simple and the children appear well dressed for this photo opportunity. Boys are sitting on one side, girls on another. A male teacher seems to enforce order on the boys' side while a woman dressed in a formal suit is supervising the girls. She might well have been Eva Schulhoff, the German refugee pedagogue who was Chaya Leah's favorite teacher.

The faces of the children are rather indistinct, but the girl sitting upright with eyes focused forward was much like Chaya Leah Walkin—eager to learn and mindful that she had to be an exemplar of the religious community in this secular Jewish school.

Children attending the Kadoorie School.

Looking back at herself as a student in the Kadoorie School, Chaya Leah does not dwell of hardships of war. Instead, what vivifies the voice of a child eager to learn was the high expectation of her rabbinical family:

> I loved school. I loved English as a second language. The school was a template for the British style of education. Our classes were called: Form I, upper or lower, Forum II, etc.

> We had to call our teachers ma'am or sir. We had to sit very straight in school or the teacher walking down the rows of desks would walk by and tap you with a ruler so that you had to sit upright.
>
> If you needed to get the teacher's attention, you did not raise your hand and wave it, but you put your elbow on the desk, and raised your arm in the upright position and waited patiently for the teacher to call you.

Here, we hear the oldest sibling among the Walkin children describe an orderly universe quite unlike the one on Liaoyang Road. In this classroom, Chaya Leah is not the innovator of games for little children. Here, she is not the girl who helped to clean chickens and to make kosher the pots for Passover. Here, she is a refugee from Poland who understood the good fortune of a British-style education that had fallen upon her during hard times:

> Our curriculum was very advanced.
> At ten or eleven we were doing trigonometry, algebra, and world history. Sports were very important and we had relay racing, soccer hockey, and croquet. Gymnastics were important. The whole school was encouraged to participate. Healthy body, healthy mind.
> We did have to take class in penmanship.
> And, of course, we eventually wrote in ink with an inkwell in our desks.

In Kobe for a few months, Chaya Leah Walkin had picked up an Asian calligraphy brush. That aesthetic experience lingered as an exotic memory in contrast to the rigors of penmanship that had to be mastered in the Kadoorie School in Shanghai.

Rav Shmuel David's daughter also took delight in the sports that were mandatory. Croquet and gymnastics had not been part of the regimen for Jewish children on Liaoyang Road. Yet, these became part of Chaya Leah's routine, opening new vistas much like the teachers who hailed from a world rather distant from that of the Polish refugees:

> We respected our teachers, and honored them. My favorite teacher was Eva Schulhoff.
> A teacher can make or break a child.
> I also remember my French teacher. His flair, his love of the language, French. The romance of the language, the love of his accent and pronunciation.

I forgot almost all the languages I spoke, but not French. When I hear French, my heart lifts.

Another teacher would walk up and down the aisle with a ruler, and would slap our hands with the ruler to discipline us. I wanted to laugh, but I had to use a lot of self-control. To me it was so funny.

To be educated at the Kadoorie School was to be exposed to the King's English. My classmates in America would make fun of my choice of words.

I felt insecure with my language and my clothing. All I had was hand-me-downs. I just felt I did not belong.

These recollections reveal both the delight as well as the insecurities that plagued a young girl among the other refugee children at the Kadoorie School. Rav Shmuel David's daughter was learning French and the King's English, while also being aware that she was different from other, more secular, students.

Her plain clothing stood out not only because it came from others, but because it marked her as an "other"—a rabbi's child who had to work hard not to laugh aloud at disciplinary measures that were not used in the Walkin family. Upstairs on Liaoyang Road, little girls might be forced to swallow unpalatable food, but Chaya Leah herself was used to a gentler touch.

The Kadoorie School in Shanghai made Rav Walkin's daughter more aware of where she came from and awoke in her a love of learning that endures to this day. Chaya Leah's last report card from "Form V" in China testifies to a hard-won excellence. She received 100 in Arithmetic and Dictation, 95 in Hebrew language, and 96 in Scripture while her conduct is inscribed as "very good." From this, we can see that Jewish subjects were also included in the Kadoorie School curriculum and that Chaya Leah excelled beyond the subjects conventionally expected in rabbinical families.

Chaya Leah's love of learning, once awakened in Kobe, became deepened in Shanghai. It continued as a passion into her married years. Even after she became a mother to five children, she was determined to get a bachelor of arts degree—which she did in June 1975 from Mundelein College, a women's Catholic institution in Chicago. From Shanghai's Jewish schools, Chaya continued to carry high expectations for reading and writing in English. Looking back, she is eloquent in describing the joys of a child who had been released from the enclosed world of Liaoyang Road. In school, it was expected that Jewish children would learn croquet, soccer, practice calisthenics, and compete in relays. Little feet trapped in ghetto apartments could be stretched and utilized in the

Kadoorie School even as correct British pronunciation was being demanded and enforced.

Lotte Lustig was a young woman who had also attended the Shanghai Jewish School. Being seven years older than Chaya Leah Walkin and a German refugee, Lotte's experiences and recollections were vastly different. Being a teenager, Lotte was acutely sensitive of the embarrassments that plagued the refugee community. She tried to avoid speaking in German at all costs, as if it were a "contaminated language and one had to be constantly on guard, fearful of its power"[2] Chaya Leah, by contrast, continued to speak in Yiddish even as she was learning to master the King's English at the Kadoorie School. It was, and remains, for her a link to the deepest layers of Jewish life both in Europe and to her family history as well.

Lotte Lustig's recollections of the school in Shanghai are also more attentive to differences among the various populations of coreligionists. Chaya Leah simply felt as an outsider in her hand-me-downs. Lotte, being older, was keenly aware of the low status indicated by her patched clothes:

> In class, we both mixed with and were segregated from a bunch of Russian, Lebanese and British children from India and Hong Kong, or the Crown Colonies, as they said. They endured our presence, our accents, our strange looks, our knickerbocker pants and Drindl dresses. Petite Esther Ashkenazi had a Rabbi for a father. She had 'class.' And Mark Tukachinski, a White Russian immigrant's kid was rich! We whispered to each other how many servants lived in his house. I was dying to be invited to a party, but the invitation never came.[3]

Chaya Leah Walkin was also never to be invited to rich immigrants' parties. Not only because she was a little girl, unnoticed by the boys and not only because she kept kosher and her parents would not sanction such an outing. It seems that she never hankered for the "class" that her family did not have. Being herself a daughter of a rabbi, Chaya Leah was part of the same crowd as Esther Ashkenazi, an older classmate she, in fact, knew well. Young as she was, Rav Shmuel David's daughter knew where she came from and she knew it was an honorable place to be cherished even in the impoverished circumstances of wartime China.

---

2   *Die Ersten Achtzig Jahre* [The First Eighty Years: A Birthday Tribute to W. Michael Blumenthal] (Berlin: Jovis Berlin, 2005), 41.
3   Ibid., 42.

Lotte Lustig's father had struggled very hard for a living and died in Shanghai in March 1945 from kidney cancer. Chaya Leah Walkin, by contrast, grew up with the protection of her father and even celebrated the birth of a new brother after the war. Life and death had very different meanings for the younger Polish refugee and for the pain-seasoned teenager from Vienna. Yet, for both of girls, the leap into the King's English was a world-shaping event. As Lotte recalls so eloquently:

> English was our academic and social 'Open Sesame.' Within six months of the school year, I passed our first grammar test. We stopped dropping English words into our German ("All right!" "So Long!") and instead dropped German words into English. ("Das war doch ganz klassisch'). I began to dream in English and when I could spell words like 'necessity' I was in heaven.[4]

For Chaya Leah, as for Lotte Lustig, mastering English in wartime China had opened new vistas, new dreams. Chaya Leah's vistas remained firmly framed in the world of Torah learning, which was the core of her home life. Expelling Yiddish from her vocabulary was not a priority. Maintaining an outward sense of being "classy" (*klassisch*) was also out of the question because of her age and background.

The "King's English" was thus more than a means of escaping the nightmares of refugees' history. In the Walkin family, it also became a tool for reconnecting with relatives once thought to be lost in the Shoah. Shortly after the war, Rabbi Walkin learned that his eldest brother's sons were alive in South Africa. Letters in English began arriving in Shanghai from Sima Valkin (one of these surviving relatives). Chaya Leah was the only one who could read these precious words. As she later recalled:

> *I was the interpreter and writer between my parents and Sima.*
> *I would read his letter, and then write what my dad wanted me to write.*
> *The simcha in the house when I came back from school and a letter was waiting for me!*
> *I took center stage.*

The family's joy (simcha) was made possible through their eldest daughter's talents. She became a key figure in reweaving fragments of the Walkin world after the war by virtue of the English she had learned in Shanghai.

---

4   Ibid.

ZAIDE YAAKOV PLANTED THOSE HUGE TREES

Lotte Lustig, by contrast, recalls how she and her friends fought the label of "refugee." Chaya Leah Walkin, embedded in a community where everyone had been on the run since the Nazi invasion of Poland, understood that home was any place where Jews could continue to learn and practice Torah. The experience of being cast out of different countries was seen as part of a larger Jewish history in which exile and redemption played powerful roles. While Chaya Leah also felt opprobrium at the Kadoorie School for her shabby clothes, she could also use her language skills in communicating with long-lost cousins in South Africa. In Shanghai (as later in life), she was proud of her identity as the little girl born in Pahost. This pride anchored her firmly onto the shores of early adolescence. Its religious roots were reinforced with the establishment of a Bais Yaakov school for girls during the war in Shanghai.

Religious education for young boys had been established immediately after the arrival of the Mirrer Yeshiva in Shanghai. The *bochrim* and some of their teachers became mentors to a Yeshiva K'tana—a full-time school for children under the age of bar mitzvah. Some of the students, such as Sigmund Tobias, transferred into the Mirrer school less out of love for religious learning and more because the food at the Yeshiva K'tana was better. One of the surviving photographs of the boys' school is dated 1944 and shows a group of thirteen pupils of mixed ages. At a time when Jewish children were being gassed by the thousands in Auschwitz, these students in shabby pants, worn shirts, and ill fitting jackets stand proudly in front of four Torah teachers—young men who were themselves struggling to stay alive while at the same time pursuing advanced studies in the Talmud during the war.

Plans for a girls' school also started to develop soon after the Mirrer Yeshiva arrived in Shanghai in the fall of 1941. One of the founders of this institution, Yehudit Cohn Goldbart, recalled how posters bean appearing in Hongkew during the holiday of Sukkot inviting mothers to a meeting intended to explore a new kind of education for their daughters. Interestingly, these meetings were held mostly in the German refugee areas, in the crowed *heims* that dotted Ward Road, Chaofoong Road, and Wayside Road.

Perhaps there was no need to make an argument for a Bais Yaakov school on Liaoyang Road, since the rabbinical families were already familiar with the innovative educational initiative pioneered by Sarah Schenirer (1883–1935) in Poland before the war. Long before the Nazi invasion, this modest seamstress became aware of the dangers faced by Jewish girls who were being sent to public schools. While the boys had been benefitting from the high level of Torah studies available in yeshivot, young women were being left without a strong foundation in Jewish learning.

Rebbetzin Tzivia was clearly an exception to this pattern since she had an excellent background in both secular and religious studies. It did not take much to persuade her to seek a similar education for her daughters. The Kadoorie School was more than adequate for general learning. The newly established Bais Yaakov of Shanghai provided an anchoring in Torah knowledge and values that was deemed necessary for a Jewish woman who held the spiritual future of her family in her hands.

Holocaust researcher Dovid Roidel, who edited Yehudit Cohn Goldbart's memoir about the Bais Yaakov in Shanghai, concludes the volume with a suggestive essay about the visionary effort entailed in cultivating giant trees. Without referring of *Shir Ha'Shirim*, this conclusion also pays tribute to the flourishing of Jewish life in China during the war. Going down into the walnut grove to see the ripening of grapes and pomegranates bespeaks an eagerness and love for Jewish learning. Similarly, Roidel points to the Jewish experience after the Exodus from Egypt, when Jews are suddenly called upon to build a tabernacle for the divine. Where are they to find the giant pillars for this structure? According to the midrash, the third patriarch of the Jewish nation had the foresight to plant seedlings even before the need arose:

> Imagine the scene during the darkest days of Egyptian slavery. A father and son drag themselves out of backbreaking labor. As they trudge along, the father whispers: *Son, do you see those huge trees? The Zaide Yaakov planted them so we could build a home for the Shechina when we leave this place!*[5]

"Zaide Yaakov," the grandfather of all Jews, is portrayed here as the visionary who understood the spiritual needs of his descendants long before they were deemed worthy to build a structure that would house the divine spirit in the desert. The giant trees, like the ripening vine and pomegranates, call to mind a conscious preparedness for the challenges and opportunities that lie ahead.

---

5   Dovid Roidel, *A Bridge Between Two Worlds: Bais Yaakov in Shanghai through the Experiences of Yehudith Cohn Goldbart* (Brooklyn: Kleinman Holocaust Education Center, 2014), 52.

The genius of Sarah Schenirer was to envision a Torah education guided by older teenagers and unmarried young women who could serve as teachers and mentors to younger girls. After opening the first full-time religious school for Orthodox women in Krakow in 1917, Schenirer had the seeds ready for her own giant trees. When graduates of the Bais Yaakov system arrived in Shanghai in 1941, they carried with them from Poland Sarah Schenirer's commitment to provide Jewish girls with the kind of religious education that would sustain a lifelong identity, much like that of yeshiva-educated boys.

Residents of 281 Liaoyang Road ca. 1944

The Walkin family, which had always valued education for women—as embodied by Tzivia Walkin herself—was among the first to enroll their daughters, Chaya Leah and Esther, in the Bais Yaakov of Shanghai. Unlike the Yeshiva K'tana however, this was not yet a full-time school. As Chaya Leah recalls:

> On Shabbos, we got dressed up in our Shabbos clothes and went to one friend or another, or we went to the little park. The older girls had a Shabbos meeting, and classes. That group eventually became our Bais Yaakov. It started as a Shabbos afternoon group meeting that developed into a school. The teachers

> were young girls, all volunteers. The Bais Yaakov School was held in the afternoon after the Kadoorie School. Everybody was welcome.

Chaya Leah's recollection emphasizes the gradual evolution of religious education for girls in Shanghai as well as the effort to make it nonsectarian. At first, there was no conflict between going to Bais Yaakov and to the Kadoorie School. On Shabbat afternoons, the girls wore their best clothing and so the embarrassments of the secular Jewish school were diminished. Classes and discussions revolved around the subjects that girls were conversant with from home. Friendships developed as older girls, such as Esther Bakst, became full-time mentors to the younger children. In a world in which the word "refugee" carried such burdensome connotations for Lotte Lustig and her friends, Chaya Leah found reassurance and enduring friendships.

In one of the surviving photographs of the Bais Yaakov institution in China taken shortly before the Walkin family left Shanghai, we see more than one hundred young girls gathered in a Hongkew courtyard. Two of them hold up a hand-lettered sign in Hebrew proudly proclaiming the name of their school. The girls holding the sign sit at the feet of five women, clearly their teachers. Unlike the shy, disheveled boys in the Yeshiva K'tana photograph, this large gathering is a vivid evocation of an encompassing commitment to the Torah education of women during the war in China.

The girls are also of mixed ages and a close look reveals that there are great differences among them: some are dressed in well-fitting sweaters and coats while many more wear odd looking socks, worn shoes, and overly baggy dresses. A dozen or so girls greet the camera's eye with an expected smile. The rest, scattered in the crowd, can be seen frowning, looking to the side, mostly inward and sad. These girls may have suffered starvation and even the loss of a parent. Their future was uncertain. Yet, here in Shanghai, during part of each week they had found community and gained some of the skills and knowledge needed to rebuild Jewish life after the war.

CHAYELE MAYN KIND, IKH HOB DIKH GERATEVET

The girls in the Bais Yaakov photograph, including Chaya Leah Walkin, were like a pomegranate already seeded but not quite ready to eat. Their Jewish education was a promise hurled forward in time from a painful past toward a more promising future. Yet, the past was not over, not even after 1945 when the war ended. The children's eyes betrayed shadows of fear and trauma that would take years to overcome. While the girls photographed in the large Hongkew courtyard were safe for the moment, their memories of bombings lingered vividly in their minds. In our conversations, Chaya Leah circled back to those memories with reluctance as well as the need to finally give voice to buried fears.

As the oldest sibling of the family and one of the oldest children in the Liaoyang Road compound, Chaya Leah was expected both to comply with the air raid protocol and to ensure that the other children were shepherded to safe spaces as well. The air raid bomb shelter in the front yard looms large in her recollections. The photograph with all the children and the pregnant women testifies to the hope that remained verdant despite the constant threat of death. Chaya Leah also was aware that other families had to rush to nearby public shelters, such as the local jail. The worst choice was some fragile doorway or a muddy half-basement. It all depended where one was standing when the siren shrieked.

The bomb shelter in the backyard of the Liaoyang Road compound did not only serve as backdrop for the moving photograph of life flourishing in the midst of distress. As Chaya Leah describes it decades after the war in China, it was also the dark cave in which families faced their darkest hours:

> Air raids were not unusual, both day and night. At night, we had to blacken our windows and all lights were extinguished. Although my father was a heavy smoker, he did not even dare to light a match.
> When the air raids came, we would run into the shelter or a safer place was the jail down the street from us. We could see low-flying planes.
> We could see bombs falling. When an air raid was sounded while in school, we knew the drill.
> The air raids also came during the rainy season. Because Shanghai is a delta, water levels are high.
> When we did not have a chance to run to the jail, we ran into the shelter in our yard. As we were standing there, the water started to rise and rise, but we stood there as the water rose, till the air raid was over.
> I was so scared of drowning that I don't remember if they were bombing or not, all I knew was the rising water in the congested shelter.

The child who turned nine years old in 1943 was familiar with the air raid drill from school. In the safety of teachers who imparted the King's English, algebra, and French, fears could be tamed, organized somehow. Practicing those drills was another form of calisthenics, and the pupils fell in line as expected. At home, away from the orderly routine of the Kadoorie School, Chaya Leah experienced a dread of drowning in the rising water of their private shelter. The jail, made of cement, was above ground. But getting there on time was not always possible. So Chaya Leah crowded in with other neighbors in the cave during Shanghai's rainy season, expecting to die.

Inside the shelter that figures so prominently in her favorite photograph from the war years in China, Chaya Leah also picked up the terror of surrounding adults more keenly. Here, the experience of bombings was augmented by an older dread carried from worlds left forcibly behind:

> *The air raid is blasting away. This was one of the most haunting sounds in Shanghai.*
> *When we heard it, we all started running into the shelter.*
> *When I heard that shrill howl, I knew it was a scary day.*
> *People were saying tehillim (psalms) and crying in the shelter.*
> *The women were holding their babies and crying. Little kids were saying the only prayer they knew: "Shema Israel."*
> *Smaller ones were saying "Modeh ani" and the letters of the aleph beth.*
> *I can still hear in my mind the littlest children saying aleph, beth, gimel, daled, over and over and over.*
> *A consoling sound.*
> *We reached out for yeshua (salvation) any way we knew how. The shelter was not only for the religious Jews who lived in our house. It was for whoever needed shelter.*

Here, Chaya Leah is looking back at formidable fears that marked her childhood years in Shanghai. Yes, there was a flourishing of life in the bomb shelter photograph. But what that image does not convey, Chaya Leah's words paint with the staccato rhythm of a child's endless dread.

The water level rising, the little children screaming, the "*Shema*" prayer mouthed by those who had learned it and the simple cacophony of the Hebrew alphabet from the little ones who did not even know the morning blessing called "*Mode ani.*" While nonreligious Jews also found shelter in the back of the Liaoyang Road compound, it was the voices and the values of the Torah-educated refugees that ring out loudest, at least in Chaya Leah's memory.

"*Yeshua*" was sure to come. That was an axiom of the community surrounding the Walkin family. The adults and children alike were familiar with the text of the *Megilat Esther* in which Mordechai tells the Jewish Queen that salvation for the Jews will come no matter what. The only question was whether Esther was going to play her part in the momentous plan. The little children who cried out in the crowded shelter understood that they were part of the salvation and added their voices to the adults' prayer. They had been well loved and well trained. The outcry of babes, from the time of *Megilat Esther* to Shanghai, was assumed to be more effective than all the petitions of more learned adults.

For Chaya Leah, one of the most terrifying moments in the bomb shelter had been buried until an encounter with Rebbetzin Rishel Kotler in the United States. The young woman who had been living with Rabbi Ashkenazi and who had been so ill in Shanghai was by then an aged rebbetzin, the matriarch of a distinguished family of Torah scholars in the Lakewood, New Jersey Yeshiva community. Chaya Leah, who had her own children and a prominent role in the Chicago Jewish community, made a point of visiting her childhood friend after she became a widow in 2011.

Rebbetzin Kotler, being older than Chaya Leah, had traveled the pathways of widowhood earlier and was eager to provide comfort to her friend by sharing memories of Shanghai. Among them was a day of childhood trauma that Chaya Leah had forgotten:

> *Most of what I dreaded, I have tried to forget. Like the reason I never wanted a pet. Rishel Kotler, who had been a young bride in those days, recalled for me one of my childhood traumas. After my husband passed, I visited Rishel in Lakewood and shared with her my loss. She saw my pain and difficulty. It reminded her of an incident during an air raid in Shanghai. I had totally blocked this out of my mind.*
>
> *"Chayele, mayn kind, ikh hob dikh geratevet."*
> *Chayele my child, I saved you.*
> *She, and the Master of the Universe, I now understand better…*
> *From the opening of the shelter I ran out to save my katzele, my scrawny little cat that was wandering outside.*
> *Rishel ran after me, grabbed me and struggled to get me back into the shelter. I only wanted to save my kitten.*

> *I do not remember what happened.*
> *But trauma lingers. From that day on, I never wanted a pet.*

The loss of a kitten in the midst of war may seem like a small matter to adults. But for Chaya Leah, the child, it was catastrophic. Rishel, the older girl, had been a witness to the depth of attachment the little girl had expressed for that animal. She pulled Chaya Leah back into the shelter just as she launched herself outward to save her pet.

That gesture and that moment saved Chaya Leah's life. Calling the incident to mind many years later was meant to give the widow of Rabbi Small some comfort, some hope. And it did. At the same time, it opened up a long buried box of grief. Chaya Leah had lost her husband and she also now understood why she never could befriend a pet after the war. Losses piled upon losses, with salvation clearly manifested in the gesture of a friend. Chaya Leah had been spared injury. With life thus regained came the challenge of crafting meaning out of all the other moments of *"yeshua"* that marked the years in Shanghai, as well as all those that followed as well.

TAKASHI VERSUS "THE WILD RAT" GOYA

For Chaya Leah Walkin, as for all the Jewish refugees in Shanghai, life became much harder after February 18, 1943. Once all the Shanghai newspapers and radio stations made a special announcement concerning the order to move stateless refugees into the restricted area, all Jews felt more vulnerable. With one stroke of the pen, the supreme commander of the Japanese naval forces in China had declared that those who had arrived after 1937 would now have to crowd into a small area along the banks of the Whampoo River. The Japanese declaration left little room for maneuvering. Jews were expected to restrict themselves both for residential and business purposes to the alleys bordered by the International Settlement Road. To the west of Hongkew, the boundary was limited to the Yangzhou River and on the east side the refugees were not supposed to cross George Seward Road (now East Changzhi Road).

How much did the nine-year-old Chaya Leah understand about these restrictions? Certainly the word "ghetto" was not a common parlance in the Walkins' community. Later, after the war, it would always point to some place in Poland, Ukraine, or Belarus, where members of the family were murdered. For Rav Shmuel David's family, the epicenter of this enduring grief would be the Pinsk ghetto, where his father—the Bais Aharon—had died in January

1942 and to a forest outside of Vilna, where his brother Chaim Walkin and his family were murdered trying to escape toward Palestine.

News of these deaths did not come into the Liaoyang courtyard in the winter of 1943. Although the house at number 281 remained officially outside of the restricted area, its inhabitants were sorely limited in their efforts to see doctors, donors, friends, and business associates outside of Hongkew. Chaya Leah's Kadoorie School was also close to the border of the newly restricted area; thus, children did not have to face additional checkpoints along the way. The slowly evolving Bais Yaakov had already been housed in the courtyards of Hongkew; thus, their Shabbat gatherings and afterschool learning were not affected by the Japanese order.

The group that was most indignant about these restrictions was the Mirrer Yeshiva. Its students received residence relocation orders while, at the same time, they were allowed to continue their studies in the Beth Aharon synagogue with daily passes. Given that most of the students were single men, the plan called for them to be relocated into the rather shabby Salvation Army building in the heart of Hongkew. This plan, however, met with active resistance. On May 18, 1943, five months before aged rabbis marched down the streets of Washington to protest the lack of American support for Jews condemned to be murdered in Europe, a group of yeshiva students stormed the offices of SACRA (Shanghai Ashkenazi Relief Association) to defy the relocation orders. In a world in which options for Jewish "agencies" were becoming fewer and fewer, these young men who had escaped from Vilna with the Sugihara visas discovered the potential of collective action and disobedience.

While in Europe the Judenrat and the Kappos were unable to defend fellow Jews and often not even their own families, in Shanghai a group of young Torah scholars managed to create enough havoc to be able to continue living and studying as they had before the Japanese order of February 1943. The locale of resistance was the Jewish organization charged by the authorities to implement Japanese policies in the occupied city. On May 18, a group of Mirrer *bochrim* marched into the SACRA offices and made it clear that they would refuse to move into what they believed were disreputable and unusable quarters.

Unwilling to be placated by Jewish clerks urging them to bend into the new situation, the yeshiva students smashed some chairs, causing a ruckus in a place of quiet compliance. Like the rabbis' march on Washington, this was the only public protest against the Nazi-inspired policies in Shanghai as well. In wartime China, however, unlike in FDR's America, these boys succeeded in their protest. They did not move into the Salvation Army building in Hongew and continued their daily Torah studies with the aid of special permission documents.

News of the disturbance at the SCARA spread like wildfire in the refugee community. Some, like Samuel Iwry, remembered the Mirrer protest as a show of arrogance and sense of entitlement.[6] Ironically, some of the same accusations would be hurled at the old rabbis marching in Washington as well, who were also deemed overly unruly and particularistic in drawing attention to the plight of their brethren being murdered during the *Shoah*. In contrast to Iwry, Shoshana Kahan, the secular Yiddish theater actress (who had no particular reasons to sympathize with the religious Torah students), viewed the protest of May 18 as nothing short of a "revolution":

> Today was a huge scandal in SACRA with the yeshiva students, all because of the ghetto and the scarcity of rooms. The students demolished the place and thirty-three of the Yeshiva students were arrested.
> The sadists prepared for them the "Salweishan," a camp for Chinese hooligans—thieves and criminals who were released from jail.
> The yeshiva students were opposed to this and didn't want to go there. They insisted that they will rent apartments with their own money because they must study and cannot sit in such a dilapidated house. It didn't help. The Japanese did not withdraw their demand and the order was not changed. Therefore the yeshiva students went to SACRA, whose job it is to move the refugees into the ghetto. (In the SACRA office) sat the bandit Tsutomu Kobuta very calmly… surrounded by the Jews who were quivering before him.
> The yeshiva students staged a revolution, they broke everything they found and the wealthy (Jewish) inhabitants spared no money and effort to suppress the story. With the help of the "revolution" the students did not go to Salweishan. The (Jewish) inhabitants prevailed upon the bandit Kubota to rent apartments at their own expense.
> The students were the heroes of the day. All Shanghai talked about the "revolutionaries."[7]

Here, we see an appreciation of Jewish "agency" in very difficult circumstances. Shoshana Kahan's diary depicts a more vivid, more complex scene than Iwry's

---

6   Iwry, *To Wear the Dust of War*, 115.
7   Eber, *Voices from Shanghai*, 111–12.

condemnation of the Mirrer Yeshiva's so-called arrogance. With the seasoned eye of a stage manager, the Yiddish actress recalls vividly the Japanese official ensconced in the offices of the Jewish aid agency. It was defiance that mattered and the yeshiva students were deemed brave.

As in European ghettos, the draconian hand of the oppressor was never far behind those "natives" in charge of implementing their murderous policies. In Shanghai, it was not a death sentence that the Torah students had faced. It was simply being shoved into close proximity to Chinese criminal elements in the "Salwaishan" camp. What was at stake here was not life itself, but the dignity of Torah, which these young men have been groomed to embody even before they had lined up to received the Sugihara visas in Kovno. Less than three years after demonstrating extraordinary resourcefulness in Lithuania, the Mirrer *bochrim* managed to maintain their daunting schedule of learning by remaining outside the Honkgew restricted area.

Chaya Leah was too young to have any direct contact with the Japanese Chief Director of the Shanghai Bureau of Stateless Refugees. However, she did get to know several other Japanese officers who were in charge of their neighborhood after 1943. The child's impressions of these men who were familiar figures on Liaoyang Road was markedly positive when compared to Kahan's indictment of the "bandit Kobuta." The few months that the Walkin family had spent in Japan left Chaya Leah with warm, indeed nostalgic, memories of order and cleanliness. Furthermore, gratitude to Sugihara was never far from her mind, especially as she looked back upon her family's survival after the war years in China. Sugihara remained an enduring symbol of a great salvation, while other smaller gestures of Japanese generosity surfaced from a childhood left behind:

> Acts of kindness do not have to be monumental or the outcome overcoming insurmountable obstacles.
> A single, simple action carries huge consequences. I learned this in Shanghai.
> It was on a day in which I was sick, running a fever. In our pre-penicillin years, nothing seemed to work.
> We had a young Japanese soldier named Takahashi who frequented the area. Someone told him that we were in need of some strong medicine.
> Many of us spoke Japanese because we had spent a year in Japan. We went to Japanese schools, had lots of Japanese friends, and had studied the language. The hospital was not far from our home, and Takahashi was a frequent visitor to that hospital. The next day after hearing that I was sick, Takahashi came

and handed my father a bottle. It contained sulfur. We used it for ear infections and a few days later I recovered from my pain. I have never forgotten Takahashi's kindness.

Chaya Leah's recollections of the young, plain-faced officer are filled with gratitude. Here was yet another Japanese helping hand to echo the kindness of Chiune Sugihara and Setsuko Kotsuji.

Japanese "general" with Chaya Leah, Esther, and Moshe Yoel ca. 1943.

This Jewish child's view of "occupiers" of Shanghai thus stands in contrast to many adult accounts about the horrors of Japanese rule. In another email to me, Chaya Leah reflected as follows upon a photograph taken in the middle of the war in China showing a relaxed Japanese man on a park bench with his arms stretched out protectively across the shoulders of two Jewish girls and a little blond boy: Chaya Leah, Esther, and Moshe Yoel:

> I remember the general (so we called him later).
> He came to our home, always in uniform, impeccable dressed, and lots of medals.
> He had a long blades word. And he projected an air of authority, elegance and regal demeanor. But then again the Japanese were famous for their good manners. And social grace.

> He came several times and talked with my father, I do not know what language they spoke, but they communicated and he came back.
> I think I was about ten or less in this picture, and he took us out to the park because there were no activities for us in the ghetto—Esther Moishe and I, probably springtime.
> He was not in uniform at that time.

Springtime in Japanese-occupied China finds three Jewish children on an outing with a Japanese officer. One could dismiss the photograph and the children's admiration for the "general" as ignorance of the young, who are easily impressed by swords and uniforms and the promise of an outing beyond the confines of the Jewish ghetto. Yet Chaya Leah's recollections are not so naïve. They do color the Japanese occupiers in warmer hues than the native Chinese or even the Jews who were cramped so tightly into the alleys of Hongkew. What Chaya Leah notes in the photograph is a feeling of safety, which was sorely lacking for many others in the wartime China:

> We favored the Japanese, as they were there to protect us. They controlled the city, the crime, etc. I do not remember much about this outing, but looking at the picture, a fondness. We have always had a tremendous Hakoras Ha Tov to the Japanese, Sugihara,
> The power of one.

Again and again, Sugihara comes to shape the recollections of survival long after he moved on from his position in the consulate in Kovno. Jewish memories, especially in the yeshiva community, kept this vision of gratitude (*hakarat ha tov*) and the "power of one" going long after their arrival in Shanghai. The role of Wang Guowei's puppet government in the Japanese occupation of the city was not clear to the beleaguered refugees. What they knew and saw was Japanese authorities, who were often identified with kindness since the summer of 1940 in Kovno, Lithuania.

Three years later, as the implementation of the restricted area became a daily reality in and around Hongkew, visions of the "power of one" began to take on darker connotations. Takashi and "the general" appear as friendly figures to the children on Liaoyang Road. But they also heard and knew about the terrifying Sgt. Kano Ghoya, the Japanese vice chief of the Stateless Refugees' Affairs Bureau in Shanghai, who called himself "King of the Jews."

Takashi had been an exceptionally kind young man who managed to procure the much needed sulfur. By contrast, Ghoya was a dreaded name in the Walkin household and in many other Jewish homes. Vivian Jeannette Kaplan, who was older than Chaya Leah, recalled the self-proclaimed "King of the Jews" as follows:

> Goya [sic] made Jews stand in long lines and slapped them in the face. But he let them live. He let them give concerts. He and his subordinates attended these Jewish musical soirees and actually enjoyed them.[8]

In light of news about Nazi atrocities in Europe, this account places Kano Ghoya firmly in the company of Germans who tortured Jews while enjoying their cultural performances at the same time. Ghoya's presence at Jewish musical soirees was a grim reminder of the power he wielded over Jewish lives. Yet, he never engineered such a macabre scene as that recalled by Erika Rothschild, a survivor of Auschwitz:

> Those who arrived in Birkenau were driven out of the cattle wagons and put in rows ... to this the band played, made up of the best musicians among the prisoners; they played, depending on the origins of the transport, Polish, Czech, or Hungarian folk music. The band played, the SS pummeled, and you had no time to reflect ... some were forced into the camp, the others into the crematoria.[9]

Jews who were forced to move into the restricted area in Shanghai did not suffer the naked brutality inflicted by the SS in Birkenau. Ghoya's slaps and shovings were erratic, one madman's need to assert authority in the tiny world he thought he controlled absolutely. Nonetheless, the terror of his victims was real enough.

Chaya Leah's own encounter with Kano Ghoya reveals the atrocities of this Japanese official though the eyes of a child who otherwise expressed fond feelings for Japanese officials. As the oldest child of Rav Shmuel David, she was allowed to accompany him on forays out of the restricted area. On one such occasion, in which she was sick and needed medical attention, Chaya Leah

---

8 Vivian Jeanette Kaplan, *Ten Green Bottles: The True Story of One Family's Journey from War-torn Austria to the Ghettos of Shanghai* (New York: St. Martin's Press, 2004), 146.
9 Shirli Gilbert, *Music in the Holocaust: Confronting Life in the Nazi Ghettos and Camps* (Oxford: Oxford University Press, 2005), 213.

Walkin witnessed the abuse of her beloved and respected father in a manner that struck truck terror into the child's heart. Whereas Vivian Jeannette Kaplan noted that the cruel Japanese officer allowed Jews to live, Chaya Leah's recollection dwells upon fear and humiliation of living under Ghoya's thumb:

> *The opposite of Takahashi's kindness was embodied in the merciless ghetto chief, Ghoya. He was in charge of policing the Ghetto. Ghoya was very short. In my memory, he appears as a midget filled with self-importance. He could be cruel and in some unpredictable moments kind. He was especially mean to the Europeans who were tall. We had to get a permit from him every time we needed to visit the doctor.*
>
> *One day in Shanghai, I had terrible stomachaches. After several days of relentless pain, we chose a doctor out of the ghetto to see me. (We also had doctors and nurses in the ghetto.) Standing in line in Ghoya's office, then being interrogated as to why you had to go out of Hongkew was a humbling and also a humiliating experience.*

Here, Rav Walkin's daughter recalls what it was like to be sick and unable to get the kind of help that Takahashi had provided with one bottle of sulfur. It seems that Chaya Leah's relentless pain could not be diminished even by German doctors and nurses who had been forced to relocate into Hongkew.

Rav Walkin was determined to get help for his daughter, the same way that he had been determined to obtain a rare banana for his little son when he suffered from tapeworms. Now, he stood tall before the small and angry Japanese official. All of Chaya Leah's old fears welled up in that dreadful moment:

> *During the escape and long journey from Poland to Asia, we as children were taught not to make a sound lest we were discovered by the enemy. The fear of authority was ingrained in all of us.*
>
> *My father was a tall man with a long beard. He made a very dignified impression. Ghoya was sitting in his chair and came around his desk and told my father to put his head on the table. My father obeyed.*
>
> *He reached for his saber and pulled out the blade from its shield. Raising the weapon above his hand, he let it swish down loudly.*
>
> *I heard a terrifying ripping even though my eyes were very tightly shut.*
>
> *Then I heard the insane giggling, and Ghoya scurrying like a wild rat, laughing hysterically. He had chopped off my father's beard.*
>
> *My father was safe. His head remained in place,*

> *I was too scared to cry. I was shaking, but stood still.*
> *I did not want to go to the doctor, I held on tight to my father's hand all the way home.*

The sound of a saber on wood and human hair. The howling of a wild rat. The swallowed terror of a child who learned to say nothing during the escape from Poland and across the frozen tundra of Siberia. These are the memories that Chaya Leah carried with her from Shanghai along with recollections of Takahashi's kindness, of calisthenics at the Kadoorie School, of the bomb shelter photograph as well as the forgotten pet, which her friend Rishel Kotler placed into its own traumatic context.

The war years in China during which Chaya Leah Walkin went from being a shy seven-year-old to a war-scarred eleven-year-old were a time of greening, ripening, and terror, too. While Shanghai was nothing like the walnut grove in *Shir Ha'Shirim*, it became the setting of Jewish flourishing nonetheless. This time of growth was marked by some internal conflict within the community of Jewish refugees as well as by acts of generosity and resistance that may be likened to budding vines and reddening pomegranates. These embodied the promise of Jewish revival after the hardships of war in China.

Even as a child, Chaya Leah had sensed this promise. But she also knew its darker underside, given voice in a simple Yiddish song about a little bird. Although the song was written in 1947 (at a Bais Yaakov summer camp in America), it continues to speak about the trauma of the *Shoah* for survivors such as Chaya Leah who were far from the death camps of Europe. The lyrics and the mournful tune of this song describe the predicament of a vulnerable animal trying to alert the world about its endangered fate.

Hope lingers in these verses despite the despair. Not giving up, Chaya Leah told me so often, was a fundamental article of her Jewish faith. Redemption does glisten in the midst of the darkest exile, again and again. Survival in wartime China, in her view, was one step in that redemption—hence, the aptness of the song about the little bird:

> The little bird is calling,
> It wishes to return.
> The little bird is wounded,
> It cannot fly but yearn.
> It's captured by the vultures,

Crying bitterly,
Oh, to see my nest again,
Oh, to be redeemed…
The little bird is Yisroel,
The vultures are our foes,
The painful wound is Golus,
Which we all feel and know,
The nest is Yerushalaim.
Where we yearn to be once more,
The eagle is Moshiach
Whom we are waiting for.

When the war ended, Chaya Leah Walkin and her family did not end up going to Yerushalaim—Jerusalem. Heading toward the unknown shores of America, they carried with them the wounds of *Golus*, an exile that stretched from Pinsk and Radin to Kobe and Shanghai.

Along with the pain, however, came the strength and vision gained during the war years in China. Chaya Leah was not the same child who had jumped rope so freely in Japan. She was no longer simply running errands for Shabbat and for the holiday needs of her family. Poised on the threshold of young adulthood, Rav Shmuel David's daughter had become a verdant grove about to display its plentiful fruit.

CHAPTER 7

UNDER THE APPLE TREE:

End of the War, End of Refuge in Shanghai

*Who comes up from the wilderness
Leaning upon her beloved?
Under the apple tree I awakened you,
There, where your mother birthed you.*

Shir Ha'Shirim 8:5

News of D-Day—June 6, 1944—took a long time to reach Jewish refugees in Shanghai, and even longer to give them hope. Their own predicament had worsened with the Japanese proclamation of February 1943. Severe food shortages and scarcity of funds to supplement the meager aid coming in from abroad plagued German and Polish Jews alike. Slowly, painfully slowly for many, things got a bit better by the end of 1944.

During this same year, far from the crowded, hungry Jews of Shanghai, the Chinese Expeditionary Forces recaptured northern Burma. This had been a key area in the war against Japan and the focus of General Joseph Stillwell's valiant efforts to open up a passage from Mandalay to Siquan in 1942. In the communist-held area of Yenan, Mao Zedong tried to sound a conciliatory note when meeting with American envoy Patrick Hurley in November 1944. A national Chinese unity government was one of the highest American priorities –although not Mao's, as the subsequent civil war showed.

On May 7, 1945 news of Germany's surrender traveled much faster than D-Day had during the previous year. The large number of German refugees in Hongkew followed the course of this defeat through radios, word of mouth, and gossip animated by a thirst for news from the European capitals left behind.

Japan's defeat also appeared imminent. The promise of genuine liberation from the sufferings of war in Shanghai was now palpable among the refugees and Chinese citizens alike. For the Jews, there was even a wild whiff of hope that they may see long lost family members again.

These hopes were cruelly dashed by the July 17, 1945 bombing of the Hongkew ghetto. On this day, American aircraft targeted a Japanese military radio station at the heart of the "restricted area." In an eerie parallel to the strategy adopted decades later by Israel's enemies in the Gaza strip, civilians became cannon fodder in a ruthless war. When Hamas willfully installed rocket launchers into schools and hospitals, they were following the model of the Japanese occupiers who had thought it safe to gather radio intelligence in a part of the Chinese city where Jewish refugees congregated and which was deemed safe from air attacks.

The July 17 bombing left scars beyond the lives and buildings that were destroyed. The shock and devastation lingered, as can be seen in Deborah Strobin's recollection of the horror six decades after the event. The child of German refugees, she was close to the epicenter of disaster on that day:

> The impact. I felt the vibrations through the earth. Buildings exploded. The sirens and the screaming and the sound of destruction. Hell. It was indescribable. The Americans were trying to hit a radio station, but they couldn't see anything with the sky solidly overcast. They based their drop on their flying time. Two hundred and sixty-three bombs dropped on Shanghai. Each of the bombs weighed one hundred pounds. They landed on the market… The devastation was incomprehensible. Men ran past dragging rickshaws, pedaling pedicabs transporting the injured. There were fire trucks and ambulances, arms and legs scattered among the debris. I saw a man with half his foot hanging off and the other foot missing entirely… I was ten. If I really stop to look at it, the fear of that day is freshly conjured as if the miles from San Francisco to Shanghai do not exist. As if the years between the little girl I was and the woman I am today never passed, and if, in the background, I happen to hear a police siren or an ambulance zooming past my building, I still shake. I shake, and I shake.[1]

---

1 Deborah Strobin and Ilie Wacs, "The Liberation of the Shanghai Jewish Ghetto." *The Huffington Post*. January 27, 2012, accessed September 6, 2017, http://www.huffingtonpost.com/ilie-wacs/the-liberation-of-the-shanghai-jewish-ghetto_b_1236647.html.

Among the two hundred and fifty cadavers on the streets of Shanghai on July 17, there were thirty-one Jews, seven of them from the Polish community closest to the Walkin family.

Chaya was only one year older than Deborah Sorbin in the summer of 1945. She did not live in the heart of Hongkew, as did Sorbin with her younger brother and parents. Yet—like them—Chaya Leah, too, continues to shudder with memories of that particular bombing so close to the end of the war. She understood that life and death hung on a very thin thread indeed. Deborah Sorbin called her own survival "a lucky accident" because she had refused to go shopping at the market on July 17, 1945. Chaya Leah would look back and call the same event a miracle and revelation of divine kindness.

The eleven-year-old child of the Walkin family heard the sound of the July bombing and shared her parents' grief at the news of those killed. What lingers in the mind's eye more vividly, however, is Rav Walkin sitting on a low stool mourning news of his own father's death and the rest of his family in the ghetto of Pinsk and in the forests where the Nazis had carried out their extermination campaigns.

Mourning one's kin, sitting *shiva* on a low stool, had started in Shanghai even before the actual end of the war on September 7, 1945. Two days before the Rosh Hashanah, the celebration of the Allies' victory had already taken center stage in the refugees' magazine called *Unsern Leben/Our Life*. Yet, not far from this rejoicing, the journal revealed the more complex emotions of a refugee community caught between joy and grief. Four years earlier, the Mirrer Yeshiva and other Polish refugees had been shipped to Shanghai from Kobe. Memories of that forcible transfer to the *unterwelt* remained fresh in the minds of Chaya Leah's parents along with the relief that there would be no two-day Yom Kippur, as some had feared in Japan. Now, in September 1945, the sense of relief was even deeper while at the same time Jews were frantically seeking news about their relatives back in Europe. Since Rosh Hashanah was also known in Hebrew as *Yom Ha Zikaron*—"Day of Remembrance"—the editors of *Our Life* added the following banner on the first page of its September 7 celebratory issue:

> "Let's be Faithful to the Memory of Millions of Jewish War Victims!
> Let's Achieve Liberty and Happiness for Our People!"[2]

In the Walkin household, grief and joy had already been intermixed before September 7, 1945. By the time of the July 17 bombing, Rebbetzin Tzivia

---

2 Eber, *Voices from Shanghai*, 174.

Walkin was cradling a new pregnancy. Her son Chaim was born on September 11, one day after Rosh Hashanah, during *"Tzom Gedalia"*—a day of fasting that commemorated the murder of the last governor of the Jews in the Land of Israel after the destruction of the first temple. The new Walkin infant was named after Rav Shmuel David's brother, the last dean of the Volozhin Yeshiva who had been killed in the Ponary Forest in Lithuania. Survivors who had reached America by 1945 confirmed news of Rav Chaim Walkin's murder. The fate of the Bais Aharon, by contrast, was not known until much later; therefore, his name was not be given to the new baby boy born at the end of the war in Shanghai.

A family photograph taken in the fall of 1945 (probably right after the infant boy's circumcision, *brit mila*) shows a growing family that managed to survive the war with renewed hope and vigor. Here, Rebbetzin Walkin is portrayed smiling, her head covered, her stomach still rounded after the birth of baby Chaim, who lies peacefully asleep in her arms. Rabbi Walkin, no longer young, looks into the camera with a vivid, focused gaze. Between the parents stands Moshe Yoel, serious in his dark clothes, the youngest sibling before this birth and one not likely to appreciate being displaced as the only son. The Walkin daughters frame the parents on each side. Esther is grinning broadly next to her mother. Chaya Leah, the closest to her father, also smiles—but with the self-aware restraint of the oldest sibling.

Chaya Leah's embroidered sweater suggests that the parents had enough resources at the end of the war for some new clothes. Her short, beribboned hair is a sign that even with the upheavals of a new baby, Rebbetzin Walkin did not miss this opportunity to groom her daughters so that they could be as presentable as possible. *"Malbushim Kavod"*—the garments of honor—reminded the girls of the special role that Jewish women and girls played in upholding the royalty of Torah itself.

Looking back, Chaya Leah recalled her baby brother's birth in Shanghai with clarity and pride. Even as a twelve-year-old child, she understood that this had been a blessing, even if it strained family resources, including the precious little space that was available in the one-room "salon" on Liaoyang Road:

> Our brother Chaim was born in Shanghai.
> He was born in the Jewish hospital, which was several blocks down from our entrance.
> Ma stayed there several days then came home and spent several weeks recuperating in bed.

> At first Chaim was kept in a wooden drawer and thence got a green cast iron crib to use till the next baby born would need one. Ma slept in the big bed with a huge down blanket in the room off the living room, which was a sun parlor. The bris was held in the living room, and my mother in the sun parlor, the kimpeturin.
> In those days, the norm was to rest and rest. Different from the Chinese who worked in the rice fields, had their babies, picked them up, and continued working.
> A kimpeturin was treated like a fragile and delicate child.
> My mother nursed Chaim. He was gevikelled (bundled tightly) in a blanket—only his head was exposed. He looked like a mummy, a tiny mummy.
> I do not know the reason why the Europeans did it.
> When my children were infants, I vickelelled them also, so tight and secure.

In the details of the wooden drawer and the green iron crib, we glimpse the shortages that still affected new life at the end of the war. Chaya Leah's recollection is colored by the Yiddishism that enveloped her mother after all the previous births, and after one more "lying in" in New York upon leaving China.

A *kimpeturin*, according to the Jewish traditions carried from Europe to China, is a woman who has just given birth and needs extra care in recovery. In Torah communities today, there are special organizations called "Kimpeturin Aid" providing this measure of additional support for new mothers. In an age of self-sufficient women who are forced by insurance considerations to leave the hospital shortly after giving birth, this Yiddish term may seem quaintly old-fashioned. But in Shanghai after the war, it shows both the will and the necessity to care for a woman who had just given birth, no matter how hard it was to find the resources for extra help. A *kimpeturin* lies in bed for long days, like a queen bee at rest. Chaya Leah, the oldest daughter, had to take the lead in the extra care that her mother needed after Chaim's *brit*. In New York, after the birth of yet another baby girl, Chaya Leah assumed the burden of nearly full-time care both for her mother and her two youngest siblings.

Chaim's birth was followed by a wave of engagements and marriages among the Walkin family friends. This created a taste for rejoicing and hope like the one celebrated in the eighth chapter of *Shir Ha'Shirim*. During the harshest years of the war, hope had sprung from the "wilderness," from barren rocky as it were. Jewish refugees had to discover the arts of endurance on their own. To be sure, help came from unlikely benefactors such as Chiune Sugihara and Avraham

Kotsuji as well as concerned benefactors who donated to the Vaad ha-Hatzala in New York. All these rescuers had helped Jews to survive, yet the meaning of survival had to be found and affirmed from within. It was under these circumstances that the uninterrupted music of Torah learning in Kobe and Shanghai had brought solace and created a sliver of light in the darkest of times.

With the end of the war came a wave of more exuberant rejoicing. Births and marriages provided those occasions. Much like the Egyptian exile, war in China had challenged Jewish women like Tzivia Walkin to muster the courage to bring new life into the world. As in *Shir Ha'Shirim*, they too had managed to find their way "under the apple tree"—where new hope could be claimed. In Egypt, the pharaoh had decreed that every boy who was born had to be flung into the Nile to die. The Jewish men, according to the Midrash, gave up hope and separated from the women. They fell pray to despair and wondered what was the point of bringing children into the world if their fate was darkly sealed? The Jewish women, by contrast, had not lost a vision of the future. They crafted strategies to meet their hard laboring, exhausted, dispirited husbands in the field and enticed them into love and procreation.

When the time for birthing came, they went out—again—under the apple trees to bring their children into the world. From that time onward, the expression *tachat ha tapuach* (beneath the apple) calls to mind the will to love, to go on despite all difficulties and practical considerations that appeared stacked against the perpetuation of the Jewish family and of the Jewish people.

Tzivia Walkin, too, had become pregnant with her fourth child even before the end of the war was in sight. She lived through the terrible bombing of July 17, 1945. Younger women who were in Shanghai also found hope despite the war. Some, like Rishel Kotler, now followed through with engagements contracted before the war. The only challenge left was to get well enough physically to travel in the hope that a commitment made before Rishel became a poor orphan in Shanghai would be honored in America.

Other young women also found love and marriage in China. Even before the war was officially over, engagements and weddings began to take place in the Walkin "salon" and in the Ohel Moshe shul not far away. The Torah injunction to be fruitful and multiply was heard loud and clear in the last year of the war. For the young men, this injunction carried the force of a *mitzvah*. For their brides, it was an opportunity to dream of building families in a world still shadowed by despair and loss. Young Chaya Leah was an intimate witness to this arousal of hope "beneath the apple tree." Even as her body began to show hints of womanly transformation, she took note of the many joyful couplings that were lifting the gloom from war-torn Shanghai.

NOT A "FINISHED PEOPLE"

Giving birth under difficult circumstances was no metaphor in Shanghai at the end of the war. One photograph that Chaya Leah treasures, along with the one taken at the bomb shelter in the backyard of 281 Liaoyang Road, is not of her own family. Rather, it comes from the archives of the American Jewish Distribution Committee (known as Joint or JDC). It is labeled simply: "Mothers with baby carriages provided by the JDC in Shanghai, c. 1946." It shows nine women with recently born babies, one pushing a double stroller, most likely for twins. A portly nurse stands closest to the camera, probably the head of the obstetrics nursing staff at the Jewish hospital in Hongkew. This hospital had a good reputation since most of the doctors had fled Hitler's Europe and were glad to provide high-quality medical care in Shanghai.

Tzivia Walkin also gave birth in this medical center, staffed and run by refugees. Located inside the Hongkew area, close to Liaoyang Road, the hospital was a source of solace and help to all who had fled the *Shoah*. In the Chinese paintings done for the global exhibition, it is not Jewish mothers or German refugee doctors who take center stage. Instead, the focus is upon a young Chinese nurse—as if it were her kind ministrations and not Jewish self-help that led to the saving of lives in Shanghai during the war. The "agency" of Jews is once more diminished in this portrayal of three sick men relying upon the care of a single Chinese civilian.

In Chaya Leah's recollections of her mother's weeklong stay in the Jewish hospital, it is the German doctors and nurses who loom larger. Their skilled care for mother and infant ensured the survival of both. After the end of the war, the American Joint Distribution was able to step in once again and help refugees coming home from the hospital by defraying the cost of baby carriages containing the most concrete testament to the Jewish will to thrive in the wake of disaster and trauma.

The desire to bring new life into the world, however, was not equally apparent in all parts of the refugee community. Even with the Torah injunction to be fruitful and multiply, getting pregnant and giving birth was a difficult decision in Shanghai. One German survivor, Yvonne Daniels, recalling the life-threatening dangers of malnutrition during the war years, was honest enough to recall that "many women who found themselves pregnant aborted their babies because it was so difficult to nurture an infant."[3]

In the Torah community, abortion was not an option, as we can see from the pregnant bellies in the bomb shelter photograph. The birth of a boy named Chaim quite literally added vigor (*chayim* meaning "life") to all the refugees who came to celebrate his circumcision. Their warmly expressed hopes for this infant came to fruition as he grew up to become a major Talmudic scholar. Looking back, Rav Chaim Walkin recalls movingly how his name continues to evoke tears and appreciation from older scholars who never forgot his illustrious uncle murdered in the prime of his life during the Holocaust.

One month before Chaim Walkin's birth in Shanghai, a German woman who had also given birth in 1945 told an interviewer "we are a finished people."[4] These are the words of a refugee who had lived through the bombing of July 17 and who most likely just started to hear details of lives lost in the *Shoah*. Her despair was augmented by the exhaustion of being a refugee who did not know where she might find food to feed her baby. Looking back upon her arrival in China, this woman saw only bleakness for the Jewish people. She did not abort her infant. At the same time, the German refugee harbored no enthusiasm for the new life.

A very different note of exuberation can be seen in the September 1945 pamphlet entitled "Good-bye Mr. Ghoya" preserved in the archives of Yad Vashem in Jerusalem. Here, a German cartoonist named Fredrich Melchior takes delight in portraying the pockmarked Japanese official who had controlled the fate of Jews as he was leaving the Hongkew ghetto. No sooner was the war won that a Jewish survivor could look back and mock the source of terror that once plagued the minds and hearts of his fellow refugees. Not content to document the murderous sayings of Ghoya, Melchior also included a personal letter to the "late Japanese official of the Stateless Refugees' Affairs Bureau":

Sir,
You called yourself "King of the Jews" assuming your position unshakable. Yet we knew better, and in spite of your beating us and your

---

3   Joanne Miyang Cho, "German-Jewish Women in Wartime Shanghai and their Encounters with the Chinese." In *Gendered Encounters between Germany and Asia*, edited by J. Cho and D. McGetchin D, 171–91. Palgrave Series in Asian German Studies. London, Palgrave Macmillan
4   Gao Bei, *Shanghai Sanctuary*, 127.

> humiliating men and women, we knew you pretty well—a malicious frog you were and a ridiculous clown.
> We want to smile on you, oh King, and that's why I pinned you down just as we saw you, and just as we shall remember you—a maniac, a nightmare but a ridiculous fool as well.

Here is a Jewish voice talking back to history, reasserting agency in a way that was inconceivable among survivors of the Holocaust in Europe. In Shanghai, it was possible to assert agency through sharply worded humor and a determination to remember the terrors of war in a lighter vein. Hitler could not have been portrayed as a malicious frog, a ridiculous fool. He had too much power and had killed too many Jews to be seen as a fallen "king of the Jews."

Whereas Melchior's witty pamphlet reflected one aspect of the agency of Jews in Shanghai, the Walkin family's *brit mila* was its more traditional, more enduring, counterpart in the Torah community. Chaya Leah Walkin may not have seen the cartoons in "Goodbye Mr. Ghoya," but she knew intimately the relief that his departure brought to the refugees. They were free from his tyrannical moods, free to build new lives quite literally out of the ashes of the *Shoah* because its terrible news was enveloping Shanghai right after the end of the war.

That is why Chaya Leah treasures the photograph of the baby carriages preserved in the archives of the Joint Distribution Committee. It is more than a sigh of relief at the departure of Ghoya. It shows Jewish women who may have endured humiliation but managed at the same time to affirm the potential for life in a way that remains unquenchable by the brutality of the Japanese occupation of Shanghai. The baby carriages display the faith and strength of Jewish women as well as the renewed aid coming into China at the end of the war.

On August 30, 1945, the Joint Distribution News in New York described with jubilation the release of its Shanghai representative, Mr. Manuel Siegel, from a Japanese internment camp. Siegel had arrived in China in November 1941 (around the same time as the Walkin family) to help with the relief efforts organized by Laura Margolis on behalf of the German refugees. Both Margolis and Siegel were interned by the Japanese after February 1943 and could not be of direct help during the harshest months of the war. The photograph with baby carriages dated "c. 1946" reflects the renewed inflow of financial help.

With the bombing of Hiroshima on August 6, 1945, the surrender of Japan was firmly in sight. Jewish organizations such as the Joint lost no time in renewed efforts to help the refugee community in Shanghai. Clearly, the disastrous impact of the July bombing was known and now could be addressed with funds from abroad. A young girl like Chaya Leah did not have to carry out any more *"lokshen"* runs. She and her family were free to join in the celebration of new life and to plan their departure from Shanghai.

In this planning, too, help from abroad was essential. Entry visas into the United States, Canada, and Palestine were as precious as the exit visas from Kovno and Soviet Russia had been five years earlier. The future loomed uncertain, but it had lost some of its hue of terror. The shadows of the trauma, however, endured lingered longer, many years after the refugees left Shanghai.

Our Simcha Hall

Among the students of the Mirrer Yeshiva, hope was fed by the miracle of survival itself. Even before the dropping of the atomic bomb, which heralded the end of hostilities in Asia, the *bochrim* had looked at the events of July 1945 with eyes informed by religious faith. Many of these young men were close to the site of the American bombing and recalled years later how the ground shook under their feet.

Astonishingly, the building in which they were learning remained standing, while others all around it collapsed. One student, Yehuda Dickstein, had dozed off in an adjacent apartment next to the study hall. When the bomb hit, the floor of his room collapsed. The young man managed to claw his way out of the rubble and told his friends that from that day on his name would become "Zayin Menachem Av"—the Hebrew date on which his life was spared.[5]

The senior rabbis mentoring the young men had been intensely aware of the increasing dangers of remaining in Shanghai during the last year of the war. When talk of moving further north to the coastal city of Tianjin came up, Rabbi Yechezkel Levenstein (1895–1974) argued against the interruption of Torah study. As the debate intensified, a group of students resorted to the mystical device called the *"Goral Ha Gra,"* which dated back to the Vilna Gaon (Rabbi Elijah Ben Solomon Zalman, 1720–97). This "lottery" had been used before, when the yeshiva decided to submit their request for exit visas in Lithuania. Now, in the last months of the war in Shanghai, the "response" was again unequivocal. By counting various passages in the Hebrew bible, the "lot" fell upon a key line in the prophet Isaiah that stated: "I will defend the city, to save it for my own sake, and for the sake of David, my servant." (37:35).

---

5 A. Bernstein, "The Final Days of the War in the Pacific and the Jews of Shanghai." *Dei'ah ve Dibur: Information and Insight*. December 14, 2005.

The Mirrer Yeshiva stayed in Shanghai and its students and teachers were spiritually ready when the war ended. Along with all the other jubilated refugees, this group was convinced that its uninterrupted Torah study had aided the survival of fellow Jews. Here, again, was a sense of agency acquired from within the community's own traditions rather than granted by the Japanese or Chinese authorities who had controlled physical aspects of everyday life.

Survival, however, was not an end itself. Building up a new generation of scholars had always been the central goal, even before the yeshiva fled to Vilna. The most concrete way to actualize this goal was marriage. Thus, Shanghai—and the Walkin home in particular—became the site for new kinds of celebrations. Even before the *brit mila* of the new infant, Chaya Leah's family was engaged in the business of *simcha*, of bringing joy to new couples who—despite all odds—had found each other in war-torn Shanghai.

The commandment to rejoice at weddings was observed in China with much zeal. While less observant refugees might skimp on celebrations and make do without much fanfare, in Chaya Leah's world a bride and groom were to be honored at all costs. According to Torah law, a man must seek a wife soon after reaching maturity. In *Bereshit* (*Genesis*), God himself declares that "it is not good for man to be alone" and busies himself with fashioning a helpmate suitable for Adam's unique soul. In Shanghai, it was Rabbi Ashkenazi and the rabbis of the Mirrer Yeshiva who busied themselves with finding suitable matches. The exigencies of war added to this quest since one young man's visa could easily save the life of a bride to be or vice versa. For the Walkin children, news of a new engagement was cause for special rejoicing. They immediately understood that their simple room would be transformed into a "*simcha* hall"—a place of celebration with wine and sweets and whatever else could be procured to raise the spirits of the new couple. The art of crafting joy even in dark times was not lost on children and adults alike.

One photograph captures this hard-won joy in Shanghai. It is dated September 19, 1944—a full year before the end of the war. It shows a small gathering of friends for the wedding of Hilda and Joseph Eisenstein outside the Ohel Moshe shul. On the day of this celebration, war was still ripping through Europe and Asia. In Holland, for example, the town of Eindhoven was bombed by Luftwaffe planes on September 19. One crowded shelter took a direct hit, with 227 people killed in one day. In China, the Japanese fought one of their fiercest battles in the city of Changsha in September 1944—deploying 360,000 troops against a Chinese population left without adequate defenses by the Nationalist armies.

Under the Apple Tree: End of the War, End of Refuge in Shanghai • CHAPTER 7 | **185**

In Shanghai's Jewish community, by contrast, Chaya Leah Walkin stands bedecked in her one and only Shabbos dress for the wedding of Yosele and the "Daishke." The groom was a family friend since the time when he had carved a bar of soap on the Trans Siberian railroad to help Rav Walkin take his $100 bill out of Soviet Russia. The bride had been coming to the Liaoyang Road courtyard for months. A very young woman herself, Hilda had at first resented the children's enthusiastic calls announcing, "the little German is coming."

Jewish wedding in wartime Shanghai ca. 1944.

In this photograph, however, she is a paragon of beauty and composure. Chaya Leah's reflections on the picture augment the affection that wove together this "mixed marriage" between a German Jewish bride and her Polish, yeshiva-educated groom. Only Shanghai could have brokered this special match:

> *The wedding took place in 1944. Here you have the Choson and Kallah. Next to the choson is my father, and next to the kallah is her friend and then her mother from Vienna. The kallah's father died in Shanghai and is buried in Shanghai.*
> *Hilda had told me that they travelled to Shanghai by boat for four weeks. Half of their passage was paid by relatives in America. They booked their own passage, since no visas were necessary.*
> *In the first row is my sister Esther; next to her is Rebbetzin Esther Levine, the Rosh Yeshiva's wife from Telshe Yeshiva. Her grandfather was the mashgiach in the Shanghai Mir. Then my brother Moishe, then I.*

Looking at the wedding photograph more than seven decades after the event, Chaya is mindful of the hardships that brought this German bride into the yeshiva community. Like the plight of Lotte Markus, Hilda's father had also died in Shanghai. He left behind a widow and daughter who were not only bereft but also struggling ever harder for survival. Relatives who had helped finance the boat travel could not send further support as the Japanese war against the Allies became ever more fierce. Marrying into this yeshiva community provided a sense of belonging as well as increased security. No wonder that both the bride and her mother look a little shy in this unfamiliar world.

Rebbetzin Tzivia Walkin, by contrast, stands in the first row, looking elegant and confident. As Chaya Leah herself noted:

> *I think one picture is worth a thousand words. When you see my mother—her poise, her demeanor, her smile, her presentation—you can see the influence she had on our behavior and home.*
> *The third row is mainly bochrim. The one other girl in the photograph is Chaikele Potachnick… I love to tell the story of Chaikele, who never talked about the war but always lived next to my parents' home. All her life. In New York, they lived across the street; in Queens, they lived next door.*
> *Chaikele was my mother's good friend, but she never addressed her by name. It was always "the Rebbetzin."*

Under the Apple Tree: End of the War, End of Refuge in Shanghai • CHAPTER 7

> They were contemporaries, but it was always the Rebbetzin. Chaikele related to me once that they were running through the forest, they were tired and hungry, and they had no food for several days. Then they saw an apple tree, they wanted desperately to eat the apple, but they were not sure if it was still Shabbos or not so they would not tear down an apple. This was *mesirat nefesh* for Shabbos. So they ran off hungry.

Chaya Leah's description helps us enter the photograph with the eyes of the future. Esther, the little sister with a matching dress, becomes Rebbetzin Poupko. The small girl next to Moshe Yoel became the Rebbetzin of the Telshe Rosh Yeshiva. The one older girl among the group of young men behind the bride is called affectionately "Chaikele" and it is she who jumps out in memory's eyes. This young woman and her brother were the sole survivors of an observant Jewish family. Many years after the refuge in Shanghai, Rav Shmuel David's daughter takes note of the orphans' respect for their parents as well as their efforts to keep the laws of Shabbat despite the hunger and dangers of surviving on the run. This fidelity to traditional Judaism colors memory as much as the central couple in the wedding photograph.

By the time Hilda became a bride with a borrowed dress and a wilting bouquet, she had buried her father in Shanghai. Like other impoverished German refugees, her mother had become a widow in black. The only truly radiant visage in this picture is Rebbetzin Walkin. Her stylish dress, white pocketbook, gloves, and crown-like hat bespeak more than religious observance. They convey dignity and joy at being able to witness the continuity of Jewish life during the war.

Not yet pregnant, she knows herself to be the embodiment of the "*Eshet Hayil*"—the woman of valor celebrated by King Solomon at the conclusion of Proverbs. Her husband is the long-bearded, generous-spirited elder in this group, smiling behind her. Tzivia Walkin's well-dressed and well-mannered children glow next to her. There is hope here despite the dark hour. Even the little basket at the feet of Esther Levine carries this message. Although there was no time for a rose-strewn stroll, a new couple was nonetheless celebrated with flowers in Shanghai. Here was rejoicing both in the moment and also for the sake of the Jewish life that this couple would build after the war.

As a growing girl in China, as the oldest of her siblings and the most "seasoned" among the children in the Liaoyang courtyard, Chaya Leah was most aware of cultural differences among the refugees. She was endlessly fascinated by various border crossings effected by marriages in China. The little ones probably would not have cried out "Daitcheke" if Chaya Leah had not been aware of the difference in Hilda's German accent. The Viennese young woman looked and sounded very different from the Polish and Lithuanian refugees on Liaoyang Road. Yet, here she was, the bride of a Mirrer *bocher*.

Another marriage that remained engraved in Chaya Leah's memory was that of Cyril Kaplan (who had also attended the makeshift Bais Yaakov in Shanghai) with a Sephardi boy, Chaim Benoliel. Chaya Leah knew about the fabulously wealthy and generous Sephardim who had endowed the Kadoorie School and who helped out with her father's fundraising when he visited their palatial mansions in the International Settlement. But to actually marry one of the "oriental boys" was almost unheard of.

To change one's *mama loshen* (native tongue) and Eastern European customs took courage and implied risk. Yet, Shanghai during the war had prompted a broadening of minds. So much of what one carried from back home in Poland had been lost, taken away, or sold for survival. All that remained was an unshakable commitment to Torah traditions. For Cyril and her family, that was enough. When this refugee girl married Rabbi Chaim Benoliel in Chicago after the war, it was an alliance that flourished beyond all expectations. Returning from Cyril Benoliel's funeral in January 2016, Chaya Leah recalled the border crossings that had been ignited in China during the war:

> *Today is a sad day.*
> *After the funeral, everyone talked about the little girl and her journey to Shanghai.*
> *The impact of life in Shanghai on that little girl.*
> *The Sephardi she married. And built a yeshiva.*
> *That took second place.*
> *The Shanghai story and life first.*

This is no mere chronological recollection. Praise for the *Yeshiva Mikdash Melech* (the first Sephardic Yeshiva founded in the Western Hemisphere by Rabbi Benoliel) came after memories of the girl who had traveled from Poland to Kobe and Shanghai. Cyril Benoliel had dared to cross cultural lines, and Chaya Leah remains convinced that it was Shanghai that made this match possible despite the fact that the "mixed" wedding took place after the war.

Another reason that Shanghai played matchmaker among the refugees was the need for papers. Even as a child, Chaya Leah was aware that some people were slightly safer than others, despite bombings and poverty. Those who had some documentation about their place of origin were less likely to be ostracized and perhaps expelled as stateless. In recalling the marriage of Blima and Rabbi Uri Hellman, Chaya Leah looks back and sees the bond forged by a need for documents, and more:

> I visited Rebbetzin Blimele Hellman in New York, and she related to me her wedding in Shanghai. It seemed that she did not have the proper papers to stay in Shanghai. Rabbi Hellman being a German Jew had the right papers, so it was a perfect match.
> The rebbetzin had nothing for a wedding, so we borrowed a dress, got a veil, a coat, flowers, and made her look as beautiful as a kallah (bride) should be. She and her groom, like other couples, married in our home. The table was set with linen, glasses, wine, flowers, all kinds of cookies, and we had a Chupah (wedding canopy).
> It was a beautiful simcha, with everyone attending.
> Picture this l'chaim. Celebrating engagements, weddings that kept the flow of life meaningful in Shanghai.
> We are in our living room. Esther, Moishe, and I are standing at the back.

In the photograph of the Hellmans' engagement party (known simply as "le'Chayim,") shows a beaming pre-teen Chaya Leah, with her more serious-looking younger siblings in the far back. Maybe the children had climbed up on stools so that they could make it into the group photograph. Rav Shmuel David's oldest daughter was old enough to grasp what memory's eye made clear in the decades after Shanghai: that engagement and marriages such as that of Blima and Rabbi Uri Hellman made life not only safer for a refugee but also much more meaningful.

As in other photographs in Chaya Leah's China albums, Rabbi Walkin sits at the head of the table. His long, graying beard and kippa set him apart from the young Mirrer students wearing hats and European suits. Rebbetzin Walkin, with her head in a scarf, stands smiling broadly in the back. The unmarried young women crowd around her, wearing their hair in the latest Shanghai curling fashion. The bottle of wine and refreshments on the table bespeak an effort to make life meaningful and more gracious in difficult times.

Rabbi Hellman did not marry Blumele simply because she needed papers. The bride and groom had actually known each other in Germany and had escaped together from Vilna. Nonetheless, responding with love to the needs of a fellow refugee was not uncommon in this community.

The Walkin family's "*simcha* hall" glowed with celebrations such as the Hellman wedding. A borrowed dress and veil, some flowers, and a tablecloth were enough to make the moment memorable—not just for the bride and groom but also for Chaya Leah, the Walkin daughter who stands tallest at this gathering. She was absorbing the *Keddusha*, the holiness of this event in Shanghai, and would reenact its message and recall its significance again and again in her later life as Rebbetzin Small—when she herself organized wedding celebrations for unlikely couples in Chicago after the war.

The other Shanghai weddings that remained inscribed in Chaya Leah's mind were that of Rabbi Hershel and Mania Milner and that of her beloved mentors Rabbi Simcha and Mira Elberg. The Milner wedding is memorialized in one of the family photographs since Rabbi and Mrs. Walkin were once again among honored guests:

> *When Manya reached marital age, Rabbi and Rebbetzin Ashkenazi made the shiddach for her with Reb Hershele Milner. Hershele was the best boy in the yeshiva—handsome, smart, with a kind heart. A catch. When Reb Hershel came to America, he went into the textile business and became very successful.*
>
> *This picture shows the choson and kallah and some of their friends. These people became lifelong friends and family. The bridal photograph does not show a war picture—rather, a well-dressed, well put together group of people.*

Here, again, Chaya Leah looks back and sees a world about to be rebuilt despite the scarcities of war. The Milner wedding took place on January 1, 1944—at a terrifying time in world history. Nonetheless, in Shanghai, seeds of the future were ebulliently sown.

> *Were the outfits borrowed? Were they made? Who knows? But I do remember my parents talking about the beautiful wedding.*
>
> *You can also see here Benny Fishoff. He liked to be called Yehiel. He was about eighteen years old in the ghetto at that time. Somehow, he gravitated to our family. My mom and dad loved him like a son, and I have always considered Benny my oldest brother. Benny considered my parents his parents.*
>
> *When my dad went to olom habo, it was Benny who took his beloved father to the final resting place. His first child born was named after my father.*
>
> *As close as he was to our family, Benny always called my dad Rabbi Walkin and my mother Rebbetzin. My parents walked him down the aisle when he got married.*

Looking back to China, memory's gaze travels forward to Benny Fishoff, the beloved adopted son of the Walkin family. This "well-put together group" had shared hardships, celebrated joys together and remained lifelong friends. Rabbi and Rebbetzin Walkin made room in their lives for Yehiel, the orphan refugee. They brought him to the marriage canopy after the war and lived long enough to share in his joys as he built up a family as well as a very successful business in America after the war.

As a budding young woman in Shanghai, Chaya Leah was learning what was considered a "catch" in her own community. Being smart, kind, and learned in Torah were the first criteria. There was no question of wealth here. The fact that Rabbi Milner went into the textile business in America underscores for Chaya Leah that there is more than one path of life for a Torah scholar. As she put later:

> Reb Hershel, the big Talmud chocham, learned and went into business. He was very successful in the textile business in Manhattan. In those years, it was—
> TOV TORAH IM DERECH ERETZ.
> It is good to learn but you must also provide, work.
> I believe it strongly.

The capital letters are Chaya Leah's choice and her determination to affirm a key principle from the ancient text of *Pirkei Avot*: Torah learning is most enduring when coupled with a worldly occupation. The daughter of a rabbi and later the wife of a rabbi, Chaya Leah viewed men like Reb Hershel with admiration and honor. As her later reflections reveal, the girl in the back of the *"simcha* hall" on Liaoyang Road did not miss any opportunity to observe and to define what she came to hold dear on her own terms after the war.

The wedding of Rabbi Simcha and Miriam Elberg was memorable for Chaya Leah as well. Here was another highly accomplished Torah scholar who would go on to become one of the leaders of Talmudic scholarship in America as chief editor of *Ha Pardes*. Chaya Leah was too young to have read or understood Elberg's 1941 poem "Three Countries Spewed Me Out." She knew that Miriam was from Harbin, a city to the north, which also housed a Jewish community during the war. It was not Rabbi Elberg's distinguished roots in pre-war Warsaw that impressed young Chaya Leah. (He had been ordained by the famous Rabbi Menachem Ziemba, and was thus among the older *bochrim* to arrive with the Mirrer Yeshiva in Shanghai). It was the warmth that the new couple lavished upon the oldest Walkin daughter that lingered in the mind from China and served as Chaya's anchor in the years after the war:

> *Mirishka always considered me as the child she did not have.*
> *She was the one who guided me when I started to date my husband.*
> *She was always there for me.*
> *My father and Reb Simcha were very close.*
> *Reb Simcha was always "out of the box."*

A childless marriage forged in Shanghai thus had room for a young woman like Chaya Leah. Simcha and Miriam Elberg became trusted mentors and models for what constitutes a vibrant, loving marriage.

It was a mark of Chaya Leah's trust that she could turn to Rebbetzin Elberg when a more senior rabbinical student came to court her in the 1950s. The age difference between the Elbergs opened the door for more intimate conversation about the relationship of a younger woman to an older man. Having been a very young bride herself, Rebbetzin Elberg reassured Chaya Leah that she carried inner treasures that would enrich a marriage beyond her husband's age and scholarly accomplishments.

The importance of building a foundation for future generations of Jews was the essential message from Shanghai to New York, especially when conveyed so emphatically by a childless woman who had been a close friend of the Walkin family during their refuge in China. "Birthing under the apple trees," to use the words of *Shir Ha'Shirim* did not always result in an infant. Enduring friendships and the establishment of vibrant Torah institutions in America and Israel were also manifestations of the flourishing that had been seeded by refugees at the end of the war in China.

BUBBLING WELL ROAD

In 1945–46, new growth marked Chaya Leah's world. Too young in China to become a bride, the budding teenager's days unfurled like a verdant tree after a harsh winter. There was a new brother to coo over and care for. Weddings and engagements were celebrated with more flourish than had been possible during the shortages of war. The twelve-year-old daughter of Rav Shmuel David was now allowed to venture beyond the Hongkew enclosure without fear of Kano Ghoya or the restrictive orders enforced by the Chinese puppet government.

There was a sense of freedom in the air, and Chaya Leah took advantage of it to explore Shanghai in ways not possible during the war.

Two photographs taken around the time that she turned twelve show Chaya Leah Walkin going to the movies with her friend, Bella Kerner. The two girls and two adults are standing on a bridge with the Shanghai Bund towering behind them. Bella's parents, well-dressed Europeans, are sporting summer clothes. They do not look like they belong to the yeshiva community that was Chaya Leah's home on Liaoyang Road.

Indeed, the Kerner family was not part of Rav Walkin's circle. Although they had fled the Holocaust through Vilna as well, Bella's parents were among those who had heard about the Sugihara visas simply by word of mouth. They were not Torah-observant Jews before or after Shanghai. Yet they respected their daughter's friend and opened for Chaya windows onto a larger world after the war. It was also a tribute to Rabbi and Rebbetzin Walkin's open-mindedness that they trusted their eldest child to know who she was and what her family's values were even during a deepening friendship with a fellow refugee.

The two girls are wearing short dresses (knees showing in a way that would be deemed unseemly in strictly observant communities after the war). Bella is looking straight at the camera; Chaya Leah gazes off into a more distant vista. The close-up of the two girls reveals a physically maturing Chaya Leah. She faces the camera with a half-smile. Her rounded bossom and shapely face hint already at the womanly beauty that marked the young bride seven years later.

Chaya Leah Walkin had arrived in Shanghai as a small, thin child from Poland and Kobe in the fall of 1941. The five years she spent in China were crucial for unfurling her incipient womanhood as well as for consolidation of traditions that she would carry forward into married life. Going to the movies on Shanghai's famous Bubbling Well Road had been a new thrill for the two young girls. Chaya Leah's parents had trusted their young daughter to venture out of the Liaoyang Road compound into the bustling world of the International Settlement. Bubbling Well Road was a large, tree-lined boulevard leading to the Jingan Temple, which extended past the crowded part of Nanjing Road near Hongkew.

Many foreign residents considered this particular street to be the prettiest road in Shanghai. It was known to be the best place to show off new automobiles long before the outbreak of war with Japan. This boulevard was also famous for the great mansions of high-born British subjects—such as Sir Elly Kadoorie, who resided at 1783 Bubbling Well Road. Further down the street from the palatial Kadoorie residence were some of Shanghai's best movie theaters, such as The Embassy and The Grand.

When Chaya Leah met up with Bella in Florida seventy years later, the joys of Shanghai's cinemas bubbled up in their conversation. Recalling those delights led to a broader appreciation for the various cultural pursuits that had marked the lives of German refugees in China during the war:

> *The arts remained important to them. There was a theater, there was an orchestra, artists continued to paint. Little cafés opened all over Shanghai to sit and schmooze, to play chess, to chat, and bond with old friends. There was everything for a normal life except we were surrounded by filth, poverty, and a lack of money, of food.*
>
> *Yet, we made do. The Eastern Europeans who came to Shanghai were from small shtetluchs, small, modest communities, not the big city. We were accustomed to a more humble lifestyle than those who came from the larger urban centers.*

Thinking about movies led to this more seasoned reflection about the differences between refugees like the Walkin family, who hailed from small towns in the Polish countryside, and Bella's family, which had been used to the life of the European cafés.

Both Polish and German refugees had experienced a shocking reduction of mobility after February 1943. The palpable relief experienced at the end of the war comes across strongly as Chaya Leah recalls meeting another fellow refugee now residing in a nursing home in New Jersey. As with Bella, memories of the Bubbling Well Road cinemas hold center stage:

> *I recently met an amazing woman who is ninety years old and has the memory of a computer. She is articulate, smart, and a go-for-it personality.*
> *She came to Harbin in the 1920s and then Shanghai. She lived in the International Settlement near Bubbling Well Road. When she mentioned to me Bubbling Well Road, I got all excited.*
> *"Goldie, do you remember the movie house there?"*
> *I went with my friend Bella to that cinema to see a Shirley Temple movie. I was so absorbed in the action that when Shirley cried, I cried. When she smiled, I smiled and I took on the role of her character.*
> *I was on a high. My two heroes were always Superman and Shirley Temple. As much as I did crave dolls, I never wanted to get a Shirley Temple doll.*

> *I followed her life as an actress, as a married woman, as a mother, and as an ambassador. Shirley Temple, who in the 1940s gave a little girl in Shanghai some joy and motivation.*
> *She taught me that life is not always the way we plan it. There are times that we smile, cry, laugh, and feel sad. I am remembering as I am writing this, and feel such nostalgia for the movie, the fantasy escape.*
> *For just for a short time, but it was a good tranquilizer.*

Looking back at the twelve-year-old girl gazing off beyond the Bund in 1946, one may glimpse the longing and the fears, which were calmed by a Shirley Temple movie in Shanghai. It is the older woman looking back who knows that life does not follow expected patterns. Nonetheless, that little bit of joy, the "tranquilizer" provided by Shanghai movies, remains vividly in Chaya Leah's mind beyond the war in China.

Goldie's conversation with Chaya Leah in the nursing home brought back the delicious specificity of place and time. In her own musings, Chaya Leah tends to dwell on the larger themes, such as the contrast between the *shtetlach* Jews and the more cosmopolitan German-speaking refugees such as Bella's parents. There is no negative judgment in this comparison, merely a keen appreciation for the world that had enclosed and nurtured her own self-becoming. Going to the movies with Bella, like reminiscing with Goldie in a nursing home, enabled Chaya Leah to open new angles of vision upon her own inner world.

When I asked Chaya Leah to reflect directly about entering adolescence in China, she came up with a couple of morsels that reveal the well-maintained boundaries erected by Rabbi and Rebbetzin Walkin for their daughter. Going to the movies was acceptable. Not thinking much about the physical maturation of one's own body was also the norm. Yet, once in a while, the protected child glimpsed some disconcerting occurrences, which did not fit into the familiar expectations:

> *Looking back to my entering adolescence, I did not feel any different.*
> *My mother never had a private talk preparing and educating me for a change.*
> *I saw birth, death, illness, and distress and looked at it as part of the clumsiness of life.*
> *Flowers whither, leaves fall, people fall and hurt themselves, animals fight for food, men and women fight for food, for their domain, or to express their frustrations and desires.*

> One thing made me uncomfortable, I was not aware why, but I knew something was not right. I just could not put my finger on the emotion I felt.
> It was a different scent.
> It was right after the war, and I was in class.
> One of my classmates came to class wearing ruby red lipstick, makeup, and a not little-girl dress. She looked different acted different, and was yawning all the time.
> She was not a friend, but a classmate.
> It was later that I found out that she was a lady of the night.
> And I, so naïve, did not know what profession that was. There were many soldiers in Shanghai after the war, soldiers who have not been home for years. It seemed that overnight every store became a bar or a house of ill repute.

In this recollection, Chaya Leah Walkin reveals both her innocence and the deep way in which she had absorbed her family's values. Even without knowing, she had a keen sense of what was right and wrong. She did not need the word "prostitute" to understand that her classmate had fallen into a tough predicament. Calling her "a lady of the night" was a sign of respect. Thus, Chaya Leah was imbued with a sixth sense for propriety that never left her.

Unlike Chaya Leah's modest bearing in the photograph taken during the movie outing, this classmate came to school wearing something not appropriate for a young teenager. None of classmates were truly little girls anymore. Yet, even with knees bared and a loose-fitting blouse, Chaya Leah knew how to look and behave as a Jewish girl groomed for royalty according to her mother's traditions. The classmate, who was yawning and sporting lipstick, appeared different. Chaya Leah did not know why. She simply sensed something out of place.

Again, there is very little negative judgment against this Jewish refugee who had become a call girl. Rather, Chaya Leah is choosing to reflect more deeply about her own naïveté. While she had indeed witnessed illness and death in wartime China, these events appeared like the withering flowers or the hum of instinctual drives that was part of the "clumsiness" of life. While being aware of soldiers and bars, Chaya Leah Walkin had no idea of the business transactions carried on around them. These were beyond the realm of the experience and even imagination of Rav Shmuel David's eldest daughter, raised with such care during the war years in China.

Another incident also surfaced when I asked Chaya Leah to reflect on becoming a teenager in Shanghai. Interestingly, this, too, centered upon her newly gained freedom to wander beyond Liaoyang Road. In one of her walks after the war, Chaya Leah Walkin came across a gracious building in the European fashion. Having meandered into Buddhist and Shinto temples in Kobe, the Jewish teenager saw no reason for concern in entering a building that emanated quiet introspection:

> Suddenly, I felt a sense of foreboding.
> Like an alarm going off in my brain, a flight of immediate danger, and that was when I was looking into a beautiful building and I saw nuns.
> They tried to invite me into their courtyard, but a warning went off in me and I knew this too is not right. I ran away as quickly as I could, and never ventured into that direction.
> Temptation and curiosity. God protected me and watched over me.

Again, this is a memory augmented by a sixth sense alerting Chaya Leah that she was in the wrong place. She did not know much about Catholicism or about proselytizing nuns. Later, as a married woman and a mother of five with her hair covered, she enjoyed being mistaken for a "nun" as she struggled to finish her bachelor of arts degree at Mundelein College in Chicago. But in Shanghai, as an innocent girl being invited into a place of Christian worship, Rabbi Walkin's eldest daughter had only a semiconscious "scent" to guide her. Looking back, Chaya Leah attributed her escape from the nuns to divine protection. But in that moment in Shanghai, it was family upbringing and a gently articulated religious code that gave the young girl the courage to act.

SUPERMAN IN SHANGHAI

The end of the war brought new freedoms, glimpses of the forbidden, and packages from abroad. Jewish refugees, who had been cut off from family and overseas material support, now began receiving news and material goods from America and Europe. The news was heartrending. The realization of how many lives had been lost during the *Shoah* began to sink in among the Jewish survivors in China.

With that realization came mourning and uncertainty. Many of the Mirrer Yeshiva students, like Benny Fishoff, realized that they had become orphans. Rabbi Walkin himself found out that many more of his family members were murdered beyond the beloved brother whose name he had already bestowed upon his China-born son.

At the same time, American soldiers arrived bringing a sense of buoyancy and hope beyond the negotiations with call girls at the bars. For Chaya Leah Walkin, the arrival of these victorious heroes was associated with the availability of new foods, including chocolate:

> In Shanghai, when the American military came, there were truckloads of marines, sailors. I used to love it when they called out "Hi ya, baby!" It sounded so much like my name. I was so proud that they knew it. Little did I know that "Hi ya, baby" was an American expression of greeting.
> When in the fifties and sixties people would ask me how do you pronounced your name, I would answer: "Well, men in the military always used to call out 'Hiya! Hiyah, baby.' You can call me 'hiyah' but not 'baby.'" It always got a chuckle.
> I don't know how I had the strength to hold on firmly to my name.
> Today, it is common to use unusual names. But then, and I was so young. I stuck to my guns. The vanity plate of my car proudly, of course, reads CHAYA. In Shanghai, the payoff for our dutiful eating of oatmeal was a sliver of chocolate. Papa would take out a paring knife and scrapped a sliver off from the short end of the bar. A tiny little slice (only one slice!) would fall on the table. We would wet our fingers in our mouth and then gently tap on the chocolate to pick it up and savor the taste. What a beautiful reward!
> The American soldiers also gave us canned food. But we did not have can openers, so we used a hammer and nails to get to the food. We also bartered and traded. Many of the foods in the cans were not kosher, so we exchanged them for what was edible by Torah standards.

Again, Chaya Leah's memories of food and freedom are linked with each other, even as it becomes apparent in her effort to hold on to a Jewish name. At first, the budding teenager was thrilled to have American soldiers call out "Hi ya." Though well-educated in English pronunciation, Rav Walkin's daughter was unfamiliar with this American expression. Yet, she never gave up the name that was given to her in memory of the Bais Aharon's mother back in Pinsk.

Recalling Rabbi Walkin's slivers of chocolate after the dutifully eaten oatmeal augments the pleasure of the taste that lingers in the mind's eye. In the same way that Chaya Leah would not change her name, the family insisted on keeping the high *kashrut* standards even as new foods began pouring into Shanghai after the war.

Under the Apple Tree: End of the War, End of Refuge in Shanghai • CHAPTER 7 | 199

In addition to goodies gained from the American military, refugees began receiving packages from abroad. Chaya Leah recalls these treasured boxes coming to Rabbi and Mrs. Naiman and could not help but wonder when the Walkins, too, would open such a gift. With her own father mourning so many relatives, it seemed that there was no one left to send the Walkin children one of those packages that glistened "like a Christmas treat" at the post office. One day, Chaya Leah's wishes seemed to have been suddenly answered:

> One day, we had a notice that there was a package also for us from America. Our first thought was that it was a ploy, but after much reflection, our curiosity won over.
>
> It was not an easy matter to go and get the package. We had to go through several channels to get permission.
>
> Papa finally went to get the coveted package. Someone from Colorado, a friend of my father's, had read the survivors list and sent us a gift. We could not wait to open it. Oh, the anticipation! The anticipation!
>
> Finally, we opened it and the whole box was filled with Superman comic books and a large bag of pecan nuts.
>
> Of course, we did not know who Superman was but we enjoyed the nuts and shared them with friends. The same hammer and nails that served to open cans of food now served us to break open pecan shells.

At the movies on Bubbling Well Road, Chaya Leah had loved Shirley Temple and Superman both. But in the packages from Colorado, the comic books were as if from another world, unrecognizable. The pecans were cracked open the hard way and shared with the families on Liaoyang Road, much like the one-pot meals that had been shared with the Chinese amah and the German nanny during the war. Nonetheless, Chaya Leah Walkin could not hide her disappointment after the long-awaited gift arrived from abroad.

A disheartening note also colors Chaya Leah's memories of American clothing arriving in Shanghai after the war. Having worn only second-hand clothes for many years, the budding young woman naturally dreamed of better fitting, more stylish outfits:

> On another day at the end of the war, we were summoned to come to the courtyard of the Ohel Moshe. There were truckloads of clothing from America. We went to look at the fashions.

> "Oh no, we will not wear such dresses," we thought, imagining ourselves selecting out some of the dresses.
> "America has no taste in fashion."
> "Paris they are not," we murmured even before we got there.
> It turned out to be truckloads of sleepwear.

Having seen her own mother bedecked in fashionable dresses after the war, Chaya had rushed to the Ohel Moshe courtyard hoping for nice new clothes. She and her friends were already a little contemptuous of American goods. These girls did not expect to find Paris fashions, but were willing to make do with anything that was new.

The sleepwear—practical, like the oatmeal that preceded her father's chocolate shavings—did not satisfy the longings of the young women. As with much else in those heady months after the war, Chaya Leah learned to make do with what was. Such bending into the inevitable was made easier by the thrilling news that the Walkin family would finally be leaving Shanghai and heading toward Palestine.

ANI MA'AMIN—I BELIEVE!

In the summer of 1946, Shanghai was abuzz with departures. Jewish refugees who had made contact with close relatives were able to obtain guarantees of support and got ready to leave soon after the war. Others were waiting for various organizations, such as the Joint and the Vaad ha-Hatzala to arrange the necessary papers. Obtaining a visa was always a difficult process. Endurance and persistence were the key.

In the Walkin family's yeshiva circle, acquiring and distributing visas required an extra measure of communal consideration. Rabbi Chaim Shmuelewitz, for example, had obtained visas for himself and his family shortly after the arrival of the Mirrer Yeshiva in Shanghai during the High Holidays of 1941. Nonetheless, this mentor of refugee scholars refused to make use of the precious papers. Instead, he declared that he could not leave China until all his students received their visas as well. This ended up costing the Shmuelewitz family an extra five years in Shanghai—years they came to see in retrospect as filled with miracles and blessings.

Another 1941 visa had been obtained for Moshe Abba Kamien, the troubled young man who had been engaged before the war and had suffered mental anguish after his bride was killed. Yet, Kamien did not leave. Watched over with care by fellow students, he journeyed with them from Kobe to Shanghai, joining the exodus to America only after the war.

In the months after the birth of his new son, Rabbi Walkin was among the first of the Torah leaders to receive the precious documents that would enable his family to leave China. They were supposed to be on the very first ship carrying refugees from Shanghai to Palestine. What delayed the family's long-awaited departure and changed its destination was a glass of boiled water:

> My mother would always soak her merlekh (carrots) in a pitcher of water to keep them crisp and ready to make merelach tzimmes, for Shabbos.
> Days before we were supposed leave Shanghai for Palestine, my mother or the amah forgot to spill out the water from the pitcher.
> My father took a glass of water, and got dysentery. We missed that first boat. We ended up on a later one leaving for the States. Because of my father's dysentery, we could not get permission to leave Shanghai immediately.

Keeping Shabbat had been the foundation of Walkin family life in China. Washing carrots and other vegetables was just what one had to do to stay safe in this setting. Keeping another pitcher of boiled water for drinking was equally essential. Confusion between the carrots' container and the drinking water made a world of difference for the Walkins.

Looking back at that pitcher, Chaya Leah does not blame the amah. That would have been the easiest way to deal with the radical change forced upon the Walkin family—blame the servant. But neither Chaya Leah nor her family took that path. There was doubt. It could have been Rebbetzin Walkin who forgot to dump the water from the carrots and boil up a fresh pot before Shabbat. In the haste and excitement of departure, mistakes could happen. They did happen. Memory's gaze grants them a forgiving framework.

The change in the family's destination, in the end, was not caused by a glass of water. Chaya, like her parents, came to believe that they ended up where providence led them, where each member of the Walkin family was to fulfill a purpose beyond what they had anticipated in Shanghai in 1945–46. One of the last family photos taken in China reveals this readiness for the unexpected. Here, Rebbetzin Walkin is holding a plump, ten-month-old Chaim in her arms. Next to the mother stands Mrs. Nash, the nanny hired by the Walkins to help with the new baby and with family preparations for departure. Esther, with a large bow in her hair, looks like the child Chaya Leah was years earlier. Moshe Yoel is wearing a sailor suit ready for the sea journey they would take to yet another foreign country. Chaya Leah is outfitted with a new suit, tailored for her changing figure.

Mrs. Nash and Rebbetzin Tzivia with baby and older children.

Gone are the girlish bows and the loose shirt. Here is a young woman, the oldest sibling, bedecked for travel and for taking on responsibilities far beyond her age. Just how daunting these new duties were to become did not become clear until Mrs. Walkin gave birth to yet another child, Rachel, in New York.

The Shanghai travel suit heralded a speedy maturation for the twelve-year-old girl gazing out into the distance in the summer of 1946. Rabbi Walkin, recovering from dysentery, is not in this photograph. The change in direction from Palestine to the United States was already in the works. What remained was the challenge of finding tickets for one of the American military ships leaving Shanghai after the war.

While waiting to book passage to America, Rav Shmuel David busied himself with helping the remaining refugees. He stayed in close contact with Rabbi Shmuelewitz about ways to aid as many of the Mirrer students with their papers as possible. As recently ordained rabbis, these young men were to be placed in various pulpits and educational institutions in which they thrived and rebuilt Torah life after the war. Each visa was precious. Yet, due to Rabbi

Walkin's generosity and Rabbi Shmuelewitz's efforts, they were not limited only to the small circle of the yeshiva community.

One such visa to America that Rabbi Walkin helped to process was for Samuel Iwry. Although he had had a Talmudic education before the war, Iwry was not one of the young rabbis ready to take up the Orthodox pulpit of a synagogue in America. Chaya Leah's father wanted to help Samuel Iwry, but at the same time, he worried that a visa for a nonobservant young man would appear fraudulent in the eyes of the American authorities and thereby endanger the prospects of other rabbinical students. He sought advice from Rabbi Shmuelewitz.

The older mentor urged Rabbi Walkin to go ahead and arrange a visa for Iwry and affirmed his many positive qualities. From a starting point in Baltimore, Samuel Iwry managed to build a distinguished academic career in the Near Eastern Studies Department of Johns Hopkins University. When he looked back upon his China years in a memoir entitled *To Wear the Dust of War*, Iwry made no mention of help from Rabbi Walkin or Rabbi Shmuelewitz in obtaining the precious visa to come to the United States. Instead, he told a more romantic tale in which an American GI friend arrived to his wedding in Shanghai, bearing a closed envelope. Iwry's marriage to his refugee sweetheart Nina took place in a spacious Shanghai apartment at the end of 1945. Rabbi Ashkenazi, who had been so dedicated to the welfare of all the refugees, came to perform the service. Unlike the yeshiva community weddings that had been held in the Walkin "*simcha* hall," this was a different kind of wedding. Iwry recalls how the GI apologized for not bringing a bouquet for the bride while handing the groom an envelope:

> I did not like this. Nina understood that this was the American way, putting a check of some amount in an envelope and giving to the young people. In Europe, we did not do this, ever. Besides, we did not need it. At the time, we had a very small income, we made our way through the war, and we knew we would continue to manage. But when we opened it, it was not a check. It was a little note from the consulate. "Come, Monday 10:00AM to get your visa for immigration to America."[6]

Where does the truth lie? Memory wears many veils and there may be no need to rend one for the sake of the other. Rabbi Walkin and Shmuel Iwry ended up traveling different paths, both in China and in America.

---

6 Iwry, *To Wear the Dust of War*, 137.

What to the Orthodox rabbi's mind was a useful position in a Conservative synagogue ended up for Iwry to be a career-launching opportunity. Perceptions differed but not the bonds of affection and responsibility that led Chaya Leah's father to help out fellow refugees. To this day, Chaya Leah remains in contact with Iwry's son, without any need to obtain gratitude for what happened in Shanghai after the war. Sharing memories is, in her mind, enough of a gift.

On July 5, 1946, the Walkin family finally boarded their ship out of Shanghai. Like Iwry's boat a few months later, this was a "liberty ship" built to carry American soldiers during the war. It was called the USS General Meigs, in memory of the Quartermaster General who had served with distinction in the Union Army during the Civil War. The USS Meigs was famed for carrying over 5,200 troops at one time during the war. Now, it was ferrying 1,500 passengers to San Francisco.

On one of the surviving pages of the ship's List of Alien Passengers for the United States appear the six names of the Walkin family. Samuel David Walkin, aged 52, is listed as "Professor." Cila Walkin, 36, is listed as "housewife." Chaja Lea, 12, bears the label "student"—as did Ester, 11, and brother Moizse Jojel, 8. Chaim, the latest addition to the Walkin family, is listed simply as a ten-month-old "child." With these misspelled, half-Americanized names, and with a fancy professorial title attached to his own name, Rav Shmuel David's family finally ended the China chapter of their turbulent life.

Walkin family before leaving Shanghai ca. 1946.

Leaving Shanghai, as Chaya Leah recalls, was an intensely emotional affair. Those on board the USS Meigs, as well as well-wishers at the dock, sensed the

Under the Apple Tree: End of the War, End of Refuge in Shanghai • CHAPTER 7 | 205

finality of the moment. Everyone had been changed by the war years in China. Everyone still recalled the arduous journeys that required leaving behind homes in Europe and Asia for an unknown destiny in America. On the eve of this momentous departure, Jews were asking themselves: What had enabled us to get this far? How did we ever withstand the harrowing trials of flight and war? How are we to go on after so many of our relatives were murdered in cold blood by the Nazis?

The values and traditions that had strengthened the Walkin family and their friends now came to the fore once again. As the ship pulled out of the Shanghai harbor, Chaya remembers an intensely emotional affirmation of Jewish faith:

> *The boat we boarded carried other refugees who also got permits to leave Shanghai. The whole Jewish community came out to bid us farewell. The hope was that they too will soon be redeemed and go to a new world to start their lives again, rebuild from ashes.*
>
> *We were on the deck, and there was a sea of people on shore. As the ship started to move, you could hear the loud sounds of the haunting and somber words of the Ani Ma'amin.*
>
> *And as the ship was moving, the waves carried the melody.*
>
> *We stood on deck waving to those on shore. I can never get that moment out of my head.*
>
> *The memory of hope, faith, endurance, sadness, and resilience. I cry every time I hear the Ani Ma'amin being sung.*
>
> *So somber, so haunting, so full of faith.*
>
> *The Ani Ma'amin was our farewell to Shanghai and also our greeting to a new life in America.*
>
> *Yes, we survived and lived in Shanghai because we are ma'aminim. We are believers. We are believers in Hakodosh Boruch Hu. And have been for thousands of years, in spite of all our sufferings.*

The twelve-year-old student of the Kadoorie School and of Bais Yaakov had been familiar with the words of this song from teachers as well as from her parents. She knew that they had been penned by the Rambam (Maimonides, 1138–1204) more than eight hundred years earlier when he codified key principles of the Jewish faith.

Yet, when Chaya Leah looked back to the moment when the USS Meigs pulled out of the harbor, she heard not only the well-known words but also a longing for redemption that went beyond the trials of refuge in

Shanghai. She now understood that within those very trials were embedded the seeds of a faith that had survived and was strengthened by the war years in China. The Jewish people had not been abandoned after all. They had not drifted aimlessly on the gray spume that now licked the shores of the Whampoo River.

Jewish refugees like the Walkin family had witnessed more miracles than ordinary language could convey. The *Ani Ma'amin* song condensed their hopes, prayers, and their determination to craft new meaning out of a history about to unfold beyond limited lives:

> *Ani ma'amin,*
> *Be'emuna shelema*
> *Beviat hamashiach ani ma'amin*
> *Veaf al pi sheyitmuhmehu*
> *Im kol zeh, achake loh*
> *Im kol zeh, im kol zeh, achake loh*
> *Achake bechol yom sheyavoh*
>
> I believe
> With complete faith
> In the coming of the Messiah, I believe
> And even though he may tarry
> Nonetheless I will wait for him
> I will wait every day for him to come.

This was not a simplistic Messianism. Instead, it carried the cadence of endurance, of grief, and of resilience. The Walkin family had survived not only as refugees but also as believers. They did not feel abandoned even in the midst of their harshest trials.

This same *Ani Ma'amin* melody was also heard in the concentration camps in Europe. The tune that Chaya recalls so well dates back to the Moditzer Rebbe (Shaul Yedidya Elazar, 1886–1947) who had a special love of *niggunim* (Chassidic melodies). One of his devoted followers, Azriel David Fastag, recalled the Rebbe's favorite notes on one of the death trains to Treblinka. It used to be sung as part of the liturgy on Yom Kippur back at home in the hamlet of Moditz. During the *Shoah*, it seemed to make more sense with the Rambam's haunting words.

Once Azriel David Fastag stared humming the Rebbe's melody augmented by the Rambam's verses, the whole train started singing with him. News of this train ride reached the Moditzer Rebbe himself just before he left for his own refuge in Shanghai. There he declared:

> When they sang *Ani Ma'amin* on the death train, the pillars of the world were shaking. The Almighty said: Whenever the Jews sing *Ani Ma'amin* I will remember the six million victims and have mercy on the rest of my people.[7]

The Moditzer tune spread from Poland to China and from there to all parts of the embattled Jewish world. In Shanghai after the war, the Rambam's words had a different connotation than they had earlier on the death train to Treblinka. In Europe's murderous camps, *Ani Ma'amin* had been a desperate last cry. In the Warsaw Ghetto, it became an anthem of revolt against the Nazi occupation.

In China, the same song wove Jewish refugees back into the fabric of a larger destiny. After reading about the genesis of *Ani Ma'aamin*, Chaya Leah wrote to me:

> I also remember sleeping on a person's shoe crushed in steerage on the boat to Japan…
> My head on those shoes.

At the same time, she understood only too well the difference between a cattle train to Treblinka and the boat ride that took the Walkin family from Stalin's Soviet Union to refuge in Japan.

For Rav Shmuel David and Rebbetzin Tzivia, travelling with four healthy children, including baby Chaim, *Ani Ma'amin* was not a song of death. Instead, it represented an affirmation of life regained from the ruins of war. During the years in Shanghai, there had been survival and awakening as well.

As in the verses of *Shir Ha'Shirim*, hope had been born anew out of the ashes of war. The "apple tree" had sprouted new branches and more rugged roots in China. Faith in Jewish destiny was strengthened as these carriers of the Torah tradition started out toward America's new shores. There, they would build upon the foundation cast by previous generations. There, they would honor the memory of their murdered kin along with the promise of renewal gained during the hardships of Shanghai.

---

7   Dorfman, Yitchak. "Ani Ma'amin." Accessed August 13, 2017. http://www.chabad.org/library/article_cdo/aid/107189/jewish/Ani-Maamin.htm

CHAPTER 8

BEFORE THE SHADOWS OF NIGHT ARE GONE:

Starting a New Life in America

Before the day breathes,
before the shadows of night are gone,
I will hurry to the mountain of myrrh...

Shir Ha'Shirim 4:6

When the USS Meigs pulled out of the Shanghai harbor, twelve-year-old Chaya Walkin did not know what to expect. She certainly felt the excitement of the adults setting out to brighter shores after the war years in China. She probably intuited the vast uncertainty that enveloped her parents as they left the close-knit community of friends and refugees who had enriched their five years on Liaoyang Road. She might have even sensed the dark shadows of grief over relatives lost in the *Shoah* that accompanied the Jewish refugees on their journey to America.

What a young girl used to the company of displaced scholars could not have imagined was the growing hostility toward survivors after the war. Even though the Holocaust was officially over by 1946, the aftermath of hate and disaster remained palpable in Europe as well as in the United States. Far from compassion for the *sh'erit ha-pletah*—the battered remnant of the Jewish people—congregating in various camps, prejudice prevailed. By the summer of 1947, there were 238,000 stateless persons trapped in Germany, France, and Italy. No country rushed to take them in, and immigration to Palestine was still violently limited.

In the United States, the American Institute of Public Opinion published findings as early as January 1946 indicating that less than five percent of the public supported an increase in Jewish immigration quotas.[1] Most Americans wanted fewer Jewish neighbors and did not want their children going to school with the scarred and maimed remnants of Europe's ravaged.

In China during the same period, General George Marshall tried to keep talks going between the Nationalists (KMT) and the Communists (CCP) in the hope of averting the coming civil war. By January 1947, active hostilities between the two armies had broken out—with that began the waning of American hopes for a liberal and democratic China. In Japan, by contrast, the occupation gave the United States a stronger hand in shaping post-war politics. This influence culminated in the "Peace Constitution" enacted on May 3, 1947. This document was best known for its Article 9, by which Japan renounced its right to wage war and agreed to promote popular sovereignty in conjunction with the monarchy.

The world at large thus remained wracked by uncertainty as the Walkin family reached American shores in the early autumn of 1946. Their predicament is echoed in the words of *Shir Ha'Shirim*, in which the groom seeks to reassure the beloved, who clearly carries fear in her heart. He promises to comfort her both during the heat of the day as well as all through dusk and the darker hours that follow. Although the mountain of myrrh beckons, the shadows of night make themselves known as well.

The day breathing its last light suggests a time when reassurance is most needed. For Chaya Leah, the human groom who would anchor her firmly into a new life did not appear until seven years after the Walkins landed in San Francisco. During those years, a child's faith in the divine benevolence that had protected her family in China developed into a more mature belief in the unique destiny of the Jewish people.

While the oldest daughter of Rav Shmuel David was nearing her physical and religious maturity, America became engulfed by the frenzy of "McCarthyism." In 1950, by the time Chaya Leah was sixteen, Senator Joe McCarthy had delivered his famous speech to the Virginia Republican Women's Convention accusing the State Department of harboring over 200 known communists, many of whom shaped the policies now blamed for the "loss of China."

In 1950, Julian and Ethel Rosenberg were arrested as spies for the Soviet Union. Less than four months after Chaya Leah's marriage in February 1953,

---

[1] Wesley Greear, *American Immigration Policies and Public Opinion on European Jews 1933-1945.* (PhD diss., East Tennessee University, 2002), 20.

this infamous couple was executed, sending shudders of fear into the wider Jewish world. In Germany, the Nuremberg Trials had come to a halt by the end of 1946, with only a few high-ranking Nazis feeling the full weight of opprobrium for their crimes against humanity. Many more were helped to escape to South America or simply vanished back into Germany's civilian life.

Three short years after the Walkin family left Shanghai, Mao Zedong stood in Tiananmen Square on October 1, 1949 and declared to a largely deaf world: "The Chinese People Have Stood Up." He was using the language of nationalism, still so fluent among Communist Party officials in China today. In October 1949, Mao claimed that it was the Chinese people as a whole who had finally shaken off the chains of imperialism. This bold declaration did not acknowledge any of the brutality that his own cohort had inflicted before and during the Chinese civil war. Few among the patriots who were in Beijing or who rushed back from abroad could have imagined the murderous policies that would be promulgated, especially against the educated elites by Mao Zedong during the 1950s and the 1960s.

One year before Mao's speech in Tiananmen Square, David Ben Gurion also proclaimed the rebirth of his people with the declaration of the founding of the state of Israel in May 1948. Of all the world tremors unleashed between 1946 and 1953, Ben Gurion's proclamation had the most heartening impact upon Chaya Leah Walkin. Just how enduring that impact was did not become clear until December 2015, when Chaya Leah attended a Hanukah play with her granddaughter in Lakewood, New Jersey. Seeing a large group of talented girls singing on the stage, she remembered her own awkward, shy, and yet willing participation in a New York City ceremony marking the birth of the state of Israel in 1948:

> *Memory came knocking at me and I remember I must have been thirteen or fourteen, when I and two other students were chosen to be on stage where John Garfield, the actor, was singing a cantata. I think it might have been 1948.*
>
> *The stage was huge, the audience was overflowing, and on stage was an American flag and an Israeli flag. How proud I was to pledge allegiance to the flag and sing the national anthem, and my heart burst with joy when I sang the Hatikva.*

Here, we see Rav Shmuel David's daughter literally in new garb. She is fourteen years old, a shy teenager raised in Japan and China, walking onto a stage in America to sing a Jewish anthem quite different than the haunting *Ani Ma'amin* that had accompanied the SS Meigs out of Shanghai.

Something was changing in the world, and inside Chaya Leah Walkin as well. There was a whiff of new confidence, a new hope in Garfield's powerful voice and striking stage presence. The days of bedraggled, homeless Jews appeared to be over:

> I went alone, and was terrified and overwhelmed.
> Everyone was envious that I was one who was chosen, but I wanted to run away and hide.
> I, the little refugee girl, in a borrowed outfit made up like a mannequin, I did not want to be there. I can't sing or carry a tune. Why did they want me, what message did they try to give?
> I wanted to hide, but I did it because it was for Israel.
> I never talked about it, as I thought it was simply propaganda.
> And don't think I ever mentioned it to my husband and I told him everything.
> And now that deep buried memory is peeking out.
> I looked at all those little girls.
> But I saw only one little girl scared and frightened wearing a white blouse and a blue shirt with white bobby socks and patent leather Mary Janes (or was it penny loafers, which were the craze in my youth)?

In the winter of 2015, attending one of her great granddaughter's performances in New Jersey, Chaya Leah allows herself to recall herself as a child in 1948. One shy girl on the stage was enough to bring up memories not even shared with her husband. The shiny shoes and the white shirt call to mind the recently arrived refugee chosen to participate in a large ceremony to honor the birth of Israel. Although Rabbi and Rebbetzin Walkin did not have a Zionist outlook, they did not stop their eldest daughter from taking part in a gathering that brought honor to the Jewish people as a whole.

Looking back, Chaya recalls John Garfield's strong and beautiful voice. Was she aware that he was a fellow Jew? Born Jacob Julius Garfinkle, this son of Russian immigrants was 20 years older than Chaya Leah. Having started his career in Yiddish theater, he had changed his name once he signed a major contract with Warner Brothers. By the early 1950s, despite his Americanized name, John Garfield became the target of the House Un-American Activities Committee for refusing to name names. Subsequently, he was blacklisted in the film industry and died at the early age of 39, one year before Chaya Leah was to become the bride of Rabbi Michael Small.

UNDZER SHTUB—OUR HOME

The shadows of history's nightmares lingered in Chaya Leah's life long after the family's arrival on American shores. To be sure, the early years in New York were exciting. During those years, this China-educated teenager made her way in America more deftly than she could have been imagined possible when she used to cross Liaoyang Road during the war.

The breath of a new day was coming, but it was coming slowly, haltingly. Chaya Leah's recollection of the passage to America on the SS Meigs shimmers with girlish delight, as if the mountain of myrrh was indeed only just ahead. The hardships that followed never quite dampened the excitement of that journey, so different from the terror-filled nights that took Tzivia Walkin and her three small children out of Poland to Vilna:

> *The General Meigs was definitely not a passenger ship. My mother was seasick the whole trip, and not having kosher food we lived on apples (McIntosh) and hard-boiled eggs. But we had a little pot, so I got from the kitchen staff some cereal and we cooked it in the big kitchen. We did not have beds on the boat, but we slept in a hammock-like bed.*

Again, here is the story of the single pot. In Shanghai, one pot was all the family had to cook whatever limited supplies could feed the children, the amah, and the German nanny. Eating non-kosher food was as inconceivable on the boat to America as it had been during the food shortages of war. While Japan's welcoming tangerines had become a distant dream, the bathrooms and packaged edibles on America's shores were an immediate marvel to behold:

> *Arriving in San Francisco, we were put up in a hotel before going to New York. Imagine the shock and awe with which we viewed everything in America.*
> *A bathroom in the room.*
> *Putting coins in a slot and pulling a lever, and wow, chocolate comes out.*
> *Gum. You eat and chew, and eat and chew, eat and it just does not disappear.*
> *Stores, no open market places. Food! Varieties of food. Feast for a king.*
> *Packaged food. Heaven, gan eden.*

Chocolate from a vending machine and gum that you chew and chew and yet it does not disappear promised a future with no shadows at all. The day's breath appeared at first fresh, simply enlivening. Then came the realization that dusk and the night had not simply lifted away once the family landed in San Francisco.

In one of the first photographs to be taken in America, the shadows are apparent in the cracked background and yellowing edges that frame the Walkin family. They look like what they were: European refugees trying to make the best of a new world. Rabbi Shmuel David, at 54, faces the camera directly, with a beard that is graying and calls to mind trials endured in Shanghai as well as the challenge of making a living for the family after the war. Rebbetzin Tzivia is holding up her China-born Chaim, a well-bundled and growing infant. Esther, bedecked in bows, wears the smile of a shy girl who knows that her parents will keep her safe. Moshe Yoel sports the most open grin in a newly acquired, probably hand-me-down trench coat. A little boy trying on the vestments of a young man. Chaya Leah, the most mature of the Walkin children, is not smiling. She is gazing directly at the camera with questioning eyes. Without knowing yet, she will be her family's most vulnerable bridgehead in this new world.

The family traveled by train across a vast continent, which they knew little about. In Chicago, they spent a few hours with Rabbi Walkin's old friend from the yeshiva in Radin. Chaya Leah had little recollection of this encounter with Rabbi Isaac Smolyar and his wife Chana, who would become her in-laws seven years later. In New York, the Walkins were cared for by Jewish relief organizations overwhelmed with all the survivors pouring in from Europe, and now even from Asia.

Their first housing was in a hotel on the upper west side of Manhattan with a kosher restaurant called Schreiber's nearby. Looking back in 2016, Chaya Leah is at once the little girl delighting in candy and a seasoned woman who understands the preciousness of old-world connections in a strange new city:

> We had a room in the hotel for the entire family and I remember the room so fondly. The elevator, the lobby, the doorman, so alien to me after the ghetto. The candy machine, where you put in a dime or quarter and the candy came out.
>
> First Shabbos was spent with the Zaks family. Feigele Zaks was the daughter of the Chofetz Chaim and a friend of my mother. Her husband, Reb Mendel Zaks, had also studied at the Chofetz Chaim yeshiva. The Chofetz Chaim was in his 60s when Feigele was born to his second wife. Our second Shabbos was with my Uncle Mordecai and Aunt Malke Landinski, my mother's uncle and the Radiner Rosh yeshiva's son. Our third Shabbos we spent with the Carlebachs, Reb Shlomo Carlebach's parents.

Chaya Leah's recollections reveal how the yeshiva connections from Radin softened the family's three months in New York. Rebbetzin Feiga Zaks was a childhood friend who brought comfort to Tzivia Walkin during her first days in New York. Her husband, Rabbi Mendel Zaks (1898–1974), had been a well-known scholar before the war. He became deeply involved with the leadership of the Chofetz Chaim Yeshiva as soon as he married Feiga in 1922. In fact, Rav Mendel was held in such trust that the aged sage of Radin had sent him to the United States as early as 1925 to incorporate the yeshiva in order to facilitate fundraising.

Rejoining the community of illustrious Torah scholars was both reassuring and a necessity for the Walkin family. It gave meaning and purpose to their new life on American shores. Tzivia Walkin's uncle, Rabbi Mordechai Landinski too, had been deeply connected to the Radin Yeshiva and to the Chofetz Chaim. As a young man, he had been noted for his fervent prayers, one of which was especially effective during the illness of his beloved mentor. Upon recovery, the Chofetz Chaim blessed Mordechai to live a long life, which indeed enabled him to continue the legacy of his family's learning in the United States.

In New York City, Chaya Leah was far from the protected infant being shown off to the rabbinical families in 1934. The teenager now had to cope with secular schooling while her father made every effort to become self-supporting as soon as possible. The hardships endured in China during the war came in handy as the family learned to live with limited means in the United States.

Living in the one room in the hotel, for example, was not so different from their accommodations on Liaoyang Road. In fact, for a growing girl, the novelties beyond the hotel door multiplied daily. The elevator was thrilling after ground floor living in Kobe and Shanghai. The doorman must have echoed the role of the Chinese watchman in the little guardhouse. But here in New York City, there was no war, no debris. Only gracious greetings for the girl who passed in and out on her way to the nearby Joan of Arc Public School. The candy machine worked and dimes seem to have been available to feed the fancy of a child who had not known sweets during her war years in China.

Spending Shabbat with families who had come from Europe enabled the Walkins to share memories. In the company of their friends and family, Rabbi Walkin and Rebbetzin Tzivia were no longer refugees but rather honored guests connected to the venerable Bais Aharon. Chaya Leah does not dwell on the conversations about the Holocaust that she must have heard around these Shabbat tables. After all, everyone had lost family. Everyone knew someone who was completely orphaned; everyone knew survivors who were broken by grief. For Chaya Leah, these shadows would creep up later along with fears of uniformed officials and a growing realization that her mother carried the wounds of war deeply buried in her heart and soul.

The quest for relatives in the new world did, however, make an impression upon Chaya Leah as a growing girl. Even after the Walkins moved from Manhattan to Brooklyn, the longing to find some living relatives continued undiminished. As the oldest child, Chaya Leah was able to see this longing with some humor because she was the only one able to decode her parents' tenuous hold on their new English-language world. In one of her emails to me, she retold a story of mistaken identities as follows:

> *My mother would rarely go out. Everything was delivered to the house, and if she needed a doctor, he would come to the house. But a dentist was different. You had to go to his office.*
> *My mother got so excited when she came back from the dentist.*
> *"We found relatives, we found relatives! We all have to go meet him!"*
> *Of course, my mother did not speak English and the dentist did not speak Yiddish, and every comment my mother made the dentist shook his head in agreement.*
> *So the whole entourage went to meet our relative that our mother found.*
> *On the door of his office was a sign in large script:*
> *DR. PINES RING BELL AND WALK IN*
> *"See there it is!*
> *WALKIN, WALKIN!*
> *Our relative, WALKIN!"*

Dr. Pines treated Rebbetzin Tzivia's teeth, but could not heal her aching heart. Not being Polish, not knowing anything of the world that the Walkins had left behind, he probably did not understand the disappointment that followed after Chaya Leah translated the innocuous sign on the office door.

The depth of the longing for kin, however, was not lost upon the girl who had gained the tools of survival in English at the Kadoorie School in Shanghai. She was not only the family's translator when corresponding with Sima Valkin from South Africa but also the one designated to go meet blood relative when Tzivia's long lost brother Leibel surfaced in New York. Like many of the other grown-up tasks entrusted to her, this was not an easy assignment for Chaya Leah. But there was no way she could refuse. It took many years for her to understand the trauma of that encounter, which brought back painful recollections of how the siblings had become separated before the war:

> *I remember something about this when my mother was trying to escape Poland. On the wagon with her was her brother Liebel. They were shooting at us. Liebel, who was about twelve, jumped off the wagon.*
> *My mother was responsible for him.*
> *After the war, we heard that Liebel was alive, and was bought to America by an organization.*
> *I, all of fifteen, was the only one to meet him at the station. I still cannot get the scene out of my mind.*
> *I met him and his wife Stella. Arrangements were made for the refugees to go to a hotel to freshen up.*
> *When Liebel came out of the bathroom, his body was scared with heavy welts, across his back, his front—huge, huge cuts that never healed.*
> *I stood in shock and bit my lips.*

Tzivia Walkin thought she had lost her brother forever during the terrifying night when she crossed the border from Poland to Lithuania. The memory of that loss did not accost Chaya Leah until Leibel surfaced in New York after the war. Suddenly, the scars upon his body vividly augmented her mother's unspoken grief and guilt. Chaya Leah, who saw the dead being carted off the streets of Shanghai as a child, now stood aghast as a teenager confronted with the atrocities that had been visited upon the Jews.

> *Liebel spoke Yiddish and Stella, from Berlin, spoke German. I understood her. She never talked about meeting Liebel, but I did know that her parents were shomer shabbos, and Liebel, as young as he was, only wanted a wife from a frum family.*
> *Vera, dear Vera, I do remember the reunion.*
> *Stella, Liebel, and I were always very close.*
> *Stella was my confidant and my best friend.*
> *They had no children.*
> *Many years later, I encouraged them to adopt a child. It was difficult, because of their age, but they did adopt a boy, who was challenged.*
> *I should have written about this long ago.*

Less than three years after disembarking from the SS Meigs, Chaya Leah Walkin was sent from Brooklyn to Manhattan to meet her uncle. Nothing in

China or America had fully prepared the fifteen-year-old girl for the tortured body of a Jewish relative who had endured the *Shoah* in Europe.

Chaya Leah had seen life begin and end in Shanghai. She was not naïve about the pain of war. But the scarred body of Leibel Socharow brought back the terror she had felt as a very young child during their winter escape from Poland. That terror took many more years to acknowledge and even more to put into words.

Stella's German words connected her to Chaya Leah and must have been a welcome relief from the darkness welling up from her own childhood. Berlin was not a familiar world to graduates of Polish yeshivas. In the midst of the wreckage of war, Leibel had found a young woman whose family had kept Shabbat. He brought her into the Walkin home, where Jewish observances mattered a great deal.

With her gift for friendship, Chaya Leah maintained the bond with Liebel and Stella and understood their pain at being childless. Harsh bruises were shocking to behold and lay buried for years in memory's graveyard. But childlessness was a grief Chaya Leah felt she could address. Adopting a child might heal this brutal past. A boy who was challenged, she realized later, was both a blessing and a reminder of the broken shards embedded in all Jewish refugees who had sought new life in America.

The commitment to come to the aid of those in need remained ingrained in the Walkin home in Brooklyn, as it had been in Shanghai. Even with very limited means, Shmuel David and Tzivia sought to help the orphaned young men whom they had mentored in China by inviting them for meals and arranging for their marriages. When Rabbi Walkin finally started a small synagogue in Brooklyn, it was the Shanghai refugees who were his first congregants and his most devoted friends.

The Walkin children, as Chaya Leah recalled, were constantly imbued with the spirit of a traditional Jewish home, consciously modeled after the lofty families from Radin and in Pinsk:

> *Both my parents grew up in homes of gedolim.*
> *And I as a child was blessed with a home that was host to most of the gedolim of the dor.*
> *"Azoy hot men zikh gefirt bay undzer shtub"*
> *"This is the manner of behavior in our home."*
> *My mother said this when she wanted us to behave.*
> *This was her expression.*
> *Her memories of her home.*
> *Always.*

> "My child, this is the right way to be.
> "*Azoy past nisht*"
> "And this is unacceptable."

In this simple, often repeated refrain—"*Azoy past nisht*"—you have Rebbetzin Tzivia's main message to her children: they are descendants of Torah royalty. Therefore, they must embody both humility and respect.

"*Undzer shtub*"—"our home"—was both the Walkins house in Brooklyn and the one back in Poland, which had served as its spiritual foundation. Even with all the embarrassments and awkwardness of her adolescence in America, Chaya did not forget her mother's words. She would build her own family in due time upon a similarly strong foundation augmented by the experience of becoming a mentor to her younger siblings at the age of thirteen.

One year after arriving in the United States, Tzivia Walkin gave birth to another child. Rachel—called Rochele by her family—was born on October 21, 1947. As a result of a spinal injection administered during labor, Rebbetzin Walkin's health become greatly compromised. Debilitated by severe back pain, she needed Chaya Leah to step in and take care of house chores as well as the younger children. Being a young woman still in her early 30s, Rebbetzin Tzivia bemoaned her fate, as Chaya Leah recalls, with the following Yiddish words: "*Mayne beste un shenste yunge yorn bin ikh gelign in bet*"—"My nicest and best years of youth I spend in bed."

Chaya Leah's recollections of those years are marked by the effort to be a mother's helper, while also trying to make her own way in the bewildering world of American schooling:

> My father adored my mother and put her on a pedestal. He did all in his power to make her life easier and more comfortable. The baby, Rochele, was less than a year old and my brother Chaim, who was two years old, were left in my care while my mother went to Sharon Springs in upstate New York to take the healing baths for her back. I was left to take care of the two little ones, my father, the house, and the shul.
>
> It was a big responsibility for a youngster, but I felt so important and needed.

Here, the young girl who learned how to buy chicken and fish in Shanghai now takes on more motherly roles. Caring for two little children was not an easy matter. Rav Walkin was busy with his community responsibilities. Chaya Leah had charge of the children and took on the challenge with a fierce pride:

> My greatest thrill was being able to honor my mother and father.
> To ensure that I would take good care of my sister Rochele, my mother bribed me by telling me she would pay me a dollar for every pound Rochele would gain.
> I stuffed her like you stuffa goose —I fed her constantly.
> They were away for about a month or 6 weeks, and the day they came home, I made a major dinner. My mother and siblings came into the house and saw the festive table, all smiling. Everything was under control, the apartment was clean, everything in order.
> She walked into the bedroom where Rochele was napping and saw this fat little baby. She had gained five pounds.
> I would get five dollars, a fortune.

In the end, Chaya Leah had managed to care for two small children and her father as well. It was not the "fortune" of those five dollars that made the deepest impact on her memory. Rather, it was the privilege of carrying out the key Torah commandment of honoring her father and mother.

Beyond fulfilling a moral dictum that she held dear, Chaya Leah found emotional satisfaction in caring for her "little ones." From the Shanghai days through today, Chaim and Rochele have a special link to the oldest sibling of the Walkin family. When they were little, Chaya Leah took them to doctors, attended their school conferences, and delighted in witnessing their unfolding talents. One memorable visit to a heart specialist with six-year-old Chaim (because he had a heart murmur) reveals the depth of caring and worry that set Chaya apart from the care-free teenagers of her time:

> I was walking with Chaim down Empire Boulevard holding his hand and crying bitter tears, praying, please God let this be nothing, not another one with a heart problem, tears running down and me squeezing his hands.
> He was OK. Chaimke, the doctor said, is OK. I always wondered if that four-block walk with my crying all the way had any effect on the outcome. We never talked about it, but I always wondered.
> Till today, I still feel that emotion I felt that warm summer day. How scared I was and fervently I was mispallel (praying).

A girl's fervent prayer lingers in Chaya Leah's mind as a sign of how she helped weave together a family burdened by war. Doctors' visits were no simple matter for Chaya Leah, who had seen how easily illness brings death in its wake in Shanghai.

Walking down Empire Boulevard in Brooklyn, gripping Chaim's hand, she turned to God because this was the first and last resource in times of terrifying need. When she was less scared, Chaya Leah could attend to her siblings' more ordinary needs:

> I also stepped in for my mother in all school functions. My mother bedridden, my father so busy all the time, school plays "ah narishkeit" (pointless trivialities), birthday parties "ah narishkeit." To me, it was important so I was there for all their "narishkeits."

This willingness to be present for "trivialities" earned Chaya Leah her younger siblings' lifelong love and respect. When she started to earn a little income from babysitting jobs outside of "Undzer shtub," Chaya Leah bought Rochele her first doll carriage. It was Chaya Leah, too, who bought Chaim's first bicycle and sought to assuage Rebbetzin Tzivia's worries about what might happen if he got hurt.

Reassurances from a daughter did not sink in as well as words of advice offered by a visiting friend, who had allowed her son to ride his bike more freely than Rebbetzin Walkin dared to imagine. The visitor, too, had a child after coming to America. Nonetheless, she counseled: "Iz dos kind shuldik, az ikh hob im geboyrn azoy shpet in lebn? Fundestvegen, a kind iz a kind un er muz hobn a normaln lebn" —"Is it the child's fault that he was born so late in my life? But a child is a child and he must live a normal life."

Chaim Walkin's journey to a "normal life" took a very public turn in 1954, when the boy of eight was featured in a *New York Times* photograph signing his own citizenship papers at the United States District Court in Brooklyn. Among the many Jewish refugees becoming naturalized citizens, this child captured a journalist's attention. The tide of McCarthyism was turning. After the execution of Julian and Ethel Rosenberg in 1953, fear and negative attention veered away from the Jewish community. By the end of 1954, Joseph McCarthy would be censured by the United States Senate for deliberate deception and fraud. The time was ripe for a journalist to turn his camera upon a Jewish boy who is eager to become a citizen in this land of the free.

Wearing special new clothes for the occasion and a white kippa, Chaya Leah's "little one" wields the pen with serious effort. The hand of the court officer rests reassuringly on the documents. The caption identifies the boy as the son of Rabbi Samuel Walkin. "Born in China, Chaim now lives in Brooklyn." Who could have known that the child photographed in 1954, would become a major educator and author in his own right, retaining a lifelong passion for fountain pens? Rabbi Chaim Walkin's collection of such pens holds pride of place in his study in Jerusalem inside a Chinese style cabinet surrounded by photographs of his illustrious grandfather, the Bais Aharon and the Chofetz Chaim.

"*Undzer shtub*" gained new meaning in the life of each of Tzivia's children, in America as well as in Israel. Just how formidable she was in her home (and beyond) became immortalized in Chaim Grade's short story, "The Rebbetzin." Born in Vilna in 1910, Grade had been an avid Talmudic scholar in his youth and had studied for a number of years with Rabbi Avrohom Yeshaya Karelitz, better known as the "Chazon Ish" (1878–1953). In 1941, Grade had managed to flee from Vilna into the Soviet Union while his first wife and mother were left behind and killed during the *Shoah*.

Chaim Grade did not journey to Kobe and to Shanghai, but he did become a frequent guest in the Walkin home after the war. The key figure in his story entitled "The Rebbetzin" is a brilliant and ambitious woman who plots for the success of her husband, the spiritual leader of a small-town congregation. The rancor and machinations of the fictional rebbetzin are nothing like Tzivia Walkin's gracious welcome to one and all. Nonetheless, Chaya Leah insists that Grade's inspiration for the portrayal of this highly educated, charismatic female character came largely from "*undzer shtub*"—the home that most reminded the Yiddish refugee writer of the world he left behind:

> *Our mother was completely opposite from his narration, but Chaim Grade would always say "I wrote The Rebbetzin and I thought of you." Grade was brilliant. Inna, his second wife, looked like she was at least 40 years his junior. Like the cellist Pablo Casals's wife, she adored him and his work. I know that he was a brilliant yeshiva student and abandoned it all. Was it the hard life of poverty, who knows? He would come often to the house and the conversation was always lively. Inna watched him like a hawk.*

In the home of Rabbi and Tzivia Walkin, Chaim Grade, a secular survivor of the *Shoah*, found solace and inspiration. Chaya Leah's recollection mirrors her own parents' affection for the writer, without a trace of negative judgment against a man who had turned against the Torah teachings of his youth. The question of why Grade left the traditions of his youth is left unanswered. What matters in the telling is that the Yiddish writer was welcomed in her parents' home and found something in Rebbetzin Walkin that fueled his imagination.

Unlike the fictional rebbetzin, Tzivia Walkin's "plots" were mostly focused on the well-being of the orphaned young men who continued to come to her home after the war. Benny Fishoff was just one of many who clung to "*undzer shtub*" as if it were his own home. Another yeshiva *bocher* man whom Chaya Leah recalls fondly is Reb Osherke Chechik, who was in his thirties, like the rebbetzin herself. Because he was older and slightly unkempt, he did not get many offers for marriage. Here was a problem that the rebbetzin was determined to solve:

> *One night, the doorbell rang and we heard my mother say*
> *to the person who rang the bell:*
> *You have the wrong floor, you need the first floor.*
> *Mommu, we asked who was it?*
> *Her answer:*
> *A perfection of a girl*
> *A beauty.*
> *Perfect for Osherke.*

Chaya Leah recalls her mother's quick pronouncement with amazement. She even recalls daring to challenge Rebbetzin Walkin's conclusions:

> "But Mamma, you did not see her, it was dark in the hall."
> "Foolish child" she said, "when I say perfect it is perfect, after all she is a girl and he is a boy."
> *Luba was young and beautiful.*
> *She was a blue-eyed blonde with a beautiful complexion.*
> *The night she rang the doorbell, she wore a gray skirt and a pink Angora sweater. A vision of loveliness.*

Chaya Leah describes the young woman with the admiring glance of a teenager who was just discovering the powers of her own beauty. What amazed her more than Luba's beauty was the promptness with which Tzivia Walkin went into action to actualize the marriage:

> *My mother made arrangements for Luba and reb Osherke to go out.*
> *She called Osherke and told him he has a date. First, she gave orders:*
> *"Go to the barber and get a haircut.*

> *Buy yourself a new shirt and a snipst (tie), cut your nails.*
> *Do not look like a shnorer, Osherke."*

Telling a young man from Shanghai how to take care of himself was second nature to Rebbetzin Walkin. She cared about her "boys" and would stop at nothing in order to ensure their happiness. Osher Chechik had little choice and it seems he was not reluctant after meeting the beautiful Luba. But he thought she was out of his reach, so he began to show disinterest. This was not to be in Tzivia's mind. So, the engagement was promptly orchestrated. Chaya Leah recalls it with humor and wonder, echoing all the *simchas* in Shanghai:

> *Our living room had no furniture, so everything took place in the dining room:*
> *Papa's sitting like a king at the head of the table and to the right the Mame and the rest around the table.*
> *My mother, knowing Osherke, was afraid that he would panic, get cold feet. She had to make a drastic move.*
> *She went to the kitchen and took out a bottle of shnaps from the pantry, filled several glasses with the shnaps, and said:*
> *"Let us make a Chaim! Osherke, Mazel tov—you are a chosson, Luba. Mazel tov!"*

From Shanghai to Brooklyn, the Walkin "*simcha* hall" continued to draw young couples. The rebbetzin's plotting for an orphan's marriage is a positive counterweight to the darker ambitions portrayed in Chaim Grade's short story. For Tzivia Walkin, the idea of a good man remaining single was painful beyond the Torah's injunction that humankind must multiply. Despite her aching back and five children, she found time and ingenuity to orchestrate the meeting of Reb Osherke and Luba.

Chaya Leah, the oldest daughter who witnessed these plots, looks back with admiration. Even as a growing teenager, she seems to have intuited that the Rebbetzin who engineered so many marriages would not wait long to find her own daughter a groom. Even as a schoolgirl, she understood the road ahead, but not the details or challenges that would accost her. The direction was clear, though. Having imbued the values of "*undzer shtub*," she would have to start building her own home before too long.

MY NAME IS CHAYA LEAH

Blooming into full adolescence in a foreign land is not easy. I know this from my own experience as an immigrant from Romania arriving in America shortly before I turned fourteen. How to deal with bras, menstruation, and boys was a mystery that only deepened with time and brought terrible embarrassment and missteps. My parents, like Chaya Leah's, were too busy trying to navigate the strange tongue in which they now had to make a living even though they were no longer young. Once I was sent to school, it was as if society took over—except that "society" was a cacophony of voices and temptations. Unlike Chaya Leah Walkin, I lacked a clear Torah framework at home and became more vulnerable to the confusions of the 1960s.

Chaya Leah, being a refugee child in the late 1940s, saw the world differently. She was more like Dr. Ruth, a survivor of the Kinder Transport out of Germany. Six years older than the Walkin's oldest daughter and not religiously observant, this sex guru touched Chaya Leah's heart and mind because she was able to voice the embarrassments they had shared as adolescents in America:

> *Dr. Ruth—very outspoken, very heavy accent, very bright, and her radio and television shows were beloved. I used to love listening to her. In her interview, she talks about her diary that she wrote into every night, and how she kept waiting for her parents.*
>
> *She was young and ended up in an orphanage; after the war she went to Israel and lived on a kibbutz. She was Zionistic, but the kibbutz life was not for her, came to America, worked, and was able to go to school on a scholarship.*
>
> *When she talked about her awkwardness, my ears perked up. I guess the hand-me-down clothes, the different mode of dress, feeling that you stick out.*
>
> *I spoke the King's English and everyone was laughing at me. Or so I thought.*

This honest, striking identification with Dr. Ruth came as a surprise to me. Born in Germany in 1928, Karola Ruth Westheimer had been the only daughter of a traditional family. As Chaya Leah knew well, this diminutive woman had gone to Palestine at age seventeen and became a scout and a sniper. Immigrating to the United States in 1956, she earned a master's degree in sociology from the New School and began giving her sex talks in the 1960s. By that time, Chaya Leah was a married woman, living a fully Orthodox life. Nonetheless, she identified with Dr. Ruth because of her acknowledgment of the embarrassments that plagued young Jewish refugees in America.

Without higher degrees, Chaya Leah understood instinctively that here was someone who spoke like her—who spoke for her, as it were. Speaking with an accent, wearing clothes that were borrowed or given by others was no fun. It made one feel ostracized from the crowd of native-born girls who always seemed "in" and could afford to act generously toward the refugees. When recalling hand-me-down dresses, Chaya Leah was particularly fond of her friend Chana, the daughter of the well-known philanthropist Irving Bunin (1901–80). Having been born in Volozhin (Lithuania), Chana's father was deeply familiar with the yeshiva world and became a key support of Rav Aharon Kotler in rebuilding Torah education in the United States. Mr. Bunin also became one of the close friends of Rav Shmuel David in New York and made sure to visit each Purim to honor the scholar from Shanghai.

Although his daughter Chana was taller than Chaya Leah Walkin, the hand-me- down dresses were of such high quality that they were accepted with gratitude:

> *Wearing Chana's clothes, I did not feel awkward but rather important.*
> *Today it might be called designer labels syndrome.*

A seasoned woman who loves fine clothes to this day looks back at herself as a refugee teenager and departs from Dr. Ruth's embarrassments. Chaya, trained to appreciate *"malbushim ha kavod"*—vestments of dignity from the war years in Shanghai, recognized the value of being dressed in the clothes that came from the well-to-do Bunim household.

At the same time, thinking of Shanghai's simpler outfits led Chaya Leah to a darker meditation on what had been her family's predicament back then. Thinking of how girls made fun of her in New York, she let thoughts wander around the theme of mirth more generally:

> *Speaking about laughter, there was no laughter that I can remember, no laughter in Shanghai.*
> *Singing, celebrating, yes.*
> *But spontaneous, boisterous laughter I do not recall.*

The absence of laughter in China was but one of the sorrows buried deep within until the start of this book project. When these sorrows surfaced, Chaya Leah started recalling more than a laughter-less childhood.

She allowed herself to recall the song about the trapped little bird—somehow, a symbol of her own younger self. The modest celebrations in the Walkin family's *"simcha* hall" in Shanghai also lingered in mind. And in their wake comes fear of erasure that an adolescent girl did not realize until she recalled herself as an object of derision among American classmates.

When Chaya was enrolled at the Joan of Arc Public School on the upper West side, the first thing the staff tried to do was to Americanize her name. On the streets of Shanghai, she had already heard GIs call out "*hi ya, baby*" and was at first thrilled to think they all knew her name. The realization that she was wrong came later, in private, so it caused no embarrassment. In public school in New York, however, the pressure became direct. The teachers there gave her several choices to replace her difficult sounding Jewish name:

> I had beautiful choices. Helen was one and I visualized Helen of Troy, her era. Then they came up with Carolyn. I did not choose Helen or Carolyn. I told them my name is Chaya Leah.
> They told me that Carolyn covers both names.
> I answered that I was not interested.
> They insisted on calling me by this English name; I refused to respond to them.
> "My name is Chaya and Chaya it will be."
> I am sorry to this day that I did not use my full name.

Refusing to be called either Helen or Carolyn, Rabbi Walkin's daughter stood her ground. Chaya Leah had turned thirteen in America and already exhibited the kind of courage that the Jewish people had discovered within themselves during the early years of the Egyptian exile. There, too, Jews had been encouraged to change their names as the first step in adapting to the customs of a new land.

Long before slavery, these early refugees from a land of hunger knew that their Jewish names carried a precious legacy, which later provided a pathway to redemption. Rav Walkin's daughter stood in this lineage with pride. Her retrospective regret that she did not keep her full name reveals the tenacity of the belief that when we are born, our parents are gifted with a touch of prophecy. Chaya Leah, named after the Bais Aharon's revered mother, knew the preciousness of the family legacy. She would not compromise with public school teachers, though she let "Leah" lapse for a while.

After public school and its vicissitudes, Chaya Leah attended attend high school in a more Jewish context. Her education now continued at a makeshift academy that later became the well-known Yeshiva University High School for Girls. The way she tells the story, happenstance played a great role in this experiment as well as the dedication of Stephen Klein (1901–78), the philanthropist and founder of the Barton's Candy Company.

Born in Austria into a family of candy makers, Klein managed to flee to America as a refugee in 1938. During the war, he became an active member of the Vaad ha-Hatzala, which worked to save Torah scholars trapped by the Holocaust in Europe and Asia. In 1946–47, just as public opinion rose against Jewish immigration, Stephen Klein personally helped to bring to the United States over five hundred rabbis and scholars and their families who had fled the Nazis by way of Shanghai and Paris. Among those directly aided by Klein was Rabbi Shmuel David Walkin.

'TIS STRANGE BUT TRUE

When Stephen Klein's own daughter Jeannette reached high school age, he was not eager to let her go to a public high school. The only other option was the Bais Yaakov seminary in Williamsburg, which Klein did not feel offered enough of a secular education. So he pulled together a small group of Jewish girls who had previously been registered in public school and started a new school. That first cohort included Rav Shmuel David's daughter as well:

> There were nine girls in the first class and no name.
> The school gave the girls the option to pick a name.
> Nine girls with ninety-nine opinions was not the ideal situation.
> One day in class, the subject of a name came up again, and we were all geared for war. When suddenly a truck went by. In large letters on the truck was the sign CENTRAL heating and air conditioning.
> Selma Rosenbloom yelled out: "I have the perfect name for the school." And that is how Central Yeshiva got its name!
> I am one of the nine, the first graduating class of Central.

Chaya Leah's recollection honors the accidental and the chaotic, which is missing in later, laudatory commemorations of the founding of Yeshiva University High School for Girls. "Nine girls with ninety-nine opinions" shows that these young women neither came from nor were forced into a one-size-fits-all model of Jewish orthodoxy. Rabbi Walkin had allowed his own daughter to try out this new school rather than following the more traditional path of the Bais Yaakov seminary precisely because he understood that she was growing into an independent-minded young woman.

The young women who graduated from Central in 1951 carried Jewish history not only in mind but in their hearts as well. The first yearbook for the Central Yeshiva High School for Girls shows nine fun loving and sophisticated heirs of a modernized Torah tradition. They had chosen to call this yearbook "Elchanette" in memory of Rabbi Isaac Elchanan Spector (1817–96), who had been chief rabbi of Kovno (Kaunas), Lithuania.

This title represented a conscious homage to this formative Torah teacher whose name also adorned the Elchanan Theological Seminary at Yeshiva University. Decades before Chaya Leah and other survivors from the Shanghai refuge decided to commemorate Chiune Sugihara's sojourn in Kovno, the members of this graduating class from Central linked their own names to that of the city that had sustained Torah leadership before the arrival of the Japanese consul. These were American girls who consciously affirmed roots in the soil that had nurtured both the spiritual and physical lives of their parents in Europe.

Chaya Leah's photograph in the yearbook is both glamorous and serious. Other girls pose more self-consciously, with side looks, coiffed bangs, and camera-ready smiles. "Caja Walkin" looks into the camera more directly, her abundant curls falling generously and naturally down her white graduation collar and black robe. She is identified as Secretary to the Economics Club and described affectionately with her Yiddish nickname "Chaikie."

The girls wrote brief biographies of each other and when they came to Rav Walkin's daughter, they made a playful allusion to "Chaike's journey on a slow boat from China." One wonders how many jokes Chaya Leah had already heard in America about that "slow boat" from China. In this fun loving high school crowd, there was room to recall her tough journeys to Tsuruga, and then to Kobe and finally to Shanghai. The little refugee girl with Chinese characters on her residence permit had given way to a sophisticated young woman. There was no need in this yearbook to mention the Walkin family's fearful flight out of Poland or the freezing tundra along the Siberian railway. No need here to dwell on the cramped quarters of the SS Meigs. Instead, Chaya appears to be a girl like all the others, with an eccentric attachment to a "certain a high school history teacher."

In a nicely penned inscription, Chaya Leah's classmate Myrna Weishaut wrote: "Dear Chaiki, with a nature like yours, you'll be followed by happiness." Myrna had no way of knowing how true her words would become two short years later when Chaya Leah met Michael Small. Truth, of course, was anything but simple, as the words chosen by the girls to place beneath Chaja Walkin's picture suggest: *"Tis strange but true."* The quote in the yearbook is attributed to Blake, a forgivable mistake for girls who must have read George Gordon Byron's well-known verses:

> Tis strange—but true; for truth are always strange;
> Stranger than fiction; if it could be told,
> How much would novels gain by the exchange!
> How differently the world would men behold!
> How oft would vice and virtue places change!
> The new world would be nothing to the old,
> If some Columbus of the moral seas
> Would show mankind their souls' antipodes.

Byron's Canto 14, written in 1819, remains eerily apt for the life of Chaya Leah Walkin in high school and beyond. A girl who appeared strange to herself and to others had crossed many worlds and emerged with a pleasant disposition and a glowing beauty fired by a spirit within. Many years after the *Elchanette* yearbook memorialized the first four words of this stanza, Chaya Leah helped revive Jewish life in Chicago with verve and vision. As a full partner in Rabbi Michael Small's efforts, she went on to make her mark upon the world, becoming a "Columbus of the moral seas" indeed.

A VERTELE, A MAYSELE

One reason for Chaya Leah's successes may be found in her capacity to describe her many journeys in compelling terms. This passion for well-told tales goes back to her father, Rav Shmuel David, who had a gift for finding the right expression for the most complex ethical message that he wished to convey. During all the family's travels and troubles, he remained at the core a man of words—most often, holy words derived from the Torah and conveyed with a distinctive verve that lingers long in his daughter's memory.

In Brooklyn, as in Shanghai, Rabbi Walkin was a magnet for many different kinds of people who were drawn to his learning and his vivid usage of the Yiddish language. Looking back, Chaya Leah emphasized artful shaping of narratives as one of her father's major gifts:

> *His beautiful play on words endeared him to businessmen like Irving Bunin, Stephen Klein, and Shabse Frankel... A vertele, a maysele, as a potter at the kiln, a seamstress fondling the fabric, a glass blower breathing life into the sand,*

> an artist with a couple of strokes presenting a beautiful world, so my father with his words put beauty and understanding into the Torah. His special gift of the right word in the right way opened the eyes of so many...oh, how I miss that generation, with such strong values. It was not a "me" generation, but a "what can I do for you" generation without thoughts for rewards or recognition.

The businessmen whom Chaya recalls as her father's buddies were men of erudition. Klein had been involved in furthering Jewish education long before he became the financial force behind Central Yeshiva for girls. Irving Bunim was also a successful businessman and a key supporter of the National Society for Hebrew Day Schools. Shabse Frankel, also a wealthy businessman, ended up devoting a considerable part of his fortune to publishing the most complete and accurate edition of the works of the Rambam. Whether born in Europe or in America, each of these men sought out Rav Walkin's company and friendship because of "*a vertele*"—a little thought-provoking expression, and "a maysele"—a little story that brought to life larger ethical lessons in a vivid fashion.

Chaya Leah herself waxes poetically about her father's gift for words. The little girl who had journeyed with her parents from Vilna to Shanghai had imbibed metaphors along with the larger message of a Torah education. The potter at the kiln and the glass blower breathing life into sand come to Chaya readily from the liturgical prayers said on the High Holidays. This is a time when Jewish people remind themselves of the fragility of life and the importance of using our short interval on earth for meaningful choices.

The metaphor of the "artist with a couple of strokes presenting a beautiful world" is Chaya Leah's own. She herself had picked up brushes for painting in her middle years following a childhood fascination with the German artist next door on Liaoyang Road. As a married woman, Chaya Leah Small became more and more attentive to the alchemy of art, to how certain dabs of paint coalesce to create an image that enriches as well as challenges the viewer. Chaya Leah, the eldest daughter of a man gifted with words, grew up to be a woman gifted with language and color herself. All along, what mattered was the fact that words and color enrich the spirit. What was important was "strong values" that Chaya Leah felt were lacking in the "me generation." Like her father, she also aimed to craft a meaningful life around "what I can do for you."

One photograph from Rav Shmuel David Walkin's years in America reveals the inner grandeur that accompanied his calling to be of help to others. In this image, Chaya Leah's father glows with a long white beard that went beyond the custom of certain religious Jews. In Chaya Leah's words, Rav Shmuel David's "*hadras panim*"—perhaps best translated as "facial glory"—was a sign of inner beauty. This glow did not depend on a beard alone. In a story told about Irving Bunim, a Chassidic rebbe rebukes his followers who condemned this generous donor for not sporting facial glory: "When you ascend to give a divine accounting, you will be asked: 'Beard, where is your Jew?'" Rav Walkin's good friend Irving Bunim did not have a beard. What is noticeable about both men is the care they took to make sure that inner values flourished along with the "*hadras panim*" that characterized Chaya Leah's father.

In America, as in China, Rav Walkin also maintained the custom of wearing a special robe (called a *schlafrock*), especially on Shabbat. To honor this divinely ordained day of rest, one's outward garment had to show a higher degree of refinement. In a photograph taken before Shabbat, Chaya Leah's father is dressed in a long robe made of Chinese silk. First worn by China's emperors with coiling dragon motifs, this kind of brocade became popular in many Chinese silk factories. From Shanghai to Brooklyn, Rabbi Walkin carried this taste for refinement, both inward and outward. When I visited his son Rabbi Chaim Walkin in Jerusalem, the same kind of robe graced his Shabbat as well, setting a tone of spiritual elevation through threads of silk woven on the soil that had nurtured the Walkin family's refuge during the war.

Custom and tradition combined to create a special mood in the Walkin household. Rav Shmuel David's youngest child, Rachel, who lingered longest at the table of her aged father, recalled this unique atmosphere. In an email to Chaya Leah, she wrote:

> I would awake Shabbos morning to hear the beautiful niggun of the papa learning. I would come into the kitchen and see the table covered with many sforim and hear the beautiful melody as the papa was learning. I can still see the papa, the seforim, and the glazele tea next to it, a sense of such serenity and beauty.[2]

It was not only the Chinese robe that set the tone for Shabbat in the Walkin household. The holy books and the melody of learning augmented the beauty recalled by Chaya Leah's sister.

With this sweetness and loftiness in mind, all five of Rav Shmuel David's children stayed close to the parental paradigm. His two sons became rabbis while his three daughters all married Torah scholars and took on the

---

[2] Rachel's email communication to Chaya Leah Small, February 16, 2016.

responsibilities and burdens of the *"rabbanut"*— rabbinical households. Each daughter married a rabbi and built a home that become a fulcrum for learning and spiritual growth for many others in their respective communities.

Chaya Leah's own journey to this destination was not an easy one. She was the daughter who was most acutely aware of the preciousness of her family's legacy carried out of the ashes of Europe. She also witnessed her father's various adaptations to the calling of a rabbi in America. After graduation from Central Yeshiva, she had set her eyes upon going to college. In this matter, "the papa"—as Rachel and all the Walkin children referred to their father—objected and put his foot down. The open-minded Torah scholar who had chosen not to send his eldest daughter to the convention-bound Bais Yaakov in Brooklyn, who had allowed his young son Chaim to see Santa Claus without opprobrium, was not eager to have Chaya Leah immersed in the world of secular studies in college.

In the end, Rav Shmuel David agreed to the college plan on the condition that Chaya Leah went first to the Bais Yaakov advanced seminary for a year. Chaya agreed and, as a result, did not fulfill her dream of going to college until two decades later, which included marriage and the birth of five children along the way. Gazing back at her post–high school year, Chaya remembers being different from other young women. She did not fit into the paradigm of those headed for modern careers.

Neither was she simply an unreflective follower of the Bais Yaakov model meant to mentor future wives and mothers. She liked to work and wanted to help others. This was her way of being keenly alive in the world. In other words, she was her father's daughter in words and deeds as well:

> *I loved helping, and caring… I remember one of my most exciting experiences. I worked for a radio program on which the social worker would interview a needy person and tried to help them out. My father got me the job to work with the social worker.*
>
> *I was her go-fer and got so excited to make calls, met people and help them with a problem… I worked with the show for about a year, and refused to take any money.*
>
> *I wanted the money to be used to help the needy… here is the little refugee girl who had nothing, helping Americans who had less.*
>
> *To give back, to be on the giving end, is so much more gratifying than to be on the receiving end.*

In this recollection, Chaya Leah shows herself to be the true heir to her parents' legacy in giving. Even in Shanghai, when there was nothing much to be gifted materially, Rav Shmuel David and Rebbetzin Tzivia took upon themselves the task of nurturing young men who had lost all their family contacts.

Working at a radio station in New York without payment was Chaya Leah's way of giving back, of continuing to serve those in need. In her circle of friends, this appeared to be foolish. Her stories about doing errands for a social worker were greeted with groans and disbelief. Yet, she persisted:

> "Here she goes again," they would say.
> Who cares? But I did care.
> I cared for every human being.
> I was sensitive to every human being.
> Maybe it was not fashionable to be like that.
> But I considered this trait a gift from Hashem.

Working for a social worker after high school was a meaningful challenge for Chaya Leah Walkin. Here was her father's credo put into action. The question of "what can you do for others?" became a moral fulcrum in Chaya Leah's life. In later years, she looked at her own capacity for caring as a divine gift, not simply the achievement of a life spent battling concrete difficulties in various cultural worlds.

Despite the groans and smirks that greeted her, Rav Walkin's eldest daughter liked to regale friends with stories from her life before New York. This came through in the Central Yeshiva yearbook with its quip about taking a slow boat to China. For the other girls, this was simply a funny reference to a popular song of that era written by Frank Loesser in 1948. They probably knew and enjoyed the opening lines far more than Chaya Leah's tales:

> I would like to get you on a slow boat to China
> All to myself alone.
> Get you and keep you in my arms evermore,
> Leave all your lovers weeping on the far away shore…

Girls in the Central Yeshiva might not have had many lovers, but romance was in the air after the war. The song was tuneful and could be used as gentle fun to describe a refugee girl's long-winded tales.

When real romance came into Chaya Leah's life, the Central girls had already drifted far away. She was now a student at the Bais Yaakov seminary, as her father had required. She also had the job with the social worker at the radio show. It was a many-sided, "out of the box" package for a rabbi's daughter. Chaya Leah herself is not shy about acknowledging the tensions within and without that shaped her last year as a single woman:

> In the beginning of the seminary year, I was rebellious and then I listened to Rebbetzin Vichna Kaplan teaching us *Shir Ha'Shirim*. She was very pregnant at that time and the heat of the summer was unbearable.
> She climbed up three flights of stairs, huffing and puffing with so much *mesirat nefesh* that
> I said to myself: "You do not have to go to class, but at least give her a little respect and pretend that you are listening."

Looking back many years later, Chaya Leah is honest enough to see the rebellious young woman she had been in a fresh light. *Shir Ha'Shirim*, the sacred poem I am using to frame this retelling of her life, was also the turning point in her seminary year.

One very talented, very pregnant teacher managed to create an awakening in the young woman. The teacher's self-sacrifice (*mesirat nefesh*) opened Chaya Leah's eyes and ears to the deeper layers of learning, which continue to inspire her to this day:

> I developed a thirst for wanting more and wanted to understand the beauty (of those words). I became insatiable. Rabbi Helman was also my teacher in Bais Yaakov. His gentleness and softness and love of every letter of the Chumash opened my heart.
> While in seminary, before my one year of graduation, our shidduch was made for us.

In the heat of summer, Vichna Kaplan, the legendary founder of the Bais Yaakov school network in America, had climbed three flights of stairs in a building that Chaya Leah recalls as being dilapidated and not very clean.

At first, Rabbi Walkin's daughter only pretended to hear Kaplan's explanations and Rabbi Hellman's impassioned emphasis on each letter of the Torah. Before the end of the year, these words took root in her echoing heart.

Shir Ha'Shirim was a text about lovers as well as a narrative focused upon the special bond between the Jewish people and the divine giver of the Torah.

Vichna Kaplan may have been the ideal mentor to open a rebellious young woman's mind to the deeper layers of this complex poem. She had been a student herself in Sarah Schenirer's Bais Yaakov Teacher's Seminary in Krakow at the age of sixteen. Orphaned at the young age of eleven, Vichna was able to empathize with the inner turmoil of a refugee girl who felt herself gifted with a spirited concern for the well-being of others.

Rebbetzin Kaplan was not only teaching about love, she was also active in the project of raising strong Jewish women who would make vigorous, self-sacrificing mates for young men dedicated to a life of Torah learning. Rabbi Aharon Kotler acknowledged this great mission by saying that without Vichna Kaplan's efforts, there would be no yeshiva education for young men either. It would be pointless to nurture generations of dedicated scholars if there are no women "willing to forgo material comfort for the sake of Talmud Torah."[3]

This essential partnership of man and woman lies at the core of *Shir Ha'Shirim* as well. It is also a kind of mutuality that Chaya Leah had witnessed in her own home from her earliest years in Kobe and Shanghai. Before the end of her year in seminary, Chaya Leah Walkin was given the opportunity to build such a loving home with one of Rav Aharon Kotler's own students.

MAYN KIND, DU VEST KHASENE HOBN MIT A LEVI

The shadows of the war in Shanghai and of the *Shoah* in Europe were beginning to lift in the year of Chaya Leah's graduation from Central Yeshiva. True, her classmates were still teasing her about the slow boat to China. True, the young woman who had turned seventeen was still wearing clothes borrowed from others. At the time, however, Chaya began to sense the beauty of her own incipient womanhood, and was thrilled with plans for the senior class trip. In the words of *Shir Ha'Shirim*, the breath of a new day seemed to caress the future that lay ahead.

We can catch a glimpse of that refreshing mood in a photograph of Chaya Leah and her parents at the wedding of Benny Fishoff. This was the orphan who took Rav Shmuel David as his own mentor when he asked the older survivor from Shanghai to walk him to his chuppa. In the photograph, Rabbi Walkin is wearing a silk top hat, while his wife is bedecked with a corsage fit for the

---

3   Shaul Magid, *American Post-Judaism: Identity and Renewal in a Post-ethnic Society* (Bloomington, IN: Indiana University Press, 2013), 20.

mother of the groom. Moshe Yoel is sporting a bowtie and Chaim, now 5 years old, looks serious in his little tuxedo. Esther looks like a teenager just savoring her first long gown. Chaya Leah, in elaborate satin, looks the part of a *"kallah maidel"*—a beauty ripe enough to become a bride.

When not bedecked in satin, Chaya Leah was busy with school, caring for the little ones, household chores, and cleaning up her father's *shtibele*—the little congregation filled with refugees. She rarely complained about the multiplicity of her tasks. In school, there were the embarrassing moments when the groceries were delivered for her to take home, including chicken and fish, which smelled and drew smirks from fellow classmates. But straightening out her father's *shul* was never a burden. Chaya Leah's bedridden mother noticed her daughter's energetic work and did not miss the opportunity to bring up the subject of engagement and marriage.

She suggested quite openly that her daughter was fit for a man descendent from the house of Levites. The tribe of Levi had been builders of the Mishkan (the tabernacle in the desert) and also the singers and maintenance staff of the Temple that was erected in Jerusalem. Young Chaya Leah's work in her father's *shul* was seen as a talent for maintaining communal institutions. At seventeen, Chaya Leah herself thought she still had the luxury to laugh at this prospect, to dismiss any talk of a groom.

Then, shortly before her graduation from high school, Reb Chaim Gulefsky, one of her parents' younger friends from Shanghai, brought a prospective groom right into the Walkin home. Chaya Leah's recollection of this event is threaded with humor and captures well the loving machinations that actualized *shidduchim* in the world of Shanghai refugees now congregating in New York:

> One night, about ten o'clock, Reb Chaim called and asked if he could come over to visit, and he has a friend with him.
> We were used to having people and guests call all hours of the day or night, so that call was not unusual.
> I was already in bed; my mother walked in gently, shook me awake and said: "Someone is coming over. Please get dressed and come out. Dress nicely," she added.
> "There are so many people coming all the time, I just don't want to come out."

Unsuspecting, Chaya Leah tried to avoid the meeting. After all, the Walkin home was open to "Shanghailanders" at all hours of the day and night and she did not feel obliged to greet them all.

But Rebbetzin Tzivia was not to be deterred, and Chaya Leah most often did what her mother asked:

> *So I got dressed, reluctantly, in my one Sabbath Yom Tov dress.*
> *I had no clue. What is this all about? I was still in high school.*
> *I was finding my footing in the social life of school and the social crowd.*
> *We were planning our prom, our graduation, our field trip, and all the excitement of a teenager's rites of life.*
> *Finally, I was a little more secure with myself.*

The once shy, awkward girl who left Shanghai had blossomed into the young woman portrayed in satin at the Fishoff wedding. She was wondering aloud: Who gets dressed to put on fancy clothes at this late hour?

In *Shir Ha'Shirim*, there is a touching and tragic moment when the beloved knocks at the door and the bride answers coyly: "But I have taken off my clothes, how can I dress again? I have bathed my feet, must I dirty them?" (5:2) The lover turns away and leaves. The bride then suddenly decides to open her heart and the door, but he is gone. The watchmen of the city find her, wound her, and tear her veils.

Chaya Leah Walkin's fate turned out differently. She did get dressed. She was a good daughter doing her parents' bidding and a young woman thrilling to the unknown. Rebbetzin Walkin also left her sick bed for this late night visit. She sensed Chaya Leah's unease and knew that meaningful work was the best sedative. She asked her daughter to sit down at the kitchen table and type a letter that needed to be sent out. Finally, at 11:30 PM, the doorbell rang:

> *Reb Chaim and a young man came over. This young man was going to Lakewood Yeshiva, and his father had been a good friend of my father's in Europe. They had both learned in Radin together.*
> *When we arrived in America, we had stopped over for four hours in Chicago. It was at his parents' house that we were hosted.*
> *My mother and father welcomed their guest, and I am sitting in the kitchen typing away dressed to the nines at eleven thirty at night.*

Tzivia Walkin had already taken a shine to the promising young man from a familiar background. Therefore, she lost no time in moving things forward:

> "Come over my child. I want you to meet someone."
> You can imagine how annoyed I was, but I went into the dining room for a few minutes and sat at the table like a statue. Not uttering a word. Unbeknown to me, this is the young man Reb Chaim had in mind.
> My mother fell in love with this young man immediately. But I was not quite ready.
> Half a year later, before my eighteenth birthday, we had our first date.

The real drama of this encounter lost none of its freshness in Chaya Leah's mind many decades after the late-night typing marathon. Like the details of each room in the house on Liaoyang Road, this moment, too, sparkled with the breath of life. Chaya Leah is invited out of the kitchen. Sullenly, she sits with the guest like a statue. She, with the many tales that made her classmates groan, is speechless. She was tempted to dismiss the young man, but her mother was already in love with the prospective suitor.

Despite her mother's affection for the late night guest, Chaya Leah was allowed to make her own choice. Jewish matchmaking is often misunderstood in the secular world. It is caricatured as a shoving operation in which two strangers are pressed into matrimony without previous knowledge or choice. But in the Walkin family, daughters were highly respected. In keeping with genuine Torah tradition, a woman is always given the right of refusal. So, Chaya Leah said no at first. She knew that she was not yet ready for an encounter that had marriage as its goal. Chaya Leah Walkin aimed to cling to girlhood a little longer.

When she finally agreed to go on a date, she braced herself for conversation with a man seven years older than she was. To be sure, she had witnessed the respectful and loving relationship between her own parents, who were almost twenty years apart. She sensed that age differences could be bridged. But how? She was young and only knew that the man coming to take her out was one of the most sought after bachelors:

> My date was 25 years old. I was a kid with my childish fantasies. Mike Small was American, from a very choshoveh (important) family, a top bocher, and a brilliant, articulate speaker, knowledgeable in politics and news. A worldly, intelligent hunk of a man.

> *In the seminary, everyone wanted to have a chance at Mike Small. I was too busy being a teenager, and wanting to enjoy my fun and freedom.*
> *No heavy-duty intellectual discussion, no academia for me.*

In these jottings, a beloved wife looks back at the start of her husband's courtship with honest eyes. Chaya Leah Walkin was not "*academia*"—Yiddish for highfalutin. She was a teenager just savoring her first glimpse of freedom, and here came a stunningly attractive man, who already found great favor in her parents' eyes. She decided to give him a chance:

> *I did meet Michel Small. His blue-green eyes summed up his inner self. He loved everyone. He saw good in everyone.*
> *In the one year that we were dating, I never heard him tell a lie or blow up his importance. His honesty and integrity were what impressed me so.*

The young woman who agreed to go out was very young. She had heard conversations about this good-looking yeshiva student among the seminary girls. She was alert enough to nascent sexuality to recognize he was a "hunk." Without a doubt, chemistry sprung up between Chaya Leah and Michael from the first. And it endured all their married life.

But with that spark of attraction also came doubts. He was indeed very intelligent and excelled in his studies. When Rav Walkin made it clear that his daughter could not be engaged to a young man who did not have rabbinical ordination, Michael promptly became one of the prized students of Rav Kotler. This famous European rabbi was in the process of seeking especially brilliant, Americanized young men to train at his nascent rabbinical college in Lakewood, New Jersey. In Chaya Leah's mind, the question still remained: How was an 18-year-old girl to hold up her end of conversation with a world-seasoned 25-year-old man?

Michael Small's blue-green eyes sparkled and Chaya Leah became at ease. Taking her two youngest siblings on their dates was both a necessity and a comfort. Chaim and Rachel were too young to be left alone with their bedridden mother. So Chaya Leah took them to the movies with Michael, where he treated the little ones with candy and other delights. Still, Chaya Leah worried. The brilliant conversationalist who was her frequent date left her thrilled and also unsure about what lay ahead.

In this state of uncertainty, Chaya Leah turned for advice to an older friend from Shanghai—Mira Elberg. Ties of affection and trust had bound the little girl to a bride who then remained a childless wife for many decades after the war. Chaya Leah sensed a good marriage and knew that Mira had also faced a great age difference when she married Rabbi Elberg in China. In the Elberg's New York home, Rav Walkin's daughter could open up her heart and speak of her complex feelings for Michael Small:

> *He was brilliant, articulate, self-confident, tall, and handsome. He was strong, liked to work out in the gym. And looked to me just like Burt Lancaster, a famous movie star.*
> *When he talked about any subject, you were mesmerized by his presentation, by his clear mind and analytical manner of approaching the subject matter.*
> *He was able to glean the core of each subject, and see the important aspects rather than the trimmings.*
> *It was instant chemistry for us. But I was scared. How can I keep pace with someone like this? How can I keep him interested? How can I be a partner in life to him?*
> *I am still a kid and he is a man. When I get older, what interest will we still have together? I am not in his league.*

Mira, who had been a raving beauty, was now married to a brilliant, older Torah scholar. She reassured her young friend that there is more to a long-term relationship than intellectual conversation. She helped Chaya Leah not feel embarrassed about the sparks flying between her and Michael Small. Those sparks could build a vibrant home while a man seeking intellectual challenges would find them with his *hevruta*—traditionally, a same-gender study partner. Chaya had something to offer than no man ever could. This Mira knew from her own experience:

> *"You have nothing to worry about. Look at me. I fill a void for Reb Simcha that no one else can do. I am the candle that lights up his life."*
> *I became that candle for my husband.*
> *He always saw me as an eighteen year old.*
> *When at sixty I would get dressed for a function and would ask him, how do I look, he would embrace me and say: "My eighteen-year-old bride, you have not aged one day."*
> *In his eyes, I had not changed one iota.*

Rebbetzin Elberg helped Chaya Leah to understand that she was going to be far more than a pretty young thing who will endlessly amuse her older husband.

She was urging Rav Walkin's daughter to become the candle that illuminates her husband's inner and outer life. In conveying this message, Mira was drawing upon a tradition that describes the soul of man as God's own candle. A person who refines one's own spiritual potential becomes an illuminating force even for the divine.

A wife, too, can accomplish this alchemy of the spirit while being fully present in the flesh. Looking back on her long and happy marriage to Michael Small, Chaya Leah affirms that alchemy. She never lost her sparkle in her husband's eyes. Nor did he lose his appeal in her eyes, even after she became a master conversationalist and an equal partner in building a Torah-anchored home and community.

A photograph from the 1950s shows Michel—called Michael in English—as a very handsome young man flexing his biceps on the beach, revealing a well-sculpted body. His smile shows confidence. Here was a totally American young man, wooing a European-born girl who had been a child refugee in Kobe and Shanghai. There was more than an age difference between them. There were worlds of memory and trauma that subsequent decades would reveal, and also soften. Michel Small became an anchoring force, a translator of American realities for a bride who still shuddered in the face of uniformed authorities. Chaya Leah became his candle that burned ever brighter, just as Mira Elberg had predicted.

The shadows did not fully lift from the war years. But the breath of new life was palpable as the young couple headed for their *chuppa* (wedding canopy) on February 23, 1953.

CHAPTER 9

UNTIL IT RIPENS:

Marriage, Community, and the Arc of Return

> *Daughters of Jerusalem, swear to me*
> *By the gazelles, by the deer of the field*
> *That you will never awaken love*
> *Until it ripens.*
>
> Shir Ha'Shirim 2:7

The ripening of spring is linked in Jewish thought with redemption, with Passover, and with the unleashing of creative energies from the narrow straits of self-doubt. For Chaya Leah Walkin, as for the bride in *Shir Ha'Shirim*, the awakening of love in springtime opened a world of agency that she had not tasted consciously before. Through her marriage, Chaya Leah became a builder of values and visions within her family as well as in her community.

At the same time, as a daughter of refugees, she carried memories of war and deprivation that took years to acknowledge and decades to overcome. The world beyond Chaya Leah's crowded wedding hall remained in the shadows of political violence. In February 1953, President Eisenhower had declared that the island of Formosa (Taiwan) could be used for staging actions against communist China. Even as the brutal Korean War was winding down (with American causalities thinning somewhat), the seeds had been sown for three decades of altercation with the Soviet Union and other communist regimes.

In China, 1953 dawned with more and more repressive policies aimed to bring the country firmly under the control of the party led by Mao Zedong. After four years of state building, Mao took the collectivization of agriculture to a higher level, demanding more and more resources from impoverished peasants. Intellectuals, too, had to be coerced to follow the party line with several campaigns aimed to discredit liberal scholars who had studied abroad before 1949.

A decade later, more violent policies were inaugurated to build upon this contempt for the educated elites. In time, these policies led to the frenzied attacks in the name of the Cultural Revolution (1966–76). In Japan, post-war reconstruction suffered a setback with the terrible floods of June 1953, which led to the death of over 400 civilians and left more than a million homeless in the northern province of Kyushu.

It was into this battered decade that Chaya Leah Walkin took her first steps as Michael Small's new wife. Their grand wedding on February 22, 1953 was celebrated by eight hundred people. As Chaya recalls, Rebbetzin Tzivia had *"invited everyone, even the garage people. Azah simcha!"* Benny Gelfish, one of the yeshiva students from Shanghai, drove the bride and her family to the lavish wedding hall in a fancy new red Cadillac. This affair was nothing like the small gatherings on Liaoyang Road during the war.

The huge crowd, the beaded gowns and silk top hats testified to a new material wealth earned by Rav Shmuel David through the support and advice of young businessmen such as Benny Fishoff and Benny Gelfish. For the bride, these old friends from Shanghai were like the gazelles and deer in *Shir Ha'Shirim*. Fellow refugees who had shared the hard times and were now present to witness the flowering of new love. These young men, who had survived the war and the grief of losing their families to the *Shoah*, understood the dangers lurking even in blossoming fields. They stood guard around the Walkin family. With the darker past still in mind, they knew when the time was ripe for celebration. That day was now at hand.

Chaya Leah sparkled in the official photograph taken with her parents, the groom, and her four siblings. In the portrait of the bride alone, one can see the hard-won strength of the little girl who had escaped death during a winter's night in Poland. Chaya Leah's gaze is serious. Her rounded chin carried echoes of the child who had posed with inner dignity for her Chinese residence permit. In Shanghai, "C. Walkin" had been labeled a "Polish refugee." Here, a Jewish bride stands her ground as the granddaughter of the Bais Aharon, wearing her great-grandmother's name, a gown of satin as well as the muted fears of a young woman who turned nineteen shortly after the wedding.

In a photograph taken with her groom, Chaya Leah's look remains serious and inward, while the handsome 26-year-old groom in a tuxedo is beaming as he holds his wife's elbow with protective intimacy. This was a new turn in life's journey and Chaya Leah now had both a partner and a protector for the challenges that lay ahead.

This Walkin wedding was not just a show that included even "the garage people." It was primarily a tribute to the Torah personalities from the Shanghai years who now gathered to bless the new couple. These giants of Jewish scholarship now surrounded Rabbi Walkin and his Americanized groom. The Amshenover Rebbe—who had accompanied the refugees from Kobe to Shanghai—was there, looking very old and European with his long white beard and Chassidic garb. Next to him, closer to the groom, sat Rabbi Aharon Kotler, the Rosh Yeshiva who had fled to America in 1941 and was in the midst of building a new community of young married men in Lakewood, New Jersey. This *kollel* would become the foundation for the largest yeshiva on American shores. Present at the Walkin celebration, too, was Rabbi Eliezer Silver (1882–1968, the tireless activist of the Vaad ha-Hatzala who had dedicated his energies to saving scholars during the Holocaust.

On the groom's side, the most distinguished guest was Rabbi Moshe Feinstein (1895–1986), Michael's uncle, already a world-renowned authority on Jewish law. It was to this man, his mother's brother, that Michael Small and his wife would turn to in the future for advice about decisions that affected family and work. Chaya Leah's own recollections of these great Torah teachers are filled with awe.

These guests from her wedding added depth of meaning to the predicament of being a "Jewish refuge." Each of these men had been nurtured in distinguished European institutions that were destroyed during the Holocaust. Each carried a passion for blowing fresh life into the cinders of the past. Each become an embodiment of spiritual greatness that the young Rebbetzin Chaya Leah Small sought to honor and to emulate in her own family:

> *I remember our home with Rabbi Kalmanowitz, Rabbi Silver, and Rabbi Hutner. And even though it was common for them to be in our home, I had great fear and respect for them.*
> *I trembled in their presence.*
> *As a Kallah, I visited my uncle Moishe (Feinstein), and he in his gentle way asked me questions.*
> *I trembled with awe and respect.*
> *Who I am to sit next to Reb Moishe?*
> *How was I zoche (worthy) for him to take time out to talk to me?*
> *But that was the behavior of a Godol in those years.*
> *The anivus (humility) and the kovod habrios (honor of others).*

Until it Ripens: Marriage, Community, and the Arc of Return • CHAPTER 9 | **245**

I was afraid to go into his study and take time away from him, even though I grew up in a similar home.
I was in awe.
Do we have that today?

Chaya Leah on her wedding day.

Looking back, Chaya Leah paints for us a picture of a trembling young bride. It was not simply her age that led to this feeling of awe. It was also due to the Walkin family upbringing. Each of the rabbis who came to her parents' home had struggled to keep learning alive during war and exile. Though she was barely nineteen, Chaya had imbued the respect due to scholars who managed to sustain Jewish tradition in the harshest times.

A "*Godol,*" in her view, was not only a Torah giant. He also a man who could speak softly, gently to a young bride. As a college-educated married woman looking back, Chaya Leah is able to describe the "anivus"—the innate humility of Rabbi Moshe Feinstein. The expression she used to sum up Reb Moishe's character is, in fact, a mission statement of Chaya Leah's own life: "*kavod habrios.*" Pronounced *kevod ha briyot*, in modern Hebrew, this term expresses an inner commitment to honor all human beings as divine creations. Affirming and nurturing the dignity of each and every person who came into the Small household became Chaya Leah's animating passion throughout her marriage to Michael Small.

Photo of the bride and groom.

I CHOSE THE RABBANUT

Chaya Leah's married life began in Lakewood, New Jersey—a place that she recalls as a small city of survivors. Here, the revered Aharon Kotler was bent upon gathering a group of young men dedicated to full-time Torah study. Rav Kotler knew firsthand the destruction caused by the *Shoah*. He had been a student in the Slobodka yeshiva before the war and then became an assistant to his father-in-law, who was a mentor in the yeshiva of Slutsk.

With the outbreak of war, many yeshivot relocated to Vilna. The vast majority of the students and teachers of these centers of Torah learning, unlike the Mirrer Yeshiva, could not obtain visas to leave and ended up being murdered by the Nazis. Rav Kotler himself managed to come to America in 1941 with the aid of the Vaad ha-Hatzala, the same year as the Walkin family was making its journey to Kobe and Shanghai.

In 1943, in the middle of the most murderous time, Rav Kotler started a new American center for Torah learning with only 15 students. From this modest and beleaguered seedling would grow the distinguished Talmudic academy, called Yeshiva Gevoha. This center was animated by Rav Kotler's masterful scholarship and intense dedication to each of his *talmidim*. Although he himself was European born and trained, Aharon Kotler had envisioned new possibilities for Torah learning on American soil.

Like many renowned rabbis before the Holocaust, he also had deemed the United States to be a country that promoted assimilation. Nonetheless, Kotler became determined to revive Jewish learning on these unlikely shores. The success of this vision depended upon the recruitment of native-born young men such as Michael Small. As Chaya Leah recalled, Kotler's dream, it appeared to run against the grain of American notions of the "good life":

> Here is a giant of Torah who started to approach "Yankee doodle dandies" with a new concept.
> Here is a man who does not speak English, a man who wears a long frock, black hat, and is engrossed in so-called archaic studies.
> His goal is wooing the American youth.
> After the war, we all wanted the good things in life. We wanted education. We wanted the money that will give us the goodies we never had. We wanted the freedom to make our own choices.

Chaya Leah is honest enough to recall the aspirations of ordinary young people in the first decade after the *Shoah*. This was a time to leave behind the deprivations of war and to start savoring the abundance of secular knowledge and material wealth that finally became available to Jewish youth.

The idea of full-time yeshiva study simply did not fit into this paradigm. But Rabbi Kotler was determined to change the paradigm. As Chaya Leah recalls, the founder of the Lakewood institution fought the tide of assimilation with more vigor and vision than other religious leaders who brooded over the sad fate of American Jewry:

> *And yet, Reb Kotler gets the finest and the best. This was Yad Hashem at work.*
> *What magic did he have?*
> *What made some of the finest minds in America to gravitate toward him?*
> *To respect him? To emulate him?*
> *They called him "My Rebbe."*
> *He gave them a meaningful life.*

Here, Rav Shmuel David Walkin's daughter and Michael Small's wife looks back and ponders a question few survivors had asked before. Why did American-born boys flock to Rav Kotler's nascent center for full-time learning?

When Chaya Leah points to *Yad Hashem*—to the hand of the Almighty—she is not evading or softening the question. Instead, she is pushing herself to reflect upon the quest for a meaningful life that managed to overcome the desire for material wealth among survivors of the *Shoah*. Rav Kotler inspired a small cohort to make a different choice in a world framed by postwar liberties.

Chaya Leah herself had been groomed for a Torah-centered life. Despite this training, she made a conscious choice to live that life more fully. The decision to dedicate her energies to the building of Jewish community in Chicago was her own. Like Kotler's yeshiva students, she too chose a path that was different from most Americans bent upon acquiring material "goodies" after the war. Becoming a rabbi's wife, as she knew from home, required far more than looking pretty, cooking well, and showing up at public events. It was a choice that required ongoing sacrifice of personal comfort in favor of something bigger, something more meaningful. Looking back, Chaya Leah acknowledged that this was a difficult choice.

A seemingly small decision made in Lakewood illuminated the broader path that Michael Small's young bride would take in later years. The decision concerned her hair. This was an intimate matter and a source of pride for the nineteen-year-old girl who had stood under the bridal canopy surrounded by the greatest rabbis of the generation.

Chaya Leah knew that after the wedding she and Michael would be heading for Lakewood. There the groom was expected to finish his studies and gain rabbinical ordination. In Rav Kotler's proximity, it was expected that young brides would cover their hair. Chaya was willing to comply, but only for a while:

> *At our wedding, Reb Aron Kotler gave me a Brocho.*
> *Those sharp blue, fiery eyes stopped me from uncovering my hair.*
> *How can I do that to Reb Aron?*
> *How can I make jest of my husband Rosh Hayeshive?*
> *After the wedding, I went into the bathroom all ready to fix up my hair.*
> *I had told my husband that I would not keep my hair covered when we leave Lakewood.*
> *In those days, I had auburn wavy hair, like fire. Long and thick, this was the hair that my husband fell in love with.*

A young bride walks into the bathroom after the wedding mindful of the natural beauty that had attracted her husband in the first place.

Now, Chaya faced a choice: To keep her auburn tresses uncovered, like many married Jewish women did at that time? Or follow an old-fashioned tradition of covering her hair?

> *When I walked out of the bathroom with my tichel (scarf) the look in his eyes told me everything.*
> *How proud he must have been.*
> *It took many years to put on a shaitel (wig). I always wore a hat or a kerchief.*
> *In those early days of my marriage, a shaitel was totally unheard of.*

Chaya Leah put on a scarf because Rav Kotler's fiery blue eyes bore into her consciousness. In addition, she sensed that her husband would appreciate this break with American conventions.

This decision, however, represented far more than a mindless acquiescence to others' expectations. It was part of a larger, conscious choice to live a life dedicated to spreading the teachings of the Torah. In Chaya Leah's view, this choice had been brewing beneath the surface of her girlhood even before she married Michael Small.

It had its origins in the war years, during which she had witnessed her own family's unswerving loyalty to Jewish traditions. These war years had strengthened Chaya Leah's character while also leaving scars of trauma that became more apparent during her life as a married woman. It was in Lakewood, as she recalls, that the young bride began to confront memories of terror from Shanghai:

> *The first year we were married, my husband learned in the kollel with other married men.*
> *One evening, I was making dinner when an alarm went off. It sounded like an air raid.*
> *I took everything breakable object off the table, got a blanket, covered myself, and lay down on the floor.*
> *Only then did I realize that my husband had not been in the war. He would not know what to do in case the bombs came.*
> *So I ran out of the house up to the yeshiva to save and protect him.*

A siren goes off, and Chaya Leah is brought back to the bomb shelter on Liaoyang Road. In China, she had been drilled for air raids. Now she rushes off to impart this hard-earned knowledge to her American husband:

> *As I was running up the street, I saw him running down the street, to get me.*
> *He knew that an air raid was a sound that would trigger memories and panic in me. He explained to me that Lakewood does not have a fire department. When there is a fire, all the volunteers are notified by the alarm.*
> *The hidden fears had been lying dormant.*
> *I ran up the hill to save my husband and he ran down the hill to save me knowing how I would react, and we met halfway.*

As the son of refugees from Europe, Michael Small understood the scars of war. He ran to reassure his bride, to bring her back to the present, which was thrown into the shadows by the terrors of the war.

Chaya Leah was simply trying to cook dinner when the fire alarm took her back to Shanghai. With no bomb shelter nearby, she lay on the floor covered with a blanket. These were the years in which American children were being taught how to hide under desks in case of a Russian attack. For Chaya Leah, these were not children's tales but rather a matter of personal experience.

She overcame her own fears to run and protect her husband. Michael Small knew that certain sounds and sights provoked his bride's childhood panic. These dormant fears would become apparent again and again during their early years in Chicago. Nonetheless, working together, Chaya Leah and Michael managed to build a vibrant marriage that was able to withstand both the trauma of war and the challenges of living in a city lacking in traditional observance.

POALEI TZEDEK—LABORERS IN RIGHTEOUSNESS

The young couple arrived in Chicago in 1955, with a young baby girl called Sarah, and nicknamed Dubby. By January 1956, Chaya Leah gave birth to another girl, named Shaindy Rachel. In the winter of 1957, Rabbi Small and Chaya Leah welcomed their first son, named Aharon (Ari) in honor of Chaya Leah's distinguished grandfather, the Rav of Pinsk. Two more boys followed, Shaul Moishe, born in April 1959, and Avruhum, born in December 1961.

Thus, in six short years, Chaya Leah had become the mother of a large family as well as the anchoring rebbetzin of a fledgling Jewish community. All along, she kept in close touch with her "little ones"—the younger Walkin siblings who remained her charges as Tzivia Walkin's poor health prevented active engagement with the children's education.

In Chicago, Michael Small finished a law degree while helping with his father's communal responsibilities as rabbi of the Poalei Tzedek congregation. Rabbi Isaac Ha Levi Smolyar (1899–1977) was born in Russia and studied at the Chofetz Chaim Yeshiva with Rav Shmuel David Walkin. In 1925, he married the daughter of Rabbi Dovid Feinstein and became involved with the previous Lubavitcher Rebbe's efforts to build and maintain yeshivot under the Soviet regime. Persecuted by the communist authorities, he and his wife fled to America where their son Michael was born in 1927.

In 1928, this European-born Torah scholar finally found a position as a pulpit rabbi and also changed his name to Small. The story that Chaya Leah tells about this transformation centers on the difficulty of acquiring a telephone line in the 1920s. To shorten the long waiting time, Rav Smolyar decided to try using the last name of the current governor, Lennington

"Len" Small (1862–1936). It worked. The family got a telephone number and Michael Small was able to grow up as the kind of "Yankee doodle dandy" that Rav Kotler was looking for when he started to build his Lakewood Yeshiva.

Looking back at her early years in Chicago, Chaya Leah acknowledges the tough challenges as well as the loneliness of being a young mother of a large family. Living far from parents made her long for the close knit world of her childhood in Shanghai:

> We came to wilderness in Chicago. I am so proud of the community that is here now. Everything in the city started in our shul. In Chicago at that time there was no kosher bakery, nor a decent Mikva and no one wore their hair covered. It was so lonely in the beginning.
> I was all of nineteen years old. My whole family was in New York. Telephones were expensive and travelling was out of the question. With small children and many community commitments, friends were so few.
> Actually, almost no one.
> But I knew from the moment I married a Levi that my job was to serve.

Here, Rabbi Shmuel David Walkin's daughter confesses the difficulties she faced in the beginning of a life dedicated to communal service.

Yes, her in-laws lived near by. Yes, Rabbi Isaac Small was a strong voice in the effort to combat Shabbat desecration and *kashrut* violations in Chicago. Nonetheless, Chaya Leah missed the gentle touch of her parents, who had nurtured the community in Shanghai. Chicago was a different kind of "wilderness" from the *unterwelt* she had known in China. It required a new vision for building Jewish life.

As the young Rebbetzin Small, Chaya Leah found she had what it took to meet the challenge in spades. With five little children and a husband who worked both as a lawyer and a rabbi, Chaya Leah became an inspirational exemplar for women taking on mitzvoth, such as going to the mikva and covering their hair. She knew the struggle these women faced from within and mentored each with unique attention and care.

At the same time, Chaya continued to carry the burden of war memories hidden deep within. Shanghai was never far from her mind, even if it was only a shadow framing long days as mother and community leader. Like the fire alarm in Lakewood, any chance event could awaken terror. One such moment

Until it Ripens: Marriage, Community, and the Arc of Return • CHAPTER 9 | 253

occurred in the wake of a break-in at their home in Chicago. The police were called and Chaya Leah became immobilized by fear:

> When I would see anyone in uniform, or government officials, memories and fear made me freeze.
> When I was interviewed and questioned, I was terrified.
> My husband explained where I grew up, and how the impact of my youth has affected me.

Again, as in New Jersey, Michael Small stepped in to protect his wife from slipping into a past that was threatening to engulf the present. He kept on "translating" his wife for strangers who did not understand the impact that the war year had upon a Jewish child coming of age in China.

In Chicago, however, after the break-in, there seemed to be less need for explanations. The investigating policeman had his own share of China tales:

> "Shanghai!" the officer exclaimed, "I was in the marines when we landed in Shanghai after the war. I was in the ghetto in a rabbi's house. I remembered him." Jack Muller had been one of the few military men who spoke Yiddish. He was the one who told us that in America you cannot buy such silverware like we had. We had a nice reunion and I showed him family pictures.

> I do not know if he was telling us the truth or not, but after that I always had a warm feeling toward this American coming into our home, speaking Yiddish. It was mind boggling.

This chance encounter with a uniformed official threatened to bring back the trauma of escaping Poland, of traveling through Siberia, of Ghoya's brutalities in Shanghai.

What turned terror into a family visit was the police officer's own recollections of China. Jack Mueller brought unexpected solace into the Small household after the break-in. He spoke Yiddish and allowed Chaya to recall the irony of the Walkin family "treasures." Battered silverware surfaces as a balm over Chaya Leah's fears. What she saw as "mind boggling" went beyond the fact that a policeman spoke Yiddish and that he could be invited safely into one's home. In the mother tongue of her youth, Chaya Leah discovered that the past could hold more than buried grief.

As far as the present was concerned, there was much work to be done. Chaya Leah joined her in-laws' efforts to build Jewish community with her own vision and verve. When the young bride arrived in Chicago, she knew that she was to join the elder Rabbi Small in his efforts to invigorate the foundations of Torah life in the Midwest. What she could not have imagined, however, is just how hard and how rewarding that challenge would become in her own life with Michael Small.

As in *Shir Ha'Shirim*, the newlyweds had to learn first how to bide their time, how to wait, how to plant slowly and keep vigil over the fields until the time was ripe for Torah learning and observance. Looking back, Chaya Leah herself uses the metaphors of planting seedlings to recall the landscape of Chicago that she and Michael helped to make more congenial for a meaningful Jewish life:

> *Sixty years ago, we transplanted a seed in West Rogers Park. The old Yiddish-speaking rabbi believed in the future of that barren piece of land, where all have said:*
> *"No, this cannot be done, the man is old and the soil is barren; what can come of a pipe dream, his mentality of the shtetl is not in the vogue, you must keep up with the times and new technology and ideas."*
> *The people laughed and laughed at this folly, but the old man ignored them and he believed.*

The aged visionary portrayed here is Rabbi Isaac Small, who echoes the commitment that led Rav Kotler to build up the yeshiva world in Lakewood, New Jersey.

In Chicago, with its slaughterhouses, racial divisions, and largely assimilated Jews, the older Rabbi Small carried an unyielding commitment to traditional observance. The homecoming of Michael and Chaya Leah strengthened his determination to make the capital of the Midwest a center for Torah learning as well:

> *The seed was planted in the hard unproductive soil, and the old man and his son, who came to the city to help man, were determined to make the tree grow. Not with new technology, but with their bare hands. The tree took root, and with care and nurturing, that tree grew and mushroomed.*
> *And people from all walks of life came and people from all denominations came and were comfortable.*

This recollection honors the memory of Chaya Leah's father-in-law, the Yiddish speaking "old man" who railed against Shabbat desecration and shady *kashrut* dealings in the meat industry of the 1940s and 1950s. With his European background and pre-war convictions, Michael's father was savvy enough to know the potential of Chicago's "barren soil." When he needed a phone, he changed his name to Small. When he needed new vision and vigor, he made sure his Lakewood educated son would become the public face of the congregation that had served as his own pulpit for decades.

The first long-term contract with an American congregation that the elder Rabbi Small signed in Chicago is dated May 1937. Three years after Chaya Leah was born, her father-in-law had already agreed to a contract that stipulated that the rabbi himself would "contribute the sum of sixteen dollars and sixteen cents toward the purchase of an exclusive House of Worship." These were not terms that a young man called Smolyar had learned in the Chofetz Chaim Yeshiva back home.

As Rabbi Small, Chaya Leah's father-in-law was also expected to have other jobs in order to make contributions to the fledging "House of Worship" that was to be called in English "Congregation Poaly Zedeck." The letterhead of its stationery also spelled out the name of the synagogue in Yiddish, adding to it *Anshei Sefarad*—to indicate the Chassidic style of prayer practiced by its members.

The name of Rabbi Small's *shul* was not unique in America. Several congregations on the East Coast had already adopted the theme of *Poalei Zedek*, which harkened back to the biblical commandment to labor in the vineyards of righteousness. This injunction called upon Jews to follow in the footsteps of Avraham, who had practiced this distinctive virtue, which is not to be confused with "charity." Rather, *poalei tzedek* connoted justice and mutual aid.

In fact, the first *Poalie Zedek* (an older form of Romanization) was founded as a mutual aid society in Brunswick, New Jersey in 1901, at a time when Jewish immigrants could count only on each other's benevolence for survival in the new land. The elder Rabbi Small kept the name and its spelling even after the synagogue moved to its new building in West Rogers Park. By 1956, the congregation *Poalie Zedek* moved once again to a new home on Albion Avenue where, as a local newspaper declared:

> Rabbi Yechiel Michael Small assumed the mantle of rabbinic leadership from his father, Ha Rav Yitzhak Ha Levi Small.[1]

The news of this English-speaking, modern-looking young rabbi made it into the newspapers of Chicago, along with the other great event of 1956—the

---

1 "What is New in Chicago" section, *Chicago Tribune*, December 20, 1956 [cut from original newspaper by Chaya Leah Small, no author].

seizure of the Suez Canal by Gamal Abdel Nasser. Just as Great Britain began losing its influence in the Middle East and the Suez Canal remained closed for over five months, the younger Rabbi and Rebbetzin Small expanded their activities in Chicago to promote Torah learning and observance among Americanized Jews.

Like his father, Rabbi Michael Small was expected to work at other jobs as well as care for all the needs of his varied congregation. It is this challenge that Rebbetzin Chaya Leah faced with the force of vision that she had gained during her family's sojourn in Kobe, Shanghai, and New York. In 2004, when the Yeshiva Women of Chicago honored Chaya Leah in their tribute booklet, it was clear that this Rebbetzin Small was the heart and soul of a now vibrant community.

The write-up about Chaya Leah noted that she had plenty of *"Yichus"*—a Yiddish term for lofty rabbinical lineage. She was, after all, the granddaughter of the Pinkser Rav, the niece of Rabbi Sorotzkin of the Telshe Yeshiva, and a niece by marriage to the renowned Rabbi Moishe Feinstein. But *"yichus"* did not explain why this woman dedicated so many decades of her life to the community to the point that anyone in need turned to her for guidance, warmth, and wisdom.

The booklet described Chaya Leah as a real estate broker who also taught kindergarten in various Jewish day schools and was a respected activist on behalf of children with special needs. By quoting her own words, the dinner journal summarized Chaya Leah's legacy as follows:

> *I love being a Rebbetzin and doing for the community... I paint, love art, decorating and crafts, cooking, and entertaining.*

Behind this modest façade was a woman of many talents and tireless compassion. As the tribute booklet emphasized, Chaya Leah had also played an active role in Bikur Cholim (an organization for visiting the sick), in the Bais Yaakov schools, and in the Chicago Mikva Association.

This list, however, does not capture the prolonged, tough struggle to establish a mikva in the community, to urge women to return to the practice of family purity. Instead of dwelling on her own accomplishments, Chaya Leah took the opportunity of the tribute dinner to pay homage to an entire generation who had endured the hardships of the *Shoah*:

> *I am a Holocaust survivor who grew up in Shanghai, China during World War II. Those impressions from formative years have greatly influenced my life, ideals and values. I came to Chicago in the 1950s and settled in West*

> Rogers Park. I was 'zoche' to be a small link in the Yiddishkeit we hope will be continued with our children.

With these modest words, Chaya Leah acknowledges that she was *zoche*—privileged—to participate in building up Torah life in Chicago. By 2004, it was clear that all five children of Rabbi and Rebbetzin Small were following in the footsteps of their parents. They, too, had become laborers in the vineyards of righteousness with the eldest son, Rabbi Aron Small, serving as congregational leader of the community today.

Looking at the chain of transmission, it might appear as if the Small legacy had been handed forward smoothly. In fact, this transmission was filled with challenges that could not be detailed in a tribute booklet or even in the news story that appeared in the *Chicago Tribune* on March 14, 2016[2]—marking the sixtieth anniversary of *Poalie Zedek*. Described as an "open, friendly congregation," the *shul* is, in fact, struggling to survive while Chaya Leah's commitment remains unflagging, despite her husband's death in April 2011.

Behind the headlines lay Michael Small's own struggles to be a rabbi who worked as a lawyer while also holding fast to Torah principles. He had succeeded in earning a degree from John Marshall Law School in 1963. Like Rabbi Berel Wein, another renowned Chicago Jewish leader, Michael Small consciously chose a Catholic institution that would accommodate his religious observance better than the more prestigious University of Chicago Law School. Rabbi Wein recalled his own decision to attend a Catholic college as follows:

> I felt much more at home in the Catholic school than in an atheistic, agnostic, hedonistic liberal arts college.[3]

Like Michael Small, Rabbi Wein also faced a dilemma at graduation: the degree-granting ceremony was to take place in the largest Roman Catholic cathedral in Chicago, with the cardinal himself handing out the diplomas. Tempted to say he was sick, Berel Wein ended up telling the truth about his

---

2 Allan Busch, "No small matter at Rabbi Small's shul," *Chicago Tribune*, March 14, 2016.
3 Berel Wein, *Teach Them Diligently to Your Children: The Personal Story of a Community Rabbi* (Jerusalem: Maggid Books, 2014), 38.

own religious observance, which prevented him from attending this Catholic ritual. Lawfully excused from attending, he concluded:

> I learned an important, life long lesson. The most successful lie is always the truth.[4]

Rabbi Michael Small faced a similar dilemma during the ninety-third commencement of his law school. Originally, the ceremony was scheduled for Saturday at noon before the end of Shabbat. In order to accommodate Rabbi Small, however, the law school rescheduled the ceremony for a later evening time and even honored this Jewish scholar with a photograph at the graduation podium in its journal, entitled *Briefcase*.

The generous spirit of accommodation that prevailed at John Marshall did not carry over into the work world. As a lawyer, Chaya Leah's husband had to find jobs that accommodated religious observance—not an easy challenge in the 1960s. Eventually, Rabbi Small became corporate counsel for the Chicago police department and was involved in the litigation issues surrounding the Democratic Convention of 1968.

Even though he was willing to work without a kippa in the courtroom so as not to prejudice the case against the clients whom he represented, Michael Small found his path barred when he considered running for a judicial position. In addition to public resistance to an obviously observant Jew, he also discovered that his uncle, Rabbi Moishe Feinstein, was hesitant about a judicial career for Michael. Asked directly for permission to be processed, this authority on matters of Jewish law only shook his head and told his nephew "*nu… nu.*" Both Michael and Chaya Leah understood Rav Moshe's noncommittal response was actually sage advice against actively campaigning for the position of judge in the Chicago elections.

Chaya Leah herself expanded the "rebbetzin" paradigm when she started to work for a college degree while being the mother of five young children. Like her husband, Chaya Leah opted for a Catholic school—Mundelein College. This was the women's division of Loyola University and an institution that accommodated her religious observance as well as offering classes for part-time students. Chaya Leah Small took a full decade to get her coveted bachelor of arts degree, often appearing like the nuns on campus with her hair covered and her modest bearing.

---

4 Ibid.

Until it Ripens: Marriage, Community, and the Arc of Return • CHAPTER 9

The effort and the will that it took to persevere in these college studies came through in an email that Chaya Leah sent me a year after we started working on this book project:

> *In those years, there were no carpools, no social services, no Pampers, no two-car families. Being the only one needed for help by my in-laws, I was very, very busy. But I wanted to get the piece of paper.*
> *It took me ten years and I did it.*
> *When it came to homework, I looked for every shortcut to save time as possible. Once, I had a thirty-page assignment about what is the most important role in your life…*
> *Horror of horrors, I don't have time to write a short note with a couple of sentences, how will I manage thirty pages?*

Here, Chaya Leah recalls how difficult it was to take care of her aging in-laws, her children, and her community while also working for a college degree. She was determined to get that "piece of paper." Clearly, the bachelor's degree represented more than an empty formality. The woman who had excelled at the Kadoorie School in Shanghai, who had faced snickering classmates at Central in New York, was not to be deterred:

> *So I cheated.*
> *I used thirty parts of the body and had thirty pages….For example: Eyes, ears, nose, legs, arm, fingers…*
> *And I wrote:*
> *"The most important role of my life is that which is needed now. I used all the parts of the body:*
> *Eyes to see danger.*
> *Legs to run when necessary.*
> *Arms to embrace. Lips to kiss.*
> *Hands to sew and cook and paint.*
> *Fingers to play music.*
> *Mother when a child needs one.*
> *Lover, a wife. Compassion.*
> *Ears to listen.*

Whether Chaya Leah actually wrote this poetic essay for her college class is not clear. What she did craft, without doubt, is a paradigm-breaking model for female leadership in her community. She was an extraordinary woman who inspired many not only because she helped others but because she radiated energy and vision.

Many of the little children who grew up in Rabbi Michael Small's *shul* on Albion Avenue are grown up now and bring their own children to meet the inspirational rebbetzin. When the children were little, Chaya Leah used to straighten out their clothes, tie up their hair ribbons, and give them special Purim gifts. The traditions continue even as a widowed Chaya Leah observes with concern the endangered fate of the community that she built up with her father-in-law and husband.

Looking back, she delights in the little details that do not fit the expectation people might have had about "an old man who spoke Yiddish" and who railed against *kashrut* violations in Chicago during the 1950s.

One morsel concerns Thanksgiving in the household of the younger Rabbi and Rebbetzin Small. Though born in Europe, Chaya Leah had embraced with vigor the customs of the new land and liked to serve a turkey dinner, which was considered a non-Jewish tradition in those times. The elder Rav Small had little interest in newfangled ways, but, for the sake of his vivacious and devoted daughter-in-law, he broke rank with scholars who wanted no part in any custom that lacked Torah precedent:

> *I remember my father-in-law, whom I revered and adored, and respected.*
> *When he was around, I behaved and held back out of kovod to him.*
> *One Thanksgiving, when my mother-in-law was out of town, he came for dinner.*
> *Vera, he was so wise, and knew the essence of each and every person, as though he saw right through them.*
> *I was not sure if turkey would be acceptable and proper, so I had meat and chicken.*
> *But I also made a turkey for the holiday tradition.*

Here, Michael Small's bride expresses both her great respect for the older Rabbi Small as well as a determination to honor American customs. Thanksgiving was not a Jewish tradition and turkey was shunned by some rabbinical authorities. Nonetheless, Chaya Leah cooked the big bird and her father-in-law honored her choice. He washed his hands and blessed the bread, as befits a celebratory meal, and then asked:

> "*Vu iz die tourkey?*" (how he pronounced it).
> "Where is the turkey?"

> *I told him I did not know if he would want to have some.*
> *"Mir voynen (we live) in America," he said, "and this is a tradition, it is not a religious rite.*
> *We have to be thankful for all the freedoms we have in this country,*
> *So of course I will have tourkey."*
> *I loved him.*
> *And from that time on he always had "tourkey" for Thanksgiving.*
> *All our children laughed—"Zaidy is eating tourkey."*
> *"Yes, zaidy is eating tourkey."*
> *I think he did it for me.*

Here, a snippet from a family dinner in the Small household gains a larger dimension. The conversation was in Yiddish, Chaya Leah's native tongue. The food on the table was novel. The beloved father-in-law gains dignity in Chaya Leah's eyes. And he ate the "tourkey" with full honors, saying a blessing before and after—grateful for the new land which nurtured a flourishing of Jewish life and helped to put an end to the family's dislocations in China and Japan.

The same "Yiddish-speaking old man" looms large in Chaya Leah's retrospective summary of what she herself accomplished in Chicago. Again, the metaphors of seeding, planting, and growing come to the fore as the "tree" of Jewish life continue to bear fruit, most importantly Chaya Leah's own gratitude for having been part of the Small family's spiritual enterprise:

> *The tree with its many leaves and blossoms nurtured all the neighborhood,*
> *where the former institutions are gone and modern ones are taking their place.*
> *Our old-fashioned way is booming.*
> *How proud the tree is to see all that came out of it.*
> *The tree is old, the leaves have fallen, and the blossoms are gone, but the roots are still there—proud to know that all the saplings that came from its seeds are thriving.*

Chaya Leah, now an octogenarian herself, looks back and sees herself as part of the root network that continues to nourish Jewish life in Chicago. She was an important part of Isaac Small's vision of Jewish revival and takes special solace from its vibrancy as a survivor of the Holocaust:

> *This is the nechama, after the Shoah.*
> *We dare not think that we cannot plant a seed in barren land. With our bare hands we have to rebuild the old-fashioned way for our future.*

> *This is what gives me meaning in life.*
> *This is my hakarat ha tov to Hakodosh Boruch Hu for what he has done for me.*

The seedling planted by her father-in-law has become part of Chaya Leah's own mission. After the *Shoah*, there is no room for doubt about what needs doing. As a survivor, the younger Rebbetzin Small had joined the planting effort with all her might.

Looking back, Chaya Leah sees herself as an aged tree. Chicago now has many Torah institutions, each more vigorous than the old congregation that once was called *Poalie Zedeck*. She knows fully well that she is part of the root system that accounts for this enduring vigor. She also understands that her own hard labors in the vineyard of righteousness were a source of *nechama*, of comfort for an entire generation after the Holocaust. Chaya Leah's toils were a way of thanking the Master of the Universe for all the good that came her way not only in China but in Chicago's seemingly barren land as well. Rebbetzin Small, like her parents and in-laws, was grateful to have had a share in rebuilding Torah life after the war.

In the metaphorical framework of *Shir Ha'Shirim*, the senior Rabbi Small, along with Michael and Chaya Leah, were exemplars of skillful timing. They knew when to awaken and how to awaken the love of *Yiddishkeit*—of traditionally anchored Jewish identity in Chicago after the war. Their initiatives bore fruit precisely because they brought affection, tact, and commitment to the "beloved" without a forcible arousal. Michael Small's father knew when to bend into the winds of change, when to pass on the mantle of leadership to his English-speaking son and vibrant daughter-in-law.

A SHTUB OF CHESED: THE PASSING OF A GENERATION

During the same years that Rabbi Michael and Chaya Leah were building their family and community in Chicago, Rav Shmuel David and Rebbetzin Tzivia were busy caring for Holocaust survivors in New York. The Walkins' *shul* and home had been moved into one gracious building in Queens. This remained a gathering place for the Shanghai *bochrim*, middle-aged men with their own families, and often painful memories that could only be shared with those who had tasted the trauma of war.

In the 1960s, Rav Shmuel David became a prominent member of the Agudas Harabanim, the most respected council of Orthodox rabbis in America presided over by Rav Moshe Feinstein, Michael Small's uncle and counselor.

From this position of honor, Rav Walkin became active in many different *kashrut* organizations. One of the positions that enabled him to entertain Chaya Leah and her husband was as *mashgiach* (*kashrut* supervisor) for the Olympia cruise lines—one of the luxury travel agencies that catered to observant customers.

Several photographs in Chaya Leah's family album portray a regally robed Rav Shmuel David with his famously flowing white beard and the elegantly dressed and coiffed Rebbetzin Tzivia at the captain's table on the cruise ship. On the deck, a more relaxed and shapely Rebbetzin Small sits next to her father in shirt sleeves, clearly each cherishing this relaxed moment away from the pressures of community and public life.

These were also years during which Professor Avraham Kotsuji was a visitor in the Walkin home and delighted in Esther Poupko's recollection of the Japanese rope jumping song. Away from the public eye, memories of Japan and China had a quiet second life, even as Rav Walkin became a public figure honored alongside Rav Moshe Feinstein and Rav Joseph Soloveitchik at weddings and other gatherings of Torah scholars. When the death of Chaya Leah's father was recorded in the *New York Times* on August 27, 1979, it was the *Shoah*, again, that featured prominently in the byline: "*Rabbi Samuel Walkin of Queens; Helped Thousands Escape Nazis.*"

More than a survivor himself, Rav Walkin was memorialized for the physical and spiritual help he had provided for fellow victims of the world's madness, both in Shanghai and beyond. The importance of maintaining and strengthening Torah life was a secondary theme, as if escaping the Holocaust and creating a meaningful refuge for survivors were two separate events. Yet, as Chaya Leah's life story reveals, these were twin branches of a single tree rooted in the values that Rav Walkin and his daughter carried from Europe to China and on to New York and Chicago as well.

Twenty years later, when Tzivia Walkin passed away on the fourth night of Hanukah (in December 1999), it was the religious press that paid extensive homage to "The Rebbetzin." The English-language magazine *Hamodia* dedicated a full page to the life and values of Chaya Leah's mother, dwelling both on her "royal" lineage in the Torah world and her own regal bearing and compassion to all those in need. In *Yatid Ne'eman*, it was noted that though Rebbetzin Tzivia passed away on Hanukah, when traditionally eulogies are not given, this custom was abrogated by rabbinical decree in order to pay due respect to a woman who had embodied the most cherished ideals. Both in Borough Park in Brooklyn and later in Jerusalem, noted public figures gathered to speak about this Rebbetzin whose wisdom had built up not only her large family of scholars but so many others who came through her home in China and in America:

> To many broken hearted and needy, it was her house that became known as a *shtub of chesed* (a home of refuge and kindness)… At the end of the war, she and her husband arrived in the United States, where she helped hundreds of refugees from China rehabilitate. She made *shiduchim* for 75 of the refugees.[5]

Here, the formidable woman who had impressed a secular Yiddish writer in the 1950s is recalled as a source of comfort for many other refugees in their hours of need. Those who eulogized Tzivia Walkin also recalled her inner refinement as well as her close connection to the Chofetz Chaim. She was deemed to have been a true *tochter* (daughter) of the Radin Yeshiva, who was scrupulous to never speak ill of others and merited being called affectionately "Tzivinka" by its founding sage.

As the oldest child of this *shtub of chesed*, Chaya Leah was entrusted to carry on the traditions. She had intuited this weighty charge as a little girl in Kobe and Shanghai. It became her conscious mission in Chicago as a rebbetzin in her own right. Yet, on looking back at her parents' lives, it was small incidents of kindness that linger in the mind's eye. These reveal the distinctive refinement of spirit that carries her forward to this day:

> *When my father left this world and people came to make shiva calls, many would ask:*
> *"Ver vet mir itster makhn a glezele tey?"*
> *"Who will make for me now a glass of tea?"*
> *Whenever my father had a guest, he would personally serve him. When I came to visit from Chicago, my father would make breakfast for me.*
> *"Can someone else make it?"*
> *His answer was:*
> *"True she is my daughter, but she is also my guest."*

Who will make "*a glezele tey?*" is not just one's guest's question nor simply a daughter's nostalgic longing for the special dishes that her father made just for

---

5   Betzalel Kahn, "Rebbetzin Tzivia Walkin o"h." *Dei'a ve Dibur*. December 22, 1999.

her, even after she was a married woman and mother. This question itself leaves an ethical directive for the next generation. Young people may not have time or take the time to cherish each visitor no matter the visitor's social standing. A personally offered cup of tea soothed so many broken spirits in the Walkin home because it came with a listening ear and an empathetic heart. Here, trauma could be shared and Torah values affirmed in order to lift a burden that few Americanized Jews bothered to fathom or to understand.

In April 2011, when Chaya Leah herself faced the loss of her husband, there were no parents, no *glezele tey*. Chaya Leah got the news while she was in Israel attending the wedding of one of her nephews. As the older sister of Rav Chaim Walkin, she had made a point of never missing an important family gathering, no matter the effort or the cost. Her deep love and respect for her little brother and his self-sacrificing wife made Chaya Leah a constant presence despite the geographical distance between Chicago and Jerusalem.

Rabbi Michael Small had been visiting their daughter in New Jersey when he suffered his fatal heart attack. Chaya Leah, shaken and brokenhearted, waited in Jerusalem for the children to accompany the body for burial in Har Ha Menuhot—the Mountain of Consolations. In that cemetery, there is a special *Chelkat Ha Rabonim*—a special section for prominent Torah teachers. There, Rebbetzin Tzivia Walkin is buried next to her husband, who, in turn, lies right next to Rabbi Soloveitchik and his family. Nearby are the graves of Rav Aharon Kotler and his family, Rabbi Chaim Shmuelevitz and family, Rav Moshe Feinstein and his family, as well as the graves of Chaya Leah's great uncle, Zalman Sorotzkin and his family.

In this one corner of Jerusalem are buried all the *gedolim* whom Chaya Leah knew and loved. They are gathered here and continue to provide inspiration and solace far beyond the circle of their immediate mourners. Learning to go on as a widow and as a guardian of her generation's memories has not been an easy challenge for Chaya Leah. Recalling, writing, and speaking about her experiences during the war has become a passion and a calling in her years of widowhood.

This lonelier time, in the words of *Shir Ha'Shirim*, has become "ripe" for another kind of soul journey. As a widow, Chaya Leah discovered that the road leads back into her personal past, back toward the child who had been part of the Jewish refugee experience. China and the trauma of war had been part of her daily life all along. But the need to memorialize that past became compelling after 2011, as Chaya entered the years of her widowhood.

Before that year, journeys back in time had been marked by echoes of the trauma that she had endured as a child. Now, the journey back in time has become part of a conscious effort to make room for the past in the present.

Taking one more trip back to Shanghai and working on this book project has enabled Chaya Leah to paint her own corner on the broader canvas of Holocaust memoirs. The result is a more vivid and more complex picture than she had imagined possible during her younger years as a daughter, then mother and wife.

BACK TO LIAOYANG ROAD

When I went to visit Chaya Leah at her home in Chicago in the fall of 2015, I sensed a painful absence beneath the plethora of Chinese vases, cabinets, and silks. The death of Michael Small was still a palpable loss after four years in the house that had served as the family haven. Living alone now, with her son Rabbi Ari down the block, Chaya Leah was well cared for and deeply immersed in collecting fragments of her China memories.

Yet, neither the plentiful mementos nor the constant love of family and friends could mute the gnawing question that came out during one of our afternoon conversations:

> *I am not sure that what I remember so vividly is real…*
> *I can't seem to find any record of our house in Shanghai.*

I sensed a deep disquiet in Chaya Leah's words. She recalled the exact address on Liaoyang Road, each room of each refugee family, the sound of the hawkers, and the names of little children in the compound. Yet, something was missing.

I promised to look into the history of Liaoyang Road. A year later, my Chinese research assistants were still unable to locate any physical remains of the street that had framed Chaya Leah's childhood in China. In 2007, however, when Chaya Leah first went back to Shanghai, a broken wall still stood outside number 281 on Liaoyang Road. Chaya Leah's daughter Dubby, who was the sole companion on this journey back in time, recalls:

> My mother basically wanted a chance to go back and see where she had spent in a place that was so significant in her life. Even in America, being a Shanghai refugee defined her—the Shanghai extended family being so central to their lives.

> At first, I think she was horribly disappointed—she couldn't find a landmark that resembles anything from her past.
>
> The alleyways of the middle of the ghetto were not like the house she grew up in at the farther edge of the ghetto; she couldn't see her old school, which was now a restricted government building; the shops were different, etc. Time did not stand still.
>
> But then we came to the *shul*. The building was the same and suddenly an onslaught of memories and feelings.
>
> I think her emotions were very strong because she couldn't even articulate them to me.[6]

Here, Chaya Leah's oldest daughter is a living witness to a flood of recollection long held back. China had shadowed Chaya Leah's life for decades. Now she was there, and the only place that opened a window to the past was the Ohel Moshe synagogue, which serves as a museum today.

Precious as that window was, Chaya Leah needed more. Her daughter recalls the relentless longing for the familiar compound:

> She had a very strong desire to find her childhood home on Liao Yang Rd, but the communists changed the street names. Mr. Wong tried to help and took her to the area he said was her block—but the homes had been razed. Because she couldn't reconcile her memories to what is there now, she started doubting some of her own memories. It's a major reason she seeks confirmation of what it was like from other Shanghailanders.[7]

The ruined neighborhood around Liaoyang Road left a chasm of unassuaged grief. Mr. Wong, the guide mentioned by Chaya Leah's daughter, probably spared the two Western ladies the details of the larger ravage that had scarred Shanghai since the 1960s. The dilapidated buildings that remained in 2007 behind the broken wall were the only mute witnesses to the missing Jewish history as well as to Chinese memories of the Cultural Revolution. This decade-long tragedy was too awful to mention aloud, especially to foreigners.

---

6   Sarah (Dubby) Pollak, personal correspondence, April 21, 2016.
7   Ibid.

Chaya Leah Small looking for her home on Liaoyang Road, 2007.

Despite the visible ravage, Chaya Leah found a tiny bit of solace in the ruined landscape:

> When I went back to Shanghai in 2007, the little shoe store was still there. Looking back at our family photographs from Shanghai, in those pictures I see the care that was taken to preserve the life of each and every garment...
> I also know how to darn socks.
> My children laugh at me—in our throwaway society—but the joy of fixing something usable is a lost treasure.

One old shack near the broken wall on Liaoyang Road was enough for Chaya Leah to recall the effort taken with small possessions during the family's refuge in war-torn China. The darning of socks had been a necessary skill among all the poor people who had crowded into Shanghai during the Japanese occupation. Chinese and Jews alike had no choice but keep on patching old clothes.

For the European refugees who had a Torah background, this attention to salvaging seemingly small possessions had the added significance of the Jacob narrative. This founding father of the Jewish people had made a great effort to cross a dangerous river in the dead of night to bring back small vessels that belonged to his family. In Shanghai, *Bnei Israel*—the children of Jacob, who was also known as Israel—had used thread and needle to sow together clothes as well as the past left behind in Europe and in Asia.

A true *Bat Yaakov* (daughter of Jacob), Chaya Leah does not see herself as part of today's "throw-away society." The joy of fixing something usable, as she puts it so well, has become indeed a "lost treasure." The search for such treasure, however, took on a different, very loud public tone during Chaya Leah's second return trip to Shanghai in the spring of 2014. Whereas mother and daughter had traveled as ordinary tourists in 2007, the journey in the company of Rav Chaim Walkin in 2014 became an event amply noted both in the Chinese and Jewish presses.

On the Chinese side, the official media was hungry for good news. On March 25, 2014, the day before the Walkin family's arrival in Shanghai, the government-sponsored newspaper called *China Daily* printed a feature story about 29 people who had been murdered and 130 injured in the most violent knife attack in post-Mao society. The crime had taken place in Kunming, one of China's most prominent cities of refuge during the Japanese occupation. With the news from the southwest being so awful and the threat of anti-state terror still unmentionable, Chinese readers needed something upbeat. The arrival of a gracious rabbi from Jerusalem who had been born in Shanghai served this purpose quite well.

Rabbi Chaim Walkin and his sister Chaya Leah made good copy since they were portrayed as coming back to express their gratitude to China for saving their lives during the war. An article written by Chinese journalist Jiang Yebin on March 26, 2014 about the Walkin visit was entitled "Jewish Delegation Thanks Shanghai." The large photograph that opened the essay showed Chaya Leah and her younger brother, now sporting a long white beard and black coat, standing in the courtyard of the Ohel Moshe synagogue. It was labeled as follows:

> Members of a Jewish delegation tour the Shanghai Jewish Refugees Museum Wednesday during their visit to thank Shanghai and its people for sheltering Jewish refugees during World War II.[8]

---

8   Jiang Yebin, "Jewish Delegation Thanks Shanghai," *The Global Times*, March 26, 2014.

Gone is the questioning tone and the doubt-filled quest that Chaya Leah's daughter had recalled from 2007. Here was an important opportunity for Chinese officials to launch a public campaign for the seventieth anniversary of the Allied victory against Japan.

In this campaign, it was important to show China—that is, the Communist Party—in the most positive light possible as a defender of Jewish victims during the Holocaust. Although Mao's Party had nothing to do with the refuge that the Walkin family had fashioned on Liaoyang Road, its representatives were eager for words of thanks from the illustrious rabbi and his vivacious older sister. Chaya Leah's story was especially poignant, thus she became the centerpiece of Jiang Yebin's essay:

> One of the five former refugees in the delegation, Chaya Small now lives in Chicago, Illinois in the USA. She came to China in 1934 [sic] as a seven-year-old. Although she left when she was 12, she never forgot the city that sheltered her. "Life has changed here," she said. "Children are still running around me just like in the years when I lived here.
> A small photograph taken in Shanghai shows her mother, the two sisters and her Chinese nanny. "My nanny was just like my mother. Although she did not speak our language, she gave us comfort when things were difficult," Small said. She shed tears when she mentioned her Chinese nanny and hoped someone could help her locate the woman.[9]

It was these tears of gratitude that the Chinese official media courted and needed from Chaya Leah and her family in 2014. Readers probably would not pick the error that Chaya had not arrived in China as early as 1934. They would be simply reminded that a Jewish woman could not forget China and loved the feel of children running around, just like in her youth. The fact that those children had been Jewish friends and fellow refugees did not have to be mentioned.

It was the gilded present that was the focus here. The old, torn photograph of the nanny served the Communist Party propaganda best. Here was a "working class" Chinese woman who had provided comfort to foreigners in trouble. Gratitude to the nanny was also featured in the March 27th issue of the Chinese language newspaper entitled *Laodong Bao (Labor Daily)*. Although the main photograph here focused upon the white bearded rabbi expressing "gratitude" to China (and by implication, the Communist Party), it was the nanny who had

---

9 Ibid.

Until it Ripens: Marriage, Community, and the Arc of Return • CHAPTER 9 | 271

the last word. Here, too, her story fit best with the new narrative being organized for the seventieth anniversary of the "liberation to the Shanghai Ghetto."

Newspapers in Israel also carried extensive stories about the Walkin trip to China. Here, too, gratitude to China was featured in bold Hebrew type declaring: *"Toda Shanghai"* Thanking the Chinese government these days is good for the booming business that Israelis are doing in techonlogy, argriculture, and intelligence sharing about Muslim terror. Although the source of terror could not be named in Kunming in 2014 (and remains a rather obscure topic in the Chinese media even today), the image of the bearded rabbi and his family made great copy for strenghtening Israel–China relations.

In one of the lengthiest essays in the Hebrew press, Rabbi Chaim Walkin's photograph is accompanied by the snapshot from the *New York Times* featuring the little boy with a kippa on the day that he received American citizenship. Next to these images was an essay about Chiune Sugihara, who also contributed to the survival of the Jewish refugees. As in the Chinese press, Israeli newspapers also quoted Chaya Leah Small about the details of the family's survival during the war. Although other Torah scholars who were trapped in Shanghai during the war were mentioned as well, the emphasis was upon how the Walkin family had benefited from the aid of the Chinese people.

Even in Hebrew, there is little emphasis upon the homegrown values and inner sense of community that had created a uniquely Jewish refuge in a world gone mad. *Toda* (הדות) in Hebrew, like *xiexie* (謝謝) in Chinese, are simple words for "thank you." These echo like a theme song in most public commemorations of the Jewish experience in China during the war. The song goes on and on despite the fact that Rabbi Chaim Walkin, like Chaya Leah, had tried to convey a more complex, more spiritual description of Jewish refuge during the *Shoah*.

In the Hebrew-language press, the photograph of Rabbi Walkin at the official reception in China in 2014 clearly shows him addressing the audience on the following theme (written upon a banner in English): "Commemorating 70 Years of the Miraculous Escape to Shanghai." The "miracle" intended here had little to do with the Chinese Communist Party and much with the Divine Providence that Rabbi Walkin believes had guided the Mirrer Yeshiva community to the shores of Shanghai.[10] This was also the

---

10 Vera Schwarcz, "Who Can See a Miracle? The Language of Jewish Memory in Shanghai," in *The Jews of China: Historical and Comparative Perspectives*. Volume 1, ed. Jonathan Goldstein, 185-210. New York: M. E. Sharpe, 2000.

perspective on which he elaborated when I visited him at his Jerusalem home in February 2016.

Pulling off a well-thumbed volume from the bookshelf, he pointed me to a passage by Rabbi Chaim Leib Shmuelevitz, which said:

> An entire book could be written on the miracles that took place during every single day of our refuge in Shanghai.[11]

Rabbi Walkin, like his older sister, was showing me this passage in order to underscore the spiritual context for survival during the *Shoah*. Shanghai had been what Chaya Leah had called the *unterwelt*—the underbelly of an ugly, violent world in which Jews had not been abandoned by their Creator. Nor did they forsake the teachings that gave meaning to survival beyond professions of "gratitude" welcomed so eagerly by the regime ruling China today.

Chaya Leah's own journeys into the vociferous world of public commemoration began in earnest after the death of Rabbi Michael Small. Ritualized remembrances of the Holocaust were, of course, not novel events in the twenty-first century. Almost every Jewish community sponsors some sort of *Yom Ha Shoah* ceremony in the spring following the Israeli government's decision in 1953 to mark the twenty-seventh day of the Jewish month of Nisan as an official day of remembrance for the victims of the Holocaust. From the 1950s onward, the Orthodox community has been reluctant to embrace this date since the Chief Rabbinate had declared that the tenth of Tevet (marking the siege of Jerusalem by Nebuchadnezzar) and the ninth of Av (marking the destruction of both the First and Second Temples) as more appropriate, more traditional avenues for mourning the destruction of European Jewry. With the dawn of the twenty-first century, however, more and more Orthodox Jews have been taking part in public ceremonies marking *Yom Ha Shoah*. Nonetheless, they remain a distinct minority.

When Chaya Leah Small began to take an active role in Holocaust education and Holocaust commemorations in the Chicago area, she was a rarity. With the opening of a new Holocaust Museum and Education Center in Skokie in 2009, she became a better-known figure. At first, she was uncertain about how to frame her own narrative. After the first trip back to Shanghai in 2007, memories and doubts had surfaced but had yet to be voiced in public. During the next

---

11 Shmuelevitz, *Pirkei Chayim*, 123.

five years, however, Chaya emerged as one of the most eloquent witnesses to the Shanghai refugee experience in a way that captured the public imagination.

In August 2013, when the Chicago-based Spungen Foundation sponsored a gathering of survivors from the Shanghai Ghetto, the *Chicago Tribune* featured Chaya Leah's story complete with details of the family's one-room dwelling on Liaoyang Road and their "insane" plan for escape through Vilna and Kobe. The largest photograph in the *Tribune* article about the gathering of survivors was reserved for the Walkin family "ca. 1944" showing Rabbi Shmuel David and Rebbetzin Tzivia with Chaya Leah, Esther, Moshe, and the newly born Chaim. The small details of the war years—including the fact that Chaim was born in 1945—were of little significance in this public celebration of Jewish survival and Chinese generosity.

The ripple effect of the 2013 gathering of Shanghai survivors in Illinois continued to bring Chaya Leah into the public eye, as well as into my own life and work. One of those attending the gathering had been David Sokal, son of Dr. Robert Sokal, the noted scientist whom I had interviewed years earlier. It was David who introduced me to Chaya Leah and suggested that I may be of help in the telling of her story. Out of the national publicity that had accompanied the gathering of Shanghailanders in 2013 came the reunion between Chaya Leah Small and Bella Tresser, the other girl in the photograph depicting Jewish moviegoers after the war.

Tresser was living in Florida when she read a news item about Chaya Leah Small's story. She did not recognize the last name but the face on the residence certificate from Shanghai was familiar. After a Google search, the two women spoke at length on the phone and, by August 2015, they were featured in an Orlando newspaper article entitled "Survivors of the Shanghai Ghetto reunite after 70 years."[12] The photograph that accompanied the story showed two aged and refined ladies sitting close to each other nearly embracing, each holding up a memento from her childhood in Shanghai. The following quote attributed to Chaya Leah Small framed the photograph of the two friends: "It was a total miracle that this happened. I get very emotional about it."

An intense emotional tone and the language of spiritual gratitude are Chaya Leah's distinctive contributions to the increasingly voluminous literature about survival in Shanghai. Just how miraculous the reunion of Chaya

---

12 Susan Jacobson, "Survivors of the Shanghai Ghetto reunite after 70 years," *Orlando Sentinel*, August 5, 2015.

Leah and Bella turned out became fully apparent a couple of months later, when the *Orlando Sentinel* carried the obituary for Mrs. Tresser.

The two girls who had shared the joy of movies after the war in Shanghai and who were far apart in religious observance and family background had nonetheless forged a bond that defied time and geography. Chaya Leah had been determined to make the trip to Florida in the summer of 2015, despite her own family's concern for her health and well-being. Chaya Leah went to visit Bella because both had been beneficiaries of "miracles." Seeking out fellow survivors was Chaya Leah's way of continuing to give deeper meaning to the Jewish life during her childhood years in China.

In this journey to visit Bella, one can glimpse again the apt wisdom of *Shir Ha'Shirim*. When the time becomes ripe, it is important to act. Chaya Leah understood and acted almost instinctively upon this sense of timing, arousing affection from the past and for the past. Memories had to be cherished and renewed or they would disappear altogether.

This is not a nostalgic pursuit of recollection but rather a conscious effort to bear witness to a world in which the creator of the universe continues to guide and shape Jewish destiny. The same drive to seek out and take note of "miracles" led Chaya Leah Small to visit older Shanghai survivors who now reside in various nursing homes in the New York area. Chaya Leah thrills with every new detail of the past regained, confirmed, and enhanced by the unfolding of current history.

One of the most vibrant threads in the fabric of Chaya Leah's unfolding memory brocade comes from Leo Melamed, a prominent Chicago attorney and businessman. Born in 1932, Leo and his family also fled from Poland through Vilna, Siberia, and Japan. As Chairman of the Chicago Mercantile Board since 1969, Melamed is a prominent sponsor of Holocaust commemorations and figures prominently in Akira Kitade's book *Visas for Life*. Chaya Leah has known about Leo Melamed for many years, but their friendship is deepening as Chaya Leah's widowhood opens up more time to cement shared recollections.

After an April 2016 visit with Leo Melamed and his wife, Chaya Leah sent me a moving series of emails describing their conversation in Yiddish about the past. In that familiar *mama loshen*, there were fewer barriers to the welcome waves of memory and grief:

> It was such a special afternoon.
> The best part of all, the whole time off camera was spent speaking Yiddish.

> Facts I learned:
> The train station, Vagzall was not in Vilna, but Moscow, going from Moscow to Vladivostok.
> The chaos and fear, Melamed's mother worrying about going to Siberia. Same with us.
> "Don't talk to anyone!" Same with us.
> Sitting on the one suitcase. Almost same with us.
> Chaos and fear. Getting off the train en route, bitter cold winter. Same with us.

The pain of memory is here lifted by the relief of mutual recognition. Chaya Leah is thrilled to hear from Leo Melamed details that she knows well from her own experience. Articulated here by a powerful public figure who can still speak Yiddish, Chaya Leah's fears from the past become a source of joy.

Sharing this delight, she is nonetheless careful to note differences between the Walkin family and that of Melamed:

> His father was academia and a Bundist.
> He was on the threatened list of refugees.
> His life was in danger because of his political convictions.
> The American government gave 100 visas as asylum, his father was one of the recipients, and therefore went from Japan to US…
> You can be the CEO of the Mercantile Exchange.
> You can sit at dinner with the Emperor of Japan.
> You can give lectures on the futures market.
> But nothing beats the joy of remembering the vagzahl, the Siberian bitter cold winter and the rickety smelly boat...
> The joy of a man who has it all remembering the simple things
> His home is filled with treasures, but the one treasure he was proudest of was in seven pictures hanging on a wall.
> Seven pictures of his mother, father, and sister.
> Pre-war pictures. His most valued treasures.

In this email, Chaya Leah described both her own joy and that of her wealthy host—who was a fellow survivor. Leo Melamed's father had been a mathematics teacher and a secular supporter of the *Algemeyner Yidisher Arbeter Bund*, founded in Russia in 1897. As a result, the elder Melamed qualified for one of the few precious US visas that brought Jewish refugees directly from Japan to the United States.

Leo Melamed had not shared the Shanghai years that had shaped Chaya Leah's childhood and adult life. He became a successful CEO in America. He had dined with the Japanese emperor and could afford to buy treasures far more valuable than the Chinoiserie that adorns Chaya Leah's own home.

And yet, what is most precious in the home of Leo Melamed, as in Chaya Leah's life, are the pre-war photographs of the family. There was no photograph of the distinguished Pinsker Rav or the Chofetz Chaim in this home. Leo Melamed's parents were ordinary Jews who nonetheless provide a living link back to a world that continues to nurture survivors who miraculously escaped being exterminated during the *Shoah*.

One way in which Chaya Leah herself honors that miracle on a daily basis is by wearing her father's gold cufflinks on a gold chain around her neck. Manufactured in Shanghai during the war, they are embossed with the character *fu*—福— which connotes "blessing" as well as "happiness" and "good fortune." This is no fortune cookie amulet. Rather, it represents a daughter's ceaseless effort to pay homage to a past that was hardly "happy" but nonetheless contained blessings that continue to unfold in the lives of Rav Shmuel David's descendants.

Another piece of jewelry also links Chaya Leah with her Chinese childhood. It is a large pendant, tastefully designed to enclose the "Shanghai Memory" medal minted by the Spungen Foundation in 2013 in time for the gathering of survivors in Illinois. Danny Spungen is a friend and admirer of Chaya Leah Small. He is also the president of "Why Not Collectibles" of Lincolnshire, Illinois. It was Danny's family foundation that sponsored the reunion of survivors and also worked with Chinese authorities to design a commemorative object that would honor the "humanitarian efforts by China to offer safe refuge for those who fled Europe in the 1930s."

Danny Spungen gained the cooperation of the Shanghai Mint officials for this project. Chaya Leah Small was one of the first to be awarded this medal made of pure silver. Each medal has been etched with a limited edition number to ensure its authenticity and value. Needless to say, Chinese authorities were eager for a positive spin concerning their role in rescuing Jewish refugees.

The designer of the medal that Chaya wears on all public occasions was "Rocky" Zhao—the same artist who had created the commemorative coins for the 2008 Beijing Olympics as well as the gold "Panda Medals" for diplomatic use by the Chinese government since 2011. Not surprisingly, the Spungen-sponsored medal confirms an official reading of the past that emphasizes Jewish gratitude for China's beneficence during war.

On the front of the large coin, Zhao depicted a Chinese lady dressed in a traditional *qipao* (the tight silken attire with side slits favored by the upper classes). She is holding a protective umbrella over a little Western girl, who, in turn, clutches a toy panda bear. By implication, the Jews are small and powerless while a generously female and mature China extended kindness in the inclement weather of war. Behind the little girl and the compassionate mother figure bending over her are a row of gates and doors that suggest all the closed options that faced Jews trying the escape the Holocaust during the later 1930s.

The four Chinese characters above the two figures—上海記憶—suggest a double meaning: "Shanghai remembers" as well as "Memories of Shanghai." They hint directly at the protective generosity of China while acknowledging rather obliquely the Jews, who had added such vitality to Shanghai before and during the war.

The other side of the silver medal is engraved with the English words "Shanghai memory" and depicts a huge boat entering the Whampoo River—supposedly depicting the SS Conte Biancamano, one of the steamer ships that brought refugees to China. The foreground of the commemorative coin also shows two Westerners dressed in Victorian attire as well another foreigner riding in a rickshaw pulled by a Chinese coolie.

The message is not quite clear: Are these Westerners Jewish refugees? Victorians of the earlier Sasoon generation? Is this a Chinese condemnation of "imperialism"? Or maybe an indirect acknowledgment of how much Westerners had contributed to China beyond the discourse of expected gratitude?

Needless to say, this medal says nothing about the role of the Japanese occupation, which is directly responsible for the residence permits obtained by the Jewish refugees in Shanghai. There is no hint here that the Chinese protection symbolized by the kind lady's umbrella was nothing but a reflection of Wang Jingwei's puppet regime. The Western gentleman and lady are stick figures who convey none of the distinctively Jewish values that had enabled Chaya Leah Walkin to survive and thrive in the community on Liaoyang Road.

Chaya Leah wears this medal with pride and continues to relish a deepening friendship with Danny Spungen and his family. Again, as with so many other threads in her China network, Chaya Leah's enthusiasm extends to all who take an interest in memorializing the refugee experience. Chaya sees and affirms the good that the Spungen Foundation does in Holocaust education and she is a willing participant in its efforts to cast a positive light upon Chinese efforts to "save" the Jews.

Between Rabbi Walkin's cufflinks and the Spungen medal lies a world of difference. The first was forged during the actual times of hardship and spiritual miracles. The second represents a belated narrative meant to satisfy disparate constituencies eager to claim that they gave a helping hand to Jews during the war. The same retrospective gaze also leads Japanese officials to seek out Chaya Leah in their current efforts to honor Chiune Sugihara and to build more memorials in his hometown. She is willing to wear the Spungen medal in honor of the Chinese as well as to meet with Japanese politicians in New York City. She continues to speak in Chicago public schools and appeared at the 2015 premiere for *Persona Non Grata,* a film about the lifesaving visas handed out by the Japanese consul in Kovno during the the summer of 1940.

All these activities underscore an instinctive grasp of the wisdom embedded in the words of *Shir Ha'Shirim*. It was only when time was "ripe" had Chaya Leah and the Walkin family managed to escape from Vilna to Kobe and beyond. It was only when time was ripe that Danny Spungen was able to cooperate with Chinese authorities in paying homage to Jewish survival with silver medallions. It was only when time was ripe that Japanese authorities found it useful to memorialize a courageous diplomat whom they had ignored for decades.

The ripening of these different temporalities depended on human effort. Chaya Leah Small has been both a witness and an agent in the maturation of public memory. The disparities in Chinese, Japanese, and Jewish commemorative narratives, in turn, allow us to glimpse the distinctive resources that refugees themselves had used to shape a meaningful survival during the *Shoah*.

These days, Chaya Leah wears her father's old cufflinks as well as the new Shanghai medal while she waxes eloquently about Japanese aid to Jewish refugees—all this in order to create new bridges between past and present, between what can be said and what remains still hidden in unspeakable grief.

Conclusion

SEEKING YOUR VOICE FOR THE SAKE OF THE UNBORN

You who dwell in gardens—
Our companions seek your voice,
Enable me to hear it.

Shir Ha'Shirim 8:13

Finding the right cadence for the Chaya Leah Walkin story was no easy challenge. Numerous public commemorations of the Jewish survival in Shanghai during recent years made the task even harder. Something quieter, more intimate, waited to be excavated out of the debris of memory and frequently told tales. Like the dove hidden in the crook of the rock, this story too trembled on the verge of silence.

Chaya Leah Small and the author, December 2017, NYC.

In *Shir Ha'Shirim*, the lover compares his beloved to a quivering bird who has taken refuge in mountain crags. When a stranger draws near, she does not make any sound at all, she does not even risk a flutter of wings. Describing the predicament of this dove perched upon a steep cliff, Professor Yehuda Felix likens her to the opening lines of Psalm 56: "Upon the dumb dove (*yonath elem*) cause me to hear, that is: let me hear your voice."[1] We all long to hear and be heard. But the *yonath elem* has a darker and more urgent predicament. She wants to sing her song, but fear chokes her voice. If she remains silent, the beloved will never come. If she cries out, the wrong people may hear and redemption will be delayed forever.

Survivors of the *Shoah*, as I learned in the course of writing this book, face a similar dilemma. They, too, have been struck dumb by history. Even before meeting Chaya Leah, I sensed that my own parents and grandparents had swallowed so much dread that they could impart to me only fractured bits of an unspeakable tale. How was I to create a cohesive narrative out of such shards?

At first, I thought that all I had to do was to encourage Chaya Leah herself to write. That would be my contribution to her story. Later, I realized that I had to enter the narrative, to craft the very voice that I was seeking to hear. This act required drifting away from all the eager "companions" in the public realm who are seeking to capitalize upon Jewish recollections of the Shanghai refuge. I had no choice but to look for inspiration far from the familiar landscape of China at war. In Vladimir Nabokov's novel *The Real Life of Sebastian Knight*, I discovered techniques to affirm the details of a single life, to trust that in the very messiness of its tapestry may be found an organic coherence that clarified larger dilemmas. As Nabokov put it: "There is only one real number: one. And love, apparently, is the best exponent of this singularity."[2]

In working with Chaya Leah, I was privileged to encounter such loving singularity. Our correspondence and conversations were marked by generous attention to the differences in our visions of Jewish as well as Chinese history. This acknowledgment enabled me listen more effectively to the story that I needed to tell. A world gone mad was to be part of my narrative about refuge with dignity. In writing about Chaya Leah, I could not help but account for the history that has led me to notice what I did, to record what I must. Perspective, I learned, was everything and had to be used explicitly. In the words of the Ramchal (Rabbi Moshe Chaim Luzzatto, 1707–46), I found

---

1   Felix, *Shir ha-shirim: Teva, alila ve alegorya*, 122.
2   Nabokov, *Sebastian Knight*, 37.

further encouragement: "Every man shall gather what belongs to him and build."[3] This is not only a description of the human predicament but also of an ethical obligation. Especially as a writer, I had to face up to the unique challenges, dangers, and opportunities that were my distinctive calling.

In this work, I aimed to build up the story of one refugee family who did more than survive the *Shoah*. Here, I found both particularity and a larger prism with which to focus upon the Jewish values that had bolstered a meaningful existence in the harshest circumstances of war. The Chaya Leah Walkin story became for me an antidote to generalizations about the Jewish experience in Shanghai that are replete in both the scholarly and the commemorative literature.

BEYOND THE HELLISH NOISE OF HISTORY

I had been seeking such an antidote for years. During the 1990s, when I was doing research for a new book in China, I had already circled the Shanghai story. I had already begun to interview survivors, such as Dr. Robert Sokal. At that time, I started to pay closer attention to Nietzsche's warning in "Thus Spoke Zarathustra":

> *Believe me, friend Hullabaloo!*
> *The greatest events are not our noisiest, but our stillest hours.*
> *Not around the inventors of new noise, but around the inventors of new values,*
> *does the world revolve; inaudibly it revolves.*[4]

The hellish noise of history back then seemed to me focused upon Chinese effort to magnify certain patriotic events of the past and wash away the proximate grief of the Tiananmen events of 1989. To counteract this public din, I began to explore memory studies as an alternative paradigm for healing the wounds of history.

Now, in the second decade of the twenty-first century, the Shanghai story has gained many more lives and much public significance. The establishment of the Shanghai Jewish Refugees Museum in 2007 and the publicity surrounding the painting exhibition entitled "Love Without Borders" were all part of the "Hullaballoo of History." Nietzsche's warning about the inventors of new noises

---

3   Chaim Walkin, *The World Within: Contemporary Mussar Essays* (Jerusalem: Targum Press, 2000), 207.
4   Vera Schwarcz, *Bridge Across Broken Time: Chinese and Jewish Cultural Memory* (New Haven, CT: Yale University Press, 1999), 186.

echoed in my mind as I tried to give voice to the values of the Walkin family, which had defined a distinctively Jewish dignity in a world gone mad.

Although these are anything but "new values," they remained nearly inaudible in the new museum as well as in scholarly literature, which condemns Orthodox Jews for focusing upon their own kind during the war. Books published in the yeshiva circles similarly ignore the complexities of survival by dwelling upon the "miracles" of Shanghai, leaving out the tough and prolonged effort to wrest some sense of agency out of loneliness, despair, and crushing poverty.

In September 2014, Shanghai resident Kenneth Lubovitch began to sound the call for a quieter, *soto voce* version of the Shanghai refuge experience in an article about the bronze sculpture in the Shanghai Museum that commemorates 13,732 Jewish names. Lubovitch's essay noted the absence of any representative from the Japanese government at the ceremony sponsored by Chinese officials as well as by the Spungen Foundation. Although Chaya Leah's name is among those carved in metal and her friend Danny Spungen tried to speak about the darker aspects of the war experience, what remains canonized in this narrative is that Shanghai saved the Jews. Like the painting of refugees behind barbed wire and the medal of the little girl beneath a kind lady's umbrella, this is a story focused upon the generosity of China as a "haven"— which today is conveniently associated with the communist government.

Another critical voice was raised by a young Chinese researcher, LuPan, in an essay entitled: "Remembering the Pain of Others: The Shanghai Jewish Refugees Museum and Beyond."[5] This essay was published on a scholarly website called *Writing the War in Asia*—which is part of a collaboration between the Universities of Essex, Hong Kong, and Konstanz. In her essay for this project, Lu Pan posed a series of serious questions both about historical veracity as well as the narrative framework of the Jewish story portrayed in Shanghai.

The starting point of Lu's critique is the overly "symbolic" space that Jewish refugees have been placed in by the Communist Party in its politicized narrative of World War II. By magnifying the "pain of others" and erasing the complexity of both the Chinese and Jewish suffering during the war, the Shanghai museum fits nicely into a sanitized version of the past, which leaves

---

5 Lu Pan, "Remembering the Pain of Others: Reflections on the Shanghai Jewish Refugee Museum and Beyond," in *Writing the War in Asia: A Documentary History*, accessed October 15, 2017, https://www.polyu.edu.hk/cc/images/Article/Doc/paper/dissertation/panlu/06_dissertation_PanLu.pdf.

the communists as the guardians of the nation. Embedded between the lines, there is a message suggesting that the party had acted magnanimously toward refugees:

> Shanghai is depicted as an abstract symbol of the tolerance of China toward Jewish refugees in the just cause of the fight against fascism. However, claiming that anti-Semitism did not exist in wartime China is inaccurate, although the majority of the Chinese population did not harbor strong resentments against the Jews. No large-scale persecutions occurred during the Japanese occupation of Shanghai and the degree of hostility towards Jews, as exhibited by Japan or by the pro-Japanese Chinese government, was largely motivated by immediate political interests. In the museum narratives, "the Chinese people" are depicted solely as a humanistic and generous collective, which aided the foreigners in surviving warfare and persecution.[6]

Lu Pan is not alone in recognizing that there was anti-Semitism in China and that the Jews survived mostly because of the complex machinations of the Japanese occupation, which controlled the Wang Jingwei puppet government. An overly generalized category of the "Chinese people" allows the government to create an idyllic vision of history while subtly appropriating both Maoist discourse and a victimization narrative borrowed wholesale from the Holocaust memorial in Berlin.

An even more sharply worded critique of the Shanghai Museum was penned by Lotte Marcus, a German-speaking survivor who was a few years older than Chaya Leah in Shanghai. Marcus's poignantly titled essay "The Marshmallow Museum" takes issues with the sanitized and politicized narrative projected in the old Ohel Moshe synagogue. She is unambiguous in denying extensive "friendships" between Chinese and Jews during the war. Like Chaya Leah Walkin, but from a secular point of view, Lotte Marcus describes Jewish refugees as staying mainly within their own world. The Chinese, contrary to images on the commemorative medal, did not alleviate the hardships of the Jews' daily circumstances.

If there was a "life umbrella," it was not one provided by China but rather was created by the refugees themselves. Funds from co-religionists beyond

---

6   Ibid.

Shanghai kept life going, along with the resourcefulness of the Jews trapped by the war:

> We were never fed by any Chinese organizations. No Chinese philanthropist or organizer sat on any of our committees. The one and only true Chinese rescuer was Dr. Shen Fang Ho, about whom I have written elsewhere … . It is not merely the fact of historical errors that are bothersome. They are correctable. What is most bothersome is an emotional tone that is repetitive, insistently bland and ultimately false. The Chinese history re-writers boldly trivialize daily life of the people (both Jews and Chinese) in war conditions. These tales dull the imagination.[7]

Dr. Lotte Marcus's eloquent indictment comes from a fidelity to the facts of her own experience as well as an insightful understanding of what is being covered over in the bland tone of the Shanghai Museum. By recalling the supposed goodness done for the Jews by China, the communist regime is, in fact, encouraging the public "to not remember its own travesties."[8]

Dr. Marcus, like Lu Pan, is urging us to look beyond official history—to hear afresh the neglected voices of survivors, both Jewish and Chinese. This message calls to mind the ethical imperative articulated by Liu Binyan (1925–2005), a much persecuted journalist who never lost his commitment to digging up the unremembered past in China. In a courageous address to fellow writers shortly after the death of Mao Zedong, Liu insisted:

> We have no right to be auditors in the courtroom of history. The people are the judges as well as the plaintiffs. We must supply them with scripts. But before we can provide answers, we must learn. We must understand more about social life than the average person.[9]

Liu Binyan's call to conscience was addressed specifically to fellow intellectuals, who had been forced to cower during the Mao regime. But the injunction against becoming "auditors in the courtroom of history" is relevant to all of us who seek to make sense out of the terrible events of the twentieth century. Listening to

---

7   Lustig Lotte Marcus, "The Marshmallow Museum: Holocaust Lite," *Points East* (November 2015), 2.
8   Ibid., 3.
9   Liu Binyan, *Two Kinds of Truth: Stories and Reportage from China*, ed. Perry Link (Bloomington, IN: Indiana University Press, 2006), 137.

the voices of survivors, providing new paradigms of interpretation for their suffering is something that we can and must do in the twenty-first century.

Liu Binyan had asked fellow writers to become *dai yan ren* (代言人)—literally "carriers of the word"—from the benumbed commoners to a regime still mired in deafness to the particulars of a brutal history that the regime itself had created. This mission is one that I also took to heart in telling the Chaya Leah Walkin story as it unfolded in a world gone mad. Although the survival of Jews in China during the war has been gaining much publicity, its particularities are in danger of being erased. The subtler, more autonomous resources for endurance have been neglected in favor of grandiose praise for the governments of China and Japan and for heroic rescuers such as Shen Fang Ho and Chiune Sugihara.

Jewish survivors of the *Shoah* have contributed to public commemorations out of their own need to express gratitude. Listening to their voices amidst the loud din of what Nietzsche called the "Hullabaloo of History" requires attentiveness to something beyond praise. Retrospectively giving thanks for one's life is, in itself, a creative, spiritual gesture that challenges official versions of survival during the war.

HAKARAT HA TOV—THE OBLIGATION TO EXPRESS GRATITUDE

Looking beneath rescuer narratives, one glimpses a distinctly Jewish concern with *hakarat ha tov*—a conscious effort to express indebtedness in a world devoid of concern for refugees. When I first started to work on this book, I did not fully understand the force and impact of this concern. I had not yet begun to think about it as a *mitzvah*—an obligation grounded in Torah sources, as opposed to what might be construed as survivor guilt.

At first, as I began to delve into the voluminous memoir literature, it seemed to me that Chaya Leah and fellow Shanghailanders were driven by an intense quest for an address (almost any address) where they could offer their thanks for having avoided the fate of other Jews killed during the *Shoah*. Going back to Shanghai to visit the Refugee Museum in a widely publicized journey and attending meetings with Japanese officials eager to have the United Nations commemorate Chiune Sugihara were all part of Chaya Leah's effort to express her gratitude to places and peoples that helped her family survive.

Yet, the obligation for *hakarat ha tov*, I came to understand, goes beyond the quest for an outward address where one could say "thank you" to public authorities. It is a distinctive pathway for deepening one's own humanity by recognizing the good that has been done by others. One of the first occasions in the Torah for this recognition to shine through occurs in Egypt. Here, Jews are in exile and oppressed. Moses, their rescuer, is charged with bringing about the plague of blood by striking the Nile. This was the very river that had saved his life as an infant, and so the prophet is reluctant to enact an act of violence toward it. Instead, it was Moses's brother Aharon who carried out the task of striking the river with his staff. If even a part of the natural world deserves gratitude, how much more so human beings who go out of their way to help others in need!

In the end, *hakarat ha tov* does not end with the river or with the kindness of men. It is, in fact, a force that expands the capacity for empathy within the very person who seeks to express gratitude for the acts of others. This Jewish obligation of voicing one's gratitude is embedded in the *amidah* (the standing prayer repeated three times each day) in which we find the words of "*modim anachnu lach*" (we thank you …). Rabbi Eliyahu Dessler (1892–1953) pointed out in one of his essays about seeking truth that the *modim* prayer represents a constant acknowledgment that we have been granted the capacity to express *hakarat ha tov*—our gratitude for each and every moment and action that enables to go on strengthened in our task of bettering the world.

A similar emphasis upon ethical refinement through the expression of one's indebtedness may be found in the Chinese character *en*—恩—which is comprised of "reason" over the ideograph for "heart." This word is most often linked to actions that honor one's parents by showing gratitude for the simple fact of life itself. Since we are not the authors of our own existence, each of us is obligated to express thanks to those who came before us, who made it possible for a child to enter the world. Within the Chinese word *en* may also be glimpsed an enlargement of the self through the very act of conveying appreciation for being alive. This is no simple challenge. It requires one to delve deeply into the gratitude-giving self and find there the core of what enables us to go on enriched beyond survival.

In light of both *en* and *hakarat ha tov*, I now see Chaya Leah's expressions of gratitude afresh. When she writes or speaks about Sugihara, for example, she is doing more than thanking one man for signing those life-giving visas in Kovno during the summer of 1940. She is, in fact, appealing to posterity and asking us to reflect upon all the various forces that converged to make survival possible for Jews who were spewed out of Europe by violent hatred. To be sure, commemorations of Sugihara's actions, much like celebrations of Jewish refuge in Kobe and in Shanghai, are good for business relations as well as diplomacy.

Nonetheless, what matters most is that we hear what kindness is possible and that hatred need not have the last word, even in a world gone mad.

The poet Naomi Shihab Nye articulated this faith in one of her works entitled "Kindness." Without any reference to *hakarat ha tov*, she manages to capture the cadence of gratitude that allows us to hear hope in the midst of grief and despair:

> Before you know kindness as the deepest thing inside,
> You must know sorrow as the other deepest thing.
> You must wake up with sorrow.
> You must speak to it till your voice
> catches the thread of all sorrows
> and you see the size of the cloth.[10]

Chaya Leah Walkin, too, had spent much of her girlhood as a refugee waking up with sorrow. Even as a seasoned rememberer, she continues to catch the thread of grief while expressing gratitude for the kindness of her parents, Sugihara, Kobe, and even Shanghai. Above all, she continues to take note of the critical values that comprise the expansive "cloth" of survival with dignity.

This dimension of "kindness" has not received its due attention in commemorations of Jewish refuge during the war. Scholars who survived the *Shoah* in China and Japan often give gratitude to divine providence for their survival. Academic scholars such as Ephraim Zuroff, by contrast, critique the "particularism" that led Orthodox Jewry to focus upon the rescue of various yeshivas during the *Shoah*. Neither point of view accounts fully for the inner resources that enabled Jews to survive the war and to vivify the expression of *hakarat ha tov* even today.

Chaya Leah herself focused upon this inner dimension by using an old Yiddish saying: *Ikh veys nisht ver trogt vemen af vemens pleytses—I don't know who is carrying whom on their shoulders.* She quoted this expression during our prolonged conversation in Chicago in the spring of 2015. We had been circling stories of sacrifice by ordinary Jews in support of Torah scholars—stories that included her father's help in supporting his youngest son (and his family) while Chaim continued full-time learning.

---

10 Naomi Shihab Nye, *Words Under Words: Selected Poems* (New York: Eighth Mountain Press, 1995), 46.

Asked as a question—"*Ikh veys nisht ver trogt?*"—enabled Chaya Leah to reflect more deeply upon the spiritual symbiosis that sustained many different kinds of Jews in China and beyond. For a while it seemed that donors from America and the wealthy community of Sephardim in Shanghai, deserve the most explicit gratitude for Jewish survival. Later, as accounts of Asian rescuers multiplied, it was heroes such as Dr. Ho and Sugihara who became the target for gratitude. In the end, however, there is a more subtle meaning to the question of "who is carrying whom upon their shoulders?" The query itself points to a mutuality of concern that sustains the Jewish people even today.

Sacrifice and survival were two sides of the coin in China, two aspects of a kindness that operated beyond the raw needs of physical endurance. The Walkins were recipients of beneficence from many sources; they, in turn, provided support for refugees far beyond the circle of the Mirrer Yeshiva and the residents crowded into the compound on Liaoyang Road. The Torah values which they carried from Radin and Pinsk to Kobe and Shanghai gained new depth during the war. Chaya Leah's use of the saying *"Ich veys nisht ver trogt vemen oif vemens pleytses"* showed me how one can be carried and be a carrier at the same time.

Chaya Leah herself pointed to Rav Shmuel David Walkin as the embodiment of this ideal. Coming from "Torah royalty" before the war, he never rested upon the laurels of that past. All his life, he insisted on reaching out to all kinds of Jews, providing each with whatever aid was needed. By way of illustration, she recalled the following encounter: As a young married woman, Chaya Leah was visiting her parents and noticed a scantily dressed Sephardi lady coming out of her father's study. She had come to ask some question about Torah law, which the rabbi promptly adjusted to her concrete situation and level of observance.

When Rav Walkin's daughter asked what the questions had been, the father demurred, respecting the privacy of a rabbinical encounter. He simply repeated a mantra that became Chaya Leah's guiding light as well: *a yid ist a yid*—a Jew is a Jew no matter what. Like the Torah's description of Israel as a "chosen people," this is not a claim of privilege but rather a call to higher responsibility.

Scholars who had taken upon themselves the challenge of focused learning in times of great historical trauma did not do this to satisfy personal intellectual curiosity. Rather, they firmly believed that their efforts were benefitting the whole Jewish nation, especially during the darkest hours of the *Shoah*. Looking back at her childhood, Chaya Leah emphasized this concept of responsibility and self-sacrifice:

> As a teen, I was privileged to have lived in a generation of Gedolim.
> I saw incredible Mesirat Nefesh.
> Done with so much ahavas Hashem.
> We do not have this today.
> Everything is available.
> It is so easy to be a religious Jew today, but we don't always see the ahava ben adam le'chavero.

Here, we have the deeper layers of "who is carrying whom." In Chaya Leah's mind, it is not enough to learn Torah, to keep kosher, and to observe the Shabbat. When she speaks of the greatness witnessed as a child, she dwells upon the willingness for self-sacrifice out of genuine love of God—*ahavat Hashem*. How do we express this sacred affection? Not only by clinging to ancient texts or the prestige of rabbinical positions. Rather, through the careful expression of respect for each human being that we are privileged to encounter.

In a world of material plenty and spiritual insensitivity, Chaya Leah's story stands as a reminder that we cannot, *must* not, turn aside from those in need. Her own gratitude to previous generations enables me now to express my own *hakarat ha tov* for the guidance received in the course of working on this book. Without Chaya Leah's constant encouragement and many-sided kindness, I could not have grasped the deeper meanings of survival in China. In writing this account, I glimpsed once again the gift of the *gedolim*. Their towering virtues were honed not simply from the study of ancient texts but also from a willful cultivation of affection for others.

SEEING LIKE SEURAT

This kind of affection, as Chaya Leah noted, seems hard to find in the post-*Shoah* generation. Whether it is material wealth or a paucity of moral imagination, we have yet to embrace fully the "gift of the *gedolim*." Geoffrey Hartman (1929–2016) also acknowledged this failed communication in his book, *The Longest Shadow: In the Aftermath of the Holocaust*. Here, a German survivor a bit older than Chaya Leah had used literary theory and oral testimony to analyze the gap between those who knew the trauma of war firsthand and the rest of us. After cataloguing all the devices used after the *Shoah* to both diminish and at times deny enduring grief, Hartman concluded that there remains a permanent precipice between those who had been engulfed by the war and those of us who seek to understand them from the other side: "Their art makes us feel something that cannot be presented... the unutterability of their memories."[11]

Chaya Leah Walkin Small's own jottings and this book represent an effort to cross a seemingly unbridgeable gap. It is also a reminder that surviving the Holocaust in Shanghai was nothing like enduring the *Shoah* in Auschwitz. Survivors in Chaya Leah's circle managed to carve out spheres of dignity and generosity that were inconceivable in Europe during the war. Nonetheless, the dilemmas of memory transmission outlined by Geoffrey Hartman also haunt this work.

Using the words of *Shir Ha'Shirim* has been one of the strategies used to bridge the gulf between my generation and that of Chaya Leah Walkin. Like the companions of the lover, I, too, engaged in a quest for the voice hidden in the crook of the rock. I also know that seeking the voice is not enough. Hearing—taking it to heart—is an altogether different challenge.

As a daughter of survivors, I had been shielded by my parents from looking into the gas chambers, which had claimed my mother's parents in Europe. An urge to hear their cries carried me, unknowingly, to China and led to years of work on intellectuals who had been tortured during the Cultural Revolution. With Chaya Leah, I was able to find yet another way of hearing the sorrows of history. Her jottings contained a gentle invitation to come close to Jewish refugees during the war. Following Chaya Leah's childhood through the alleys around Liaoyang Road, I managed to find a story and a voice that countered the madness of a heartless world.

The voice that found me was that of the little girl who carried a small bag of *"lokshen"* to deliver to Rabbi Walkin's contacts in Shanghai. The child had no idea that this was foreign currency used to save and sustain lives. Only later, much later, did Chaya Leah wonder aloud:

> *I did know I had to be very careful with the bag and why would a little girl be asked to take a small bag of lokshen (noodles) and deliver them to friends?*
> *My father was also in charge of giving out money, but odd that a little girl should make deliveries. Either there was barter and exchange, or I had to deliver money to someone not on the yeshiva list.*
> *I know my father helped others.*
> *But me delivering money?*

---

11 Geoffrey H. Hartman, *The Longest Shadow: In the Aftermath of the Holocaust* (Bloomington, IN: Indiana University Press, 1996), 129.

Conclusion: Seeking Your Voice for the Sake of the Unborn

The voice that drifted off the page here was one that pulled me in. It was a voice I could trust precisely because it was not looking for answers. I could join its cadence, follow where it led to unexpected associations.

> *The bag was small, but I did not think much about it…*
> *I remember a chocolate bar lasting a long time.*
> *A sliver on the smaller end of the bar was doled out if we ate the horrific breakfast.*
> *So a small bag of precious lokshen is not impossible.*
> *I simply had to give it only to the designated person.*

Here, memory speaks its tale full of hesitation, uncertainty and wonder. Chaya did not mask her confusion—both back during the war and later, looking back. The link between noodles and a sliver of chocolate created a unique picture of what refuge looked like inside the Walkins' world in Shanghai. Conveying that picture with its unexpected details became my challenge—and opportunity.

Precisely at a moment in time when public commemorations washed over the minutiae of Jewish survival, I was privileged to be immersed in the complexities of personal recollection. As we kept up our intense correspondence during the writing of this book, Chaya Leah herself kept reminding me of the hardships faced by a small child who had lived through war, yet was not defined by its cruelties:

> *Circumstances made me a mother at twelve or thirteen.*
> *Your little girl that you are trying so hard to find…*
> *Circumstances.*
> *Your little girl who never had a childhood.*
> *I am stronger for it, but in reality I never had a childhood.*

Here, the *lokshen*-carrying child speaks with the voice of a woman seeking to fathom what lies buried in one word: circumstances. It was that word which drew me in. I knew that I could expand its meanings, paint its layered colors, and thereby bring back a childhood that never was. Responsibilities, both familial and communal, had engulfed Chaya Leah and her parents even before she suffered terror on the Trans Siberian railway. I could describe that and also a few idyllic months in Japan. I could try to follow the threads of a rope-jumping song learned in Kobe long ago.

As I wrote this book, I glimpsed far more than the little girl who grew up in Shanghai during the war. A strong and wise woman became part of the picture as well, an octogenarian who looks upon the past in all its murkiness. The key to clarity lay in the grainy details. I learned to cherish those details even as Chaya Leah herself sought an overarching theme:

> *Today, I am philosophical about existing and living.*
> *We lived in Shanghai a Torah true life, in spite of all the hardships and pain.*
> *The seforim were our souls…*
> *We shared our food to nourish the body. We shared our seforim to nourish the soul.*
> *Simple. We made life simple and meaningful.*
> *That was the key to our survival. Achdus.*
> *A community. A group of friends with the same goals.*
> *One helping the other.*
> *One loving the other unconditionally.*

"Unity" was Chaya Leah's one-word summary for life during the war. I came to see why this was indeed an apt description of the bomb shelter where she had been the tallest child and all the women from the yeshiva community were pregnant or holding infants in their arms. Here, indeed, was a picture of resilience and hope. But also terror. I had to find ways to make room in a narrative focused on community for the girl who recalled the rising water in the bomb shelter, the screams of little ones trying to remember the Hebrew alphabet when prayers failed to come to mind.

My goal, aided by Chaya Leah's jottings, was to let the cacophony of the past come through even as I sought to make sense of its confusions. No single explanation sufficed, no single theme could sum up this rich narrative of survival. I had to find a way to honor complexity. Again, an email from Chaya Leah helped to guide me in this quest:

> *We do not know the masterpiece of the creations of the hand of God. But we believe that everything is for a reason whether we understand it or not.*
> *A good example that comes to mind.*
> *The Seurat painting hanging proudly in the Chicago Museum of Art.*
> *A bunch of tiny dots from close up and when you back away and study the painting, you see a masterpiece.*

I had not been asking for a lesson in Jewish theology when I received this email. Chaya had long ago told me that she did not want the book to be *"fa'chnyoket"*—unctuously religious. Yet, here she was telling me how to glimpse a pattern in the tapestry of life.

Conclusion: Seeking Your Voice for the Sake of the Unborn

I never thought of pointillism as a form of historical explanation before. Yet, in this snippet of existential rumination, I glimpsed a technique for telling my part of the story. As a member of the generation born after the war, I know that it is time to add up the dots. How are we to move far enough from the canvas to see each color in its own context and also the larger image they create?

How to see history as Seurat did in his well-known work entitled "A Sunday on La Grande Jatte" composed in 1884? In this painting, I found a world as different from Shanghai during the *Shoah* as it is possible to imagine: a suburban island along the Seine river lies frozen in time with ladies and gentlemen relaxing in attitudes of distant contemplation as they stroll along the slow moving river of time. Only one dark dog in the foreground is busy rooting for something in grainy grasses.

Like that hound, I am looking for nourishing morsels through this willfully stilled fragment of the Chaya Leah Walkin story. Georges Seurat had used countless horizontal brushstrokes to create a palate of complementary colors and later added the tiny dots that appear solid and luminous and form shapes discernible only from a distance. Pointillism, once called "divisionism," broke up the presumed unity of subject and observer. Both the painter and the viewer have to work hard to recompose the painting, much like Chaya Leah and I did during the creation of this book.

Each of us took turns as "painter" and "viewer." Chaya Leah's jottings consisted both of horizontal strokes attributing meaning to the past and dots—like the bag of noodles—that don't quite fit yet add depth of perception. I used the horizontal lines of world history between 1934 and the 1950s to create a palate that not so much explained as questioned the meanings of Jewish refuge during the war. The details of Chaya Leah's life and the words of *Shir Ha'Shirim* are dabs of color aimed to pull you, the reader, into picture.

If I succeeded at all, you will have to step back and recompose the picture in your own mind's eye. The very subjectivity of the voice—the *zhu guan* 主觀—created on these pages demands participation. This book, then, is a glance into how we create meaning out of the details of contemporary history in a world only somewhat less crazed than the one that had shaped the Chaya Leah Walkin story. If we listen to the subject creatively enough, we may be able to see ourselves afresh:

> A dot here, a dot there, a mish mash.
> Each of our lives is a personal painting, each life is a masterpiece.
> But you have to see the painting as a whole, not as a bunch of little dots.

Bibliography

Adika, Alon. "Tsuruga: Truly a port of humanity," *The Japan Times*. February 1, 2014.
Akabori, Anne Hoshiko. *The Gift: A Biographical Account of Japanese Diplomat, Chiune Sugihara Whose Legacy Continues to Burn Brightly Through the Lives of Those Who Received His Gift of Life*. Sacramento, CA: Edu-Comm Plus, 2005.
Altman, Mira. "From Shanghai to the ICC Jerusalem," *The Jerusalem Post*. May 20, 2015.
Bachrach, Susan and Anita Kassof. *Flight and Rescue*. Washington, DC: The United States Holocaust Museum, 2000.
Birnbaum, Ervin. "Evian: The Most Fateful Conference in Jewish History, Part II" *Nativ: Ariel Center for Policy Research*. February, 2009. Accessed August 13, 2017. http://www.acpr.org.il/nativ/0902-birnbaum-E2.pdf.
Barrett, David and Shyu, Larry eds. *Chinese Collaboration with Japan, 1932–1945: The Limits of Accommodation*. Stanford, CA: Stanford University Press, 2001.
Bauer, Yehuda. *Rethinking the Holocaust*. New Haven, CT: Yale University Press, 2002.
Bauer, Yehuda. *The Death of the Shtetl*. New Haven, CT: Yale University Press, 2009.
Belkin, Herbert. "When 400 Rabbis Marched on Washington." *Moment Magazine*. October 6, 2015.
Ben-Canaan, Dan. "Nostalgia vs. Historical Reality: Imagined Communities. Imagined History. Accessed August 13, 2017. http://kehilalinks.jewishgen.org/Harbin/Nostalgia_vs._Historical_Reality.pdf.
Ben-Sasson, Haim Hillel. "Grodzinski, Ḥayyim Ozer." In *Encyclopaedia Judaica*. 2nd ed., Vol. 8., 91–92. Detroit, MI: Macmillan, 2007.
Bernstein, A. "The Final Days of the War in the Pacific and the Jews of Shanghai." *Dei'ah ve Dibur: Information and Insight*. December 14, 2005.
Blair, Margaret. *Gudao: The Lone Islet: The War Years in Shanghai—A Childhood Memoir*. Bloomington, IN: Trafford Publishing, 2009.
Blesser, Yisroel. "Still Singing: Reb Yechiel Benzion Fishoff." *Mishpacha*. December 12, 2012.
Bloch, Chana, and Ariel Bloch. *The Song of Songs: A New Translation, Introduction and Commentary*. New York, NY: Random House, 1995.
Bobker, Joe. *The Rabbis and the Holocaust*. Jerusalem: Gefen Publishing House, 2010.
Bunim, Amos. *A Fire in His Soul: Irving M. Bunim, 1901–1980, the Man and His Impact on American Orthodox Jewry*. New York: Feldheim Publishers, 1964.
Busch, Allan. "No small matter at Rabbi Small's shul." *Chicago Tribune*, March 14, 2016.
Cho, Joanne Miyang. "German-Jewish Women in Wartime Shanghai and their Encounters with the Chinese." In *Gendered Encounters between Germany and Asia*, edited by J. Cho

and D. McGetchin, 171–91. Palgrave Series in Asian German Studies. London, Palgrave Macmillan.

Die Ersten Achtzig Jahre (The First Eighty Years: A Birthday Tribute to W. Michael Blumenthal) Berlin: Jovis Berlin, 2005.

Dorfman, Yitchak. "Ani Ma'amin." Accessed August 13, 2017. http://www.chabad.org/library/article_cdo/aid/107189/jewish/Ani-Maamin.htm.

Dwork, Deborah and Robert Jan van Pelt. *Flight from the Reich: Refugee Jews 1933-1946.* New York: W. W. Norton, 2012.

Dunn, Leslie and Nancy Jones, eds. *Embodied Voices: Representing Female Vocality in Western Culture.* New York: Cambridge University Press, 1994.

Eber, Irene. *Voices from Shanghai: Jewish Exiles in Wartime China.* Chicago: University of Chicago Press, 2008.

Eber, Irene. *Wartime Shanghai and the Jewish Refugees from Central Europe.* Berlin: De Gruyter, 2012.

Elberg, Simcha. "Hagaon Harav Shmuel Walkin zt"l." *Hamodia.* August 27, 2014.

Farbstein, Esther. *Hidden in Thunder: Perspectives on Faith, Halachah and Leadership during the Holocaust.* Translated by Deborah Stern. New York: Feldheim Publishers, 2007.

Farbstein, Esther. *The Forgotten Memoirs—Moving Personal Accounts of Rabbis Who Survived the Holocaust.* New York: Shaar Press, 2011.

Fackenheim, Emil. *God's Presence in History: Jewish Affirmations and Philosophical Reflections.* New York: Jason Aronson Inc., 1970.

Fatal-Knaani, Tikva. "The Jews of Pinsk, 1939-1943, Through the Prism of New Documentation." Accessed August 13, 2017. http://www.yadvashem.org/odot_pdf/Microsoft%20Word%20-%202283.pdf.

Chani. "Feeling a Friend's Pain," *Binah Bunch*, July 4, 2016, 3.

Felix, Yehuda. *Shir ha-shirim: Teva,alila ve alegorya* (The Song of Songs: Nature, plot and allegory). Jerusalem:Ha-hevra le-heker ha-mikra, 1974.

Findeisen, Raoul David and Martin Slobodník, eds. *Talking Literature: Essays on Chinese and Biblical Writings and Their Interaction.* Wiesbaden: Harrassowitz Verlag, 2013.

Fine, Jacob E. "Refugee Awareness." My Jewish Learning. Accessed August 13, 2017. http://www.myjewishlearning.com/article/refugee-awareness/.

Fogelman, Eva. *Conscience and Courage: Rescuers during the Holocaust.* New York: Anchor Books Doubleday & Company, Inc, 1994.

Frankfurter, Yitzchok. "A Conversation with Rav Chaim Walkin." *Ami Magazine.* November 5, 2015.

French, Paul. *The Old Shanghai A to Z.* Hong Kong: Hong Kong University Press, 2010.

Frodon, Jean-Michel. *Cinema et la Shoah.* Paris: Cahiers du cinéma, 2007.

Gao Bei. *Shanghai Sanctuary: Chinese and Japanese Policies toward European Jewish Refugees during World War II.* Oxford: Oxford University Press, 2013.

Gilbert, Shirli. *Music in the Holocaust: Confronting Life in the Nazi Ghettos and Camps.* Oxford: Oxford University Press, 2005.

Greear, Wesley. *American Immigration Policies and Public Opinion on European Jews 1933-1945.* PhD diss., East Tennessee University, 2002.

Grescoe, Taras. *Shanghai Grand: Forbidden Love and International Intrigue on the Eve of the Second World War.* New York: St. Martin's Press, 2016.

Grodinsky, Yitchok. "The last moments of Rav Elchonon Wasserman Before His Murder." *The Yeshiva World*, April 10, 2010.

Goldman, Shimon. *From Shedlitz to Safety: A Young Jew's Story of Survival.* New York: S. Goldman, 2004.

Glowacka, Dorota. *Disappearing Traces: Holocaust, Testimonials, Ethics and Aesthetics.* Seattle, WA: University of Washington Press, 2012.

"Hakaras HaTov After 75 Years: Emotional Gathering At The Mirrer Yeshiva With Mr. Nobuki Sugihara, Japanese Hero." March 2, 2015. Accessed August 13, 2017. https://www.theyeshivaworld.com/news/headlines-breaking-stories/287899/hakaras-hatov-after-75-years-emotional-gathering-at-the-mirrer-yeshiva-with-mr-nobuki-sugihara-japanese-hero.html.

Harris, Samuel R. *Sammy: Child Survivor of the Holocaust.* Chicago: CreateSpace, 2013.

Hartman, Geoffrey H. *The Longest Shadow: In the Aftermath of the Holocaust.* Bloomington, In: Indiana University Press, 1996.

"Hebrew Printing in Shanghai, 1941-1946 – Mirrer Yeshiva and Others," *Fishburn Books.* London, 2011, accessed November 4, 2017, https://www.fishburnbooks.com/catalogs/Shanghai%20HebrewLatestsbFinalJF.pdf

Hochstadt, Steve. *Exodus to Shanghai: Stories of Escape from the Third Reich.* New York: Palgrave, 2012.

Hoffman, Yair. "Rebbetzin Rishel Kotler." *The 5 Towns Jewish Times.* July 22, 2015.

Huang Yuan. "Jews in Shanghai: A Japanese Officer Cut off Rabbi Walkin's Beard in a Swoop." *Shanghai University International Studies.* September 16, 2016.

Iwry, Samuel. *To Wear the Dust of War: From Bialystock to Shanghai, to the Promised Land--an Oral History.* New York: Palgrave, 2004.

Jaffe, Maayan. "The under-the-radar story of Far East Jewry." *JNS.* March 8, 2014.

Jiang Yebin. "Jewish Delegation Thanks Shanghai." *The Global Times*, March 26, 2014.

Johnson, Naula. "Cast in Stone: Monuments, Geography, and Nationalism." *Environment and Planning in Society and Space* 13 (1995): 51–65.

Johnston, Tess. *A Last Look: Western Architecture in Old Shanghai.* Hong Kong: Old China Hand Press, 1993.

Kahn, Betzalel. "Rebbetzin Tzivia Walkin o"h." *Dei'a ve Dibur.* December 22, 1999.

Kapner, Daniel and Stephen Levine. "Jews of Japan." *Jerusalem Center for Public Affairs.* March 1, 2000.

Kaplan, Vivian Jeanette. *Ten Green Bottles: The True Story of One Family's Journey from War-torn Austria to the Ghettos of Shanghai.* New York: St. Martin's Press, 2004.

Kaufmann, Max. *Churbn Lettland: The Destruction of the Jews of Latvia.* Edited by Gertrude Schneider and Erhad Roy Wiehn. Kostanz, Germany: Hartung-Gorre, 2010.

Kirshner, Sheldon. "When 'Shang' was Yiddish for 'life'," *Jewish World Review.* February 3, 1998.

Kitade, Akira. *Visas for Life and the Epic Journey: How the Sugihara Survivors Reached Japan.* Tokyo: Chobunsha, 2014.

Kotsuji, Setsuzau Abraham. *From Tokyo to Jerusalem.* Jerusalem: Bernard Geis Associates, 1964.
Kozak, Warren. *The Rabbi of 84th Street: The Extraordinary Life of Haskel Besser.* New York: HarperCollins, 2004.
Kranzler, David. *Japanese, Nazis & Jews: The Jewish Refugee Community of Shanghai, 1938–1945.* New York: Yeshiva University Press, 1976.
Kranzler, David. "Orthodoxy's Finest Hour." *Jewish Action.* October 13, 2002.
Kranzler, David and Gutta Sternbuch. *Memories of a Vanished World: Studies in Halacha and Jewish Thought Presented to Rabbi Prof. Menachem Emanuel Rackman on His 80th Anniversary.* Ramat Gan: n.p., 1994.
Lau, Israel Meir. *Out of the Depths: The Story of a Child of Buchenwald.* Jerusalem: Jerusalem Publications, 2009.
Leitner, Yecheskel. *Operation Torah Rescue: The Escape of the Mirrer Yeshiva from War-Torn Poland to Shanghai, China.* New York: Feldheim Publishers, 1987.
Levine, Hillel. *In Search of Sugihara: The Elusive Japanese Diplomat Who Risked his Life to Rescue 10,000 Jews From the Holocaust.* Lexington, MA: Plunkett Lake Press, 2012.
Lewin, Alyza D. "How my grandmother's chutzpah helped Sugihara rescue thousands of Jews." *Jewish Telegraphic Agency (JTA).* April 25, 2016.
Leys, Simon. *Chinese Shadows.* New York: The Viking Press, 1977.
Lingis, Alphonso. *First Person Singular.* Evanston, IL: Northwestern University Press, 2007.
Liu Binyan. *Two Kinds of Truth: Stories and Reportage from China.* Edited by Perry Link. Bloomington, IN: Indiana University Press. 2006.
Livni. Itamar. *The Gelbe Post: A Shanghai Immigrant Paper 1939.* Jerusalem: Hebrew University, 2008.
Loenen, Eva. "A Fresh Perspective on the History of Hasidic Judaism." *New Horizons.* No. 20. September 2012.
Lubowich, Kenneth. "Saved by Shanghai." September 16, 2014. Accessed August 13, 2017. www.cjss.org.cn/a/English/Related_Works/2014/0916/226.html.
Magid, Shaul. *American Post-Judaism: Identity and Renewal in a Post-ethnic Society.* Bloomington, IN: Indiana University Press, 2013.
Mandelbaum, David and Yechiel Benzion Fishoff. *From Lublin to Shanghai: The Miraculous Exile of Yeshivas Chachmei Lublin.* New York: Mesorah Publications, Ltd, 2012.
Marcus, Lotte Lustig. "Speak Memory! (Refugees, Trauma & the (Long) Road to Recovery)". Unpublished ms. Courtesy of the author.
Marcus, Lotte Lustig. "The Marshmallow Museum: Holocaust Lite." *Points East.* November, 2015.
Margolick, David. "Haunting photo of Nazi victim stirs debate," *Chicago Tribune*, June 20, 1982.
Mead, Margaret. *Coming of Age in Samoa: A Psychological Study of Primitive Youth for Western Civilization.* New York: William Morrow and Company, 1928.
Meir, Yoshor Moses. *Chafetz Chaim: The Life and Works of Rabbi Yisrael Meir Kagan of Radin*, rev. ed. Translated by Charles Wengrov. New York: Mesorah Publications 1986.
Melamed, Leo. *Escape to the Futures.* Hoboken, NJ: Wiley, 1996.

Mendelsohn, John. *Jewish Emigration from 1933 to the Evian Conference of 1938*. New York: Garland Publishing, Inc., 1982.

Messmer, Matthias. *Jewish Wayfarers in Modern China: Tragedy and Splendor*. New York: Lexington Books, 2012.

Meyer, Maisie J. *Shanghai's Baghdadi Jews: A Collection of Biographical Reflections*. London: Blacksmith Books, 2015.

Meyer, Maisie J. *From the Rivers of Babylon to the Whangpoo: A Century of Sephardi Jewish Life in Shanghai*. New York: University Press of America, 2003.

Miller, Judith. *One by One by One: Facing the Holocaust*. New York: Simon and Schuster, 1990.

Mitter, Rana. *China's War with Japan, 1937-1945: The Struggle for Survival*. London: Penguin, 2014.

Nabokov, Vladimir. *The Real Life of Sebastian Knight*. New York: New Directions Publishers, 1941.

Nye, Naomi Shihab. *Words Under Words: Selected Poems*. New York: Eighth Mountain Press, 1995.

Pagis, Dan. *The Selected Poems of Dan Pagis*. Translated by Stephen Mitchell. Berkeley, CA: University of California Press, 1996.

Pan, Lu. "Remembering the Pain of Others. Reflections on the Shanghai Jewish Refugee Museum and Beyond." *Writing the War in Asia: A Documentary History*. https://www.polyu.edu.hk/cc/images/Article/Doc/paper/dissertation/panlu/06_dissertation_PanLu.pdf

Pardes, Ilana. *Agnon's Moonstruck Lovers: The Song of Songs in Israeli Culture*. Seattle, WA: University of Washington Press, 2013.

Piotrowski, Tadeusz. *Poland's Holocaust: Ethnic Strife, Collaboration with Occupying Forces and Genocide in the Second Republic, 1918-1947*. Jefferson, NC: MacFarland 2007.

Orwell, George. "Looking back at the Spanish Civil War." In *Collected Essays and Journalism 1940–1943*, London: Secker & Warburg, 1961.

Ristaino, Marcia. *Port of Last Resort: The Diaspora Communities of Shanghai*. Stanford, CA: Stanford University Press, 2003.

Roidel, Dovid. *A Bridge Between Two Worlds: Bais Yaakov in Shanghai through the Experiences of Yehudith Cohn Goldbart*. Brooklyn: Kleinman Holocaust Education Center, 2014.

Rosenblum, Jonathan. "Anatomy of a Slander." *The Jewish Observer*. August, 2005.

Rosenstein, Neil. *The Unbroken Chain : Biographical Sketches and the Genealogy of Illustrious Jewish Families from the 15th-20th Century*. New York: CIS Publishers, 1990.

Sacharaw, Abraham. "Letter from Rabbi Abraham Sacharaw of Traby, Poland addressed to Chjrew." *YIVO Digital Archive on Jewish Life in Poland*. February 4, 1932.

Sakamoto, Pamela Rotner. *Japanese Diplomats and Jewish Refugees: A World War II Dilemma*. Westport, CT: Praeger Publishers, 1998.

Sato, Izumi. *A History of the Kobe Jewish Community*. Paper presented at the American Anthropological Association, Washington, DC. November 21, 1997.

Schlosser, Markus. "Agency." In *The Stanford Encyclopedia of Philosophy*, edited by Edward N. Zalta. Fall 2015. https://plato.stanford.edu/archives/fall2015/entries/agency/. Accessed August 22, 2017.

Schwarcz, Vera. "Who Can See a Miracle? The Language of Jewish Memory in Shanghai." In *The Jews of China: Historical and Comparative Perspectives*. Volume 1, edited by Jonathan Goldstein, 277–98. New York: M.E. Sharpe, 1999.
Schwarcz, Vera. *Bridge Across Broken Time: Chinese and Jewish Cultural Memory.* New Haven, CT: Yale University Press, 1999.
Shaw, Gary. "Agency and Language in the Postmodern Age." *History & Theory.* (December 2001), 1–9. Shmuelevitz, Chayim. *Pirkei Chayim* (Chapters of a Life). Jerusalem: Yeshivat Mir, 1989.
Shmulovich, Michal. "Saved in Shanghai—a young girl's story highlights a rare WWII place of refuge." *The Times of Israel.* August 25, 2012.
Silberstein, Michael and Anthony Chemero. "Dynamics, Agency and Intentional Action." (2011), accessed November 4, 2017, https://www.semanticscholar.org/paper/Dynamics-Agency-and-Intentional-Action-Silberstein-Chemero/7cb6c46b9c5e464bfe60f5a59af982f7e82d2d1f
Sofer, D. "The Japanese Convert." *Yated Neeman.* October 21, 2004.
Soloveitchik, Joseph B. *And from There You Shall Seek.* New York: KTAV Publishing House, 2009.
Stampler, Ann Reddisch. *Shlemazel and the Remarkable Spoon of Pohost.* New York: Clarion Books, 2006.
Starck, Israel. *A Boy Named 68818*. New York: Feldheim Publishers, 2015.
Strobin, Deborah and Ilie Wacs. "The Liberation of the Shanghai Jewish Ghetto." *The Huffington Post.* January 27, 2012. Accessed September 6, 2017, http://www.huffingtonpost.com/ilie-wacs/the-liberation-of-the-shanghai-jewish-ghetto_b_1236647.html.
Sugihara, Hiroki. *Puppe's Story: A Five-Year-Old Child Remembrance of His Father's Remarkable Rescue of 6,000 Jewish Refugees during the Holocaust.* Sacramento, CA: Edu-Comm. Plus, 1996
Sugihara, Seishiro. *Chiune Sugihara and Japan's Foreign Ministry.* Translated by Norman Hu. Lanham, MD: United Press of America, 2001.
Taniuchi, Yukata. *The Miracle Visas.* Jerusalem: Gefen Publishing House, 2001.
"The Chofetz Chaim's Obituary in the NY Times (1933)." Beyond Teshuva website, accessed November 4, 2017, http://www.beyondbt.com/2006/11/03/the-chofetz-chaims-obituary/
Tobias, Sigmund. *Strange Haven: A Jewish Childhood in Wartime Shanghai.* Champaign, IL: University of Illinois Press, 1999.
Tokayer, Marvin. *The Fugu Plan: The Untold Story of the Japanese and the Jews During World War II.* New York and London: Paddington Press, 1979.
Thompson, Vivian Alpert. "David Bloch." *A Mission in Art: Recent Holocaust Work in America.* Mercer, GA. Mercer University Press, 1988.
Twain, Mark. "Concerning the Jews." *Harper's Magazine.* June–November, 1899.
Vamos, Peter. "Home Afar: The Life of Central European Jewish Refugees in Shanghai During World War II." *Pacific Rim Report.* November, 2001.
Verba, Eliezer. *Sefer yizkor le-kehilat Lokatsh, Polin* (*The Book of Remembrance of the Community of Lokatsh, Poland*), edited by Shimon Matlofski. Jerusalem, Yad Vashem, 1993.
Walkin, Ahron. "Cheirus." *Matzav.* April 9, 2009.

Walkin, Chaim. *The World Within: Contemporary Mussar Essays*. Jerusalem: Targum Press, 2000.

Walkin, Shmuel David. *Sparks of Light: Jewels from the Chofetz Chaim*. New York: Kol Publishers, 2012.

Wang Jian. *Taowang yu Zhengjiu* (Escape and Rescue). Shanghai: Jiatong daxue chubanshe, 2016

Wein, Berel. *Teach Them Diligently to Your Children: The Personal Story of a Community Rabbi*. Jerusalem: Maggid Books, 2014.

Wein, Berel. "Rabbi Aharon Walkin." In *Guide Through The Dark Years—10 Lectures*. Audio compilation. Jerusalem: RabbiWein.com, 2012.

"We Remember Jewish Pinsk!" Translated by Ellen Stepak, from the Pinsk Yizkor Book (1966), accessed November 3, 2017, www.zchor.org/pinsk/pinsk.htm.

"What is New in Chicago" section. *Chicago Tribune*, December 20, 1956 [cut from original newspaper by Chaya Leah Small, no author].

White, Theodore. "The desperate urgency of flight," *Time* 40, no. 17 (October 26, 1942), 38.

Young, Dwight. "Stephen S. Wise to Franklin D. Roosevelt." In *Dear Mr. President: Letters to the Oval Office from the Files of the National Archives*. Edited by Dwight Young, 70–71. Washington, DC: National Geographic.

Yaakovson, Tzvi. "Rav Chaim Shmulewitz on his Holocaust Rescue." *Yated Ne'eman*. December 24, 2014.

Yamada, Jundai. 命のビザを繋いだ男—小辻節三とユダヤ難民. (Inochi no biza wo tsunaida otoko —Kotsuji Setsuzo to Yudaya nanmin, The man who anchored the transit visa lifeline: Setsuzo Kotsuji's aid to Jewish Refugees). Tokyo: NHK Shuppan, 2013.

Yoshor, Moshe M. *Chafetz Chaim: The Life and Works of Rabbi Yisrael Meir Kagan of Radin*. New York: Mesorah Publications Ltd, 1986.

Zuroff, Efraim. *The Response of Orthodox Jewry in the United States to the Holocaust: The Activities of the Vaad ha-Hatzala Rescue Committee 1939-1945*. New York: KTAV Publishing House, 2000.

FURTHER READINGS

Ariyeh, Yehuda. "Rebbetzin Tzivia Walkin, A.H." *Yated Ne'eman*. December 31, 1999, 96.

Jakubowicz, Andrew. "Cosmopolitanism with Roots: The Jewish Presence in Shanghai before the Communist Revolution and the New Metropolis." In *Branding Cities: Cosmopolitanism, Parochialism and Social Change*, edited by Stephanie Hemelryk Donald, Eleonore Kofman, and Catherine Kevin, 12–28. New York: Routledge, 2009.

Jacobson, Susan. "Survivors of the Shanghai Ghetto reunite after 70 years," *Orlando Sentinel*, August 5, 2015.

Kotsuji, Abram S. *Hiburugo genten nyumon: bunpo, kobunpo, honbun kaisetsu tsuki* (A Hebrew Grammar with Syntax and Chrestomathy: Being the First Work in Japanese) Tokyo: Nichiei-do, 1936.

Kranzler, David. *Thy Brother's Blood: The Orthodox Jewish Response to the Holocaust*. New York: Mesorah Publications, 1987.

Lustig Marcus, Lotte. "Contradicting Revisionist History." *Points East* 29, no. 1 (March, 2014): 1–3.

Margolis, Laua. "Race Against Time in Shanghai." *Survey Graphic* 33, no. 3 (March 1944): 168–90.

Medzini, Meron. *Under the Shadow of the Rising Sun: Japan and the Jews During the Holocaust Era.* Boston: Academic Studies Press, 2016.

Shai, Aharon. "China's 1939 Plan to Settle Persecuted European Jews," *Points East* 32, no. 3 (November 2017): 1, 11.

Shohet, Azriel. *The Jews of Pinsk 1881-1941*. Translated by Faigie Troppes and Moshe Rosman. Stanford, CA: Stanford University Press, 2013.

Simmons, Shraga. "The Rabbi from Shanghai." January 3, 2015. Accessed November 11, 2017 from http://www.aish.com/jw/s/The-Rabbi-from-Shanghai.html

Sterelny, Kim. *The Evolution of Agency and Other Essays.* Cambridge: Cambridge University Press, 2001.

Index

A
Agudas Yisrael, 12–13
Aharon (Ari), 251
Akiva, Rabbi, xxx–xxxi
altruistic personality, 39–40
Ani Ma'amin song, 206–207, 210
anti-foot-binding campaign, 103
Ashkenazi, Rabbi Meir, xxvi, 121–123, 131–134, 184, 203
Atlantic Charter, 53
Auschwitz–Birkenau concentration camp, xviii, xxiii, 58, 82, 102, 113–114, 146, 170
Axis agreement, 1940, 64

B
Baghdadi Jews, 125
Bais Yaakov school network for girls, 172, 227, 232–235, 256
Bais Yaakovin Shanghai, 157–160, 165, 188, 205
Bar-Ilan, Rav Meir, 30
Bei, Gao, xxv
Bella, 274
Ben Gurion, David, 210
Benoliel, Cyril, 188
Berlin, 40
Berlin, Rabbi Yehuda, 12
Beth Aharon Beit Midrash, 127
Beth Aharon Synagogue, 125
Birobidzhan (Jewish republic), 50
Blair, Margaret, xxiv
Bloch, David, 141
Blumenthal, Michael, 116
Bolshevik Revolution, 1917, 126
Bunin, Chana, 225
Bunin, Irving, 225, 229
Byron, George Gordon, 229

C
Central Committee for Religious Education, Vilna, 4

Central Yeshiva High School for Girls, 228
Chanin, Leo, 72
Chechik, Reb Osherke, 222–223
Chevra Kadisha (Sacred Burial Society), 136
China Daily, 269
China's role in rescuing Jewish refugee, xxi
Chinese Exclusion Act of 1882, 146
Chinese Expeditionary Forces, 174
Churban Eyrope, xix, xx
Churchill, Winston, 53
Coming of Age in Samoa (Margaret Mead), xxiii
Cultural Revolution (1966–76), 243

D
Daniels, Yvonne, 181
Day of Remembrance, 176
Decker, L. P. J. de, 43
Dickstein, Yehuda, 183
Dokshitz, 130
Dos Vort (The Word), 86
Dwork, Deborah, xvi

E
Ederman, Rabbi Yaakov Yehuda, 120
Eichmann, Adolf, 53
Eisenstein, Joseph, 185
Elazar, Shaul Yedidya (Moditzer Rebbe), 206–207
Elberg, Miriam, 190–192, 239–241
Elberg, Rabbi Simcha, xxix, xxviii, 85–87, 190–192, 240
Emergency Committee for the Rescue of Displaced Yeshivot, 29

F
"face," Japanese concept of, 65
Fackenheim, Emil, xix, xviii
Fain, Yonia, 139
Fastag, Azriel David, 206

Feinstein, Rabbi Moshe, 244, 251
Fine, Rabbi Jacob E., xxvii
Fishoff, Benny, 28–30, 140, 191, 197, 243
Flight from the Reich: Refugee Jews 1933–1946, xvi
French, Paul, 88
From Lublin to Shanghai (David Mandelbaum), 130
Fugu Plan, 54

G

Garfield, John, 211
gedolim, 116–123
Germany-Poland non-aggression pact, 1
Ghoya, Kano, 170–171, 182, 192
Goldbart, Yehudit Cohn, 157
Goldie, 195
Greater East Asia Co–Prosperity Sphere, 80
Grodinski, Chaim Ozer, 28, 31, 42
Gudao: The Lone Islet (Margaret Blair), xiv
Gudze, Wolfgang, 45
Gurwith, Nathan, 43

H

Handel, Ernst, 140–141
Hanukah, 36, 210, 236
Hardoon, Silas Aaron, 124–127
Hardoon, Luo Jialing, 126–127
Harper's Magazine, 131
Heimann, Max, 137–138, 141
Hellman, Blima, 189
Hellman, Rabbi Uri, 189, 234
High Holidays of 1941, 76
Himmler, Heinrich, 53
Hirohito, Emperor, 3
Hiroshima bombing, 1945, 183
Hitler, Adolf, 2
Hochstadt, Steve, xxv
Holocaust education, 116, 272, 277
Hongkew "ghetto," 148
July 17, 1945 bombing, 175–176
Hurley, Patrick, 174

I

irei miklat, 24, xxvii
Iwai, Masahiro, xiv, 70
Iwry, Samuel, xxiv–xxv, 20, 47–48, 50, 59, 134, 166, 203
To Wear the Dust of War, 203

J

Japanese authorities, role in saving Jewish lives, xxi
Japanese ethical code for samurai, 37

Japan Travel Bureau, 56
Jerusalem, xx, 17, 25, 30, 65–66, 135, 173, 181, 221, 231, 236, 263, 265, 269, 272
Jewish Distribution Committee (JDC), 180, 182
Jewish Holocaust Museum, Berlin, 116
Jewish life in Poland and Belarus, 10
Jewish matchmaking, 238–241
Jiang Kai-shek, 3. 79, 113, 146
Joan of Arc Public School, 214, 226
"Joint" (American–Jewish relief agency), 49
Joint Distribution News, 182
Judische Gemeinde (Communal Association of Central European Jews), 136

K

Kadoorie, Horace, 151
Kadoorie, Sir Elly, 193
Kadoorie School, 152–155, 158, 172, 205, 215, 259
Kagan, Rabbi Israel Meir (Chofetz Chaim), 15–19, 84, 107, 214, 219–220
Kahan, Shoshana, 84–85, 111
Kalish, Rabbi Shimon Shlomo (Amshenover Rebbe), 71–72, 131, 143
Kalmanowitz, Rabbi Avraham, 35, 104, 147, 244
Kamien, Moshe Abba, 120, 200
Kaplan, Rebbetzin Vichna, 235
Kaplan, Vivian, xxiv
kashrut, 13, 60, 107–109, 198, 252, 254, 260, 263
kosher, 61, 106–108, 125, 132–133, 138, 143, 153, 155, 198, 212–213, 252, 289
mashgiach, 186, 263
Kaufmann, Max, xx
Churban Lettland, xx
Kerner, Bella, 193–194
kimpeturin, 178
King's English, 151–156, 162, 224
Kiskilov, Rabbi Moshe Aharon, 64
Kitade, Akira, 55–56, 58
Klein, Stephen, 226
Klein, Jeannette, 227
Kobe, 23, 52, 54, 58, 62, 66, 78, 85, 92, 120, 131, 154, 173, 193
Kohen, Rabbi Yisrael Meir Kagan Ha, 15
Chofetz Chaim, Seeker of Life, 15
"Kolibri" (hummingbird), 2–3
korban, xix
Kotler, Rav Aahron, 76, 122–123, 225, 232, 239, 244, 247–248, 252, 254, 265

Kotler, Rebbetzin Rishel, 122–123, 163–164, 172, 179
Kotler, Shneur, 122
Kotsuji, Setsuko (Avraham ben Avraham), 62–66, 68, 77, 86, 127, 168, 263
From Tokyo to Jerusalem, 64
The True Character of the Jewish Nation, 64
Kovno, 40–44, 78, 169
Kramer, Rabbi Ariyeh Leib, 74
Kranzler, David, xxvi
Kumauchi Shinto shrine, 68

L
Landinski, Rabbi Moishe, 5–6, 11, 19
Landinski, Rabbi Mordechai, 213–214
Levenstein, Rabbi Yechezkel, 183
Levine, Esther, 187
Levine, Hillel, 39–40, 44–45
Levites, 236
Levi-Yitzhok, Rabbi, Kaddish of, 112
Lewin, Alyza, 43
Lingis, Alphonso, xxii
Lithuania, 28, 32, 39, 45, 52
 Soviet invasion of, 1940, 42
Lithuanian *Shoah,* xx
Liu Binyan, 284–285
Loesser, Frank, 233
The Longest Shadow: In the Aftermath of the Holocaust (Geoffrey Hartman), 289
Lubovitch, Kenneth, 282
Lukatch, xxviii, 20–22, 26, 30
Lukatz Kreuz, 10
Lu Pan, 282, 284

M
Malbushim Kovod, 97–101
Manchurian Jewish community, 64
Maoist "Great Leap Forward" of 1959–60, 114
Mao Zedong, 3, 80, 174, 210, 242, 284
Marcus, Lotte Lustig, xxi, 95, 155–156 283–284
Margolis, Laura, 183
Matsuoka, Yosuke, 73–74
McCarthy, Joe, 209, 220
 McCarthyism, 209, 220
Mead, Margaret, xxiii, 26
Melamed, Leo, 274–276
Melchior, Fredrich, 181–182
Meyer, Maisie, xxv
Miller, Judith, xv–xvi
Mirrer Yeshiva, xix, xxiv, 44, 49, 62, 66, 73–74, 76–77, 86, 92–93, 117, 122, 124–126, 157, 165, 167, 176, 183–184, 247, 271
Moishe, Shaul, 251

Molotov–Ribbentrop agreement, 25, 40
Mueller, Jack, 253
Mukden Incident of 1931, 3

N
Naiman, Rabbi Yaakov, 93
Nationalist Government (KMT), 79–80, 87
Nazis and Jews: The Jewish Refugee Community of Shanghai 1938–1945 (David Kranzler), xxv
Novardok Yeshiva, 6
Nuremberg Trials, 210
Nussbaum, Felix, 141

O
Ohel Moshe synagogue, 121–122, 132, 179, 184, 199, 200, 267, 269, 283
oil paintings of Jewish life, xx
One by One: Facing the Holocaust (Miller), xv
Operation Torah Rescue (Yecheskel Leitner), 62
Orwell, George, 114
Osaka Asahi Kaikan Museum, 74
Osako, Tatsuo, 56
otherness, xxxii

P
Pagis, Dan, 51
Passover (Pesach), 98, 108, 115, 121, 131–133, 138, 146, 153, 242
Pawlowitz, Olgierd, 42
Pearl Harbor attack, 1941, 71, 78–79
Pelt, Robert Jan Van, xvi
pikuach nefesh , 35, 40
Pinsk, 1, 3, 14, 22, 32, 53, 62, 124
Pinsk Ghetto, 53
Poalie Zedek, 255
Pohost, 1, 3, 9, 32
Poland, 24–25, 28, 32, 36, 38, 52–53, 193
Prague, 40
"Protocols of the Elders of Zion," 55
Puyi, Emperor, 3

Q
Qing dynasty, 3

R
Radin, 6, 10, 14–19, 99, 124, 133, 137, 173, 213–214, 217, 288
Radin Yeshiva, 19, 264
rape of Nanjing, 1937, 55
The Real Life of Sebastian Knight (Vladimir Nabokov), 280
The Response of Orthodox Jewry in the United States to the Holocaust (Ephraim Zuroff), xxvi

Ristaino, Marcia, xxv
Rodsko, Reverend Waclaw, 4
Roidel, Dovid, 158
Romania, x, 41, 48–49, 89, 223
Roosevelt, Franklin Delano, 21, 53, 146
Rosenberg, Ethel, 209, 220
Rosenberg, Julian, 209, 220
Rosenberg, Rabbi Yosef, 107
Rosenblum, Jonathan, xxvi
Rosh Hashanah, 25, 76, 87, 176, 177
Rothschild, Erika, 170
Ryushoji Temple, 68

S
Saburo, Nei, 55
Samuels, Yoshiko, 68
Schenirer, Sarah, 157, 159, 235
Schmidt, Samuel, 29
Seurat, Georges, 293
Shanghai
Bais Yaakov school for girls, 157–160
Bubbling Well Road, 192–197
Chinese watchman of, 100–103
observance of holy days in, 107–109
poverty of, 83–84
schools in, 151–156
shopping in, 104–109
streets of, 87–94
survival as Jews, 113–145
unterwelt in, 83–87
Shanghai, meaning of term, xxvi–xxvii
Shanghai Ashkenazi Relief Association (SACRA), 165–166
Shanghai Grand (Taras Grescoe), 84
Shanghai Jewish Refugees Museum, 281, xxi
Shanghai Jewish School, 151
Shanghai memoirs, xxiii–xxv
Shanghai survivors in Illinois, gathering of, 273
Shapiro, Rabbi Shlomo, 72
Shatskes, Rabbi Moshe, 72–73
Shavuot, 36
Shaw, Gary, xviii
Shimanowitz, Berele, 115
Shimanowitz, Mushka, 93
Shimanowitz, Rabbi Yeshaya, 76, 93
Shimon bar Yochai, Rabbi, 130
Shintoism, 59
Shir Ha'Shirim, xxix
shmatkeles, 133
Shmuelevitz, Rabbi Chaim Leib, 49, 66, 117, 131, 200, 202, 272

Shoah (Holocaust), xv–xvi, xviii, xxv–xxvii, xxxi, 9, 20, 27, 29, 35, 41, 46, 51, 136–137, 149, 172, 197, 206, 235, 247, 272, 281, 285
Siberia, 46, 57
Siegel, Manuel, 183
Silver, Rabbi Eliezer, 35, 244
simcha hall, 184, 190
Small, Aharon (Ari), 251, 266
Small, Avruhum, 251
Small, Rabbi Michael, 5, 9, 100, 211, 239–240, 250–253, 257–258, 266, 272
Smolyar, Rabbi Isaac, 213, 251
Socharow, Rabbi Avrohom (Trabe Rav), 4, 31–32, 34
Socharow, Leibel, 32, 215–217
Society for the Safeguarding the Health of the Jewish Population, 4
Sofer, Rabbi Moshe, 27
Sokal, David, 173
Sokal, Dr. Robert Reuven, 143–144, 173
Soloveitchik, Rabbi Chaim, 6
Soloveitchik, Rabbi Joseph, xxxii
And From There You Shall Seek, xxxii
Song of Songs (Shir Ha'Shirim), xv, xxix, xxx–xxxii, 4, 25, 37, 52, 54, 75, 78, 80, 115, 148, 172, 207, 209, 234, 254, 262, 266, 278, 280, 290
Sorotzkin, Rabbi Boruch, 75
Sorotzkin, Rabbi Zalman, 75
Soviet invasion of Lithuania, 1940, 42
Soviet Secret Service, 46
Spector, Rabbi Isaac Elchanan, 228
Spungen, Danny, 276
Spungen Foundation, 273
St. Louis, a ship, 22, 24
Starck, Israel, xxii–xxiii
A Boy Named 68818, xxiii
state of Israel, founding of, 210
Stella, 217
Sternheim, Leo, 43
Stillwell, Joseph, 80, 174
Strange Haven: A Jewish Childhood in Wartime Shanghai (Sigmund Tobias), xxiv
Strobin, Deborah, 175
Sugihara, Chiune, 25, 36–47, 49, 54–56, 59, 62, 65–66, 70, 78, 86, 120, 127, 167–169, 178, 228, 271, 278, 285–288
issuing of Japanese visas, 25, 45, 47, 55, 63, 120, 126, 139, 165, 167, 193
personality, 40
postings, 40–41
Sugihara, Hiroki, 36–37

Index

Sugihara, Seishiro, 41
Sukkot, 131, 133–134, 136, 157
Sun Ke, 80

T
Takashi, 169–170
Talmudic learning, 6, 75, xxvii
Talmudic scholarship, xix
Tanpei Photography Club, 74
Ten Green Bottles (Vivian Kaplan), xiv
Tiananmen events of 1989, 281
Tobias, Sigmund, 142, xxiv
Torah, *passim*
  Bereshit (*Genesis*) 185,
  Bamidbar (the *Book of Numbers*), xxvii
Torah learning, xix, 4, 7, 19, 23, 25, 75–77, 93, 116, 123–126, 132, 156, 179, 191, 235, 247, 254, 256
Torah observance xxii–xxiv, 60–61, 71, 74, 76, 83, 95, 99, 127, 144, 194, 254, 256
Torah scholarship, xx, xxvi, 3, 12, 75, 130–131
To Wear the Dust of War (Samuel Iwry), xxiv
Trabe, 4, 5, 8–10, 31
Trans–Siberian Railway, 46, 50, 291
Tsuruga, 56–59, 62, 78, 85
Tsuruga museum, 58–59
Tsuyoshi, Inukai, 3
Twain, Mark, 131
tzelem elokim, 134, 136–137, 139, 141

U
Undzer Lebn (Our Life), 86
United States, xv, xxvi, 6, 10, 13, 15, 20–21, 53, 63, 75, 77, 80, 87, 104, 114, 118–120, 123, 143 146, 163, 183, 202–204, 208–209, 314, 218, 220, 224–225, 227, 247, 264, 275
United States Holocaust Memorial Museum, 10
Unsern Leben/Our Life, 176
unterwelt in China, 83–87

V
Vaad ha–Hatzala, 35, 49, 104, 179, 200, 227, 244, 247
 Rescue Committee, xxvi
Vilna, 23, 25–26, 28–31, 34–36, 43, 92, 193, 230
Visas for Life (Akira Kitade), 55, 274
Vladivostok, 50
Volozhin Yeshiva, 12, 30, 177

W
Walkin, Chaim, xiii, 178, 181, 221, 231, 266, 269, 271

Walkin (Small), Chaya Leah, xv, xvi–xvii, xx–xxi, xxii, xxiii–xiv, xxv, xxxi
  about Siberia's ten locks, 47
  affection of Trabe Jews, 31–32
  amah, 94–100, 112, 121
  American schooling, 218
  as an artist, 137–142
  birth and childhood, 1–2
  childhood, xxviii
  childhood resident certificate in Shanghai, xxx, 82–83
  Chinese woman's services, 97–100
  commitment to Holocaust education, 116–117
  concept of responsibility and self-sacrifice, 289
  day of her landing in Japan, 57
  dimension of kindness, 287–288
  efforts to build Jewish community in Chicago, 253–262
  end of the war and, 179
  experience of bombings, 161–162
  on father's arrest on the Romanian border, 48–49
  home on 281 Liaoyang Road, 87–94, 115–116, 121, 129, 136, 149, 161–162, 165, 177, 267–268, 290
  Jewish survival during the war, 127–128
  Jewish wedding in wartime Shanghai, 185–192
  life among the *gedolim,* 116–123
  life in America, 208–241
  living standards of yeshiva community, 142–143
  Lukatch before disaster, 20–22
  marriage, 5, 9, 209–210, 242–246
  medals, 276–278
  memories of American clothing, 199–200
  memories of food and freedom, 198–199
  parents, 4–5, 7–8
  recollection of Shabbos preparation, 104–109, 131–133
  recollections of nine months in Japan, 54–55
  recollections of Shabbat in Kobe, 68–69
  rope-jumping song, 69–71
  schooling in Japan, 66–67, 69–70, 74
  schooling in Shanghai, 114–115, 151–160
  sense of well-being, 102
  spirit of a traditional Jewish home, 217–218
  Torah-centered life, 246–251
  university education, 225–226
  view of "occupiers" of Shanghai, 164–173
Walkin, Esther, 9, 95, 159, 168, 177
Walkin, Moshe Yoel, 9, 20, 35, 168, 187

Walkin, Rabbi Aharon (BaisAharon), 5–6, 9–15, 17, 22–23, 28, 30, 70, 75, 109, 124, 129, 164, 177, 198, 214, 221, 226, 243

Metzach Aharon, 22, 128–131, 145

Walkin, Rabbi Shmuel David, v, xxv–xxvi,, xxviii, 1–2, 6–11, 15–20, 22–23, 25, 27–31, 35, 39, 42–43, 46, 48, 61, 63, 68, 76, 79, 83, 85, 91, 104, 117–118, 120–122, 125, 127–129, 135, 137, 140–143, 150, 153–155, 164, 170, 173, 192, 202, 204, 207, 209, 213, 217, 225, 227, 229–233, 235, 243, 248, 251, 262–263, 273, 288

Sparks of Light: Jewels of Wisdom from the Chofetz Chaim, 15

Walkin, Rachel (Rochele), 218–219, 231

Walkin, Rav Chaim, 12, 30–31, 49, 177, 181, 265, 269

Walkin (nee Socharow), Rebbetzin Tzivia, v, 1–2, 4–5, 7–10, 15, 17–18, 21, 23, 31–37, 57, 69, 150, 158–159, 176, 179–180, 186–187, 202, 207, 212–218, 220–223, 233, 237–238, 243, 251, 262–265, 273

Wang Jingwei, 82–83

Wansee Conference, 1942, 113

Warhaftig, Zerach, 49

Warsaw Uprising, 115, 146

Wasserman, Rabbi Elchonon, 5–7, 28

Wein, Rabbi Berel, 12, 14

Weishaut, Myrna, 228

White, Theodore, 113–114

White Terror of 1927, 3

Wise, Rabbi Stephen, 146–147

Y

Yad Hashem, 126–127, 135, 248

Yad Vashem, 136, 139, 181

Yamada, Jundai, 63

Yasue, Norihiro, 55

Yebin, Jiang, 269–270

Yeshiva Gevoha, 247

Yeshiva K'tana, 157, 159–160

Yeshiva University High School for Girls, 227

Yochanan Ben Zakkai, Rabbi, xix–xx

Yom Kippur, 76–77, 93, 147, 176, 206

Z

Zaks (nee Kagan), Rebbetzin Feiga, 15, 214

Zupnik, Moshe, 44–45, 49

Zuroff, Ephraim, 142

Zwartndijk, Jan (Zwartendyk), 43–44